THE MAMMOTH BOOK OF TRUE WAR STORIES

Jon E. Lewis was born in Hereford, England, in 1961 and studied History at the Universities of Kent and Wales. His previous books include the anthologies *Red Handed* and *The Mammoth Book of the Western*. He works as a freelance writer and critic, and lives in South Wales.

The Mammoth Book of
TRUE WAR STORIES

May 30, 2013

Edited by
Jon E. Lewis

Books To Look Into/Get

Kid's books: Night Light by Nicholas Blechman (Ages 2-4)

Frog Song by Brenda Guiberson (Ages 4-6)

A Little Book of Sloth by Lucy Cooke (Ages 6 and up)

Brief Thief by Michael Escoffier (Ages 4 and up)

Carroll & Graf Publishers, Inc.
New York

Carroll & Graf Publishers, Inc
260 Fifth Avenue
New York
NY 1001

This collection first published in Great Britain 1992
First Carroll & Graf Edition 1992

ISBN 0-88184-756-9

Printed and bound in Great Britain by
Cox & Wyman Ltd, Reading, Berkshire

Contents

ACKNOWLEDGEMENTS

My thanks are due to the following people for their help and advice in the preparation of this book: Phil Lucas, Julian Jenkins, John Tomlinson, the staffs of the British Library and the Imperial War Museum, Nick Robinson, Alex Stitt, Stephanie Maury and, of course, Penny Stempel.

Permissions Acknowledgements:

The editor has made every effort to locate all persons having any rights in the selections appearing in this anthology and to secure permission from the holders of such rights. Any queries regarding the use of material should be addressed to the editor c/o the publishers.

'Survival' by John Hersey is from *The New Yorker*, 1944. Copyright © 1944 *The New Yorker*.

'Tank Battle on the Golan Heights' is an extract from *The War of Atonement* by Chaim Herzog. Copyright © 1975 Chaim Hertzog. Reprinted by permission of Weidenfeld & Nicholson Ltd.

'Doodlebugs in July' is an extract from *Few Eggs and No Oranges* by Vere Hodgson. Copyright © 1976 Vere Hodgson.

'Knight of the Crusades' is an extract from *Chronicles of the Crusades* by Joinville & Villehardouin. Copyright © 1963 MRB Shaw. Reprinted by permission of Penguin Books Ltd.

'Dogfight over Lille' is an extract from *Wing Leader*. Copyright © 1956 J.E. Johnson. Reprinted by permission of Random Century.

'The Sinking of HMS Hood' is an extract from *Pursuit* by Ludovic Kennedy. Copyright © 1974 Ludovic Kennedy. Reprinted by permission of Harper Collins.

'Convoy' is an extract from *The Corvette Navy* by James B. Lamb. Copyright © 1977 James B. Lamb. Reprinted by permission of Macmillan of Canada.

'Blowing Up a Train on the Hejaz Railway' and 'Torture' are both excerpts from *Seven Pillars of Wisdom* by T.E. Lawrence. Copyright © 1926, 1935 by Doubleday & Co. Inc. Reprinted by permission of Doubleday.

'The S.B.S. Raid on Simi' is an extract from *The Filibusters* by John Lodwick. Copyright © 1957 John Lodwick. Reprinted by permission of the Octopus Publishing Group plc.

'The Merrimack and the Monitor' is an extract from *Battle Cry of Freedom* by James McPherson. Copyright © 1980 James McPherson. Reprinted by permission of Oxford University Press.

'Carve Her Name With Pride' is an extract from *Carve Her Name With Pride* by RJ Minney. Copyright © 1989 RJ Minney. Reprinted by permission of Harper Collins.

'The Naval Battle of Guadalcanal' is from the *History of United States Naval Operations in World War II* by Samuel Eliot Morison. Copyright © 1959 Samuel Eliot Morison. Reprinted by permission of Oxford University Press.

'The Great Escaper' is an extract from *The Flying Sword*. Copyright © 1964 Tom Moulson. Reprinted by permission of Macdonald & Co.

'Merrill's Marauders' is an extract from *The Marauders* by Charlton Ogburn. Copyright © 1956, 1959 and 1982 by Charlton Ogburn. Reprinted by permission of William Morrow and Company, Inc.

'The Spanish Front' is an extract from *Homage to Catalonia* by George Orwell. Copyright © the Estate of Eric Blair 1938, 1953. Reprinted by permission of the estate of the late Sonia Brownell Orwell, Martin Secker & Warburg and Harcourt, Brace, Jovanovich.

'Diary of A German Paratrooper on the Eastern Front' is an extract by from *Heaven and Hell* by Martin Pöppel. Copyright © 1967 by Martin Pöppel. Reprinted by permission of Spellmont Ltd.

'Home Run from Colditz', is an extract from *The Colditz Story* by PR Reid, MBE, MC. Copyright © 1952 by PR Reid. Reprinted by permission of Hodder & Stoughton Publishers.

'The Amazing Colonel Doolittle' is an extract from *The Amazing Mr Doolittle* by Quentin Reynolds. Copyright © 1953 Quentin Reynolds.

'Strafing the Drachens' is an extract from *Fighting the Flying Circus* by Captain Eddie V. Rickenbacker. Copyright © 1965 Doubleday & Co. Inc. Reprinted by permission of Doubleday & Co., Inc.

'Hot Day, Hot Night' is an extract from *The Red Baron* by Manfred von Richthofen. Copyright © 1963 Doubleday & Co, Inc.

'The Retreat from El Alamein' is an extract from *The Rommell Papers*. Copyright © 1953 BH Liddell Hart, renewed 1981 by Lady Kathleen Liddell Hart, Fritz Bayerlein-Dittmar and Manfred Rommell.

'Scud Hunting' was originally published as 'Racing Through the Darkness in Pursuit of Scuds' by Eric Schmitt in the *New York Times*, February 1991. Copyright © 1991 the *New York Times* Reprinted by permission of the *New York Times*.

'The Bombing of Baghdad' is an extract from 'The Bombing of Baghdad' by John Simpson, *The Observer*, January 1991. Copyright © 1991 *The Observer*. Reprinted by permission of *The Observer*.

'The Destruction of the Athenian Expedition' is an extract from *The Peloponnesian War* by Thucydides. Translation Copyright © 1954 Rex Warner. Reprinted by permission of Penguin Books Ltd.

'The Lost Corsair to bring Down a MiG' is from *Corsair* by Barrett Tillman. Copyright © 1979 United States Naval Institute, Annapolis. Reprinted by permission of the United States Naval Institute.

'The Last days of Hitler' is an extract from *The Last Days of Hitler* by Hugh Trevor-Roper. Copyright © 1986 Hugh Trevor-Roper. Reprinted by permission of Macmillan Ltd.

'Nuts' is an extract from *Eisenhower's Lieutenants* by Russell F. Weigley. Copyright © 1981 Russell F. Weigley. Reprinted by permission of Sidgwick & Jackson Ltd and of Indiana University Press.

T.E. LAWRENCE (LAWRENCE OF ARABIA)
Blowing Up a Train on the Hejaz Railway

As the British leader of an irregular Arab army fighting the Turks during World War One, much of the activity of T.E. Lawrence—better known as Lawrence of Arabia—was aimed at sabotaging the Hejaz Railway, the main Turkish supply line in the Palestinian desert.

NEXT MORNING WE RETURNED ON our tracks to let a fold of the plain hide us from the railway, and then marched south across the sandy flat; seeing tracks of gazelle, oryx and ostrich; with, in one spot, stale padmarks of leopard. We were making for the low hills bounding the far side, intending to blow up a train; for Zaal said that where these touched the railway was such a curve as we needed for mine-laying, and that the spurs commanding it would give us ambush and field of fire for our machine-guns.

So we turned east in the southern ridges till within half a mile of the line. There the party halted in a thirty-foot valley, while a few of us walked down to the line, which bent a little eastward to avoid the point of higher ground under our feet. The point ended in a flat table fifty feet above the track facing north across the valley.

The metals crossed the hollow on a high bank, pierced by a two-arched bridge for the passage of rain-water. This seemed an ideal spot to lay the charge. It was our first try at electric mining and we had no idea what would happen; but it stood to our reason that the job would be more sure with an arch under the explosive because, whatever the effect on the locomotive, the bridge would go, and the succeeding coaches be inevitably derailed.

The ledge would make an admirable position for Stokes.* For the automatics, it was rather high; but the enfilade would be masterful whether the train was going up or down the line. So we determined to put up with the disadvantages of plunging fire. It was good to have my two British responsibilities in one place, safe from surprise and with an independent retreat into the rough: for to-day Stokes was in pain with dysentery. Probably the Mudowwara water had upset his stomach. So few Englishmen seemed to have been endowed by their upbringing with any organic resistance to disease.

Back with our camels, we dumped the loads, and sent the animals to safe pasture near some undercut rocks from which the Arabs scraped salt. The freedmen carried down the Stokes gun with its shells; the Lewis guns; and the gelatine with its insulated wire, magneto and tools to the chosen place. The sergeants set up their toys on a terrace, while we went down to the bridge to dig a bed between the ends of two steel sleepers, wherein to hide my fifty pounds of gelatine. We had stripped off the paper wrapping of the individual explosive plugs and kneaded them together by help of the sun-heat into a shaking jelly in a sand-bag.

The burying of it was not easy. The embankment was steep, and in the sheltered pocket between it and the hill-side was a wind-laid bank of sand. No one crossed this but myself, stepping carefully; yet I left unavoidable great prints over its smoothness. The ballast dug out from the track I had to gather in my cloak for carriage in repeated journeys to the culvert, whence it could be tipped naturally over the shingle bed of the watercourse.

It took me nearly two hours to dig in and cover the charge: then came the difficult job of unrolling the heavy wires from the detonator to the hills whence we would fire the mine. The top sand was crusted and had to be broken through in burying the wires. They were stiff wires, which scarred the wind-rippled surface with long lines like the belly marks of preposterously

* *T.E. Lawrence's two British assistants were nicknamed Stokes and Lewis after the makes of machine-gun they were in charge of respectively.*

narrow and heavy snakes. When pressed down in one place they rose into the air in another. At last they had to be weighted down with rocks which, in turn, had to be buried at the cost of great disturbance of the ground.

Afterwards it was necessary, with a sand-bag, to stipple the marks into a wavy surface; and, finally, with a bellows and long fanning sweeps of my cloak, to simulate the smooth laying of the wind. The whole job took five hours to finish; but then it was well finished: neither myself nor any of us could see where the charge lay, or that double wires led out underground from it to the firing point two hundred yards off, behind the ridge marked for our riflemen.

The wires were just long enough to cross from this ridge into a depression. There we brought up the two ends and connected them with the electric exploder. It was an ideal place both for it and the man who fired it, except that the bridge was not visible thence.

However, this only meant that someone would have to press the handle at a signal from a point fifty yards ahead, commanding the bridge and the ends of the wire alike. Salem, Feisal's best slave, asked for this task of honour, and was yielded it by acclamation. The end of the afternoon was spent in showing him (on the disconnected exploder) what to do, till he was act-perfect and banged down the ratchet precisely as I raised my hand with an imaginary engine on the bridge.

We walked back to camp, leaving one man on watch by the line. Our baggage was deserted, and we stared about in a puzzle for the rest, till we saw them suddenly sitting against the golden light of sunset along a high ridge. We yelled to them to lie down or come down, but they persisted up there on their perch like a school of hooded crows, in full view of north and south.

At last we ran up and threw them off the skyline, too late. The Turks in a little hill-post by Hallat Ammar, four miles south of us, had seen them, and opened fire in their alarm upon the long shadows which the declining sun was pushing gradually up the slopes towards the post. Beduin were past masters in the art of using country, but in their abiding contempt for the stupidity of the Turks they would take no care to fight them. This ridge was visible at once from Mudowwara and Hallat Ammar, and they had frightened both places by their sudden ominous expectant watch.

However, the dark closed on us, and we knew we must sleep away the night patiently in hope of the morrow. Perhaps the Turks would reckon us gone if our place looked deserted in the morning. So we lit fires in a deep hollow, baked bread and were comfortable. The common tasks had made us one party, and the hill-top folly shamed everyone into agreement that Zaal should be our leader.

Day broke quietly, and for hours we watched the empty railway with its peaceful camps. The constant care of Zaal and of his lame cousin Howeimil, kept us hidden, though with difficulty, because of the insatiate restlessness of the Beduin, who would never sit down for ten minutes, but must fidget and do or say something. This defect made them very inferior to the stolid English for the long, tedious strain of a waiting war. Also it partly accounted for their uncertain stomachs in defence. To-day they made us very angry.

Perhaps, after all, the Turks saw us, for at nine o'clock some forty men came out of the tents on the hill-top by Hallat Ammar to the south and advanced in open order. If we left them alone, they would turn us off our mine in an hour; if we opposed them with our superior strength and drove them back, the railway would take notice, and traffic be held up. It was a quandary, which eventually we tried to solve by sending thirty men to check the enemy patrol gradually; and, if possible, to draw them lightly aside into the broken hills. This might hide our main position and reassure them as to our insignificant strength and purpose.

For some hours it worked as we had hoped; the firing grew desultory and distant. A permanent patrol came confidently up from the south and walked past our hill, over our mine and on towards Mudowwara without noticing us. There were eight soldiers and a stout corporal, who mopped his brow against the heat, for it was now after eleven o'clock and really warm. When he had passed us by a mile or two the fatigue of the tramp became too much for him. He marched his party into the shade of a long culvert, under whose arches a cool draught from the east was gently flowing, and there in comfort they lay on the soft sand, drank water from their bottles, smoked, and at last slept. We presumed that this was the noon-day rest which every solid Turk in the hot summer of Arabia took as a matter of principle, and that their allowing themselves the pause showed that we were disproved or ignored. However, we were in error.

Noon brought fresh care. Through my powerful glasses we saw a hundred Turkish soldiers issue from Mudowwara Station and make straight across the sandy plain towards our place. They were coming very slowly, and no doubt unwillingly, for sorrow at losing their beloved midday sleep: but at their very worst marching and temper they could hardly take more than two hours before they reached us.

We begun to pack up, preparatory to moving off, having decided to leave the mine and its leads in place on chance that the Turks might not find them, and we be able to return and take advantage of all the careful work. We sent a messenger to our covering party on the south, that they should meet us farther up, near those scarred rocks which served as screen for our pasturing camels.

Just as he had gone, the watchman cried out that smoke in clouds was rising from Hallat Ammar. Zaal and I rushed uphill and saw by its shape and volume that indeed there must be a train waiting in that station. As we were trying to see it over the hill, suddenly it moved out in our direction. We yelled to the Arabs to get into position as quick as possible, and there came a wild scramble over sand and rock. Stokes and Lewis, being booted, could not win the race; but they came well up, their pains and dysentery forgotten.

The men with rifles posted themselves in a long line behind the spur running from the guns past the exploder to the mouth of the valley. From it they would fire directly into the derailed carriages at less than one hundred and fifty yards, whereas the ranges for the Stokes and Lewis guns were about three hundred yards. An Arab stood up on high behind the guns and shouted to us what the train was doing—a necessary precaution, for if it carried troops and detrained them behind our ridge we should have to face about like a flash and retire fighting up the valley for our lives. Fortunately it held on at all the speed the two locomotives could make on wood fuel.

It drew near where we had been reported, and opened random fire into the desert. I could hear the racket coming, as I sat on my hillock by the bridge to give the signal to Salem, who danced round the exploder on his knees, crying with excitement, and calling urgently on God to make him fruitful. The Turkish fire sounded heavy, and I wondered with how many men we were going to have affair, and if the mine would be advantage enough for our eighty fellows to equal them. It would have been better if the first electrical experiment had been simpler.

However, at that moment the engines, looking very big, rocked with screaming whistles into view around the bend. Behind them followed ten box-waggons, crowded with rifle-muzzles at the windows and doors; and in little sand-bag nests on the roofs Turks precariously held on, to shoot at us. I had not thought of two engines, and on the moment decided to fire the charge under the second, so that however little the mine's effect, the uninjured engine should not be able to uncouple and drag the carriages away.

Accordingly, when the front 'driver' of the second engine was on the bridge, I raised my hand to Salem. There followed a terrific roar, and the line vanished from sight behind a spouting column of black dust and smoke a hundred feet high and wide. Out of the darkness came shattering crashes and long, loud metallic clangings of ripped steel, with many lumps of iron and plate; while one entire wheel of a locomotive whirled up suddenly black out of the cloud against the sky, and sailed musically over our heads to fall slowly and heavily into the desert behind. Except for the flight of these, there succeeded a deathly silence, with no cry of men or rifle-shot, as the now grey mist of the explosion drifted from the line towards us, and over our ridge until it was lost in the hills.

In the lull, I ran southward to join the sergeants. Salem picked up his rifle and charged out into the murk. Before I had climbed to the guns the hollow was alive with shots, and with the brown figures of the Beduin leaping forward to grips with the enemy.I looked round to see what was happening so quickly, and saw the train stationary and dismembered along the track, with its waggon sides jumping under the bullets which riddled them, while Turks were falling out from the far doors to gain the shelter of the railway embankment.

As I watched, our machine-guns chattered out over my head, and the long rows of Turks on the carriage roofs rolled over, and were swept off the top like bales of cotton before the furious shower of bullets which stormed along the roofs and splashed clouds of yellow chips from the planking. The dominant position of the guns had been an advantage to us so far.

When I reached Stokes and Lewis the engagement had taken another turn. The remaining Turks had got behind the bank, here about eleven feet high, and from cover of the wheels were firing point-blank at the Beduin twenty yards away across the sand-filled dip. The enemy in the crescent of the curving line were secure from the machine-guns; but Stokes slipped in his first shell, and after a few seconds there came a crash as it burst beyond the train in the desert.

He touched the elevating screw, and his second shot fell just by the trucks in the deep hollow below the bridge where the Turks were taking refuge. It made a shambles of the place. The survivors of the group broke out in a panic across the desert, throwing away their rifles and equipment as they ran. This was the opportunity of the Lewis gunners. The sergeant grimly traversed with drum after drum, till the open sand was littered with bodies. Mushagraf, the Sherari boy behind the second gun, saw the battle over,threw aside his weapon with a yell, and dashed down at speed with his rifle to join the others who were beginning, like wild beasts, to tear open the carriages and fall to plunder. It had taken nearly ten minutes.

I looked up-line through my glasses and saw the Mudowwara patrol breaking back uncertainly towards the railway to meet the train-fugitives running their fastest northward. I looked south, to see our thirty men cantering their camels neck and neck in our direction to share the spoils. The Turks there, seeing them go, began to move after them with infinite precaution, firing volleys. Evidently we had a half hour respite, and then a double threat against us.

I ran down to the ruins to see what the mine had done. The bridge was gone; and into its gap was fallen the front waggon, which had been filled with sick. The smash had killed all but three or four and had rolled dead and dying into a bleeding heap against the splintered end. One of those yet alive deliriously cried out the word typhus. So I wedged shut the door, and left them there, alone.

Succeeding waggons were derailed and smashed: some had frames irreparably buckled. The second engine was a blanched pile of smoking iron. Its driving wheels had been blown upward, taking away the side of the fire-box. Cab and tender were twisted into strips, among the piled stones of the bridge abutment. It would never run again. The front engine had got off better: though heavily derailed and lying half-over, with the cab burst, yet its steam was at pressure, and driving-gear intact.

Our greatest object was to destroy locomotives, and I had kept in my arms a box of gun-cotton with fuse and detonator ready fixed, to make sure such a case. I now put them in position on the outside cylinder. On the boiler would have been better, but the sizzling steam made me fear a general explosion which would sweep across my men (swarming like ants over the booty) with a blast of jagged fragments. Yet they would not finish their looting before the Turks came. So I lit the fuse, and in the half-minute of its burning drove the plunderers a little back, with difficulty. Then the charge burst, blowing the cylinder to smithers, and the axle too. At the moment I was distressed with uncertainty whether the damage were enough; but the Turks, later, found the engine beyond use and broke it up.

The valley was a weird sight. The Arabs, gone raving mad, were rushing about at top speed bareheaded and half-naked, screaming, shooting into the air, clawing one another nail and fist, while they burst open trucks and staggered back and forward with immense bales, which they ripped by the rail-side, and tossed through, smashing what they did not want. The train had been packed with refugees and sick men, volunteers for boat-service on the Euphrates, and families of Turkish officers returning to Damascus.

There were scores of carpets spread about; dozens of mattresses and flowered quilts, blankets in heaps, clothes for men and women in full variety; clocks, cooking-pots, food, ornaments and weapons. To one side stood thirty or forty hysterical women, unveiled, tearing their clothes and hair; shrieking themselves distracted. The Arabs without regard to them went on wrecking the household goods; looting their absolute fill. Camels had become common property. Each man frantically loaded the nearest with what it could carry and shooed it westward into the void, while he turned to his next fancy.

Seeing me tolerably unemployed, the women rushed, and caught at me with howls for mercy. I assured them that all was going well: but they would not get away till some husbands delivered me. These knocked their wives off and seized my feet in a very agony of terror of instant death. A Turk so broken down was a nasty spectacle: I kicked them off as well as I could with bare feet, and finally broke free.

Next a group of Austrians, officers and non-commissioned officers, appealed to me quietly in Turkish for quarter. I replied with my halting German whereupon one, in English, begged for a doctor for his wounds. We had none: not that it mattered, for he was mortally hurt and dying. I told them the Turks would return in an hour and care for them. But he was dead before that, as were most of the others (instructors in the new Skoda mountain howitzers supplied to Turkey for the Hejaz war), because some dispute broke out between them and my own bodyguard, and one of them fired a pistol shot at young Rahail. My infuriated men cut them down, all but two or three, before I could return to interfere.

ROBERT GRAVES
Night Patrol in No-Man's Land

Robert Graves went from school to fight in the First World War, where he served as a captain with the Royal Welsh Fusiliers on the Western Front. Later he became one of Britain's leading writers and poets.

THE FIRST TRENCHES WE WENT into on arrival were the Cuinchy brick-stacks. My company held the canal-bank frontage, a few hundred yards to the left of where I had been with the Welsh Regiment at the end of May. The Germans opposite wanted to be sociable. They sent messages over to us in undetonated rifle-grenades. One of these was evidently addressed to the Irish battalion we had relieved:

> We all German korporals wish you English korporals a good day and invite you to a good German dinner tonight with beer (ale) and cakes. Your little dog ran over to us and we keep it safe; it became no food with you so it run to us. Answer in the same way, if you please.

Another grenade contained a copy of the *Neueste Nachrichten*, a German Army newspaper printed at Lille, giving sensational details of Russian defeats around Warsaw, with immense captures of prisoners and guns. But what interested us far more was a full account in another column of the destruction of a German submarine by British armed trawlers; no details of the sinking of German submarines had been allowed to appear in any English papers. The battalion cared as little about the successes or reverses of our Allies as about the origins of the war. It never allowed itself to have any political feelings about the Germans. A professional soldier's duty was simply to fight whomever the King ordered him to fight. With the King as colonel-in-chief of the regiment it became even simpler. The Christmas 1914 fraternization, in which the battalion was among the first to participate, had had the same professional simplicity: no emotional hiatus, this, but a common-place of military tradition—an exchange of courtesies between officers of opposing armies.

Cuinchy bred rats. They came up from the canal, fed on the plentiful corpses, and multiplied exceedingly. While I stayed here with the Welsh, a new officer joined the company and, in token of welcome, was given a dug-out containing a spring-bed. When he turned in that night, he heard a scuffling, shone his torch on the bed, and found two rats on his blanket tussling for the possession of a severed hand. This story circulated as a great joke.

The colonel called for a patrol to visit the side of the tow-path, where we had heard suspicious sounds on the previous night, and see whether they came from a working-party. I volunteered to go at dark. But that night the moon shone so bright and full that it dazzled the eyes. Between us and the Germans lay a flat stretch of about two hundreds yards, broken only by shell craters and an occasional patch of coarse grass. I was not with my own company, but lent to 'B', which had two officers away on leave. Childe-Freeman, the company-commander, asked: 'You're not going out on patrol tonight, Graves, are you? It's almost as bright as day.'

'All the more reason for going,' I answered. 'They won't be expecting me. Will you please keep everything as usual? Let the men fire an occasional rifle, and send up a flare every half-hour. If I go carefully, the Germans won't see me.'

While we were having supper, I nervously knocked over a cup of tea, and after that a plate. Freeman said: 'Look here, I'll phone through to battalion and tell them it's too bright for your patrol.' But I knew that, if he did, Buzz Off* would accuse me of cold feet.

So one Sergeant Williams and I put on our crawlers, and went out by way of a mine-crater at the side of the tow-path. We had no need to stare that night. We could see only too clearly. Our plan was to wait for an opportunity to move quickly, to stop

* *Nickname for a Lieutenant-Colonel in Graves' regiment.*

dead and trust to luck, then move on quickly again. We planned our rushes from shell-hole to shell-hole, the opportunities being provided by artillery or machine-gun fire, which would distract the sentries. Many of the craters contained the corpses of men who had been wounded and crept in there to die. Some were skeletons, picked clean by the rats.

We got to within thirty yards of a big German working-party, who were digging a trench ahead of their front line. Between them and us we counted a covering party of ten men lying on the grass in their greatcoasts. We had gone far enough. A German lay on his back about twelve yards off, humming a tune. It was the 'Merry Widow' waltz. The sergeant, from behind me, pressed my foot with his hand and showed me the revolver he was carrying. He raised his eyebrows inquiringly. I signalled 'no'. We turned to go back; finding it hard not to move too quickly. We had got about half-way, when a German machine-gun opened traversing fire along the top of our trenches. We immediately jumped to our feet; the bullets were brushing the grass, so to stand up was safer. We walked the rest of the way home, but moving irregularly to distract the aim of the covering party if they saw us. Back in the trench, I rang up brigade artillery, and asked for as much shrapnel as they could spare, fifty yards short of where the German front trench touched the tow-path; I knew that one of the night-lines of the battery supporting us was trained near enough to this point. A minute and a quarter later the shells started coming over. Hearing the clash of downed tools and distant shouts and cries, we reckoned the probable casualties.—

The next morning, at stand-to, Buzz Off came up to me: 'I hear you were on patrol last night?'

'Yes, sir.'

He asked for particulars. When I told him about the covering party, he cursed me for not 'scuppering them with that revolver of yours.' As he turned away, he snorted: 'Cold feet!'

FRANK RICHARDS
The Third Battle of Ypres, 1917

Like Robert Graves (see preceding story), Frank Richards served in WWI with the Royal Welsh Fusiliers. Richards, a signalman, fought in every major engagement on the Western Front between 1914 and 1918. He consistently refused any form of promotion, but won both the Distinguished Conduct Medal and the Military Medal.

THE THIRD BATTLE OF YPRES commenced on July 31st and our Division were sent to the Belgian coast. We travelled by train and barge and arrived at Dunkirk. A little higher up the coast was a place named Bray Dunes, where we stayed about a week, and the architect and I went for many a long swim in the sea. We moved closer to the line along thc coast and arrived at a place which the majority of inhabitants had only just evacuated. In July a British division had relieved the Belgian troops around this part. Ever since November 1914 the people had been living in peace and security in the towns and villages in this area, but as soon as the British troops took over the enemy began shelling these places and the people cleared out. In one place we were in the people were in the act of leaving and complaining very bitterly because the arrival of British troops had caused a lot of shelling and forced them to leave their homes. In one pretty village by the sea there hadn't been enough shells exploded in it to have frightened a poll parrot away, yct there wasn't a soul left there now. They were evidently not such good stickers as the French people who worried less about their lives than about their property and hung on to the last possible minute.

At Bray Dunes I got in conversation with a Canadian officer

who was in charge of some men building a light railway. He said it was a good job that the States came in the War as the French were ready to throw the sponge up. A few days later two of our signallers overheard a full colonel of the Staff telling our Colonel that he did not know what would have happened if the United States had not come in when they did. It was common knowledge among the Staff that the whole of the French Army were more or less demoralized, and the States coming in had to a great extent been the means of restoring their morale. We got wind that our Division and another had been sent up the coast to try and break through the German Front and capture Ostend. This was freely discussed by the officers, but no break through was attempted owing to so little progress being made on the Ypres front.

One of the largest concentration prison camps I ever saw was erected in this area. It was estimated to hold between ten and fifteen thousand prisoners, but all I saw in it were two solitary prisoners who must have been very lonely in so large a place.

On the night the Battalion went in the line I went on leave. It was eighteen months since I had the last one and as usual I made the most of it. I didn't spend the whole of it in pubs: I spent two days going for long tramps in the mountains, which I thoroughly enjoyed after being so long in a flat country. I was presented with a gold watch, in recognition of winning the D.C.M., which I still have, but it has been touch-and-go with it several times since the War. Probably if there hadn't been an inscription on it I should have parted with it. This time every man of military age that I met wanted to shake hands with me and also ask my advice on how to evade military service, or, if they were forced to go, which would be the best corps to join that would keep them away from the firing line. They were wonderfully patriotic at smoking concerts given in honour of soldiers returning from the Front, but their patriotism never extended beyond that.

When I landed back at Boulogne I came across the man who had been shot through his cheeks at Bois Grenier in April 1915. If anything, that bullet had improved his appearance. He now had a nice little dimple on each side of his face. We had a chat. I asked what he was doing now and he said that he had a Staff job, as a military policeman around the Docks. He told me very seriously that if it was possible, and he had the name and address of the German that shot him, he would send him the largest parcel he could pack and a hundred-franc note as well. He was having the time of his life on his present job and had one of the smartest fillies in Boulogne, who was the goods in every way. As I left him I could not help thinking how lucky some men were and how unlucky were others.

When I arrived back I found that the Division had left the coastal area on short notice. All returning leave men of the Division were in a little camp outside Dunkirk. One night some German planes came over bombing and one of our searchlights kept a plane in its rays for some time. Anti-aircraft guns, machine-guns and Lewis guns, and we with our rifles were all banging at him, but he got away with it. Whilst everyone was busy firing at that one, his friends were busy dropping their bombs on Dunkirk. It was very rare that a plane flying at any height was brought down by anti-aircraft guns or rifle-fire but we lost a lot of planes on the Somme by rifle-fire when they came down very low, machine-gunning the enemy before our troops attacked. German planes used to do the same thing and seldom got away with it either.

I rejoined the Battalion in a village near Ypres and guessed that we would soon be in the blood tub. Ricco and Paddy had been made full corporals but Paddy had taken a lot of persuading before he consented to be made an N.C.O. He was sent back to Division Headquarters for a special course of signalling and was lucky enough to miss the next show we were in. Our Colonel went on leave and missed the show too. The name of our Acting-Colonel was Major Poore. He was not an old regimental officer but had been posted to us some six months before from the Yeomanry, I believe. He was a very big man, about fifty years of age, slightly deaf, and his favourite expression was 'What, what!' He was a very decent officer. A tall, slender young lieutenant who had just returned from leave was made Assistant-Adjutant for the show. I believe he was given that job because he was an excellent map-reader. As we were marching along the road, Sealyham asked him if he had come across Mr Sassoon during his leave. He replied that he hadn't and that he had spent a good part of his leave trying to find out where he was but had failed to get any news at all. This young officer had joined the Battalion about the same time as Mr Sassoon and we old hands thought he was a man and a half to spend his leave looking for a pal. His name was Casson. I wrote it down first here as Carson, but an old soldiering pal tells me that I had it wrong. Mr Casson was said to be a first-class pianist, but trench warfare did not give him much opportunity to show his skill at that. If he was as good a pianist as he was a cool soldier he must have been a treat to hear.

During the night we passed through a wood where a Very-light dump had been exploded by a German shell. It was like witnessing a fireworks display at home. We stayed in the wood for the night. Our Brigade were in reserve and ready to be called upon at any moment. Orders were given that no fires were to be lit. September 26th, 1917, was a glorious day from the weather point of view and when dawn was breaking Ricco and I who were crack hands at making smokeless fires had found a dump of pick-handles which when cut up in thin strips answered very well. We soon cooked our bacon and made tea for ourselves and the bank clerk and architect, and made no more smoke than a man would have done smoking a cigarette. We had at least made sure of our breakfast which might be the last we would ever have.

At 8 a.m. orders arrived that the Battalion would move off to the assistance of the Australians who had made an attack early in the morning on Polygon Wood. Although the attack was successful they had received heavy casualties and were now hard pressed themselves. Young Mr Casson led the way, as cool as a cucumber. One part of the ground we travelled over was nothing but lakes and boggy ground and the whole of the Battalion were strung out in Indian file walking along a track about eighteen inches wide. We had just got out of this bad ground but were still travelling in file when the enemy opened out with a fierce bombardment. Just in front of me half a dozen men fell on the side of the track: it was like as if a Giant Hand had suddenly swept them one side. The Battalion had close on a hundred casualties before they were out of that valley. If a man's best pal was wounded he could not stop to dress his wounds for him.

We arrived on some rising ground and joined forces with the Australians. I expected to find a wood but it was undulating land with a tree dotted here and there and little banks running in different directions. About half a mile in front of us was a ridge of trees, and a few concrete pillboxes of different sizes. The ground that we were now on and some of the pillboxes had only been taken some hours previously. I entered one pillbox during the day and found eighteen dead Germans inside. There was not a mark on one of them; one of our heavy shells had made a direct hit on the top of it and they were killed by concussion, but very little damage had been done to the pillbox. They were all constructed with reinforced concrete and shells could explode all round them but the flying pieces would never penetrate the concrete. There were small windows in the sides and by jumping in and out of shell holes attacking troops could get in bombing range: if a bomb was thrown through one of the windows the pillbox was as good as captured.

There was a strong point called Black Watch Corner which was a trench facing north, south, east and west. A few yards outside the trench was a pillbox which was Battalion Headquarters. The bank clerk, architect and I got in the trench facing our front, and I was soon on friendly terms with an Australian officer, whom his men called Mr Diamond. He was wearing the ribbon of the D.C.M., which he told me he had won in Gallipoli while serving in the ranks and had been granted a commission some time later. About a hundred yards in front of us was a bank which extended for hundreds of yards across the ground behind which the Australians were. Our chaps charged through them to take a position in front and Captain Mann, our Adjutant, who was following close behind, fell with a bullet through his head. The enemy now began to heavily bombard our position and Major Poore and Mr Casson left the pillbox and got in a large shell hole which had a deep narrow trench dug in the bottom of it. They were safer there than in the pillbox, yet in less than fifteen minutes an howitzer shell had pitched clean in it, killing the both of them.

During the day shells fell all around the pillbox but not one made a direct hit on it. The ground rocked and heaved with the bursting shells. The enemy were doing their best to obliterate the strong point that they had lost. Mr Diamond and I were mucking-in with a tin of Maconochies when a dud shell landed clean in the trench, killing the man behind me, and burying itself in the side of the trench by me. Our Maconochie was spoilt but I opened another one and we had the luck to eat that one without a clod of earth being thrown over it. If that shell had not been a dud we should have needed no more Maconochies in this world. I had found eight of them in a sandbag before I left the wood and brought them along with me. I passed the other six along our trench, but no one seemed to want them with the exception of the bank clerk and architect who had got into my way of thinking that it was better to enter the next world with a full belly than an empty one.

The bombardment lasted until the afternoon and then ceased. Not one of us had hardly moved a yard for some hours but we had been lucky in our part of the trench, having only two casualties. In two other parts of the strong point every man had been killed or wounded. The shells had been bursting right on the parapets and in the trenches, blowing them to pieces. One part of the trench was completely obliterated. The fourth part of the strong point had also been lucky, having only three casualties. Mr Diamond said that we could expect a counter attack at any minute. He lined us up on the parapet in extended order outside the trench and told us to lie down. Suddenly a German plane swooped very low, machine-gunning us. We brought him down but not before he had done some damage, several being killed including our Aid Post Sergeant.

A few minutes later Dr. Dunn temporarily resigned from the Royal Army Medical Corps. He told me to get him a rifle and bayonet and a bandolier of ammunition. I told him that he had better have a revolver but he insisted on having what he had asked me to get. I found them for him and slinging the rifle over his shoulder he commenced to make his way over to the troops behind the bank. I accompanied him. Just before we reached there our chaps who were hanging on to a position in front of it started to retire back. The doctor barked at them to line up with the others. Only Captain Radford and four platoon officers were left in the Battalion and the Doctor unofficially took command.

We and the Australians were all mixed up in extended order. Everyone had now left the strong point and were lined up behind the bank, which was about three feet high. We had lent a Lewis-gun team to the 5th Scottish Rifles on our right, and when it began to get dark the Doctor sent me with a verbal message to bring them back with me, if they were still in the land of the living. When I arrived at the extreme right of our line I asked the right-hand man if he was in touch with the 5th Scottish. He replied that he had no more idea than a crow where they were, but guessed that they were somewhere in front and to the right of him. I now made my way very carefully over the ground. After I had walked some way I began to crawl. I was liable any moment to come in contact with a German post or trench. I thought I saw someone moving in front of me, so I slid into a shell hole and landed on a dead German. I waited in that shell hole for a while trying to pierce the darkness in front. I resumed my journey and, skirting one shell hole, a wounded German was shrieking aloud in agony: he must have been hit low down but I could not stop for no wounded man. I saw the forms of two men in a shallow trench and did not know whether they were the 5th Scottish or the Germans until I was sharply challenged in good Glasgow English. When I got in their trench they told me that they had only just spotted me when they challenged. The Lewis-gun team were still kicking and my journey back with them was a lot easier than the outgoing one.

I reported to the Doctor that there was a gap of about one hundred yards between the 5th Scottish Rifles and we; and he went himself to remedy it. The whole of the British Front that night seemed to be in a semi-circle. We had sent up some S O S rockets and no matter where we looked we could see our S O S rockets going up in the air: they were only used when the situation was deemed critical and everybody seemed to be in the same plight as ourselves. The bank clerk and I got into a shell hole to snatch a couple of hours rest, and although there were two dead Germans in it we were soon fast asleep. I was woke up to guide a ration party to us who were on their way. Dawn was now breaking and I made my way back about six hundred yards, where I met them. We landed safely with the rations.

Major Kearsley had just arrived from B Echelon to take command of the Battalion. The Brigadier-General of the Australians had also arrived and was sorting his men out. It was the only time during the whole of the War that I saw a brigadier with the first line of attacking troops. Some brigadier that I knew never moved from Brigade Headquarters. It was also the first time I had been in action with the Australians and I found them very brave men. There was also an excellent spirit of comradeship between officers and men.

We were moving about quite freely in the open but we did not know that a large pillbox a little over an hundred yards in front of us was still held by the enemy. They must have all been having a snooze, otherwise some of us would have been riddled. Major Kearsley, the Doctor and I went out reconnoitring. We were jumping in and out of shell holes when a machine-gun opened out from somewhere in front, the bullets knocking up the dust around the shell holes we had just jumped into. They both agreed that the machine-gun had been fired from the pillbox about a hundred yards in front of us. We did some wonderful jumping and hopping, making our way back to the bank. The enemy's artillery had also opened out and an hour later shells were bursting all over our front and in the rear of us.

A sapping platoon of one sergeant and twenty men under the command of The Athlete were on the extreme left of the bank, and the Major and I made our way towards them. We found the men but not the officer and sergeant, and when the Major inquired where they were they replied that they were both down the dug-out. There was a concrete dug-out at this spot which had been taken the day before. I shouted down for them to come up, and the Major gave the young officer a severe reprimand for being in the dug-out, especially as he knew our men had just started another attack. Our chaps and the 5th Scottish Rifles had attacked on our right about fifteen minutes previously. The Major gave The Athlete orders that if the pillbox in front was not taken in fifteen minutes he was to take his platoon and capture it and then dig a trench around it. If the pillbox was captured during that time he was still to take his platoon and sap around it. I felt very sorry for The Athlete. This was the first real action he had been in and he had the most windy sergeant in the Battalion with him. Although The Athlete did not know it, this sergeant had been extremely lucky after one of the Arras stunts that he had not been court-martialled and tried on the charge of cowardice in face of the enemy.

We arrived back at our position behind the bank. We and the Australians were in telephone communication with no one; all messages went by runners. Ricco, the bank clerk and the architect were running messages, the majority of our Battalion runners being casualties. Sealyham was still kicking and Lane was back in B Echelon; it was the first time for over two years he had been left out of the line. The Sapping-Sergeant came running along the track by the bank and informed the Major that The Athlete had sent him for further instructions as he was not quite certain what he had to do. The Major very nearly lost his temper and told me to go back with the Sergeant and tell him what he had to do. Just as we arrived at the sapping-platoon we saw some of our chaps rushing towards the pillbox, which surrendered, one officer and twenty men being inside it.

C and D Companies were now merged into one company. They advanced and took up a position behind a little bank about a hundred yards in front of the pillbox. I informed The Athlete that he had to take his platoon and sap around the pillbox, and that this was a verbal message which Major Kearsley had given me for him. I left him and the Sergeant conferring together and made my way back by a different route.

The enemy were now shelling very heavily and occasionally the track was being sprayed by machine-gun bullets. I met a man of one of our companies with six German prisoners whom he told me he had to take back to a place called Clapham Junction, where he would hand them over. He then had to return and rejoin his company. The shelling was worse behind us than where we were and it happened more than once that escort and prisoners had been killed making their way back. I had known this man about eighteen months and he said, 'Look here, Dick. About an hour ago I lost the best pal I ever had, and he was worth all these six Jerries put together. I'm not going to take them far before I put them out of mess.' Just after they passed me I saw the six dive in one large shell hole and he had a job to drive them out. I expect being under their own shelling would make them more nervous than under ours. Some little time later I saw him coming back and I knew it was impossible for him to have reached Clapham Junction and returned in the time, especially by the way his prisoners had been ducking and jumping into shell holes. As he passed me again he said: 'I done them in as I said, about two hundred yards back. Two bombs did the trick.' He had not walked twenty yards beyond me when he fell himself: a shell-splinter had gone clean through him. I had often heard some of our chaps say that they had done their prisoners in whilst taking them back but this was the only case I could vouch for, and no doubt the loss of his pal had upset him very much.

During the afternoon the Major handed me a message to take to A Company, which consisted of the survivors of two companies now merged into one under the command of a young platoon officer. They had to advance and take up a position about two hundred yards in front of them. The ground over which I had to travel had been occupied by the enemy a little while before and the Company were behind a little bank which was being heavily shelled. I slung my rifle, and after I had proceeded some way I pulled my revolver out for safety. Shells were falling here and there and I was jumping in and out of shell holes. When I was about fifty yards from the Company, in getting out of a large shell hole I saw a German pop up from another shell hole in front of me and rest his rifle on the lip of the shell hole. He was about to fire at our chaps in front who had passed him by without noticing him. He could never have heard me amidst all the din around: I expect it was some instinct made him turn around with the rifle at his shoulder. I fired first and as the rifle fell out of his hands I fired again. I made sure he was dead before I left him. If he hadn't popped his head up when he did no doubt I would have passed the shell hole he was in. I expect he had been shamming death and every now and then popping up and sniping at our chaps in front. If I hadn't spotted him he would have soon put my lights out after I had passed him and if any of his bullets had found their mark it would not have been noticed among the Company, who were getting men knocked out now and then by the shells that were bursting around them. This little affair was nothing out of the ordinary in a runner's work when in attacks.

The shelling was very severe around here and when I arrived I shouted for the officer. A man pointed along the bank. When I found him and delivered the message he shouted above the noise that he had not been given much time; I had delivered the message only three minutes before they were timed to advance. During the short time they had been behind the bank one-third of the Company had become casualties. When I arrived back I could only see the Major. All the signallers had gone somewhere on messages and the Doctor was some distance away attending wounded men whom he came across. He seemed to be temporarily back in the R.A.M.C.

The Major asked me how my leg was. I replied that it was all right when I was moving about, but it became very stiff after I had been resting. During the two days many pieces and flying splinters of shells and bullets must have missed me by inches. But when a small piece of spent shrapnel had hit me on the calf of the leg I knew all about it. I thought at the time that someone had hit me with a coal hammer. I had the bottom of my trousers doubled inside the sock on the calf and also my puttee doubled in the same place which, no doubt, had helped to minimize the blow. If it had not been a spent piece it would have gone clean through the calf and given me a beautiful blighty wound, which I don't mind admitting I was still hoping for.

Ricco in returning from running a message to Brigade had come across the ration party of another battalion who had all been killed, and he had brought back with him a lovely sandbag full of officers' rations. There were several kinds of tinned stuffs and three loaves of bread. The bank clerk, architect and Sealyham had also arrived back and we all had a muck in. The way the bank clerk and architect got a tin of cooked sausages across their chests made me wonder whether their forefathers had not been pure-bred Germans. The officers who the bag of rations were intended for could never have enjoyed them better than we did.

Just as we finished our feed Major Kearsley called me and told me to follow him. I could see we were making our way towards where we had visited the sapping-platoon, but I could not see any men sapping around the pillbox and was wondering if they had been knocked out. When we arrived at the concrete dug-out some of the sapping-platoon were still outside it and some had become casualties, but The Athlete and the Sergeant were still down in the dug-out. I shouted down and told them to come up and the Major asked The Athlete the reason why he had not carried out his orders. He replied that the shelling had been so intense around the pillbox after it was taken that he decided to stop where he was until it slackened. Then he had seen our troops advance again and he was under the impression that the trench would not be needed. The Major again gave him a severe reprimand and told him to take what men he had left and sap around the pillbox as he had been ordered at first.

Shortly after, the Major said he was going to visit the positions our companies had lately taken. We set off on our journey and when we passed through the Australians they started shouting, 'Come back, you bloody fools! They've got everything in line with machine-gun fire.' We took no notice and by jumping in shell holes now and again we reached halfway there. We had only advanced a few yards further when in jumping into a large shell hole an enemy machine-gun opened out and the ground around us was sprayed with bullets. The Major was shot clean through the leg just above the ankle. As I dressed his wound we discussed the possibility of returning to the bank. I said that it would be dusk in two hours' time and that we had better wait until then. He replied that he could not do that as he would have to hand over the command of the Battalion, and also wanted to discuss matters with the Commanding Officer of the 5th Scottish Rifles, and that we would make our way back at once. He clambered out of the shell hole and I followed. He hopped back to the bank, taking a zig-zag course and I the same. How we were not riddled was a mystery: the machine-gun had been playing a pretty tune behind us.

We met the Doctor and Captain Radford, who had been sent for some time before, advancing along the bank. They had decided to shift Battalion Headquarters more on the left of the bank and they had just shifted in time. The spot where Battalion Headquarters had been was now being blown to pieces. Shells were bursting right along the bank and for a considerable way back and men were being blowed yards in the air. The Major said that the Battalion would be relieved at dusk and he would try to stick it until then; but the Doctor warned him, if he did, that it might be the cause of him losing his leg.

He then handed over the command to Captain Radford, who said that he would much prefer the Doctor taking command, as he seemed to have a better grip of the situation than what he had. But the Major said he could not do that as the Doctor was a non-combatant, but that they could make any arrangements they like when he had left. We made our way to the 5th Scottish Rifles and met their colonel outside a little dug-out. He mentioned that only three young platoon-officers were left in his battalion. They went in the dug-out to discuss matters and when we left the Major had a difficult job to walk. The Casualty Clearing Station was at Clapham Junction and all along the track leading down to it lay stretcher-bearers and bandaged men who had been killed making their way back. Many men who had received what they thought were nice blighty wounds had been killed along this track. The previous day the track, in addition to being heavily shelled had also been under machine-gun fire. As we were moving along I counted over twenty of our tanks which had been put out of action. Mr Diamond, whom I had not seen since the previous day, passed us with his arm in a sling and said, 'Hello. I'm glad to see you alive.' He had been hit through the muscle of his arm. Shells were bursting here and there and we could sniff gas. We put our gas helmets on for a little while and it was twilight when we reached Clapham Junction.

The Major told me that the Battalion was going back to Dickiebusch after it was relieved and that I had no need to return. He wrote me out a note to take back to the transport. He then said that he would have liked to have remained with the Battalion until they were relieved but he thought it best to follow the Doctor's advice, especially when he said that he might lose his leg. I told him not to take too much notice of the Doctor, who would have made a better general than a doctor, and that I had seen worse bullet-wounds than what he had which had healed up in a fortnight's time. I hoped he would be back with the Battalion inside a couple of months. We shook hands and wished one another the best of luck and I made my way back to the transport.

The enemy bombed Dickiebusch that night but it was such a common occurence around this area and I was so dead-beat that I took no notice of it. The following morning I rejoined the remnants of the Battalion and found that Ricco, the bank clerk, the architect and Sealyham were still kicking. They thought I had gone West and were as delighted to see me as I was them. We had lost heavily in signallers, but Tich was still hale and hearty.

RITTMEISTER MANFRED FREIHARR VON RICHTHOFEN (THE RED BARON)
Hot Day, Hot Night

Manfred von Richthofen was Germany's most celebrated air ace during WWI. The nickname 'The Red Baron' derived from his affectation in having his Fokker aircraft painted brilliant red. (The rest of his squadron, or Jagdstaffel, *followed suit.) Below are two extracts from von Richthofen's memoirs of aerial combat on the Western Front.*

THE SECOND OF APRIL, 1917, was another hot day for my squadron. From our field we could hear the sounds of the bombardment, and it was certainly very heavy that day.

I was still in bed when the orderly rushed in crying: '*Herr Leutnant*, the English are here!' Still somewhat sleepy, I looked out the window and there circling over the field were my dear 'friends'. I got out of bed, quickly put my things on and got ready. My red bird was all set to begin the morning's work. My mechanics knew that I would not let this favourable moment go by without taking advantage of it. Everything was ready. I quickly donned my flight suit and was off.

Even so, I was the last to start. My comrades got much closer to the enemy. Then, suddenly, one of the impudent fellows fell on me, attempting to force me down. I calmly let him come on, and then we began a merry dance. At one point my opponent flew on his back, then he did this, then that. It was a two-seater. I was superior to him, and he soon realized that he could not escape me. During a pause in the fighting I looked around and saw that we were alone. Therefore, whoever shot better, whoever had the greatest calm and the best position in the moment of danger, would win.

It did not take long. I squeezed under him and fired, but without causing serious damage. We were at least two kilometres from the Front and I thought he would land, but I miscalculated my opponent. When only a few metres above the ground, he suddenly levelled off and flew straight ahead, seeking to escape me. That was too bad for him. I attacked him again and went so low that I feared I would touch the houses in the village beneath me. The Englishman kept fighting back. Almost at the end I felt a hit on my machine. I must not let up now, he must fall. He crashed at full speed into a block of houses, and there was not much left. It was again a case of splendid daring. He defended himself right up to the end.

Very pleased with the performance of my red 'bicycle' in the morning's work, I turned back. My comrades were still in the air and were very surprised when, as we later sat down to breakfast, I told them of my number thirty-two. A very young lieutenant had shot down his first, and we were all happy.

I then made up for the morning ablutions I had missed. Later, a good friend—*Leutnant* Voss of *Jagdstaffel Boelcke*—came to visit me, and we had a long and delightful conversation. The day before, Voss had scored his twenty-third victory. Therefore, he ranked next to me and was indeed, at the time, my most vigorous competitor.

As he flew home I accompanied him part of the way. We went a roundabout way over the Front. The weather became so very bad we gave up hope of finding more game.

Beneath us were dense clouds. Voss, who did not know the area, was beginning to get uncomfortable. Over Arras I met my brother, who is also in my squadron, and who had got lost from his group. He joined us when he recognized my red bird.

Then we saw an enemy squadron approaching from the other side. Immediately, 'Number thirty-three!' flashed through my head. However, the nine Englishmen were over their own territory and they preferred to avoid battle. (I will change the colour of my plane the next time!) But we caught them. Fast machines are an important factor in combat.

I was closest to the enemy and attacked the one farthest back. To my great delight, he also wanted to engage me in battle. Looking around, I was pleased to see he had been deserted by his comrades and I was soon alone with him. He was the same type I had fought with in the morning. He knew what it was all about and was a very good shot. I found that out very well, to my sorrow. The favourable wind came to my aid and carried us both over the German lines. My opponent realized that the situation was not to his advantage and disappeared in a dive into a cloud. It was almost his salvation. I dived after him, came out below and miraculously found myself sitting behind him. I fired, and fired, but there was no tangible result. Then—finally I hit him. I noticed it from the white vapour of fuel he left behind. Consequently, his engine stopped and he had to land.

But he was a stubborn fellow. He must have recognized that he had played to the end. If he continued to shoot, I could immediately shoot him dead, for we were only three hundred metres up. But this fellow defended himself, exactly as the fellow in the morning had, until he landed. After his landing I flew over him again at ten metres altitude in order to determine whether or not I had killed him. What did the impertinent fellow do? He took his machine gun and shot up my whole machine.

Voss said to me afterwards, if that had happened to him, he would have flown back and shot him dead on the ground. This fellow was, indeed, one of the few lucky ones who remained alive.

Very pleased, I flew home and celebrated my thirty-third.

Nights when the moon is full are the most suitable for night flights. During the full-moon nights of April 1917, our English 'friends' were particularly active in conjunction with the battle of Arras. They probably found out that we had set ourselves up quite comfortably at a very nice large airfield in Douai.

One night as we sat in the officers' mess, the telephone rang and it was announced: 'The English are coming.' Naturally there was a great hullabaloo of activity. We already had shelters; Simon, our construction boss, had seen to that. Everyone dived into the shelters and then we heard, faintly at first, the noise of a plane engine. The flak and searchlight batteries appeared to have heard the announcement when we did, for we noticed that they came to life slowly. However, the first enemy aircraft was much too far away to be attacked. We had a grand time. We only feared that the Englishmen would not find our field, for it was not at all simple at night especially since we did not lie alongside a road, or near water or near a railway line, which would make the best reference points at night.

Apparently the Englishmen flew very high. First they went once entirely around the field—we thought they were looking for another target—then suddenly one of them switched his engine off and came diving down. 'Now it is getting serious,' Wolff said. We each had a carbine and began to shoot at the Englishman. We could not even see him yet, but the noise of our shooting calmed our nerves. Then he came into the searchlight. All over the airfield there was great commotion. It was quite an old crate which we recognized immediately. He was, at most, a kilometre away from us. He flew right toward our field, coming ever closer. When he was at about a hundred metre altitude he switched the engine on again and flew right over us. Wolff said: 'Thank God, he was looking at the other side of the airfield.' But it did not take long for the first, and then other, bombs to rain down. Our 'friend' put on a wonderful fireworks display which could only impress a scared rabbit. I find, in general, bombing at night has only a moral significance. If one fills one's pants, it is very uncomfortable or embarrassing; but it is seldom more harmful than this.

We made a great joke of this and hoped that the English would come often. Subsequently, the 'lattice-tail'*[1] dropped his bombs from a fifty-metre altitude, and flew safely away, which is somewhat impertinent, for I'm sure with a full moon, I would not miss a shot at a wild boar from fifty metres. Why couldn't I hit an Englishman? It would be something to shoot down one of these 'friends' from the ground. We often had that honour in the air, but I had not tried it from the ground. When the Englishmen left, we went back into the mess and promised we would prepare a better reception for them the next night.

The next day the orderlies and other enlisted men busied themselves near the mess and the officers' living quarters, driving in poles which in the coming night would be used as machine-gun

1

* *German description of certain two-seater 'pusher' aircraft.*

stands. We adjusted the range on several captured English machine guns for night shooting and were very excited about what would happen. I will not reveal the number of machine guns, but it was enough. Each of my gentlemen was armed with one.

That night we again sat in the mess, naturally talking about night fliers, when an orderly burst in and cried: 'They are coming, they are coming!' Finishing his announcement, he disappeared, somewhat sparsely dressed, into the next shelter. Each of us rushed to a machine gun. Some of the qualified enlisted marksmen were also armed with machine guns. Everyone else had carbines. In any case, the squadron was armed to the teeth and ready to receive the English gentlemen.

The first came, just as on the evening before, at great altitude, then down to fifty metres and, to our great joy, he aimed this time at the site of our barracks. He was caught in the searchlight no more than three hundred metres away from us. The first of our men began to shoot, and we all joined in at the same time. An infantry assault charge could not have been better repelled. This poor fellow was greeted by furious ground fire which he could not have heard over the noise of his engine, but he would see the flashes of our gunfire. I thought it very plucky of him that he did not swerve but stubbornly continued on his mission. He flew right over us. The moment he was above us, we of course all jumped into a shelter, for to be hit by a stupid bomb would be a foolish hero's death for a fighter pilot. Scarcely had he passed over us when we were back at our guns, firing after him. Schäfer claimed, of course: 'I hit him!' Schäfer shoots well, but in this case I did not believe him and, besides, everyone else had just as good a chance of hitting the Englishman.

If nothing else, the enemy was forced to drop his bombs in the area without effect. One landed a few metres from '*Le petit rouge*', but did not harm it. Later that night this fun was repeated. I was already in bed and fast asleep when, as if in a dream, I heard anti-aircraft fire. I woke up only to learn that the dream was really happening. One fellow flew so low over my room that I pulled the covers over my head in fright. The next minute there was a terrific noise near my window, and the panes of glass fell victim to the bomb. Quickly I jumped into my shirt in order to get a few shots at him. Outside he was the target of vigorous shooting. Unfortunately, I had outslept my comrades.

The next morning we were pleasantly surprised to learn that we had brought down no less than three Englishmen. They landed not far from our airfield and were taken prisoner. We had hit their engines and thereby forced them down on our side. So, perhaps Schäfer had not been mistaken, after all. In any event, we were very pleased with our success. The Englishmen were somewhat less pleased, however, and they preferred not to attack our field any more.

EDDIE V. RICKENBACKER
Strafing the Drachens

Captain Eddie V. Rickenbacker led the legendary American 94th Pursuit Squadron in the skies over France during 1918.

OBSERVATION BALLOONS, OR 'DRACHEN' AS the Boches call them, provide a most valuable method of espionage upon the movements of an enemy and at the same time are a most tempting bait to pilots of the opposing fighting squadrons.

They are huge in size, forming an elongated sausage some two hundred feet in length and perhaps fifty feet in diameter. They hang swinging in the sky at a low elevation—some two thousand feet or under, and are prevented from making any rapid effort to escape from airplane attack by reason of the long cable which attaches them to their mother truck on the highway below.

These trucks which attend the balloons are of the ordinary size—a three-ton motor truck which steers and travels quite like any big lorry one meets on the streets. On the truck bed is fastened a winch which lets out the cable to any desired length. In case of an attack by shell fire the truck simply runs up the road a short distance without drawing down the balloon. When it is observed that the enemy gunners have again calculated its range another move is made, perhaps back to a point near its former position.

Large as is its bulk and as favourable and steady a target as it must present to the enemy gunners three miles away, it is seldom indeed that a hit from bursting shrapnel is recorded.

These balloons are placed along the lines some two miles back of the front-line trenches. From his elevated perch two thousand feet above ground, the observer can study the ground and pick up every detail over a radius of ten miles on every side. Clamped over his ears are telephone receivers. With his telescope to his eye he observes and talks to the officers on the truck below him. They in turn inform him of any special object about which information is desired. If our battery is firing upon a certain enemy position, the observer watches for the bursts and corrects the faults in aim. If a certain roadway is being dug up by our artillery, the observer notifies the battery when sufficient damage has been done to render that road impassable.

Observation balloons are thus a constant menace to contemplated movements of forces and considered as a factor of warfare they are of immense importance. Every fifteen or twenty miles along the front both sides station their balloons, and when one is shot down by an enemy airplane another immediately runs up to take its place.

Shelling by artillery fire being so ineffective it naturally occurs to every airplane pilot that such a huge and unwieldy target must be easy to destroy from the air. Their cost is many times greater than the value of an airplane. They cannot fight back with any hope of success. All that seems to be required is a sudden dash by a fighting airplane, a few shots with incendiary bullets—and the big gas bag bursts into flames. What could be more simple?

I had been victorious over five or six enemy airplanes at this time and had never received a wound in return. This balloon business puzzled me and I was determined to solve the mystery.

I lay awake many nights pondering over the stories I had heard about attacking these Drachen, planning just how I should dive in and let them have a quick burst, sheer off and climb away from their machine-gun fire, hang about for another dive and continue these tactics until a sure hit could be scored.

I would talk this plan over with several of my pilots and after working out all the details we would try it on. Perhaps we could make 94 Squadron famous for its destruction of enemy balloons. There must be some way to do it, provided I picked out the right men for the job and gave them a thorough training.

After discussing the matter with Major Atkinson, our commanding officer, who readily gave me his approval, I sought out Reed Chambers, Jimmy Meissner, Thorn Taylor, and Lieutenant Loomis. These four with myself would make an ideal team to investigate this situation.

First we obtained photographs of five German balloons in their lairs, from a French Observation Squadron. Then we studied the map and ascertained the precise position each occupied: the nature of the land, the relative position of the mountains and rivers, the trees and villages in the vicinity of each, and all the details of their environment.

One by one we visited these balloons, studying from above the nature of the roadway upon which their mother trucks must operate, the height of the trees along this roadway and where the anti-aircraft defenses had been posted around each Drachen. These latter were the only perils we had to fear. We knew the reputation of these defenses, and they were not to be ignored. Since they alone were responsible for the defense of the balloons, we presumed that they were unusually numerous and accurate. They would undoubtedly put up such a heavy barrage of gunfire around the suspended Drachen that an airplane must actually pass through a steady hailstorm of bullets both in coming in and in going out.

Major Willy Coppens, the Belgian ace, had made the greatest success of this balloon strafing. He had shot down over a score of German Drachens and had never received a wound. I knew he armed his airplane with flaming rockets which penetrated the envelope of the gas bag and burned there until it was ignited. This method had its advantages and its disadvantages. But another trick that was devised by Coppens met with my full approval.

This was to make the attack early in the morning or late in the evening, when visibility was poor and the approach of the buzzing engine could not be definitely located. Furthermore, he made his attack from a low level, flying so close to the ground that he could not be readily picked up from above. As he approached the vicinity of his balloon he zoomed up and began his attack. If the balloon was being hauled down he met it halfway. All depended upon the timing of his attack and the accuracy of his aim.

On June 25, 1918, my alarm clock buzzed me awake at 2:30 o'clock sharp. As I was the instigator of this little expedition, I leaped out of bed and leaned out of my window to get a glimpse of the sky. It promised to be a fine day!

Rousing out the other four of my party, I telephoned to the hangars and ordered out the machines. The guns had been thoroughly serviced during the night and special incendiary bullets had been placed in the magazines. Everything was ready for our first attack and we sat down to a hurried breakfast, full of excitement and fervor.

The whole squadron got up and accompanied us to the hangars. We were soon in our flying suits and strapped in our seats. The engines began humming and then I felt my elation suddenly begin to dissipate. My engine was stubborn and would not keep up its steady revolutions. Upon investigation, I found one magneto unserviceable, leaving me with but one upon which I could rely! I debated within myself for a few seconds as to whether I should risk dropping into Germany with a dud engine or risk the condolences of the present crowd which had gathered to see us off.

The former won in spite of my best judgment. Rather than endure the sarcasm of the onlookers and the disappointment of my team, I prayed for one more visitation of my Goddess of Luck and gave the signal to start.

At 4:30 o'clock we left the ground and headed straight into Germany. I had decided to fly eight or ten miles behind the lines and then turn and come back at the balloon line from an unexpected quarter, trusting to the discipline of the German army to have its balloons ascending just as we reached them. Each pilot in my party had his own balloon marked out. Each was to follow the same tactics. We separated as soon as we left the field, each man taking up his own course.

Passing high over Nancy I proceeded northward and soon saw the irregular lines of the trenches below me. It was a mild morning and very little activity was discernible on either side. Not a gun was flashing in the twilight which covered the ground and as far as my eye could reach nothing was stirring. It was the precise time of day when weary fighters would prefer to catch their last wink of sleep. I hoped they would be equally deaf to the sounds of my humming Nieuport.

Cutting off my engine at fifteen thousand feet over the lines. I prayed once more that when the time came to switch on again my one magneto would prove faithful. It alone stood between me and certain capture. I could not go roaring along over the heads of the whole German army and expect to conceal my presence. By gliding quietly with silent engine as I passed deeper and deeper within their territory I could gradually lose my altitude and then turn and gain the balloon line with comparatively little noise.

'Keep your Spunk Up—Magneto, Boy!' I sang to my engine as I began the fateful glide. I had a mental vision of the precise spot behind the enemy balloon where I should turn on my switch and there discover—liberty or death! I would gladly have given my kingdom that moment for just one more little magneto!

At that moment I was passing swiftly over the little village of Goin. It was exactly five o'clock. The black outlines of the Bois de Face lay to my left, nestled along the two arms of the Moselle. I might possibly reach those woods with a long glide if my engine failed me at the critical moment. I could crash in the treetops, hide in the forest until dark and possibly make my way back through the lines with a little luck. Cheery thoughts I had as I watched the menacing German territory slipping away beneath my wings!

And then I saw my balloon! The faithful fellows had not disappointed me at any rate! Conscientious and reliable men these Germans were! Up and ready for the day's work at the exact hour I had planned for them! I flattened out my glide a trifle more, so as to pass their post with the minimum noise of singing wires. A mile or two beyond them I began a wide circle with my nose well down. It was a question of seconds now and all would be over. I wondered how Chambers and Meissner and the others were getting on. Probably at this very instant they were throbbing with joy over the scene of a flaming bag of gas!

Finding the earth rapidly nearing me, I banked sharply to the left and looked ahead. There was my target floating blandly and unsuspiciously in the first rays of the sun. The men below were undoubtedly drinking their coffee and drawing up orders for the day's work that would never be executed. I headed directly for the swinging target and set my sights dead on its center. There facing me with rare arrogance in the middle of the balloon was a huge Maltese Cross—the emblem of the Boche aviation. I shifted my rudder a bit and pointed my sights exactly at the center of the cross. Then I deliberately pressed both triggers with my right hand, while with my left I snapped on the switch.

There must be some compartment in one's brain for equalizing the conflicting emotions that crowd simultaneously upon one at such moments as this. I realized instantly that I was saved myself, for the engine picked up with a whole-souled roar the very first instant after I made the contact. With this happy realization came the simultaneous impression that my whole morning's work and anguish were wasted.

I saw three or four streaks of flame flash ahead of me and enter the huge bulk of the balloon ahead. Then the flames abruptly ceased.

Flashing bullets were cutting a living circle all around me too, I noticed. Notwithstanding the subtlety of my stalking approach, the balloon's defenders had discovered my presence and were all waiting for me. My guns had both jammed. This, too, I realized at the same instant. I had had my chance, had shot my bolt, was in the very midst of a fiery furnace that beggars description but thanks to a benignant Providence, was behind a lusty engine that would carry me home.

Amid all these conflicting impressions which surged through me during that brief instant, I distinctly remember that I had failed in my mission! With the largest target in the world before my guns, with all the risks already run and conquered, I had failed in my mission simply because of a stupid jamming of my guns.

I had swerved to the right of the suspended gas bag and grazed the distended sides of the enemy Drachen. I might almost have extended my hand and cut a hole in its sleek envelope, as I swept by. The wind had been from the east, so I knew that the balloon would stretch away from its supporting cable and leave it to the right. More than one balloon strafer has rushed below his balloon and crashed headlong into the slim wire cable which anchors it to the ground.

I had planned every detail with rare success. The only thing I had failed in was the over-all result. Either the Boche had some material covering their Drachens that extinguished my flaming bullets, or else the gas which was contained within them was not as highly inflammable as I had been led to believe. Some three or four bullets had entered the sides of the balloon—of this I was certain. Why had they failed to set fire to it?

Later on I was to discover that flaming bullets very frequently puncture observation balloons without producing the expected blaze. The very rapidity of their flight leaves no time for the ignition of the gas. Often in the early dawn the accumulated dews and moisture in the air serve to dampen the balloon's envelope and hundreds of incendiary bullets penetrate the envelope without doing more damage than can be repaired with a few strips of adhesive plaster.

As I flew through the fiery curtain of German bullets and set my nose for home I developed a distinct admiration for the Belgian Willy Coppens de Houthulst. And since he had proved that balloon strafing had in fact a possibility of success, I was determined to investigate this business until I too had solved its mysteries.

Then I began to laugh to myself at an occurrence that until then I had had not time to consider. As I began firing at the sausage, the German observer who had been standing in his basket under the balloon with his eyes glued to his binoculars, had evidently been taken entirely by surprise. The first intimation he had of my approach was the bullets which preceded me. At the instant he dropped his glasses he dived headlong over the side of his basket with his parachute. He did not even pause to look around to see what danger threatened him.

Evidently the mother truck began winding up the cable at the same time, for as the observer jumped for his life the balloon began to descend upon him. I caught the merest glimpse of his face as I swept past him, and there was a mingled look of terror and surprise upon his features that almost compensated me for my disappointment.

On my way homeward I flew directly toward a French observation balloon that swung on the end of its cable in my path. Without considering the consequences of my act, I sheered in and passed quite close to the Frenchman who was staring at me from his suspended basket.

Suddenly the Froggy leaped headlong from his perch and clutching his parachute rigging with his two hands began a rapid descent to earth. And not until then did I realize that coming directly at him, head on from Germany as I did, he had no way of reading my cocards which were painted underneath my wings. He had decided that I was a Boche and did not care to take any chances at a jump with a blazing gas bag about his ears.

Fortunately for me, the French gunners below could read my insignias from the ground and they suffered me to pass, without taking any revenge for the trick I had played upon their comrade.

Arriving at the aerodrome at 5:45, I found that I was the last of my little party of balloon strafers to land. The other four were standing together, looking rather sheepishly in my direction as I walked toward them.

'Well, what luck?' I inquired as I came up to them. Nobody spoke. 'I thought I saw a big blaze over in your direction, Jimmy!' I went on, addressing myself to Lieutenant Meissner. 'Did you get him?'

'No!' replied Jimmy disgustedly. 'The balloon was not up in thc air at all. I didn't get a sight of it. I didn't even see where they had hidden it.'

'Did you get yours, Reed?' I asked, turning to Chambers.

'Hell, no!' retorted Lieutenant Chambers emphatically. 'I shot the thing full of holes, but she wouldn't drop.'

The other two pilots had much the same stories. One had failed to find his balloon and the other had made an attack but it had brought no results. All had been subjected to a defensive fire that had quite reversed their opinions of the Archibald family.

'I suppose you burned yours all right, Rick?' said Reed Chambers rather enviously as we walked up to the mess together. 'What do you think of us fellows anyway?'

'I think, Reed,' replied I, 'that we are the rottenest lot of balloonatical fakers that ever got up at two-thirty in the morning. But I am happy to discover,' I added, thinking of my one operative magneto, 'that none of us had to land in Germany.'

ROBERT GRAVES
The Report of My Death

Robert Graves (see page 11) was wounded during a German artillery barrage at the Somme in 1916.

ONE PIECE OF SHELL WENT through my left thigh, high up, near the groin; I must have been at the full stretch of my stride to escape emasculation. The wound over the eye was made by a little chip of marble, possibly from one of the Bazentin cemetery headstones. (Later, I had it cut out, but a smaller piece has since risen to the surface under my right eyebrow, where I keep it for a souvenir.) This, and a finger-wound which split the bone, probably came from another shell bursting in front of me. But a piece of shell had also gone in two inches below the point of my right shoulder-blade and came out through my chest two inches above the right nipple.

My memory of what happened then is vague. Apparently Dr Dunn came up through the barrage with a stretcher-party, dressed my wound, and got me down to the old German dressing-station at the north end of Mametz Wood. I remember being put on the stretcher, and winking at the stretcher-bearer sergeant who had just said: 'Old Gravy's got it, all right!' They laid my stretcher in a corner of the dressing-station, where I remained unconscious for more than twenty-four hours.

Late that night, Colonel Crawshay came back from High Wood and visited the dressing-station; he saw me lying in the corner, and they told him I was done for. The next morning, July 21st, clearing away the dead, they found me still breathing and put me on an ambulance for Heilly, the nearest field hospital. The pain of being jolted down the Happy Valley, with a shell hole at every three or four yards of the road, woke me up. I remember screaming. But back on the better roads I became unconscious again. That morning, Crawshay wrote the usual formal letters of condolence to the next-of-kin of the six or seven officers who had been killed. This was his letter to my mother:

> Dear Mrs Graves, 22.7.16
>
> I very much regret to have to write and tell you your son has died of wounds. He was very gallant, and was doing so well and is a great loss.
>
> He was hit by a shell and very badly wounded, and died on the way down to the base I believe. He was not in bad pain, and our doctor managed to get across and attend to him at once.
>
> We have had a very hard time, and our casualties have been large. Believe me you have all our sympathy in your loss, and we have lost a very gallant soldier.
>
> Please write to me if I can tell you or do anything.
>
> Yours sincerely,
> C. Crawshay, Lt-Col.

Then he made out the official casualty list—a long one, because only eighty men were left in the battalion—and reported me 'died of wounds'. Heilly lay on the railway; close to the station stood the hospital tents with the red cross prominently painted on the roofs, to discourage air-bombing. Fine July weather made the tents insufferably hot. I was semi-conscious now, and aware of my lung-wound through a shortness of breath. It amused me to watch the little bubbles of blood, like scarlet soap-bubbles, which my breath made in escaping through the opening of the wound. The doctor came over to my bed. I felt sorry for him; he looked as though he had not slept for days.

I asked him: 'Can I have a drink?'

'Would you like some tea?'

I whispered: 'Not with condensed milk.'

He said, most apologetically: 'I'm afraid there's no fresh milk.'

Tears of disappointment pricked my eyes; I expected better of a hospital behind the lines.

'Will you have some water?'

'Not if it's boiled.'

'It is boiled. And I'm afraid I can't give you anything alcoholic in your present condition.'

'Some fruit then?'

'I have seen no fruit for days.'

Yet a few minutes later he returned with two rather unripe greengages. In whispers I promised him a whole orchard when I recovered.

The nights of the 22nd and 23rd were horrible. Early on the morning of the 24th, when the doctor came round the ward, I said: 'You must send me away from here. This heat will kill me.' It was beating on my head through the canvas.

'Stick it out. Your best chance is to lie here and not to be moved. You'd not reach the Base alive.'

'Let me risk the move. I'll be all right, you'll see.'

Half an hour later he returned. 'Well, you're having it your way. I've just got orders to evacuate every case in the hospital. Apparently the Guards have been in it up at Delville Wood, and they'll all be coming down tonight.' I did not fear that I would die, now—it was enough to be honourably wounded and bound for home.

THUCYDIDES
The Destruction of the Athenian Expedition

Many expeditionary forces have fared badly over the course of history, but few have endured the mauling received by the Athenians in 413 BC. The Greek historian takes up the story after the Athenians have already lost a naval engagement to the Syracusans (Sicilians).

AFTER THIS HARD-FOUGHT FIGHT, in which many men and many ships had been lost on both sides, the victorious Syracusans and their allies took up the wrecks and the dead bodies, sailed back to their city, and put up a trophy. But the Athenians were so oppressed by the present weight of their misfortune that they never even thought of asking for permission to take up their dead or the wreckage. Instead they wanted to retreat at once and on that very night. Demosthenes, however, went to Nicias and proposed that they should once again man the ships that they had left and do their best to force their way out at dawn. He pointed out that they still had more ships left fit for service than the enemy; for the Athenians had about sixty ships left, and their opponents had less than fifty. Nicias agreed with this proposal, but when they wanted to man the ships, the sailors would not go on board, being so demoralized by their defeat that they no longer regarded victory as a possibility.

The Athenians, therefore, were now all resolved to retreat by land. Hermocrates, the Syracusan, suspected that this was their plan, and thought that it would be a dangerous thing for Syracuse if so large an army were to get away by land and settle in some part of Sicily from which it could wage war against them again. He therefore approached the authorities and pointed out that they ought not to allow the Athenians to escape by night, saying that, in his personal opinion, the Syracusans and their allies should go out of the city at once in full force and build road-blocks and occupy and garrison the passes. The authorities saw the force of his argument as clearly as he did himself, and thought that his plan should be carried out; however, they did not think that it would be at all easy to get their own people to obey orders, considering that they were just beginning to celebrate the occasion and were relaxing after their great victory at sea, and were also holding a festival (there happened to be a sacrifice to Heracles on that day); most of them, in fact, in their great joy in their victory, had started drinking at the festival, so that it looked as though about the last thing they could be persuaded to do at this particular moment would be to take up their arms and march out to battle. Taking all this into consideration, the magistrates decided that the idea was impossible to carry out in practice, and Hermocrates, failing to get any further with them, proceeded to put the following plan of his own into operation. What he feared was that in the night the Athenians might have the start of them and so get over the most difficult part of the route unopposed; therefore as soon as it began to grow dark he sent down to their camp some friends of his own with a cavalry detachment. These men rode up to within earshot and called out to some of the soldiers, pretending that they were friendly to the Athenians (for there were, in fact, some people who brought news to Nicias about what was happening inside the city), and asking them to tell Nicias not to lead the army away during the night, since the Syracusans were guarding the roads; instead he should retreat, in his own time and after making the proper preparations, by day. After saying this, they went away, and those who had heard them passed on the message to the Athenian generals, who, on the strength of what they were told, put off the retreat for the night, in the belief that the information was genuine.

And now, since even after all this they failed to start immediately, they decided to wait for the next day too, so that the soldiers could pack their most essential luggage as best they could; then, leaving everything else behind, they were to set off, taking with them only what was absolutely necessary for each man's personal needs. Meanwhile the Syracusans and Gylippus set out first with their land forces, built road-blocks in the country on the routes which the Athenians were likely to take, posted guards at the fords of the streams and rivers, and arranged themselves so as to be able to meet and to stop the retreating army at the points which they chose. And with their ships they sailed up to the Athenian ships and dragged them from the beach. Some had been burned by the Athenians themselves, according to their original plan; as for the others, the Syracusans towed them away as they liked, just as each one was driven ashore, and brought them, with no opposition from anyone, to their city.

Afterwards, when Nicias and Demosthenes thought that the preparations were complete, came the time for the army to move, two days after the naval battle. It was a terrible scene, and more than one element in their situation contributed to their dismay. Not only were they retreating after having lost all their ships, and instead of their high hopes now found themselves and the whole state of Athens in danger, but in the actual leaving of the camp there were sad sights for every eye, sad thoughts for every mind to feel. The dead were unburied, and when any man recognized one of his friends lying among them, he was filled with grief and fear; and the living who, whether sick or wounded, were being left behind caused more pain than did the dead to those who were left alive, and were more pitiable than the lost. Their prayers and their lamentations made the rest feel impotent and helpless, as they begged to be taken with them and cried out aloud to every single friend or relative whom they could see; as they hung about the necks of those who had shared tents with them and were now going, following after them as far as they could, and, when their bodily strength failed them, reiterated their cries to heaven and their lamentations as they were left behind. So the whole army was filled with tears and in such distress of mind that they found it difficult to go away even from this land of their enemies when sufferings too great for tears had befallen them already and more still, they feared, awaited them in the dark future ahead. There was also a profound sense of shame and deep feelings of self-reproach. Indeed, they were like nothing so much as the fleeing population of a city that has surrendered to its besiegers, and no small city at that, since in the whole crowd of them marching together there were not less than 40,000 men. Each of them carried with him whatever he could that would be useful, and, contrary to the usual practice, the hoplites* and cavalry carried their own provisions themselves while under arms, some because they had no servants, some because they did not trust the servants they had; many of these had deserted in the past, and most of the rest were doing so now. Yet even so they did not carry a sufficient amount, since there was no longer any food in the camp. And then there was the degradation of it all and the fact that all without exception were afflicted, so that, although there may be some lightening of a burden when it is shared with many others, this still did not make the burden seem any easier to bear at the time, especially when they remembered the splendour and the pride of their setting out and saw how mean and abject was the conclusion. No Hellenic army had ever suffered such a reverse. They had come to enslave others, and now they were going away frightened of being enslaved themselves; and instead of the prayers and paeans with which they had sailed out, the words to be heard now were directly contrary and boded evil as they started on their way back, sailors travelling on land, trusting in hoplites rather than in ships. Nevertheless, when they considered the greatness of the danger that still hung over them, all this seemed able to be borne.

Nicias, seeing the discouragement of the army with its hopes so totally eclipsed, went along the ranks and then did the best he could to encourage and to comfort them, and, as he went from one line to another, he raised his voice louder and louder in his eagerness to be of help and in his wish that the good that his words might do should reach as far as possible:

'Athenians and allies, even now we must still hope on. You have been saved from worse straits than these before now. And you must not reproach yourselves too much for the disasters of the past or for your present undeserved sufferings. I myself am physically no stronger than any one among you (in fact you see what my illness has done to me), nor, I think, can anyone be considered to have been more blessed by fortune than I have been in my private life and in other respects; but I am now plunged into the same perils as the meanest man here. Yet throughout my life I have worshipped the gods as I ought, and my conduct towards men has been just and without reproach.

* *Hoplite: a heavily armoured infantryman.*

Because of this I still have a strong hope for the future, and these disasters do not terrify me as they well might do. Perhaps they may even come to an end. Our enemies have had good fortune enough, and, if any of the gods was angry with us at our setting out, by this time we have been sufficiently punished. Other men before us have attacked their neighbours, and, after doing what men will do, have suffered no more than what men can bear. So it is now reasonable for us to hope that the gods will be kinder to us, since by now we deserve their pity rather than their jealousy. And then look at yourselves; see how many first-rate hoplites you have marching together in your ranks, and do not be too much alarmed. Reflect that you yourselves, wherever you settle down, are a city already and that there is no other city in Sicily that could easily meet your attack or drive you out from any place where you establish yourselves. As for the march, you must see to its safety and its good order yourselves, and let this one thought be in the mind of every man among you—that on whatever spot of ground he is forced to fight, there, if he wins it, he will find a country and a fortress. We shall hurry forward, marching by night as well as by day, since our supplies are short, and once we can reach some friendly place in the country of the Sicels, whom, because of their fear of Syracuse, we can still rely upon, then you can consider yourselves safe. We have already sent instructions to them to meet us and to bring supplies of food with them. In a word, soldiers, you must make up your minds that to be brave now is a matter of necessity, since no place exists near at hand where a coward can take refuge, and that, if you escape the enemy now, you will all see again the homes for which you long, and the Athenians among you will build up again the great power of Athens, fallen though it is. It is men who make the city, and not walls or ships with no men inside them.'

While he was speaking to the troops, Nicias was going along the ranks, and wherever he saw that they were not in close formation or were out of order, he brought them together and set them in their correct positions. Demosthenes did the same for the troops under his command and spoke to them in much the same terms. The army marched in a hollow square, the troops of Nicias being in front and those of Demosthenes at the rear; the hoplites were at the outside, and the baggage-carriers and general mass of the army were in the middle.

When they reached the crossing of the river Anapus they found a body of Syracusan and allied troops drawn up there to guard it. These they routed and, gaining control of the ford, pushed on farther, with the Syracusan cavalry attacking them on the flanks and the light troops harassing them with their missiles. The Athenians advanced about four and a half miles that day, and halted for the night on a hill. Next day they were on the march early, went forward about two miles, and descended to some level ground, where they camped, with the intention of procuring food from the houses, since the place was inhabited, and of carrying water with them from there, as for many furlongs in front of them, in the direction which they intended to take, the supply of water was not plentiful. Meanwhile the Syracusans went on and fortified the pass that lay ahead of them. It was a place where there was a steep hill with a rocky ravine at each side of it, and it was called the Acraean cliff.

Next day the Athenians went forward, and the cavalry and javelin-throwers of the Syracusans and their allies came up in great numbers from both sides, hampering their march with volleys of javelins and with cavalry charges on their flanks. After fighting for a long time, the Athenians finally went back again to the same camp as before. They no longer had the same supplies of provisions, since it was now impossible to leave the camp because of the enemy cavalry.

Early in the morning they set forward again and forced their way up to the hill which had been fortified. Here they found in front of them the enemy's infantry ready to defend the fortification and drawn up many shields deep, since the place was a narrow one. The Athenians charged and assaulted the wall: missiles rained down on them from the hill, which rose steeply, so that it was all the easier for those on it to be sure of hitting their target; and, finding it impossible to break through, they retreated and rested. At the same time there were some claps of thunder with some rain, as often happens when it gets near autumn, and this made the Athenians still more discouraged, for they saw in all these events omens of their own destruction. While they were resting, Gylippus and the Syracusans sent part of their army to build fortifications in the rear of the Athenians on the route by which they had come forward; but the Athenians sent back some of their own men to counter this move and succeeded in preventing it. Afterwards they fell back more in the direction of the plain and there spent the night.

Next day they went on again, and the Syracusans came all round them and attacked them from every side and wounded many of them, giving way whenever the Athenians charged, and resuming their attacks as soon as they retired. In particular they attacked the rearguard, hoping that, if they could rout some detachments separately, this would cause a panic throughout the whole army. For a long time the Athenians held out, fighting in this way; finally, after having advanced a little over half a mile, they halted in the plain to rest, and the Syracusans left them and went back to their own camp.

During the night Nicias and Demosthenes, seeing the wretched state in which their army was, now in want of every kind of necessity and with numbers of men disabled in the numerous attacks of the enemy, decided to light as many fires as possible and to lead their forces away. Instead of going by the route which they had intended to take, they were now to go towards the sea, in the opposite direction to the part guarded by the Syracusans. This new route, instead of leading towards Catana, would take the army to the other side of Sicily, towards Camarina, Gela and the other Hellenic and non-Hellenic cities in that area. They therefore lit a number of fires and marched away in the night. What happened to them was something which happens in all armies, and most of all in the biggest ones. Fears and alarms are apt to break out, especially when troops are marching by night, through enemy country and with the enemy himself not far away. So the Athenian army fell into confusion. The division under Nicias, as it was leading the way, kept together and got a long distance ahead of the rest, while the troops under Demosthenes—rather more than half of the whole army—lost contact with each other and marched in some disorder. Nevertheless, they reached the sea at dawn and, taking the Helorine road, marched on with the intention of getting to the river Cacyparis and following its course up into the interior, where they hoped to join forces with the Sicels whom they had sent for. When they reached the river they found that here also was a detachment of Syracusans who were building a wall and a stockade to block the crossing place. They forced their way through these troops, crossed the river, and, following the advice of their guides, marched on again to another river called the Erineus.

Meanwhile, when it was day and the Syracusans and their allies found that the Athenians had gone, most of them accused Gylippus of having deliberately let them escape, and, since there was no difficulty in finding the route which they had taken, they quickly hurried after them, and caught up with them about the time of the midday meal. The troops they came up with were those under Demosthenes, who were behind the rest and were marching more slowly and in worse order, because of the confusion which, as already mentioned, had taken place during the night. The Syracusans went into action and attacked them at once and, surrounding them with their cavalry all the more easily because they were separated from the rest, hemmed them in on one spot. Nicias's troops were five or six miles ahead of them, as Nicias was leading his men on faster, in the belief that, as things were, their safety lay not in standing their ground and fighting, unless they had to, but in retreating as fast as possible and only fighting when they were forced to do so. Demosthenes, however, had been on the whole in more continual difficulties, since the rear-guard was always attacked first by the enemy; and now, when he realized that the enemy were in pursuit, instead of pushing on, he formed his men up in battle order, and the loss of time involved in this operation led to his being surrounded. He and the Athenians with him were now in a state of great confusion. They were penned into a place which had a wall all round it, with a road on both sides and great numbers of olive trees, and they were under a rain of missiles from every direction. This method of attack was naturally adopted by the Syracusans in preference to hand-to-hand fighting, since to venture themselves against men who had been driven desperate would now be more in the interests of the Athenians than in their own; and at the same time they began to spare themselves a little, so as not to throw away their lives before the moment of victory which was now a certainty; besides, they thought that by these methods they would in any case break down the resistance of the Athenians and make them prisoners.

As it was, after attacking the Athenians and allies all day long and from every side with their missiles, they saw that they were now worn out with their wounds and with all the other sufferings they had endured. Gylippus and the Syracusans and their allies then made a proclamation first to the islanders, offering their liberty to any who would come over to them; and a few cities did so. Afterwards terms of surrender were agreed upon for all the troops serving under Demosthenes: they were to lay down their arms on the condition that no one was to be put to death either summarily, or by imprisonment, or by lack of the necessities of life. They then surrendered, 6,000 of them in all, and gave up all the money in their possession, which they threw into the hollows of shields, filling four of them. They were then immediately taken to the city. On the same day Nicias with his men reached the river Erineus. He crossed the river and halted his army on some high ground.

Next day the Syracusans caught up with him, told him that the troops under Demosthenes had surrendered, and invited him to do so also. Nicias did not believe it, and a truce was arranged so that he could send a horseman to go and see. When the messenger had gone and returned with the news that they had surrendered, Nicias sent a herald to Gylippus and the Syracusans, saying that he was prepared to make an agreement with them in the name of the Athenians that, in return for letting his army go, they would pay back to Syracuse all the money that she had spent on the war; until the money should be paid he would give them Athenian citizens as hostages, one man for each talent. The Syracusans and Gylippus would not accept these proposals. They attacked and surrounded this army as they had the other, raining missiles on them from all sides until the evening. These men, too, were wretchedly off in their want of food and other necessities. Nevertheless, they intended to wait until the dead of night and then to go on with their march. As they were taking up their arms, the Syracusans realized what they were doing and raised their paean. The Athenians, finding that they were discovered, laid down their arms again, except for about 300 men, who forced their way through the guards and went on through the night as best they could.

When day came Nicias led his army on, and the Syracusans and their allies pressed them hard in the same way as before, showering missiles and hurling javelins in upon them from every side. The Athenians hurried on towards the river Assinarus, partly because they were under pressure from the attacks made upon them from every side by the numbers of cavalry and the masses of other troops, and thought that things would not be so bad if they got to the river, partly because they were exhausted and were longing for water to drink. Once they reached the river, they rushed down into it, and now all discipline was at an end. Every man wanted to be the first to get across, and, as the enemy persisted in his attacks, the crossing now became a difficult matter. Forced to crowd in close together, they fell upon each other and trampled each other underfoot; some were killed immediately by their own spears, others got entangled among themselves and among the baggage and were swept away by the river. Syracusan troops were stationed on the opposite bank, which was a steep one. They hurled down their weapons from above on the Athenians, most of whom, in a disordered mass, were greedily drinking in the deep river-bed. And the Peloponnesians came down and slaughtered them, especially those who were in the river. The water immediately became foul, but nevertheless they went on drinking it, all muddy as it was and stained with blood; indeed, most of them were fighting among themselves to have it.

Finally, when the many dead were by now heaped upon each other in the bed of the stream, when part of the army had been destroyed there in the river, and the few who managed to get away had been cut down by the cavalry, Nicias surrendered himself to Gylippus, whom he trusted more than he did the Syracusans, telling him and the Spartans to do what they liked with him personally, but to stop the slaughter of his soldiers. After this Gylippus gave orders to take prisoners, and all the rest, apart from a large number who were hidden by the soldiers who had captured them, were brought in alive. They also sent in pursuit of the 300 who had broken through the guards during the night, and captured them as well. The number of prisoners taken over in a body by the state was not very large; great numbers, however, had been appropriated by their captors; in fact the whole of Sicily was full of them, there having been no fixed agreement for the surrender, as in the case of the troops of Demosthenes. Then a considerable part of the army had been killed outright, since this had been a very great slaughter—greater than any that took place in this war. Large numbers, too, had fallen in the constant attacks made on them during the march. Nevertheless, there were many who escaped, some at the time, and others, after having been enslaved, ran away afterwards. These found refuge in Catana.

The Syracusans and their allies now brought their forces together into one, took up the spoils and as many of the prisoners as they could, and went back to their city. They put the Athenian and allied prisoners whom they had taken into the stone quarries, thinking that this was the safest way of keeping them. Nicias and Demosthenes they put to death, against the will of Gylippus, who thought that it would be a fine thing indeed for him if, on top of everything else, he could bring the enemy generals back to Sparta. It so happened that one of them, Demosthenes, was Sparta's greatest enemy because of the campaign at Pylos and in the island, while the other, for the same reasons, was Sparta's best friend. For Nicias had done his utmost to secure the release of the Spartans captured on the island by persuading the Athenians to make peace. Because of this the Spartans were well-disposed towards him, and it was in this that Nicias himself had chiefly trusted when he surrendered himself to Gylippus. But some of the Syracusans who had been in contact with him were afraid, so it was said, that this fact might lead to his being examined under torture, and so bringing trouble on them at the very moment of their success. Others, particularly the Corinthians, feared that, since he was rich, he might escape by means of bribery and do them still more harm in the future. So they persuaded their allies to agree and put him to death. For these reasons or reasons very like them he was killed, a man who, of all the Hellenes in my time, least deserved to come to so miserable an end, since the whole of his life had been devoted to the study and the practice of virtue.

Those who were in the stone quarries were treated badly by the Syracusans at first. There were many of them and were crowded together in a narrow pit, where, since there was no roof over their heads, they suffered first from the heat of the sun and the closeness of the air; and then, in contrast, came on the cold autumnal nights, and the change in temperature brought disease among them. Lack of space made it necessary for them to do everything on the same spot; and besides there were the bodies all heaped together on top of one another of those who had died from their wounds or from the change of temperature or other such causes, so that the smell was insupportable. At the same time they suffered from hunger and from thirst. During eight months the daily allowance for each man was half a pint of water and a pint of corn. In fact they suffered everything which one could imagine might be suffered by men imprisoned in such a place. For about ten weeks they lived like this all together; then, with the exception of the Athenians and any Greeks from Italy or Sicily who had joined the expedition, the rest were sold as slaves. It is hard to give the exact figure, but the whole number of prisoners must have been at least 7,000.

This was the greatest Hellenic action that took place during this war, and, in my opinion, the greatest action that we know of in Hellenic history—to the victors the most brilliant of successes, to the vanquished the most calamitous of defeats; for they were utterly and entirely defeated; their sufferings were on an enormous scale; their losses were, as they say, total; army, navy, everything was destroyed, and, out of many, only few returned. So ended the events in Sicily.

CHARLTON OGBURN
Merrill's Marauders

Charlton Ogburn was one of the 3,000 American infantrymen who comprised the American 5307th Composite Unit, or 'Merrill's Marauders' (after their commanding officer, Brigadier-General Frank D. Merrill), during WWII. In 1944 this long-range penetration unit fought through 600 miles of Japanese-occupied Burma to open surface communication with China. Ogburn here describes life and action on the Marauders' Second Mission, the march to Shaduzup.

WE GENERALLY FARED WELL IN the neighborhood of the Chinese. We could barter cigarettes for rice and tea and often bum real coffee from the American liaison team attached to the Chinese unit. Boiled with a bouillon cube, the rice made a princely dish. Northerners, who believe rice is supposed to go into puddings, would cook it with a chopped-up fruit bar from the K ration and sugar from the liaison team and extol the result. If we were bivouacked beside a river and the situation permitted, grenades tossed into the water would bring a lot of fish, belly up, to the surface. Roasted in sections of bamboo, they were edible, if not tasty, and with the rice helped fill the stomach's void. That was always the problem. K rations would sustain life, but they provided no bulk. Even when our stomachs had shrunk, so that when ultimately we had a chance to eat a meal we could not, their incessant demands for something to work on were a torment.

For two days in Shikau Ga we ate and swam and lived mostly naked in the sun. Even the dour mules unbent and rolled in the sand. Like times of happiness in retrospect, the passing hours had an Indian-summer air, and you wanted to cling to them. At least that is how it was when we had heard what our next mission was to be.

Another, but deeper, envelopment was in order. Moving again around the eastern flank of the Japanese, we were to put in a block on the Kamaing Road below the village of Shaduzup (pronounced with the accent on the second syllable). The spot selected was about 30 miles south of Walawbum by road and was to prove to be more than 50 miles by the route we had to take. The object was to undermine the Japanese defense of the Jambu Bum. This low range of hills, with its barbaric name, formed the southern end of the Hukawng valley. When you crossed it you entered the valley of the Mogaung, which led to the Irrawaddy—and the world. By Stilwell's direction and against the advice of Merrill and Hunter, the 5307th was to be divided for the operation. Colonel Osborne having been promised that his turn would come when he was assigned a reserve role at Walawbum, 1st Battalion was given the mission of striking south on its own at no great distance from the road, with the Chinese 113th Regiment following a day behind, while the other two battalions were to swing farther out and around before hitting the road in the same vicinity. On a map, the routes of the two bodies together form a figure suggesting the outline of the state of New Jersey, with 1st Battalion threading its way down the hilly, western border and the others completing the circumnavigation of the peanut-shaped area over a more circuitous but generally easier route.

The large-scale contour maps we carried made clear at a glance what the difficulty was going to be. There was only one trail skirting the Jambu Bum on the east, where 1st Battalion was supposed to go. With only one trail to watch, it was as certain as anything could be that the Japanese would have it well in hand.

Setting out first thing in the morning on March 12, we covered over 20 miles of the flat Hukawng valley in two days. The next 30-odd miles was to take us over two weeks.

Even before the end of the second day we ran into trouble. Shortly after noon Sam Wilson's platoon, well in the van, came to a spot where a body of Japanese, patrolling northward, had turned and gone back; there were the imprints of hobnailed soles and the cloven-hoof marks left by the canvas shoes with separate big toes many of the Japanese wore. For two hours the platoon followed the steadily freshening southbound prints; it was the usual grim business of sweating out the bends. It came to a climax with a burst of Tommy-gun fire from up the trail, where the lead scout was out of sight. Then there was silence. The scout, John Sukup, when Sam had come up with him, reported that he had walked right on top of an Asiatic soldier when he had rounded a bend. The man had reached for his rifle and Sukup had turned his Tommy gun loose on him but he had got away. From ahead they could hear sounds of movement in the vegetation, and Sam, to guard against repeating the error of five days before, when we had shot up our allies, sent for one of the Chinese who had been attached to his platoon after that accident. He asked him to call out in the direction of the movement. A strange colloquy ensued, the Chinese shouting inquiries and a voice from the other side answering 'Wah . . . ? Wah?' repeatedly and hesitantly. 'Wah . . . ? Wah?' The uncertainty expressed by the voice was very human, but manifestly the man who was calling could not understand Chinese, and it was not a time to reflect upon the common destiny that makes all mankind one.

'Fire away,' said Sam to his BAR man.

The deafening clatter of the Browning automatic produced a scream and an answering fusillade. In a short time Sam's platoon was under such heavy fire from the unseen enemy that, being under orders to avoid getting pinned down, he had to pull the platoon back into the forest and withdraw it northward. On the arrival of the main body, Caifson Johnson sent two rifle platoons on through to deal with the obstruction. They succeeded in driving the Japanese across a stream that lay in our path, permitting the battalion to cross. Lieutenant McElmurray, the rangy, red-haired, taciturn Oklahoman who led one of the platoons, had a man killed in the action, and in the first and last show of emotion we ever witnessed in him wiped his forearm across his eyes with a grimace of pain. 'The first man I've lost,' he said.

That was only the beginning of our trouble with that bunch of Japanese. Their stubbornness the next morning indicated that they had received reinforcements during the night, and we had to fight eight actions to advance a mile and a half. The Japanese would hold their position on the trail until our fire began to hurt, then fall back a couple of hundred yards, set up their machine guns and mortars and wait to blaze away at us when we ran into them again. It was the chronic problem; in the narrow corridor in which we moved, only a platoon or two could find room to fight. We would rotate our lead platoons but otherwise could not make our superior numbers tell.

What we did not know—did not have the remotest suspicion of—was that our adversaries were caught in a kind of nutcracker, or must have thought they were. At the other end of their column, as we found out several days later, they were having to fight much the same kind of action we were having to fight against them, for in their rear, firing on them from ambushes, was a patrol of Kachin Rangers led by an OSS lieutenant, James L. Tilly. The Japanese, pressed between the two forces, unquestionably took it for granted that they had been artfully trapped and would have been dumfounded to learn that in actuality the two actions were as unrelated as if they had been taking place in different theaters. At that time the United States Army and the Office of Strategic Services were fighting independent wars in Burma. Far from having received the copious information on Japanese dispositions that Tilly's organization had garnered, the 5307th had never even heard of Tilly's existence. The wonder was that the Tingkrung Hka did not witness a sanguinary collision between the Marauder battalion and the Kachin irregulars of OSS's 101 Detachment.

Colonel Osborne had a tough problem. If we kept on bucking our way down the trail, it might take us forever to get where we were going. The only alternative, however, was to leave the trail and head off across country. Uninviting as this was, it appeared to promise faster progress than the present course. Accordingly, he directed the forward elements to hold off the Japanese while the rest of the battalion turned eastward into a dry stream bed, followed it as far as possible, then started cutting a path southward through the forest.

The holding action turned out to be a horrible affair that led to the relief of one of the battalion's high-ranking officers, and the award of a Silver Star to Lieutenant William Lepore. Lepore's rifle platoon was the forwardest element by some hundreds of yards, and in Sam Wilson's words was taking one hell of a shellacking while the battalion was preparing to disengage. Sam found Lepore's superior, the officer in command of the leading part of the column, in a state of near panic. He had an exaggerated idea of the strength of the Japanese and had been unnerved by the din of the fight and the dreadful sight of the wounded who were managing to get back, one clutching a hole in his chest, another voiceless from a gash a grenade had torn in his throat. He was actually preparing to abandon Lepore's platoon. 'We'll have to leave 'em!' he was crying. A hot exchange nearly ending in a knockdown fight ensued between him and Sam, after which Sam took the situation in his own hands. With Lieutenant McDowell and a radio operator carrying an SCR 300 he made his way to Billy Lepore's beleaguered unit. While the weapons platoon behind them created a no man's land behind a screen of mortar fire, Lepore gradually got his platoon extricated and with the help of Sam, McDowell, and a few volunteers brought back the wounded and a few who were paralyzed with fear. Two men had been killed. One, a Sergeant Clark, had been shot between the temples. The other was a Chinese-American with his face blown off. Sam and Billy carried Clark by his legs and shoulders. Accompanied by the bearers of the other body and the rest of the platoon, they got safely across the broad draw separating them from the parent body despite the sniper fire they attracted and the shelling they got from a Japanese mortar until the weapons platoon, responding to an appeal on the SCR 300, silenced it.

The parent body under the officer with whom Sam had had the set-to was pulling out and losing no time about it. Sam and Billy and the volunteers turned with a desperate haste to the task of burying the dead. The earth was hard—they were on a ridge—and the men had all they could do, digging frantically with the sweat getting in their eyes, to hack out grooves barely deep enough for the bodies while the two lieutenants cut some sections of bamboo and made crosses of them, binding the pieces together with vine. In the resistant ground, despite their best efforts, the crosses tilted forlornly. Only six inches of soil covered the two bodies. Sam stood on one side of the graves, fair-haired and still boyish looking though already wasted by the dysentery that dogged him through the campaign. Billy Lepore, stocky and swarthy with black hair, including a mat of it on his chest, stood on the other facing him. 'The Lord giveth and the Lord taketh away,' said Sam. 'Blessed be the name of the Lord.' Billy, a Catholic, crossed himself. 'May the Lord have mercy on their souls.' They stood looking at each other. Sam felt weary and empty—for the events of the afternoon had taken it out of him in more ways than one—and also on edge; for by now the little burial party was all alone on the ridge and the Japanese, for unaccountable reasons, had commenced to lay a thundering barrage on the hill just evacuated by Lepore's platoon. The two shook hands; Sam did not know why. Said Billy, 'Let's get the hell out of here!'

That was the end of the action at the Tingkrung Hka.

The country we had to cross in bypassing the Japanese was a conglomeration of hills resembling the patternless jumble of waves in a tide rip and often so steep your feet would go out from under you while you were climbing. ('The steeper the hill the less distance you got to fall before you hit it. So what the hell are you complaining about?') Sometimes the slopes were too much for the mules; the packs would have to be unloaded and broken up and the pieces carried up or passed up from hand to hand. The platoons took in rotation the task of hacking a passage through the towering, tangled, resistant vegetation that buried hillsides, valleys and ridges together and reduced us in scale to crawling animalcules in its somnolent depths. Within the platoons, officers shared with the men the labor of chopping. The young bamboo would slash out like saber blades when severed; the old, resisting like steel the blows of the dulled machetes, could hardly be cut at all. (The cuticle of bamboo has a high content of the material quartz consists of: silica.) Little of it would fall. You could cut a passage for hours, for days on end, and nothing would happen; the tops of the growth were too interwoven for any of it to break loose. So the bamboo had to be cut twice, at the ground and at a height above the peaks of the mules' loads. The head of the column sounded like a spike-driving crew on a railroad, but the jungle imprisoned the sound, as it did us, and within a small fraction of the column's length to the rear nothing could be heard. The men in the van struck savagely at the unyielding stems, as if the vegetation were an enemy that had to be done to death, until, soaked with sweat, their arms heavy, and gasping for breath, they would fall back to the end of the platoon and be replaced. It was like a column of slaves clearing a path for the pampered and despotic ruler of an ancient Asian empire.

We fought and toiled to reach Shaduzup as if it were salvation. But, Christ, how I hated its uncouth syllables! Shadu'zup! On to Shadu'zup! I pictured it as a cowled and sheeted figure like one of those ghoulish Moslem women. The days of that tortuous march were to remain forever living in my mind, though merged with other days of other marches that preceded or followed—not that it mattered; they were all alike anyway.

We were twelve hours a day on the trail, as a rule—whether there was a trail or not. When there was not, it was mostly a matter of standing and waiting while they slashed away up front. Pack, weapon, ammunition, knife, canteen, all grew heavier; the straps they were slung on cut into the flesh. You could sit down and lean back on your pack to rest your shoulders, but holding your head at a 45-degree angle was hard on your neck, and anyhow you might have to struggle to your feet again immediately. So usually you just stood, leaning slightly forward like an old farm horse in his harness to bring your center of gravity over your feet. If a break were ordered it would pay you to take your pack off, but the mule-leaders had little respite. The mules lived only to get the spray of bamboo leaves that was just out of reach, and the palms of the leaders' hands were burned or their shoulders jerked half out of joint, depending upon whether they were holding the halter ropes loosely or firmly. One would hardly have thought it, but the continual yanking of the mules was a major trial to those who had to control them.

While we marched, men were continually falling out beside the trail, taking care to remain in plain sight lest they be shot in trying to rejoin the column. Dysentery was already the scourge of the organization; much of the command could have been carried in the morning report as walking dead.

On everyone's uniform there were dark, stiff patches. These were of dried blood, from leech bites. The country was infested with these repulsive little rubbery monsters, black worms with suction cups at both ends able to contract to pea-sized balls or elongate themselves to a couple of inches. They did give us the pleasure of going after them with the lighted ends of cigarettes. It required nice judgment to bring the heat close enough to persuade them to disengage without cooking them before they had a chance to. Unfortunately, Mother Nature—whose passion is for equalizing odds—had endowed the little pests with the capacity of clamping on and opening a lesion without your feeling anything, especially if you were asleep. Then after you had found one of them on you and got him off you were liable to have difficulty stanching the flow of blood, for their saliva contained an anticoagulant, a heparin-like agent, according to Doc Kolodny. Caifson Johnson oozed blood for days from some leech bites and one of the platoon leaders went around for an equal length of time with a ruby-red eyeball, the result of a leech's fastening onto it during the night. All of us were more or less bloody all the time, and the mules suffered worse than we; their fetlocks were generally dark red and slimy with blood. In addition, eggs deposited in their lesions by a kind of fly hatched out into screw worms.

Compared with the combat platoons, the communications platoon had nothing to complain about. It was a fact, though, that after their work was over, at the end of the day's march, ours began. We generally had help in clearing enough of the forest to make room for our antenna, but the responsibility rested on us. The problem was a different one from opening a trail. It was not enough to hack out a tunnel; the roof of the forest had to come down. So we would cut farther and farther out and tug at the bamboo and vines, then cut some more and pull some more until a section of the canopy finally sagged to the ground. When we had cleared enough for our wire and had got it erected—and bamboo at least provided the world's best poles—we could turn to the job of producing enough current to heave our signal out through the woods and over the intervening miles to Merrill's headquarters, wherever they might be, and to our base at Dinjan, in Assam. This was done with a hand-cranked generator, which might be likened to an upended bicycle without wheels or handlebars; you sat on the seat and pedaled by hand. The drag on the crank was proportionate to the power output of the set you were working, and the AN/PRC-1 was designed to reach a long way. To keep it going was like forcing a bicycle uphill just before you have to get off and walk. It took everyone in the platoon working by turns to keep the glutton satisfied.

JOHN HERSEY
Survival

During the Second World War, John F. Kennedy, the future US president, was the captain of a Motor Torpedo Boat in the South Pacific. In the spring of 1944, Kennedy's boat was rammed by a Japanese destroyer off the Solomon Islands. The story of what happened to Kennedy and his men is related here by New Yorker *war correspondent John Hersey.*

OUR MEN IN THE SOUTH Pacific fight nature, when they are pitted against her, with a greater fierceness than they could ever expend on a human enemy. Lieutenant John F. Kennedy, the ex-Ambassador's son and lately a PT skipper in the Solomons, came through town the other day and told me the story of his survival in the South Pacific. I asked Kennedy if I might write the story down. He asked me if I wouldn't talk first with some of his crew, so I went up to the Motor Torpedo Boat Training Center at Melville, Rhode Island, and there, under the curving iron of a Quonset hut, three enlisted men named Johnston, McMahon, and McGuire filled in the gaps.

It seems that Kennedy's PT, the 109, was out one night with a squadron patrolling Blackett Strait, in mid-Solomons. Blackett Strait is a patch of water bounded on the northeast by the volcano called Kolombangara, on the west by the island of Vella Lavella, on the south by the island of Gizo and a string of coral-fringed islets, and on the east by the bulk of New Georgia. The boats were working about forty miles away from their base on the island of Rendova, on the south side of New Georgia. They had entered Blackett Strait, as was their habit, through Ferguson Passage, between the coral islets and New Georgia.

The night was a starless black and Japanese destroyers were around. It was about two-thirty. The 109, with three officers and ten enlisted men aboard, was leading three boats on a sweep for a target. An officer named George Ross was up on the bow, magnifying the void with binoculars. Kennedy was at the wheel and he saw Ross turn and point into the darkness. The man in the forward machine-gun turret shouted, 'Ship at two o'clock!' Kennedy saw a shape and spun the wheel to turn for an attack, but the 109 answered sluggishly. She was running slowly on only one of her three engines, so as to make a minimum wake and avoid detection from the air. The shape became a Japanese destroyer, cutting through the night at forty knots and heading straight for the 109. The thirteen men on the PT hardly had time to brace themselves. Those who saw the Japanese ship coming were paralyzed by fear in a curious way: they could move their hands but not their feet. Kennedy whirled the wheel to the left, but again the 109 did not respond. Ross went through the gallant but futile motions of slamming a shell into the breach of the 37-millimetre anti-tank gun which had been temporarily mounted that very day, wheels and all, on the foredeck. The urge to bolt and dive over the side was terribly strong, but still no one was able to move; all hands froze to their battle stations. Then the Japanese crashed into the 109 and cut her right in two. The sharp enemy forefoot struck the PT on the starboard side about fifteen feet from the bow and crunched diagonally across with a racking noise. The PT's wooden hull hardly even delayed the destroyer. Kennedy was thrown hard to the left in the cockpit, and he thought, 'This is how it feels to be killed.' In a moment he found himself on his back on the deck, looking up at the destroyer as it passed through his boat. There was another loud noise and a huge flash of yellow-red light, and the destroyer glowed. Its peculiar, raked, inverted-Y stack stood out in the brilliant light and, later, in Kennedy's memory.

There was only one man below decks at the moment of collision. That was McMahon, engineer. He had no idea what was up. He was just reaching forward to slam the starboard engine into gear when a ship came into his engine room. He was lifted from the narrow passage between two of the engines and thrown painfully against the starboard bulkhead aft of the boat's auxiliary generator. He landed in a sitting position. A tremendous burst of flame came back at him from the day room, where some of the gas tanks were. He put his hands over his face, drew his legs up tight, and waited to die. But he felt water hit him after the fire, and he was sucked far downward as his half of the PT sank. He began to struggle upward through the water. He had held his breath since the impact, so his lungs were tight and they hurt. He looked up through the water. Over his head he saw a yellow glow—gasoline burning on the water. He broke the surface and was in fire again. He splashed hard to keep a little island of water around him.

Johnston, another engineer, had been asleep on deck when the collision came. It lifted him and dropped him overboard. He saw the flame and the destroyer for a moment. Then a huge propeller pounded by near him and the awful turbulence of the destroyer's wake took him down, turned him over and over, held him down, shook him, and drubbed on his ribs. He hung on and came up in water that was like a river rapids. The next day his body turned black and blue from the beating.

Kennedy's half of the PT stayed afloat. The bulkheads were sealed, so the undamaged watertight compartments up forward kept the half hull floating. The destroyer rushed off into the dark. There was an awful quiet: only the sound of gasoline burning.

Kennedy shouted, 'Who's aboard?'

Feeble answers came from three of the enlisted men, McGuire, Mauer, and Albert; and from one of the officers, Thom.

Kennedy saw the fire only ten feet from the boat. He thought it might reach her and explode the remaining gas tanks, so he shouted, 'Over the side!'

The five men slid into the water. But the wake of the destroyer swept the fire away from the PT, so after a few minutes, Kennedy and the others crawled back aboard. Kennedy shouted for survivors in the water. One by one they answered: Ross, the third officer; Harris, McMahon, Johnston, Zinsser, Starkey, enlisted men. Two did not answer: Kirksey and Marney, enlisted men. Since the last bombing at base, Kirksey had been sure he would die. He had huddled at his battle station by the fantail gun, with his kapok life jacket tied tight up to his cheeks. No one knows what happened to him or to Marney.

Harris shouted from the darkness, 'Mr Kennedy! Mr Kennedy! McMahon is badly hurt.' Kennedy took his shoes, his shirt, and his sidearms off, told Mauer to blink a light so that the men in the water would know where the half hull was, then dived in and swam toward the voice. The survivors were widely scattered. McMahon and Harris were a hundred yards away.

When Kennedy reached McMahon, he asked, 'How are you, Mac?'

McMahon said, 'I'm all right. I'm kind of burnt.'

Kennedy shouted out, 'How are the others?'

Harris said softly, 'I hurt my leg.'

Kennedy, who had been on the Harvard swimming team five years before, took McMahon in tow and headed for the PT. A gentle breeze kept blowing the boat away from the swimmers. It took forty-five minutes to make what had been an easy hundred yards. On the way in, Harris said, 'I can't go any farther.' Kennedy, of the Boston Kennedys, said to Harris, of the same home town, 'For a guy from Boston, you're certainly putting up a great exhibition out here, Harris.' Harris made it all right and didn't complain any more. Then Kennedy swam from man to man, to see how they were doing. All who had survived the crash were able to stay afloat, since they were wearing life preservers—kapok jackets shaped like overstuffed vests, aviators' yellow Mae Wests, or air-filled belts like small inner tubes. But those who couldn't swim had to be towed back to the wreckage by those who could. One of the men screamed for help. When Ross reached him, he found that the screaming man had two life jackets on. Johnston was treading water in a film of gasoline which did not catch fire. The fumes filled his lungs and he fainted. Thom towed him in. The others got in under their own power. It was now after 5 a.m., but still dark. It had taken nearly three hours to get everyone aboard.

The men stretched out on the tilted deck of the PT. Johnston, McMahon, and Ross collapsed into sleep. The men talked about how wonderful it was to be alive and speculated on when the other PTs would come back to rescue them. Mauer kept blinking the light to point their way. But the other boats had no idea of coming back. They had seen a collision, a sheet of flame, and a slow burning on the water. When the skipper of one of the boats saw the sight, he put his hands over his face and sobbed, 'My God! My God!' He and the others turned away. Back at the base, after a couple of days, the squadron held services for the souls of the thirteen men, and one of the officers wrote his mother, 'George Ross lost his life for a cause that he believed in stronger than any one of us, because he was an idealist in the purest sense. Jack Kennedy, the Ambassador's son, was on the same boat and also lost his life. The man that said the cream of a nation is lost in war can never be accused of making an overstatement of a very cruel fact . . .'

When day broke, the men on the remains of the 109 stirred and looked around. To the northeast, three miles off, they saw the monumental cone of Kolombangara; there, the men knew, ten thousand Japanese swarmed. To the west, five miles away, they saw Vella Lavella; more Japs. To the south, only a mile or so away, they actually could see a Japanese camp on Gizo. Kennedy ordered his men to keep as low as possible, so that no moving silhouettes would show against the sky. The listing hulk was gurgling and gradually settling. Kennedy said, 'What do you want to do if the Japs come out? Fight or surrender?' One said, 'Fight with what?' So they took an inventory of their armament. The 37-millimetre gun had flopped over the side and was hanging there by a chain. They had one tommy gun, six 45-calibre automatics, and one .38. Not much.

'Well,' Kennedy said, 'what do you want to do?'

One said, 'Anything you say, Mr Kennedy. You're the boss.'

Kennedy said, 'There's nothing in the book about a situation like this. Seems to me we're not a military organization any more. Let's just talk this over.'

They talked it over, and pretty soon they argued, and Kennedy could see that they would never survive in anarchy. So he took command again.

It was vital that McMahon and Johnston should have room to lie down. McMahon's face, neck, hands, wrists, and feet were horribly burned. Johnston was pale and he coughed continually. There was scarcely space for everyone, so Kennedy ordered the other men into the water to make room, and went in himself. All morning they clung to the hulk and talked about how incredible it was that no one had come to rescue them. All morning they watched for the plane which they thought would be looking for them. They cursed war in general and PTs in particular. At about ten o'clock the hulk heaved a moist sigh and turned turtle. McMahon and Johnston had to hang on as best they could. It was clear that the remains of the 109 would soon sink. When the sun had passed the meridian, Kennedy said, 'We will swim to that small island,' pointing to one of a group three miles to the southeast. 'We have less chance of making it than some of these other islands here, but there'll be less chance of Japs, too.' Those who could not swim well grouped themselves around a long two-by-six timber with which carpenters had braced the 37-millimetre cannon on deck and which had been knocked overboard by the force of the collision. They tied several pairs of shoes to the timber, as well as the ship's lantern, wrapped in a life jacket to keep it afloat. Thom took charge of this unwieldy group. Kennedy took McMahon in tow again. He cut loose one end of a long strap on McMahon's Mae West and took the end in his teeth. He swam breast stroke, pulling the helpless McMahon along on his back. It took over five hours to reach the island. Water lapped into Kennedy's mouth through his clenched teeth, and he swallowed a lot. The salt water cut into McMahon's awful burns, but he did not complain. Every few minutes, when Kennedy stopped to rest, taking the strap out of his mouth and holding it in his hand, McMahon would simply say, 'How far do we have to go?'

Kennedy would reply, 'We're going good.' Then he would ask, 'How do you feel, Mac?'

McMahon always answered, 'I'm O.K., Mr Kennedy. How about you?'

In spite of his burden, Kennedy beat the other men to the reef that surrounded the island. He left McMahon on the reef and told him to keep low, so as not to be spotted by Japs. Kennedy went ahead and explored the island. It was only a hundred yards in diameter; coconuts on the trees but none on the ground; no visible Japs. Just as the others reached the island, one of them spotted a Japanese barge chugging along close to shore. They all lay low. The barge went on. Johnston, who was very pale and weak and who was still coughing a lot, said, 'They wouldn't come here. What'd they be walking around here for? It's too small.' Kennedy lay in some bushes, exhausted by his effort, his stomach heavy with the water he had swallowed. He had been in the sea, except for short intervals on the hulk, for fifteen and a half hours. Now he started thinking. Every night for several nights the PTs had cut through Ferguson Passage on their way to action. Ferguson Passage was just beyond the next little island. Maybe . . .

He stood up. He took one of the pairs of shoes. He put one of the rubber life belts around his waist. He hung the .38 around his neck on a lanyard. He took his pants off. He picked up the ship's lantern, a heavy battery affair ten inches by ten inches, still wrapped in the kapok jacket. He said, 'If I find a boat, I'll flash the lantern twice. The password will be "Roger," the answer will be "Wilco."' He walked toward the water. After fifteen paces he was dizzy, but in the water he felt all right.

It was early evening. It took half an hour to swim to the reef around the next island. Just as he planted his feet on the reef, which lay about four feet under the surface, he saw the shape of a very big fish in the clear water. He flashed the light at it and splashed hard. The fish went away. Kennedy remembered what one of his men had said a few days before, 'These barracuda will come up under a swimming man and eat his testicles.' He had many occasions to think of that remark in the next few hours.

Now it was dark. Kennedy blundered along the uneven reef in water up to his waist. Sometimes he would reach forward with his leg and cut one of his shins or ankles on sharp coral. Other times he would step forward onto emptiness. He made his way like a slow-motion drunk, hugging the lantern. At about nine o'clock he came to the end of the reef, alongside Ferguson Passage. He took his shoes off and tied them to the life jacket, then struck out into open water. He swam about an hour, until he felt he was far enough out to intercept the PTs. Treading water, he listened for the muffled roar of motors, getting chilled, waiting, holding the lamp. Once he looked west and saw flares and the false gaiety of an action. The lights were far beyond the little islands, even beyond Gizo, ten miles away. Kennedy realized that the PT boats had chosen, for the first night in many, to go around Gizo instead of through Ferguson Passage. There was no hope. He started back. He made the same painful promenade of the reef and struck out for the tiny island where his friends were. But this swim was different. He was very tired and now the current was running fast, carrying him to the right. He saw that he could not make the island, so he flashed the light once and shouted 'Roger! Roger!' to identify himself.

On the beach the men were hopefully vigilant. They saw the light and heard the shouts. They were very happy, because they thought that Kennedy had found a PT. They walked out onto the reef, sometimes up to their waists in water, and waited. It was very painful for those who had no shoes. The men shouted, but not much, because they were afraid of Japanese.

One said, 'There's another flash.'

A few minutes later a second said, 'There's a light over there.'

A third said, 'We're seeing things in this dark.'

They waited a long time, but they saw nothing except phosphorescence and heard nothing but the sound of waves. They went back, very discouraged.

One said despairingly, 'We're going to die.'

Johnston said, 'Aw, shut up. You can't die. Only the good die young.'

Kennedy had drifted right by the little island. He thought he had never known such deep trouble, but something he did shows that unconsciously he had not given up hope. He dropped his shoes, but he held onto the heavy lantern, his symbol of contact with his fellows. He stopped trying to swim. He seemed to stop caring. His body drifted through the wet hours, and he was very cold. His mind was a jumble. A few hours before, he had wanted desperately to get to the base at Rendova. Now he only wanted to get back to the little island he had left that night, but he didn't try to get there; he just wanted to. His mind seemed to float away from his body. Darkness and time took the place of a mind in his skull. For a long time he slept, or was crazy, or floated in a chill trance.

The currents of the Solomon Islands are queer. The tide shoves and sucks through the islands and makes the currents curl in odd patterns. It was a fateful pattern into which Jack Kennedy drifted. He drifted in it all night. His mind was blank, but his fist was tightly clenched on the kapok around the lantern. The current moved in a huge circle—west past Gizo, then north and east past Kolombangara, then south into Ferguson Passage. Early in the morning the sky turned from black to gray, and so did Kennedy's mind. Light came to both at about six. Kennedy looked around and saw that he was exactly where he had been the night before when he saw the flares beyond Gizo. For a second time, he started home. He thought for a while that he had lost his mind and that he only imagined that he was repeating his attempt to reach the island. But the chill of the water was real enough, the lantern was real, his progress was measurable. He made the reef, crossed the lagoon, and got to the first island. He lay on the beach awhile. He found that his lantern did not work any more, so he left it and started back to the next island, where his men were. This time the trip along the reef was awful. He had discarded his shoes, and every step on the coral was painful. This time the swim across the gap where the current had caught him the night before seemed endless. But the current had changed; he made the island. He crawled up on the beach. He was vomiting when his men came up to him. He said, 'Ross, you try it tonight.' Then he passed out.

Ross, seeing Kennedy so sick, did not look forward to the execution of the order. He distracted himself by complaining about his hunger. There were a few coconuts on the trees, but the men were too weak to climb up for them. One of the men thought of sea food, stirred his tired body, and found a snail on the beach. He said, 'If we were desperate, we could eat these.' Ross said, 'Desperate, hell. Give me that. I'll eat that.' He took it in his hand and looked at it. The snail put its head out and looked at him. Ross was startled, but he shelled the snail and ate it, making faces because it was bitter.

In the afternoon, Ross swam across to the next island. He took a pistol to signal with, and he spent the night watching Ferguson Passage from the reef around the island. Nothing came through. Kennedy slept badly that night; he was cold and sick.

The next morning everyone felt wretched. Planes that the men were unable to identify flew overhead and there were dogfights. That meant Japs as well as friends, so the men dragged themselves into the bushes and lay low. Some prayed. Johnston said, 'You guys make me sore. You didn't spend ten cents in church in ten years, then all of a sudden you're in trouble and you see the light.' Kennedy felt a little better now. When Ross came back, Kennedy decided that the group should move to another, larger island to the southeast, where there seemed to be more coconut trees and where the party would be nearer Ferguson Passage. Again Kennedy took McMahon in tow with the strap in his teeth, and the nine others grouped themselves around the timber.

This swim took three hours. The nine around the timber were caught by the current and barely made the far tip of the island. Kennedy found walking the quarter mile across to them much harder than the three-hour swim. The cuts on his bare feet were festered and looked like small balloons. The men were suffering most from thirst, and they broke open some coconuts lying on the ground and avidly drank the milk. Kennedy and McMahon, the first to drink, were sickened, and Thom told the others to drink sparingly. In the middle of the night it rained, and someone suggested moving into the underbrush and licking water off the leaves. Ross and McMahon kept contact at first by touching feet as they licked. Somehow they got separated, and, being uncertain whether there were any Japs on the island, they became frightened. McMahon, trying to make his way back to the beach, bumped into someone and froze. It turned out to be Johnston, licking leaves on his own. In the morning the group saw that all the leaves were covered with droppings. Bitterly, they named the place Bird Island.

On this fourth day, the men were low. Even Johnston was low. He had changed his mind about praying. McGuire had a rosary around his neck, and Johnston said, 'McGuire, give that necklace a working over.' McGuire said quietly, 'Yes, I'll take care of all you fellows.' Kennedy was still unwilling to admit that things were hopeless. He asked Ross if he would swim with him to an island called Nauru, to the southeast and even nearer Ferguson Passage. They were very weak indeed by now, but after an hour's swim they made it.

They walked painfully across Nauru to the Ferguson Passage side, where they saw a Japanese barge aground on the reef. There were two men by the barge—possibly Japs. They apparently spotted Kennedy and Ross, for they got into a dugout canoe and hurriedly paddled to the other side of the island. Kennedy and Ross moved up the beach. They came upon an unopened ropebound box and, back in the trees, a little shelter containing a keg of water, a Japanese gas mask, and a crude wooden fetish shaped like a fish. There were Japanese hardtack and candy in the box and the two had a wary feast. Down by the water they found a one-man canoe. They hid from imagined Japs all day. When night fell, Kennedy left Ross and took the canoe, with some hardtack and a can of water from the keg, out into Ferguson Passage. But no PTs came, so he paddled to Bird Island. The men there told him that the two men he had spotted by the barge that morning were natives, who had paddled to Bird Island. The natives had said that there were Japs on Nauru and the men had given Kennedy and Ross up for lost. Then the natives had gone away. Kennedy gave out small rations of crackers and water, and the men went to sleep. During the night, one man, who kept himself awake until the rest were asleep, drank all the water in the can Kennedy had brought back. In the morning the others figured out that he was the guilty one. They swore at him and found it hard to forgive him.

Before dawn, Kennedy started out in the canoe to rejoin Ross on Nauru, but when day broke a wind arose and the canoe was swamped. Some natives appeared from nowhere in a canoe, rescued Kennedy, and took him to Nauru. There they showed him where a two-man canoe was cached. Kennedy picked up a coconut with a smooth shell and scratched a message on it with a jackknife: 'ELEVEN ALIVE NATIVE KNOWS POSIT AND REEFS NAURU ISLAND KENNEDY.' Then he said to the natives, 'Rendova, Rendova.'

One of the natives seemed to understand. They took the coconut and paddled off.

Ross and Kennedy lay in a sickly daze all day. Toward evening it rained and they crawled under a bush. When it got dark, conscience took hold of Kennedy and he persuaded Ross to go out into Ferguson Passage with him in the two-man canoe. Ross argued against it. Kennedy insisted. The two started out in the canoe. They had shaped paddles from the boards of the Japanese box, and they took a coconut shell to bail with. As they got out into the Passage, the wind rose again and the water became choppy. The canoe began to fill. Ross bailed and Kennedy kept the bow into the wind. The waves grew until they were five or six feet high. Kennedy shouted, 'Better turn around and go back!' As soon as the canoe was broadside to the waves, the water poured in and the dugout was swamped. The two clung to it, Kennedy at the bow, Ross at the stern. The tide carried them southward toward the open sea, so they kicked and tugged the canoe, aiming northwest. They struggled that way for two hours, not knowing whether they would hit the small island or drift into the endless open.

The weather got worse; rain poured down and they couldn't see more than ten feet. Kennedy shouted, 'Sorry I got you out here, Barney!' Ross shouted back, 'This would be a great time to say I told you so, but I won't!'

Soon the two could see a white line ahead and could hear a frightening roar—waves crashing on a reef. They had got out of the tidal current and were approaching the island all right, but now they realized that the wind and the waves were carrying them toward the reef. But it was too late to do anything, now that their canoe was swamped, except hang on and wait.

When they were near the reef, a wave broke Kennedy's hold, ripped him away from the canoe, turned him head over heels, and spun him in a violent rush. His ears roared and his eyes pinwheeled, and for the third time since the collision he thought he was dying. Somehow he was not thrown against the coral but floated into a kind of eddy. Suddenly he felt the reef under his feet. Steadying himself so that he would not be swept off it, he shouted, 'Barney!' There was no reply. Kennedy thought of how he had insisted on going out in the canoe, and he screamed, 'Barney!' This time Ross answered. He, too, had been thrown on the reef. He had not been as lucky as Kennedy; his right arm and shoulder had been cruelly lacerated by the coral, and his feet, which were already infected from earlier wounds, were cut some more.

The procession of Kennedy and Ross from reef to beach was a crazy one. Ross's feet hurt so much that Kennedy would hold one paddle on the bottom while Ross put a foot on it, then the other paddle forward for another step, then the first paddle forward again, until they reached sand. They fell on the beach and slept.

Kennedy and Ross were wakened early in the morning by a noise. They looked up and saw four husky natives. One walked up to them and said in an excellent English accent, 'I have a letter for you, sir.' Kennedy tore the note open. It said, 'On His Majesty's Service. To the Senior Officer, Nauru Island. I have just learned of your presence on Nauru Is. I am in command of a New Zealand infantry patrol operating in conjunction with U.S. Army troops on New Georgia. I strongly advise that you come with these natives to me. Meanwhile I shall be in radio communication with your authorities at Rendova, and we can finalize plans to collect balance of your party. Lt. Wincote. P.S. Will warn aviation of your crossing Ferguson Passage.'

Everyone shook hands and the four natives took Ross and Kennedy in their war canoe across to Bird Island to tell the others the good news. There the natives broke out a spirit stove and cooked a feast of yams and C ration. Then they built a leanto for McMahon, whose burns had begun to rot and stink, and for Ross, whose arm had swelled to the size of a thigh because of the coral cuts. The natives put Kennedy in the bottom of their canoe and covered him with sacking and palm fronds, in case Japanese planes should buzz them. The long trip was fun for the natives. They stopped once to try to grab a turtle, and laughed at the sport they were having. Thirty Japanese planes went over low toward Rendova, and the natives waved and shouted gaily. They rowed with a strange rhythm, pounding paddles on the gunwales between strokes. At last they reached a censored place. Lieutenant Wincote came to the water's edge and said formally, 'How do you do. Leftenant Wincote.'

Kennedy said, 'Hello. I'm Kennedy.'

Wincote said, 'Come up to my tent and have a cup of tea.'

In the middle of the night, after several radio conversations between Wincote's outfit and the PT base, Kennedy sat in the war canoe waiting at an arranged rendezvous for a PT. The moon went down at eleven-twenty. Shortly afterward, Kennedy heard the signal he was waiting for—four shots. Kennedy fired four answering shots.

A voice shouted to him, 'Hey, Jack!'

Kennedy said, 'Where the hell you been?'

The voice said, 'We got some food for you.'

Kennedy said bitterly, 'No, thanks, I just had a coconut.'

A moment later a PT came alongside. Kennedy jumped onto it and hugged the men aboard—his friends. In the American tradition, Kennedy held under his arm a couple of souvenirs: one of the improvised paddles and the Japanese gas mask.

With the help of the natives, the PT made its way to Bird Island. A skiff went in and picked up the men. In the deep of the night, the PT and its happy cargo roared back toward base. The squadron medic had sent some brandy along to revive the weakened men. Johnston felt the need of a little revival. In fact, he felt he needed quite a bit of revival. After taking care of that, he retired topside and sat with his arms around a couple of roly-poly, mission-trained natives. And in the fresh breeze on the way home they sang together a hymn all three happened to know:

Jesus loves me, this I know,
For the Bible tells me so;
Little ones to Him belong,
They are weak, but He is strong.
Yes, Jesus loves me; yes, Jesus loves me . . .

HEINZ SCHAEFER
Wolfpack

Heinz Schaefer was a German U-Boat midshipman (later commander) during the Battle of the Atlantic in WWII.

OUR DESTINATION THIS TIME WAS mid-Atlantic—we had already crossed longitude 15° W., beyond which point the wireless was generally silent. This meridian was, so to speak, a frontier, and we generally referred to waters west of it as our 'Western zone'; after we had crossed it we received an increase in pay. For days on end there was the same monotonous routine; nothing different ever happened, and we began to long for something to turn up. At last there came an urgent signal, which the wireless operator laid before our Commander—it was news of a convoy.

It was still far off but coming our way, if it didn't alter its course, and we proceeded at half-speed towards our interception point. We should have sighted it in two days, but still we saw no smoke. However, it must have been a very important convoy, for the High Command sent us out a reconnaissance plane although we were 3,000 kilometres from the nearest airfield. A U-boat is a small object to make out, however, and we were doubtful if it would find us. The wireless operator tried to make contact so as to give him our exact position and, if possible, our bearing, but this wasn't an easy job, for aeroplane transmitters are not powerful.

We kept on sending out signals at short intervals, and in the end it all worked out amazingly. The plane came into view, a B.V. 138 built by Blohm and Voss for special tasks, and we flashed the probable position of the convoy. The B.V. flew away. Two hours passed, and we went ahead without any more news. Our Commander personally had not much faith in radio. Although under favourable conditions European transmissions can be picked up in America, messages from ships can normally only be picked up 20 miles away.

In the end our B.V. 138 returned, and flashed this message: *Convoy. Square 10. About 50 ships escorted by 10 destroyers.* We went full speed ahead, with the whole watch standing by, the petty-officer torpedoman checking up on his torpedoes, and the plane still flying over us. At three in the afternoon we sighted the first column of smoke. Then another, and a third. We sped ahead. Next the first masts showed up, more and more of them.

'Why, it's a whole forest,' said someone on the bridge. 'We've certainly got a job.'

'Stop chattering and get on with your work,' the Commander snapped back, without lowering his binoculars. The B.V. 138 made off, wishing us luck, and vanished.

'Those airmen don't have such a bad time. Home to mother every night. I wouldn't mind being in their shoes.'

We sent out a twenty-word signal—position of the convoy, course, speed, strength and escort—so as to put High Command in the picture. Every two hours we transmitted fuller details. We were the first U-boat to contact the convoy and our job now was to call in all other U-boats in the area, that being the whole point of our wolf-pack tactics. But I do not mean to imply by this that we were all acting under a unified command. United action in the Battle of the Atlantic merely meant calling up all available forces, for once in touch with the convoy every ship acted on its own, yet in this way we could annihilate convoys of fifty ships and more in actions that went on for days.

The night, which was pitch dark without a moon, was in our favour. But some U-boats were failing to show up. As far as we could judge from the reports we got we might be six in all by dawn. It was an important convoy—fifty ships with war materials bound for England.

'Make call-signs,' the Commander ordered.

Rather a nerve, sending out wireless messages right in among the enemy ships. If our wavelength was known we were finished. But it couldn't be helped, we had to have more U-boats.

Wireless operator to Commander: 'U X has contacted the convoy.'

Next thing we learned was that another of our boats had done so too.

So we were now three in all, and our Commander decided to attack. Bearing indications to the other ships were no longer required, as you can see the flash of a torpedo miles away, and if one ship went up in flames it would light the way for the other U-boats. We wanted to torpedo four ships, so we picked out the big ones, preparing to attack the furthest first and the rest afterwards, allotting two torpedoes to the largest ship, and one each to the others. If possible all four must hit simultaneously, so as to leave no time for alterations of course. We were quite close to the nearest ship already—650 metres perhaps.

'*Fire!*'

The ship throbbed five times—we were using our after tube along with the rest. In fifteen seconds the torpedoes should hit. We grew impatient; they seemed such very long seconds. Perhaps the tinfish hadn't run properly. Was anything wrong?

A spurt of flame and then two thuds. Sound travels through water faster than through the air. One more explosion aboard the same ship. She was breaking apart now, and in a moment she had gone down. There could be few survivors. Then came two more explosions—one torpedo had evidently missed. In a moment the convoy which had been peacefully pursuing its course sprang to action with much flashing of red and blue lights and signals to change course. The British knew their job. To handle blacked-out ships in convoy at night is no easy task, yet there was no collision. A pity for us, it would have saved us extra work.

The destroyers now pounced on their prey. Searchlights switched on, guns opened fire, depth-charges detonated. But we were not discovered, for we were still in among the convoy, which was probably the last place they expected to find us. Instead of making off or diving we went further in. Our Commander guessed they'd overlook us there, and he was right. With a small range of vision you can easily overlook a submarine from the high bridge of a merchant-ship. It's hard to make out that dark streak on the water, to distinguish it from the shadows cast by the higher waves.

The rear doors of the torpedo tubes swung open, one torpedo after another sliding in. The crew were bathed in sweat, working like mad. It was a matter of life and death, no time or place for reflection. If they found us now we were utterly lost, for without our torpedoes secured we couldn't dive. This was war—'Go in and sink'.

It lasted thirty-five minutes. Already we were making ready for the next attack.

Torpedo control officer to Commander: 'Tubes one to four ready!'

Heavy explosions. Ships were breaking up, others letting off steam and coming to a standstill, thick smoke mounting skywards. Searchlights played on the dark water and the starry blaze of oil. SOS calls never stopped going out on the 600-metre wavelength. More U-boats were coming up. Still more explosions.

'Hope we don't buy one of the "overs",' said the second officer of the watch. 'It would bc thc limit if our own people sent us all to hell.'

And it might so easily happen, seeing that we were all mixed up with the escort ships.

At last the convoy was really breaking up, ships making off in all directions. That was bad for us for we could only take one target at a time now. Besides, they'd had their warning—some were zig-zagging, others steaming on a circular course.

Hard a-starboard. Our next victim, an 8,000-ton ship, was held in the crosswires. '*Fire*!' Almost simultaneously with this fresh command a flash went up from her. But we only scored one hit, though she was listing heavily aft.

'Object ahead!'

We tried to get away—but the object moved more quickly than we could. Gradually it loomed larger. 'Watch out! They're after us!' As we rushed below we heard more explosions. We were just robots. Things were happening spontaneously, events taking charge of us.

Our High Command had warned us about fast launches shipped aboard the convoys and launched when U-boats attacked at night. Their strength lay in their small size, amazing speed and strong armament of quick-firing guns. You could only see these craft when they were right on top of you, if you saw them at all.

Down to 50 fathoms. With 40 degrees load and all our power we sank into the depths. . . . Was our engineer by any chance related to a fish? He dived the boat to the exact depth, put her on an even keel, closed the vents and finally reported 'All clear'.

'Well done,' the Commander congratulated him.

Our friend the enemy had always got a new card up his sleeve. Well, the war would be very dull if he hadn't. Anyhow, we'd know better next time. The watch on the bridge were pretty alert in my opinion.

The first depth-charges were exploding now, but a long way off. We were still too close to the convoy and the destroyers couldn't pick us up because of all the other din—a happy state that could hardly last long. The Commander gave the order to proceed at silent speed. The electric engines were almost inaudible, and the auxiliaries shut off; words of command whispered, the ratings went around in felt shoes. Everybody not needed for immediate duty went off to lie down, as in that way we expended less oxygen. Nobody knew how long we would have to survive on what we had, and you consume less lying down than standing up and talking.

The convoy was steaming away now, its propellers barely audible. But three destroyers were after us, and before long the sound of their Asdic, like fingernails run over a comb, grew all too familiar. Another of their Asdic devices rattled like peas in a tin, a third screeched like an ancient tramcar taking a curve. We weren't likely to forget this experience. I thought of the man who went out to discover what fear meant. He should have been there.

The destroyers surrounded us, their explosions sounding closer and closer, usually in threes. My action-station was cramped up aft at the speaking-tube, and every time a charge exploded I had to report if there was any damage. The tube ran between the hull and the torpedo tube, and in this minute space I had to support myself leaning on one hand and aching in every limb. There was an almighty roar, and the boat sank like a stone for 20 metres: the light went out, and the emergency lighting came on automatically. It was no joke, when the enemy had us held like this on the dials of his instruments. Engine noises got louder—and the depth-charges ever nearer. The electricians were moving about the boat repairing damage: meanwhile the lights were switched over to the second of the two ring-main electrical circuits with which the boat was fitted. It went on for hours. Our wireless operators maintained contact with the destroyers, and kept the Commander posted; when they came closer he went to the wireless room himself to give orders.

Every time a destroyer was on top of us we altered course—you have to react instinctively. Fortunately our Commander knew exactly what he was about. He betrayed no feeling, and indeed everyone gave an appearance of self-control, but we were all uneasy, myself not least. It had never been as bad as this—we couldn't see, we couldn't shoot, we just had to last it out, though it was almost more than we could stand. We counted sixty-eight depth-charges.

How long could this unreal combat, not man to man or even weapon against weapon, this inhuman strain go on, this mixture of luck, blind tactics and instinctively doing the right thing at the right time? We were caught up in a mechanism, everyone getting down to their work in a dead, automatic silence. There was something uncanny about the whole atmosphere aboard. The ratings looked like phantoms.

There is a frightful crack, just as if the boat has been struck by a gigantic hammer. Electric bulbs and glasses fly about, leaving fragments everywhere. The motors have stopped. Reports from all stations show, thank God, that there are no leaks—just the main fuses blown. The damage is made good. We are now using special breathing apparatus to guard against the deadly carbon-monoxide which may be in the boat. The rubber mouthpiece tastes horrible. This is war all right, real war, not a film-war of waving flags and blaring music.

Yet the instinct of self-preservation is active in every man of us, and if we had been asked if we really felt frightened I doubt if we could have given a plain yes or no in reply.

The hundredth depth-charge bursts. Beads of sweat stand out on every forehead. As our last hope we discharge the *Bold*—the Asdic decoy to which so many U-boats owe their survival, its chemical components creating a film which hangs like a curtain in the water and gives an echo like a submarine to the destroyer's Asdic.

Our tactics then are to turn, intentionally, broadside on to our hunters, so as to make sure they get our echo, then turn away sharply and show them our stern, sneaking away and leaving the *Bold* for the hunting pack to worry.

Our *Bold* evidently helped us, for fewer depth-charges were exploding now, and it did seem the enemy had been tricked. After counting one hundred and sixty-eight charges in eight hours, we at last began to breathe again. The destroyers were steaming away. They had to pick up their convoy, for it needed an escort for the coming night. If every U-boat had pinned down three destroyers, then only one of the ten could still be with the convoy, and things would be easier for other U-boats.

Our kind of warfare is not what the layman thinks it is, just slinking up under water, shooting and stealing away like a thief in the night. On the contrary, most ships are torpedoed in an escorted convoy by a surfaced submarine; and although the size of a destroyer doesn't allow for an unlimited number of depth-charges—I imagine that they must make do with about eighty—what they have can make things hot enough while the action lasts.

We waited for an hour and then we surfaced.

Full speed ahead.

The batteries were then recharged, which was the chief thing, for without our batteries we could not dive and in effect would cease to be a submarine. We reloaded our tubes and once more we were ready for action, only a bit worn out. I remembered our training advice on Dänholm: 'No sailor gets worn out—if you can't keep your eyes open jam matches into them.' Instead of matches we took caffeine and pervitin tablets, which wasn't ideal for our health but we had to go without sleep for days and just could not do without them.

That night we failed to overtake the convoy, and reported our success to date to headquarters: four ships sunk, 24,000 tons in all.

The Admiral replied: *Not 24,000–36,000. The ships were . . .* and he listed them. *Well done. Go on in and sink the rest.* Our intelligence service was superb, and this time they had decoded the enemy wireless signals. Altogether 100,000 tons had been sunk, and we hoped that there was something left for the following night; we had already forgotten the counterattack with depth-charges, and counted on the destroyers having exhausted their supply. But in fact we found ourselves unable to keep up with the convoy, for our fuel was almost exhausted and we had to turn back to base. Later on we learnt that the convoy had been almost annihilated.

JAMES B. LAMB
Convoy

The transatlantic convoy system was Britain's supplies lifeline during World War II (as in World War I), and thus a major target for Admiral Dönitz's U-boats. James Lamb, a Canadian, served as an officer aboard a destroyer escorting merchantmen on the Atlantic run.

GALE AFTER GALE SHRIEKS DOWN upon us, howling out of the north as we approach Cape Farewell, southernmost tip of Greenland. Fierce winds tear at our rigging, snatch the tops off waves and send them flying above our mastheads, stinging our faces and blinding our eyes. Mountainous seas crash inboard, making our upper decks impassable, sweeping over our forward gun and crashing against our superstructure with an impact that jars us to the keel. Life below is a hell of wet clothes and fitful sleep, of sandwich meals and constant violent, bruising motion. Even the plumbing is impossible; to use the toilet is to risk a cold douche as the head seas overpower valves and piping.

On a wild night watch, I see the lighter rim of the sky blotted out and realize, in a moment of mind-numbing panic, that the wall of blackness that towers ahead of us is an enormous, an unbelievable, sea, the '67th wave' dreaded by every sailor. I duck beneath the dodger as the bows rise, and commend my soul to God. There is a thunderous roar, and the whole world is blotted out in water, filled with a myriad crashes and crackings. Miraculously, the wave passes, and I emerge, soaked and scared yet unscathed. But in the sudden silence I can sense something wrong: the ship is falling off into the trough and I can get no answer from the wheelhouse voice-pipe. Mad with fright—if the ship falls broadside to the waves in this mountainous sea we shall surely be rolled right over—I dash down the ladder and burst into the wheelhouse, and into a scene of utter chaos.

The rogue sea had burst in the shutters and windows of the wheelhouse, flooding and gutting it and knocking helmsman and telegraph rating against the after bulkhead. They are still there, paralysed with fright and shock, but at the wheel is the captain, brought from his tiny sea-cabin off the wheelhouse, now spinning the wheel hard over to get the ship back head to sea. I ring the engines to emergency full ahead, and we wait, frozen in an agonized tableau, our eyes riveted on the pool of light that is the steering compass. The ship rolls heavily, deeply, right over on her side; if she gets another sea in this position we are all gone for sure. But the engine beat quickens; we can hear the stokehold bell below as the engine room opens all the taps, and at last we can see the compass card begin to move. The crisis is past; it is just a matter of shoring up our shattered wheelhouse covers and we are back in business.

The wild weather may be keeping the U-boats down, but it is also taking its toll of the convoy; under its thunderous blows, HX 142 begins to disintegrate. The gaps between ships increase as ships seek greater sea-room. There is a tremendous collision near the centre as a great bulk carrier becomes unmanageable and sheers out of line, her bows colliding with those of a new Empire vessel in the adjoining column; in the black night we hear the rending screech of fractured metal above the howling of the gale.

Fortunately, it is a glancing blow, but even so it has torn a gaping hole in the starboard bow of the Empire ship, and although the hole is well above the water-line, in this wild weather it is a dangerous wound. Both ships fall astern to examine and repair damage as best they can, and *Kamsack* is told off to stand by them until they can rejoin the convoy. But there is no respite; all the next day the gaps between ships steadily widen, although the commodore has reduced speed to a signalled four knots, which is more like two over the ground. At this speed some ships are virtually unable to maintain a proper course; they fall out of line and peel off to either side, seeking sea-room. They give us in the escorts some grey hairs, for there is nothing which can bring one's heart into one's mouth faster than the sight of a great black shape looming out of the night when one fancied oneself safely distant a mile or so from the nearest merchantman. Next morning Smoky Joe is far behind, now just a smudge of smoke astern on the horizon, and *Kamsack* is directed by *Montgomery* to take him under her wing as well. By the morning of this third day of the gale, HX 142 is scattered over miles of ocean, its shattered ranks broken into two shapeless huddles of storm-lashed ships, its escorts now running dangerously low on fuel with a thousand miles of stormy Atlantic still ahead and the U-boat gauntlet still to run.

Fortunately, at this desperate juncture the wind begins to ease; by afternoon it is no more than a fresh breeze and by nightfall the enormous sea has begun to subside. Dawn next day reveals a North Atlantic restored to something like normalcy. Immediately *Montgomery* drops back to fuel from the aftermost tanker in the centre column, signalling as she goes the rotation in which we, the other escorts, are to leave the screen to top up our depleted tanks. By mid-afternoon our turn has come; we steam down through the re-forming ranks of the convoy and approach the tanker from astern. Our fo'c'sle party grapples and picks up the long grass-line streamed behind the huge tanker, together with the empty water-breaker used as a buoy on the end of it, and haul it on the empty fuel hose, filled with air so it will float, which the tanker pays out like a great serpent astern. We close up until we are broad on the tanker's quarter, the buoyant hose streaming astern of the tanker and then up onto our fo'c'sle in a deep U-shape. The hose end is quickly fastened to the pipe-nozzle which had just been fitted for the purpose at our refit last fall, and at a flag signal from us the oiler begins pumping. We steam along at convoy speed, protected from attack by ships all about us, keeping station easily by maintaining the U in the bight of the hose, which in effect cushions any small failure in station-keeping caused by wind or sea.

This is a method of fuelling at sea developed by mid-ocean escorts in the teeth of regular-navy opposition, for in peacetime oiling had been regarded as an evolution, something to be carried out on calm seas as a display of smart seamanship. Destroyers were required to close the tanker alongside and to steam, beam to beam, a few feet apart, while a short length of hose was passed directly across. Station-keeping had to be perfect; the slightest yawing resulted in a broken hose or a collision, sometimes both together, so that the evolution became impossible with any sort of sea running. Even the astern method had its dangers; more than one escort had been covered with thick black oil from bows to bridge, from masthead to water-line, as a result of a hose breaking during fuelling and the broken end, flying madly about under great pressure, squirting tons of heavy bunker oil over everything. Such a nightmare was always possible in bad weather, but the large amount of slack in the fuel hose represented by the deep U-shaped bight provided a safe degree of leeway for any well-handled ship. In less than an hour we have topped-up, had pumping stopped, let the hose blow clear, capped it, and cast it off, and we are on our way back to our screening position on the starboard flank of the convoy.

All day HX 142 has been re-forming, the commodore maintaining slow speed while stragglers hurry back into position, and the ranks slowly close up and regain cohesion. Last to return is Smoky Joe, clouds of smoke belching from his tall, thin funnel. As night closes in, convoy speed is increased.

Next day brings a new enemy. We are approaching the area, just beyond reach of air cover from Iceland or Ireland, where the U-boats maintain their patrolling line. It is a thin affair nowadays, as more and more U-boats are hurried down to the happy hunting grounds off the American coast where American shipping, unprotected by convoy as a result of an almost unbelievable miscalculation by Admiral King and his staff, can be butchered like so many sheep. But the evening U-boat report shows plenty of activity still in our area, and the Admiralty, in a special signal to us, warn that at least three U-boats are in the immediate vicinity of our convoy.

We take every precaution; lookouts are especially vigilant, guns and depth-charges are checked out, and we close in to abjure Smoky Joe to throw on his best lumps of coal in order to keep in station and make the minimum amount of smoke. We receive the mandatory wave of the hand—reassuring? resigned? resentful? Who could say?—and return to our position on the screen, maintaining our zigzag in meticulous station. The night passes without incident.

Next day it becomes clear that we have been spotted. Unusual U-boat wireless activity from our immediate area indicates we are being tailed by at least one U-boat, and the pack is gathering. Late that afternoon, as visibility fades, *Montgomery* leaves her station and sweeps astern at high speed; half an hour later the commodore alters convoy course drastically to the northward. *Montgomery* hopes to force any shadower to submerge and thereby not be in a position to detect our new change of course. *Montgomery* returns early in the evening without having spotted anything, but it is hoped that we have shaken off, at least temporarily, any U-boat attack. It is standard practice for U-boats to maintain contact at visibility limit astern, on the surface or at periscope depth according to circumstances, steering convoy course and speed by day and surfacing at nightfall to overtake at high speed and gain an attacking position on the bow of the convoy. Attack is usually from this position on the surface, the boat trimmed down so that virtually only her conning tower is exposed. A spread of torpedoes is fired, with the attacker then either running right through the convoy, or turning to escape at high speed on the surface while the convoy steams on.

It is a black night; there will be a moon later on, if the cloud cover permits, but meantime the darkness favours us in our attempt to avoid detection. We steam on, everyone on tenterhooks; on the bridge and in the messdecks the tension is almost palpable. Yet at sea we are all fatalists; when I turn in after an austere supper—all our fresh supplies are long gone and we virtually live on Spam—I quickly fall into deep and dreamless sleep.

Good God, what was that? I sit upright in the pitch-black cabin. There it is again: the rumbling bang against the ship's side of an underwater explosion, and as I switch on the lamp there is another one. Not depth-charges, these; they can only be torpedoes, and as I fling my legs over the side of the bunk and pull on my seaboots, the alarm bells suddenly go off overhead, sounding action stations, and the whole sleeping ship explodes into pandemonium. Racing for the bridge, I cannon into dark figures, bulky with lifejackets; the night is filled with drumming feet, muttered curses, the metallic sounds of clips being loosened, hatches flung open, guns and depth-charges cleared away, and over all the insistent, mind-maddening clangour of the alarm bells.

Up on the bridge the atmosphere is tense with suppressed excitement; the captain is at the voice-pipes, bringing the ship around to point directly away from the convoy, his voice clipped, controlled, urgent. And the convoy, ah God, the convoy—

We must have been at the inner limit of our zigzag when the torpedoes struck; the dark shapes of the outer column tower darkly above us, seeming frighteningly close. But just beyond them is a terrifying sight: the leading ship of the second column is afire, and flames can be seen all along her upper deck. Even as we watch, there is a blinding flash, and suddenly she bursts into a towering pillar of flame. Across the water comes the sound of the explosion, and a new, horrifying sound: the roar of the inferno that has engulfed her. She must have been carrying high-octane petroleum as deck cargo; only this could have turned her into such a tremendous torch. It is as bright as day; the flames light up the sea all around us, throwing the ships of the intervening column into bold relief, illuminating the pale, tense faces on the bridge behind me. All eyes are on the doomed ship; nobody speaks, we are struck dumb by the fearful majesty of the terrible scene before us, by the unbelievable roar of the holocaust. Slowly, serenely, she passes down the column, isolated now from her grubby sisters ploughing past in the splendid beauty of her destruction. It is a voice up the pipe from the wireless office which breaks the spell: 'From *Montgomery*, sir: Raspberry!'

It is an order to all escorts to turn outward and illuminate their sectors with star shell—one of the new group tactical evolutions embodied in the escort 'Bible', the big blue-bound volume known as Western Approaches Convoy Instructions, or simply 'Wackey'. From our inward position, the captain swings our bows around until we are steaming directly away from the convoy, and at a word from him Falconer, our gunnery officer, calls down the foregun voice-pipe: 'With star shell and reduced charge, load! Load! Load!' There are orderly scufflings from the gun's crew, and we can hear the breech being swung open and closed, and then Falconer passes down the arc to be covered. 'Illuminate from red 45 to green 45.' The gun is trained and reported ready, and as all glasses on the bridge are readied and we cover our eyes with our hands, there comes the order 'Shoot!' A blinding flash, a hot whiff of cordite, and in the sudden blackness that follows, everyone peers intently out into the dark void on the port bow. After what seems ages, the shell bursts, high and far, and instantly turns night into day. As the magnesium flare, dangling from its parachute, slowly descends, it lights up the empty sea beneath it. Even as we watch, the gun fires again, and after another ageless interval, a second flare appears, further ahead, and now higher than the original, which has been drifting evenly down. And then another, and another; in the space of a minute we have hung a curtain of star shell over a wide arc of the sea, and as the flares drift lower they light up the surface in unbelievable detail, throwing into relief every tiny wavetop. All around the convoy the other escorts are lighting up their sectors; already we can benefit from the outermost star shell fired by *Chilliwack* ahead and *Kamsack* far astern. If, as *Montgomery* believes, the U-boat attacking us is making her escape on the surface, we should be able to catch a glimpse of her, with any luck. Luck, because the area to be covered is huge, and the arcs can never be simultaneous; the first star shell are dipping into the sea, to be snuffed out before the arc can be half completed, and the gaps between areas covered by individual escorts are many and large. And yet—there is a lot of light up there, a lot of sea laid bare for the scrutiny of hundreds of searching eyes. *Montgomery* has radar, a sort of Stone Age contraption; one of her officers told me that they don't put any faith in any object it reports unless they can actually see it, and that its main use was in giving a distance off the convoy for station-keeping, but for all of that they'll be chasing every back-echo and will-o'-the-wisp wavetop it reports right now.

And then—there it is! Far out to the right of the last star shell I catch a glimpse through the binoculars of something in the wavetops, and as my heart almost stops with excitement I see, for the first time, the unmistakable outline of a U-boat conning tower. My shout is simultaneous with that of the captain: 'There she is; green 45!' and then everything happens at once. The captain cannons into me, leaping for the voice-pipe. 'Starboard twenty!' Falconer calls for another star shell on the same bearing as the last, and Harvey rushes for the asdic set to give his operators the bearing of the surfaced enemy; the moment he dives he becomes their responsibility. As the ship steadies on her new course, heading directly for the submarine, the captain issues a string of orders. A sighting signal is cracked off to *Montgomery*, the gun's crew bangs off its last star shell and then loads with high-explosive shell and a full charge, and down in the waist and quarterdeck the depth-charge crews rush to put shallow settings on their first pattern of charges, for we hope to be up with the

U-boat before he can dive deep. The captain calls for emergency full ahead, and even on the bridge we can hear the double ring of the engine telegraphs in the wheelhouse, and up the stokehold ventilators behind us we can hear the answering bells ringing and the stokers shouting as they open all the taps.

I keep the glasses glued on the U-boat, now brightly illuminated as the star-shell flares fall closer; under our feet the ship vibrates madly as the engines reach for their full power. We are closing rapidly, but suddenly there is a welter of white water all about the tiny black conning tower towards which we are charging.

She's diving! I turn to the captain, but he has already seen for himself.

'She's blowing ballast tanks,' he mutters, and calmly takes a bearing of her over the standard compass.

In a matter of seconds, she is gone, her position marked by a swirl of foam, and moments later our last star shell dips into the sea and blackness locks us in on every side. The captain moves into the asdic house to direct the search, and as we approach the diving position we reduce speed to ten knots, our asdic beam searching beneath the surface for the vanished enemy.

'From *Montgomery*, sir; *Kamsack* to close and assist *Trail* in hunting U-boat,' reports the signal yeoman from the wireless cabin voice-pipe. This is welcome news; with two escorts, one to hold contact while the other attacks, we should be able to kill this U-boat. On the silent bridge, on the darkened decks, men stand in attitudes of tension, all minds on the softly lit compass in the asdic cabin, where a ray of light and the persistent ping! of the set indicate that our supersonic beam is probing the blind depths for the hidden killer of our ships.

'Echo bearing red 10, range eleven hundred yards!' Out on the windswept bridge, I hear the report we have been aching to hear on the chart-room voice-pipe. The report is from the operator on the set; from Clarke, his leading hand and the ranking asdic rating on the ship, comes the qualifying report: 'Echo low,' and then, after the cut-offs have been established, the confident, unequivocal report: 'Target is submarine, sir, on an opening course.'

From the captain, then, the low words that put it all together: 'Start the attack!'

The attacking signal is made to *Kamsack* and *Montgomery*, we accelerate to a fifteen-knot attacking speed, settings for depth-charges are confirmed and their crews put on standby for firing. As officer of the watch I keep a lookout on the bridge, but my mind is with the little group huddled about the soft-lit instruments inside the cabin behind me, where the operator is holding contact, Clarke, our senior specialist, is keeping the captain posted, and the deep black marks of the chemical traces mark the roll of paper on the set each time an echo is received back from the U-boat, and thus indicate its range on the marked scale.

Bang!

Jesus, what was that! I whirl around toward the convoy, and then, seconds later, comes the sound of yet another explosion. Lord, more torpedoes; we've walked into a second submarine. I pass the word to the captain inside, who simply nods, too intent on our own developing attack to waste words. Moments later, *Kamsack* is diverted from us by *Montgomery*, and detailed to sweep astern for the second U-boat. The commodore reports the pennant numbers of the latest ship attacked, and corrects an earlier report; despite those first three explosions, only two ships have been torpedoed in the earlier attack—the extra bang was just one of those things.

At six hundred yards, the captain makes a bold throw-off, based on reports from the set and our plot, where the courses of target and ship have been carefully plotted. We alter thirty degrees to starboard in order to cross ahead of our unseen antagonist, so that our charges may sink through the water in his path and, hopefully, explode as he heads right into them.

Now the reports come thick and fast, the whole intensity of our effort stepping up as the range closes quickly. This is the climactic moment of the whole attack, when this ship justifies the purpose for which she was built and for which all her crew have trained and endured. The next few seconds can make it all worth while, can redeem the endless man-hours and effort which ship and crew represent. Except for the chanted litany of the asdic team, intoning its bearings and ranges, there is utter silence throughout the ship, every man keyed up to the breaking point. In the asdic cabin, the black line of the echo traces will be moving along the paper tape, being aligned with the perspex firing bar; when they coincide with the etched line on the bar the firing will begin.

There it is: 'Fire one!' And seconds later, 'Fire two!' and then 'Fire three!'

From the blackness behind us, we hear the splash of the charges from the traps into our wake, the 'whoosh! whoosh!' of the throwers on each side as we drop our charges in an elongated diamond pattern of ten, with six charges in pairs on the centre line and four from the throwers, two on each side.

'Simultaneous echoes!' comes the report from the asdic operator; the target is so close that no ranging is possible, and moments later, as the target passes astern and our transmissions are blanked out by our own wake. 'Lost contact, sir.'

'Boom! Bang! Whoorumph!' The tremendous detonation of our charges is like a giant hammer striking our hull; the whole ship lifts and is borne aloft as a great fountain of water, sensed rather than seen, rises from astern. The ship is given a ferocious shaking, and on deck we clutch for support; in the engine room, we must have broken every pipe we have. The captain reduces speed, and we circle around to give our asdic set a clear field in which to regain contact. But in the asdic cabin there are bitter oaths; the main gyro which directs our compasses has been unseated by the explosions, and everyone works desperately to get it back in service, for without it our asdic compass is useless. The captain paces in a fury of exasperation.

How was it? we ask ourselves. In the waist, the depth-charge crews are jabbering with excitement as they reload their mortars, and all of us wait for confirmation of our success. Surely no U-boat could have survived the accurate explosion of three tons of amatol? From the plot comes confirmation that the attack seemed a good one, but still, as we circle around, comes neither contact with the U-boat nor signs of its destruction. Unless—surely that smell was not there before—surely that is the smell of oil! I call the captain out, and he sniffs excitedly, but then the smell is gone, as quickly as it came.

'Not enough for a kill; more likely she's sprung a rivet or two in her fuel tanks,' the captain cautions, and moves back to the set. At long last, our gyro is operational again, and the asdic team buckles to its job. Still no contact; we begin a square search, directed by the plot, and the minutes grow, and with them our chances of regaining contact dwindle. Time is now crucial to us, for if we are not firmly in contact we cannot delay much longer. Our convoy is under attack, our escort hard-pressed, the sea perhaps covered with survivors awaiting rescue or death, men whose life in the sea is measured in minutes.

The issue we are already beginning to agonize over is resolved in a moment by a peremptory signal from *Montgomery*. We are to rejoin at best speed, and sweep astern as we do so while *Kamsack* screens the rescue ship, lying stopped and vulnerable as she hauls shaken and sodden men from the sea.

In dejected silence we huddle at our action stations.

LIVY
Hannibal Crosses the Alps, 218 BC

The Carthaginian general Hannibal crossed the Alps with his shock-weapon, the elephant, in 218 BC. The crossing was a feat of endurance and audacity which almost succeeded in bringing the Roman Empire to its knees.

FROM THAT TIME THE MOUNTAINEERS fell upon them in smaller parties, more like an attack of robbers than war, sometimes on the van, sometimes on the rear, according as the ground afforded them advantage, or stragglers advancing or loitering gave them an opportunity. Though the elephants were driven through steep and narrow roads with great loss of time, yet wherever they went they rendered the army safe from the enemy, because men unacquainted with such animals were afraid of approaching too nearly. On the ninth day they came to a summit of the Alps, chiefly through places trackless; and after many mistakes of their way, which were caused either by the treachery of the guides, or, when they were not trusted, by entering valleys at random, on their own conjectures of the route. For two days they remained encamped on the summit; and rest was given to the soldiers, exhausted with toil and fighting: and several beasts of burden, which had fallen down among the rocks, by following the track of the army arrived at the camp. A fall of snow, it being now the season of the setting of the constellation of the Pleiades, caused great fear to the soldiers, already worn out with weariness of so many hardships. On the standards being moved forward at day-break, when the army proceeded slowly over all places entirely blocked up with snow, and languor and despair strongly appeared in the countenances of all, Hannibal, having advanced before the standards, and ordered the soldiers to halt on a certain eminence, whence there was a prospect far and wide, points out to them Italy and the plains of the Po, extending themselves beneath the Alpine mountains; and said 'that they were now surmounting not only the ramparts of Italy, but also of the city of Rome; that the rest of the journey would be smooth and down-hill; that after one, or, at most, a second battle, they would have the citadel and capital of Italy in their power and possession'. The army then began to advance, the enemy now making no attempts beyond petty thefts, as opportunity offered. But the journey proved much more difficult that it had been in the ascent, as the declivity of the Alps being generally shorter on the side of Italy is consequently steeper; for nearly all the road was precipitous, narrow, and slippery, so that neither those who made the least stumble could prevent themselves from falling, nor, when fallen, remain in the same place, but rolled, both men and beasts of burden, one upon another.

They then came to a rock much more narrow, and formed of such perpendicular ledges, that a light-armed soldier, carefully making the attempt, and clinging with his hands to the bushes and roots around, could with difficulty lower himself down. The ground, even before very steep by nature, had been broken by a recent falling away of the earth into a precipice of nearly a thousand feet in depth. Here when the cavalry had halted, as if at the end of their journey, it is announced to Hannibal, wondering what obstructed the march, that the rock was impassable. Having then gone himself to view the place, it seemed clear to him that he must lead his army round it, by however great a circuit, through the pathless and untrodden regions around. But this route also proved impracticable; for while the new snow of a moderate depth remained on the old, which had not been removed, their footsteps were planted with ease as they walked upon the new snow, which was soft and not too deep; but when it was dissolved by the trampling of so many men and beasts of burden, they then walked on the bare ice below, and through the dirty fluid formed by the melting snow. Here there was a wretched struggle, both on account of the slippery ice not affording any hold to the step, and giving way beneath the foot more readily by reason of the slope; and whether they assisted themselves in rising by their hands or their knees, their supports themselves giving way, they would tumble again; nor were there any stumps or roots near, by pressing against which, one might with hand or foot support himself; so that they only floundered on the smooth ice and amid the melted snow. The beasts of burden sometimes also cut into this lower ice by merely treading upon it, at others they broke it completely through, by the violence with which they struck in their hoofs in their struggling, so that most of them, as if taken in a trap, stuck in the hardened and deeply frozen ice.

At length, after the men and beasts of burden had been fatigued to no purpose, the camp was pitched on the summit, the ground being cleared for that purpose with great difficulty, so much snow was there to be dug out and carried away. The soldiers being then set to make a way down the cliff, by which alone a passage could be effected, and it being necessary that they should cut through the rocks, having felled and lopped a number of large trees which grew around, they make a huge pile of timber; and as soon as strong wind fit for exciting the flames arose, they set fire to it, and, pouring vinegar on the heated stones, they render them soft and crumbling. They then open a way with iron instruments through the rock thus heated by the fire, and soften its declivities by gentle windings, so that not only the beasts of burden, but also the elephants could be led down it. Four days were spent about this rock, the beasts nearly perishing through hunger: for the summits of the mountains are for the most part bare, and if there is any pasture the snows bury it. The lower parts contain valleys, and some sunny hills, and rivulets flowing beside woods, and scenes more worthy of the abode of man. There the beasts of burden were sent out to pasture, and rest given for three days to the men, fatigued with forming the passage: they then descended into the plains, the country and the dispositions of the inhabitants being now less rugged.

In this manner chiefly they came to Italy in the fifth month (as some authors relate) after leaving New Carthage, having crossed the Alps in fifteen days.

GRAEME COOK
The Raid on Saint Nazaire

The port of Saint Nazaire on the occupied west coast of France, was an important dry-dock facility for heavy German naval vessels during WWII. It was thus a major target for the Allies in the Battle of the Atlantic. The subsequent British raid on St Nazaire in 1942 was one of the most dramatic sea actions of the war.

AT PRECISELY 12.30 HOURS ON 26 MARCH, a signal came to the waiting force from Admiral Farber, 'Carry out Chariot'. The raid on St Nazaire was on. The motor launches, the MGB and the MTB lying in Falmouth harbour grunted in unison and roared into life, their engines throbbing in a fanfare. The commandos stirred as the little boats nudged out of the bay and slipped neatly into formation. They were on their way to an unknown fate.

The cluster of small boats joined forces with the *Campbeltown* and the escorting destroyers and the armada set course for the Bay of Biscay at a steady thirteen knots. The crews of the motor launches knew only too well their vulnerability. They had no armour and their wooden hulls were like paper against even the lightest German weapons. A stray bullet in the wrong place could cause a conflagration which would envelop a boat in seconds and leave those on board no time for escape. Nevertheless, the entire naval contingent was conscious of the importance of its role. Their job was to get the commandos there and back or perish in the process.

The little fleet forged on across the water towards its objective in the growing darkness. On board the commando-carrying ships, the men who would carry out the attack tried as best they could to get some sleep but the sense of expectation was so great that few managed more than brief naps.

The night passed without event and the first rays of dawn lit the sea. The men on the MLs were tired after their sleepless night but thankful that so far, all had gone according to plan. Alas the plan was about to be disrupted. . . .

The alarm was raised by a lookout on board the *Tynedale*. He spotted the shape on the horizon. It jutted like a finger from the water with a thin deck at either side. Closer examination confirmed the captain's fears. It was a U-boat. The *Tynedale* swept round and charged through the waves towards the submarine. At all cost the U-boat had to be destroyed before she could raise the alarm and alert the German defenders. The bows of the destroyer carved a furrow through the heaving sea while behind her she cast a foaming white wake. Every man on board stood at action stations, waiting for the order to unleash a fusillade of fire at the enemy. But less than a mile from the submarine, the *Tynedale* was spotted. A klaxon blared on board the U-boat and she crash-dived into the sanctuary of the depths.

Before the conning tower disappeared beneath the bubbling water, the *Tynedale* opened fire, but the shells erupted harmlessly in the sea around the plunging U-boat. She was gone but the *Tynedale* pressed on, bent upon depth-charging her to destruction.

Once in the position at which the submarine had last been seen, the *Tynedale's* depth-charges fell into the water and moments later the sea was cast into mountainous white plumes as they erupted. The *Tynedale's* captain waited after the first attack. There was no sign of the U-boat having been damaged; no oil seeping to the surface or the flotsam of a hit. Then, just as another pattern of charges was about to be fired, the surface parted in a foaming turmoil and the submarine appeared. The destroyer's guns opened fire, hitting the hull. But she had no sooner reappeared than she was gone again, down into the deep where she lay on the sea bed to play the waiting game until the destroyer had gone.

Above her, the *Tynedale* swept the area in a bid to determine whether or not the submarine had been mortally wounded; but there was no trace of the U-boat. For two whole hours, the *Tynedale* scoured the area. Nothing. The search was abandoned. But it could not be left there. Since no one could be sure if the submarine had been sunk, the destroyers changed course out into the Atlantic in the hope that, if they were observed by the U-boat they would be taken for an anti-submarine patrol. It was a clever move and one that paid off for the submarine later surfaced and reported the encounter to its headquarters. The German naval commander at St Nazaire sent out the five *Möwe* class destroyers to hunt down and attack the British destroyers. But by the time the German destroyers had reached the reported position of the British ships they were gone. The *Tynedale* and the *Atherstone* had rejoined the little fleet and were steering an erratic deception course towards the Loire.

Not long after the encounter with the U-boat, a fleet of French fishing boats was sighted and this gave Ryder cause for concern. Intelligence had warned him that some French trawlers were known to carry German observers equipped with radio. Ryder could not risk the possibility that there might be observers on some of the boats and he felt he had no alternative but to order them sunk. After taking the crews on board, two of the boats were sunk by gunfire. Then the captain of one of the trawlers assured Ryder that there were no Germans on board the other boats so after a closer look, Ryder allowed them to continue with their fishing unmolested.

That evening as the fleet drew closer to its objective, Ryder and Newman changed ships and went on board the MGB from which they would command the raid and the fleet sailed south of the Loire before making a dog-leg turn towards the target.

In darkness the fleet nosed in towards the French coast. About twenty-five miles from the Loire estuary, the submarine *Sturgeon* broke the surface. Look-outs clambered into the conning tower and peered out into the darkness, anxiously straining their eyes for the 'Charioteers'. *Sturgeon* had been on station for some time, waiting to point the way into the Loire for the fleet. At precisely 22.15 hours a signal blinked out from the submarine. It was spotted by the fleet and it changed course to run into the estuary. The *Campbeltown* and her cluster of little boats swept past the submarine while the two escorting destroyers broke off to take up patrol positions off the estuary and wait for their return.

The tension on board the ships that slid into the estuary was electric. The telling time was at hand. They were sailing into the yawning embrace of hell, the *Campbeltown* with eighty commandos, Newman and Ryder in the MGB, four motor launches equipped with torpedoes, MTB-74, and eleven motor launches with 185 commandos alert and ready for action on their decks. One of the motor launches had had to drop out due to engine failure and her group of commandos was transferred to a torpedo-carrying ML, commanded by Lieutenant Falconer.

Lieutenant-Commander Beattie, the captain of the *Campbeltown*, nursed his ship into the mouth of the Loire estuary but had no sooner done so than she ground to a halt with a sickening shudder. The event that everyone on board her feared most had happened. She was aground on a mud bank. With remarkable coolness, Beattie ordered reverse engines and after a struggle, she squirmed free, only to run aground once more. There she was exposed, caught on the bank and an easy target for the German gunners. Beattie's skill paid off and again she was free and coursing into the estuary. Below decks, the time-fuses were set on the tons of explosives. The *Campbeltown* had reached the point of no return. Nothing could now stop the explosives from blowing up.

Lieutenant Green, the fleet navigator, now had the onerous task of guiding the *Campbeltown* onto her target, the caisson at the south end of the Normandie dock. He did this from the tiny chartroom of the MGB which had taken up its position in the van of the fleet, a little way ahead of the *Campbeltown*. Flanking the *Campbeltown* were the MLs, seven on either side with an ML and MTB-74 taking up the rear.

Now, as they forged deeper into the Loire came the most testing time of all. From here onwards, the fortunes of the little boats differed greatly from that of the *Campbeltown* and chaotic confusion reigned. Even today, the events which befell some of the boats of Coastal Forces in the Loire are uncertain, for the wrath of hell descended upon them. Since the actions which follow took place almost simultaneously, it is necessary to follow the fate of each vessel individually, in the interests of clarity. Because the prime objective of the raid was the destruction of the caisson, we shall take the *Campbeltown* first. . . .

She had now to run the gauntlet of the German gun batteries before ramming the caisson and her progress to the target would be determined by the success of two important factors: the RAF's diversionary raid and her ability to fox the Germans into thinking that she was a German ship.

The sky was dark and brooding with dense black thunder clouds hanging menacingly above. While such conditions might have been a blessing for the raiders, they seriously hindered the pilots of the Wellington and Whitley bombers that were already overhead St Nazaire. They had been given explicit orders only to bomb those targets that could be seen, in order to minimise the possibility of killing innocent French civilians. If the targets could not be seen, then they were to return with their bomb loads. When the bombers arrived over the port, they found it almost completely covered by cloud. The result was that only a handful of bombs were dropped. Pencil-thin fingers of light from searchlight batteries in and around St Nazaire searched the sky for the raiders, while anti-aircraft guns threw a barrage of fire into the sky. It was 23.30 hours. Captain Mecke, commanding the anti-aircraft battery, had watched the progress of the aircraft on the radar screen, noted their unusually high altitude and the strange absence of falling bombs for such a large force of bombers—sixty Whitleys and Wellingtons. When the bulk of the bombers turned for home without dropping their loads, Mecke became convinced that this was no ordinary raid and that there was some hidden purpose behind it. He signalled to the Wehrmacht: 'The conduct of the enemy aircraft is inexplicable and indicates suspicion of parachute landings.' By then it was midnight and the last of the bombers were droning off into the distance.

The searchlights blinked and went out, returning the night sky to darkness. But even with the bombers gone, Mecke was not happy and he kept his batteries at action stations. The enemy's unusual behaviour niggled at Mecke and he warned all stations to be on the alert and keep a watchful eye, especially out to sea. Within minutes, the little fleet was spotted. Mecke immediately telephoned the harbour-master and asked him if he was expecting these ships. The answer was an emphatic 'no'. Mecke swung into action and issued a general order to beware of a landing. The entire German defence system looked towards the Loire.

On board the *Campbeltown* and the other craft of the Chariot force, eager eyes had watched the bombardment and the retaliation by the defenders. The maintenance of surprise very largely depended upon the success of the diversionary raid. It had failed, through no fault of the bomber crews who had been told nothing of Operation Chariot. Had they known, the story might have been quite different but as it was, the raid served only to alert the defenders and resulted in terrible tragedy.

But yet the force sailed on. By then it was 0120 hours, only ten minutes to go before the *Campbeltown* was due to ram. She was barely two miles from her objective now when a searchlight ignited on the north shore and caught the *Campbeltown* in its beam. More searchlights lit up, all focused on the destroyer but the Germans held their fire. They did not know what to make of her. She flew the German naval ensign and certainly had the appearance of a German ship. Trigger fingers were poised nervously on board the ships and on shore. The uneasy seconds ticked by. Someone had to make a move and it was the Germans who took the initiative when signal lamps flashed from the shore demanding to know what ship the *Campbeltown* was.

Leading Signalman Pike, on board Ryder's MGB, waited tensely to play his part in the game of bluff. Thanks to the capture of German code books during a commando raid in Norway, Pike knew the precise replies to give. He raised his signal lamp and flashed the morse code name of one of the German torpedo boats he knew operated in the area. Then he turned his attention to the other bank and signalled the same message to them and told them that he was a German naval force sailing under orders to anchor in the harbour. The deception worked and the lights went out.

No one on board the ships dared to breathe a sigh of relief but it did seem that they had pulled it off. Then suddenly one of the shore batteries opened fire on the *Campbeltown*. Pike immediately flashed the international signal indicating that they were firing on friendly forces and the guns fell silent. But their luck had been tested to the limit.

In an instant every gun on shore that could be brought to bear on the ships opened fire. The fate of the vulnerable little boats we shall see; but the *Campbeltown* was for the moment the focus of attention as she stormed up the Loire bent on reaching her target. The bluff was over and Beattie ordered them to open fire. The German ensign was struck and the White ensign hauled up. Bullets and shells tore into the *Campbeltown*, gashing her armour plating and taking a deadly toll of crew and commandos who were crouched on the deck. Now the river was a blaze of light and the multi-coloured tracer arched almost leisurely towards the boats.

Ryder's MGB fought its way courageously through the wall of fire, guiding the *Campbeltown* on target while Leading Seaman Savage, manning the MGB's pom-pom blasted away at anything that moved on the shore. The slightest shadow caught the full fury of his gun.

At last the dock gate came into sight through the fury of fire. Beattie increased speed and the *Campbeltown* fairly raced through the water at twenty knots, the exact speed at which she had to hit the caisson for maximum effect. Lieutenant Curtis, commander of Ryder's MGB, waited until the very last moment when his boat was dwarfed by the caisson before he swerved out of the *Campbeltown*'s path. The destroyer throbbed and shook and she hurtled herself at the caisson. Then, with only a few yards to go, an incendiary shell hit the fo'c'sle and burst into flames, engulfing the forward deck of the ship in a raging torrent of fire. But Beattie held her steady.

'Stand by to ram!' he yelled. Everyone on board braced himself for the impact. A second later it came. . . .

A grinding thunder rocked the ship as the bows smashed into the caisson and crumpled back thirty-six feet. The *Campbeltown* was thrust atop the caisson by the force of her impetus until she finally came to a halt. Those commandos who had not been mauled by the German fire poured off the ship to go about their business of destruction. They fought their way into the dock to their objectives and began to set their charges.

The *Campbeltown* had done her part and all that remained was for her to blow up. But while she had succeeded in ramming the caisson and off-loading her commandos, the same success was not destined to attend the motor launches. By the time the destroyer smashed into the Normandie dock, the river behind her had been transformed into a fiery hell.

Until she hit the dock, the *Campbeltown* had been attended in her course up river by two lines of motor launches, one to starboard and the other to port. Each of these lines comprised seven launches, sailing in line astern with a torpedo-carrying launch and MTB-74 bringing up the rear. Following the opening of fire from the German batteries on shore, almost total chaos reigned among the motor launches and the other small craft.

The port column of boats was destined for the Old Mole, a stone-built protrusion which jutted out into the Loire a little south of the Normandie dock. It was there that they were to off-load their commandos. But with one exception, it was not to be. The boats, in order of formation, were commanded by Lieutenants Irwin (a torpedo-carrying ML), Platt, Collier, Wallis, Horlock, Henderson and Falconer. On the starboard side, the seven craft were commanded by Boyd (another torpedo-carrying ML), Stephens, Burt, Beart, Tillie, Fenton and Rodier. Lying behind both columns was a torpedo-carrying ML commanded by Nock and MTB-74 commanded by Lieutenant Wynn.

In the van of the port column was Irwin's boat, which carried torpedoes and no commandos. His job was to seek out and torpedo any enemy craft in the Loire which proved troublesome so he surged off farther up the Loire in search of fodder but quickly came under heavy attack from the shore. A shell hit the boat, ripped through her side and shattered the steering gear, forcing her to steer a crazy course in the river. The weight of fire never let up for a moment and with his boat out of control, Irwin sensibly decided that he could do no good in the river and aimed to withdraw. After a hectic if erratic dash back down river, he succeeded in reaching the open sea.

Hot on Irwin's heels and aiming for the Old Mole was Platt's boat with her commandos who were to be landed there with the idea of neutralising the German gun positions on the Mole and securing the stretch of land between it and the southern entrance to the St Nazaire basin. Platt darted around the Mole to land his commandos on the north side but, as he reached it, the boat ran aground. He rammed the engines into reverse but already the German gunners on the Mole had a bead on him and sprayed the boat with machine-gun fire and shells, which took their inevitable toll. Then the worst happened, a bullet found the fuel tank and soon the boat was a raging inferno. Platt managed to wriggle free of the mud and the boat drifted round to the south side of the Mole; but it was clear to him that she was doomed. He ordered abandon ship and the few survivors left leapt overboard to attempt the three-hundred-yard swim to the sand by the shore. The commander of the commandos on the boat was caught in the current and swept downstream. He managed to reach the shore but died shortly afterwards. Troop Sergeant-Major Hewett struggled valiantly against the current, gulping in oily water. Finally he reached a ladder by the quayside and managed to haul his spent body to the land. But he was taken prisoner by the Germans who beat him up before dragging him off to captivity. Of the commandos and crew on Platt's boat, sixteen were drowned or killed by gunfire. The remainder were picked up by the torpedo-carrying ML leading the starboard column of boats which came to the rescue.

Collier, who followed Platt, was more successful. He swept around Platt's drifting wreck and succeeded in putting his commandos ashore. Among them was Captain Pritchard, the explosives expert, who was to run amok in the dockyard. The commandos hurled themselves along the Mole, levelling their tommy-guns at the defenders and spraying them with bullets. With his charges safely deposited, Collier retreated into midstream to wait for re-embarkation of the commandos when their job was done.

Wallis was next one in, but as his boat drew alongside the Mole, German soldiers high above threw hand-grenades into the boat. Without weapons to reply to the bombing, Wallis was forced to withdraw without landing his commandos, which comprised a small demolition team.

The three remaining boats were queueing up to get in at the Mole, all the time under heavy fire from the shore. Shells and bullets ripped at the boats as they nudged in towards the Mole bathed in the glaring light of powerful searchlights and the flames from Platt's boat. Horlock, in the lead, was forced off the Mole by the sheer weight of fire from the dockside. He determinedly roared round in a circle and tried again to no avail. The water around him was in a turmoil, lashed by bullet and shell; the accuracy of the fire forced him to break off.

Henderson, directly behind Horlock, now made his bid, but he too found the wall of fire impenetrable. He decided to try his luck farther up at a point known as the Old Entrance. But there as well the opposition was too great and he had to withdraw, with his commandos still on board. As we shall see, he was to get a fearful taste of action when he reached the open sea.

The last man in on the port column was Falconer, who, it will be remembered, had taken commandos on board his torpedo-carrying ML when another boat had had engine trouble. But his attempt to land at the Mole was also thwarted when all his guns were put out of action by gunfire which raked the deck. The fire also took its toll of the commandos and their leader Lieutenant Hodgson was dead, lying alongside other commandos who had been injured. Falconer, realising that he had an ineffective commando force on board, retreated.

Of the six boats which had attempted to land their commandos, only one had succeeded. Considering the weight of defensive fire, it was little short of a miracle that Collier's boat had succeeded in that short and bloody encounter which had lasted less than five minutes. The Mole which by then should have been in British hands was still held by the Germans.

Farther up the river at the other landing point, the Old Entrance, the boats of the starboard column were in the thick of the fighting. Boyd's torpedo-carrying ML went off in search of targets for his torpedoes farther up-stream; but when he found none, he returned to the scene of action. Not wishing to waste his 'fish', he fired at a German ship and then charged into the fray at the Old Mole. Almost immediately, his boat was hit by a shell. Both engines stopped and the boat was plunged into darkness below decks. However, the mechanic managed to get the engines operating again. Spotting Platt's burning boat, Boyd went alongside. With the air filled with whistling shells and bullets, he took off the wounded and the remainder of Platt's crew and swerved back out into mid-river. There he rescued three more men from the water before beginning the dash down-stream. Before he could get underway, however, the boat was caught in intense fire which killed and wounded many of the unfortunates on deck. At last Boyd put on speed and charged off towards the open sea.

The first of the troop-carrying boats in the starboard column was Stephens's which bore an assault party under Captain Burn. Stephens's boat had, by the time it reached the Old Entrance, already been hit by a shell which ripped the guts out of the engine room and put the boat out of control. She careered about the river and rammed the shore below the Old Mole. Stephens ordered abandon ship since it was impossible to scale the fourteen-foot-high wall they had hit. The wounded were put into rafts and cast off down river while the others jumped into the water. Of those who took to the water, several were claimed by the river. Only five of the commandos survived and four of these were quickly captured. Captain Burn managed to elude the Germans for a while and put up a valiant fight but was later captured, only to escape again and join forces with Newman.

Lieutenant Burt's boat was on the heels of Stephens's ML but the intense glare from the shore searchlights and Stephens's burning boat threw him wildly off course. Burt followed him in the boat behind and they found themselves several hundred yards from the Old Entrance. Both boats swerved round and charged at the Old Entrance where the other boats of the starboard column were already landing their commandos. Burt was first in and landed his commandos on the north side of the Entrance but the commandos leapt ashore into a barrage of machine-gun fire and many of them were killed as they jumped. The opposition was too intense for the commandos and they re-embarked, along with others who had completed their work. The German fire followed them on board and a commando and a naval rating were killed while others were wounded. Burt soared out into mid-river.

Beart suffered much the same as Burt. He too got to the shore and landed his commandos but they were forced back on to the boat. Beart was killed and the boat set on fire. Burning petrol spread over the river and when the crew and commandos leapt overboard, they did so into a flaming cauldron. Of the eleven commandos on board, only three survived.

By now, the river was alight with flaming petrol and the burning wrecks of boats strewn across it. But still the other boats forged in. Tillie was next and he caught the full force of the German fire, which set his boat alight adding to the conflagration. She drifted helplessly out of control towards the *Campbeltown* and blew up, killing most of the sailors and fifteen of the seventeen commandos on board her.

Fenton bounded in towards the Entrance but he too came under fire and was wounded, along with the officer in charge of his commandos and his first lieutenant. In addition, his steering gear was put out of action by a well-aimed shell. His position was hopeless and he withdrew to mid-stream to fight it out there.

Lieutenant Rodier was last man in the starboard column and he bolted through the blazing river and landed his contingent of commandos. Trailing behind Rodier was Nock's torpedo-carrying ML which had a roving commission to hit anything it could. For some time, Nock let fly at the guns on shore, knocking out several of them. He stopped to pick up survivors and it was then that the boat was hit and set on fire. Nock put on full speed in a bid to charge down river and gain the open sea but his flaming boat was an easy target. Shells found their mark and both his engines blew up. Nock was badly wounded and the boat sank.

By then seven boats had been forced to withdraw from the fray. Five more had been destroyed and only three remained in the river fighting it out until the time came to re-embark their commandos. These were the boats of Burt, Rodier and Collier.

Collier and Burt found each other and joined forces. Collier headed in towards the Old Entrance to take off commandos but was hit by concentrated fire and set alight. Burt had already taken off a small party of commandos and saw that Collier was in trouble. He went to his aid by coming alongside. Collier was hit by machine-gun fire and from the bridge of the ML declined Burt's offer of help, despite the fact that his deck was strewn with dead and dying. Collier, mortally wounded, remained on the bridge until he died shortly afterwards. In the meantime, Burt was forced to take his boat away from Collier's because of the risk of fire. As he did so, he came under fierce attack which put the boat out of control and wounded many of those on board. For almost an hour the boat drifted aimlessly about the river until Burt, realising she was doomed, ordered everyone to abandon ship. But most of his men were by then dead. Those who survived, Burt among them, were swept far down river and subsequently taken prisoner.

Only one motor launch remained, that of Lieutenant Rodier. Showing incredible coolness, Rodier took his boat away from the Old Entrance and over to the *Campbeltown* where he tied up alongside and began taking on the destroyer's crew, including Beattie, the captain. Then, with some fifty men crammed on-board, he set off down river. It was not long, however, before the Germans found him and brought all their guns to bear on the boat. A shell hit the bridge, killing Rodier while another wrecked the engine room and set the boat on fire. The barrage of fire directed at the boat wiped out all but a handful of the men on board before she was finally abandoned, blazing from stem to stern. Beattie was among the few who were subsequently picked up from the river and taken prisoner.

There were still two small boats in the river, the MGB headquarters boat and Lieutenant Wynn's MTB-74. After Ryder had landed Newman ashore to set up his headquarters, he boldly took the MGB alongside the *Campbeltown* and boarded her to make sure that the demolition charges had been properly set. When he returned to the MGB, Wynn's boat had joined the other. Ryder, confident that the caisson required no further attention, ordered Wynn to fire his torpedoes at the lock gates in the Old Entrance. Wynn manoeuvred out into mid-stream where he fired both 'fish'. They slammed into the lock-gates and lay on the bottom, their delayed action fuses burning to explode the charges some time later.

With his job done, Wynn took on board the remainder of the *Campbeltown's* crew and started a dash down-river at speed. He had covered six miles before he spotted some survivors in the river and stopped to pick them up. It was a fatal move. Immediately, German guns found the boat and it was quickly transformed into a blazing wreck. Not a soul escaped unscathed. Wynn was badly wounded and his left eye hung out of its socket. He was helped onto a raft with about thirty men on board. It floated down river in the current throughout the morning. During that time men slipped into the water never to be seen again. When the raft was eventually sighted at 1400 hours by a German patrol boat there were only three men left on board. Wynn was one of them. Of the men Wynn had taken on board, thirty-three had perished.

Lieutenant Henderson's boat which, it will be remembered, was forced to withdraw without landing her commandos was not to miss the action. She bolted down river and succeeded in reaching the open sea where she hoped to rendezvous with British destroyers waiting to escort the Chariot force home. Alas it was not to be. After the attack had taken place, the German naval command at St Nazaire had signalled the five *Möwe* class destroyers to return to base and it was these that Henderson met in the Bay of Biscay.

The sky was still dark when Henderson first saw the German destroyers. They were dashing at speed towards the Loire and he hoped that his small boat would not be seen in the darkness. He cut engines and lay silent, praying that they would pass. The first ship swept past. Then the second. Their luck was holding. Then came the third, the destroyer *Jaguar*, under the command of Lieutenant Paul. It was third time unlucky for the ML. It was spotted and a searchlight from the destroyer caught it in its beam. A gun opened from the ML and the searchlight was doused. But moments later another bathed the boat in light and guns from both vessels opened up. On the ML, everyone on deck was firing, including the commandos who let fly with Tommy guns and pistols while the heavier armament of the launch pumped missiles at the destroyer.

Lieutenant Paul was staggered at the intensity of the fire from the small British boat and he decided to ram it. He brought the *Jaguar* round to slice the boat in half; but Henderson saw what was about to happen and darted out of the way just in time. Throughout this manoeuvre the German gunners thrashed the decks of the ML with fire, killing and wounding commandos and seamen alike. Then the destroyer opened up with its 4.1-inch gun and gouged great chunks out of the little boat. Henderson was killed but the gallant survivors continued to fight with fierce determination. One of them was Sergeant Durrant who, although already mortally wounded, fired at the destroyer with his Bren gun. The seaman manning the ML's twin Lewis gun was killed and Durrant hauled himself across the deck and took over. Bleeding from multiple wounds, Durrant continued to lash out at the destroyer.

The outcome of the battle was a foregone conclusion but still the men in the launch continued to put up strong opposition. Lieutenant Paul saw the futility of the fight and called upon the ML to surrender. It was Durrant who gave the answer when he turned the Lewis gun on the bridge of the destroyer and sprayed it with fire, almost killing the captain. A few moments later, Durrant was hit again. His body could take no more punishment and he collapsed dying on the deck. It was only after almost all the ammunition was spent that the British reluctantly surrendered, bringing to an end one of the most gallant actions in the history of Coastal Forces.

In St Nazaire the river was still ablaze and escape for the surviving commandos all but impossible. Newman, along with the vast majority of his men, was captured but not before he had the satisfaction of hearing demolition charges exploding throughout the dockyard. They were held captive in St Nazaire until arrangements could be made to take them to prisoner of war camps. One thought was uppermost in their minds during these early hours of captivity—would the *Campbeltown* blow up? She obliged at 1030 hours. The explosion blew off the front third of the ship and knocked the caisson halfway off its rollers. The resulting flood carried the *Campbeltown* halfway down the dock where she sank to the bottom. The Normandie dock was a shambles and remained out of action for about ten years. The *Tirpitz* never did reach the Atlantic.

The raid on St Nazaire had been a success but at a terrible cost in lives and ships, particularly the little boats of Coastal Forces. Of the entire force of motor launches that took part in the raid, only three reached England, having fought off fighter and bomber attacks on the way. Lieutenant Wynn's two delayed-action torpedoes blew up some days later, throwing the Germans into a further panic.

Of the 611 men who took part in the raid, 169 were killed, many were seriously wounded and the majority taken prisoner. The other survivors were taken home on board the *Atherstone* and the *Tynedale*.

The Victoria Cross was awarded to five of those who took part in the raid. Newman, Ryder and Beattie were each decorated with their countries highest award for bravery. It was also posthumously awarded to Able Seaman Savage and Sergeant Durrant, the first soldier ever to be awarded a VC in a naval action . . . and he won it aboard a launch of Coastal Forces.

The Raid on St Nazaire was unquestionably the most valiant moment in the history of the small boats.

JOHN LODWICK
The SBS Raid on Simi

The Special Boat Section was set up in 1941, as an irregular British hit-and-run force. It was active in North Africa, Italy, Jugoslavia and the Greek Islands. (The Alistair Maclean novel, The Guns of Navarone, *is based on the exploits of the SBS in the Aegean.) John Lodwick, one of a trio of authors who served with the SBS in the Mediterranean (the others being Eric Newby and John Verney) describes the SBS's most famous action, the raid on the occupied Greek island of Simi in 1944.*

THE SIMI OPERATION HAD BEEN considered for some time, but as long as the enemy possessed destroyers in the Aegean, it had never looked practicable. Destroyers can interfere with landing operations, even at long range and at short notice. At the beginning of the year, there had been four destroyers in the Eastern Mediterranean. Only very gradually were they eliminated.

The German navy in those waters seldom put to sea.

In March, one of these ships was damaged by a British submarine. Later, a second received a bomb amidships from a Beaufighter. Two remained lurking in Leros. In this emergency, Brigadier Turnbull requested London to send him out a small party of Royal Marine Boom Commando troops. A wise move, for though there were still many men in the SBS to whom folboating was second nature, the art of infiltration by canoe had undoubtedly declined since the days of 'Tug' Wilson. Folboats, when used at all, were now used to land personnel, their role being no more aggressive than that of a gondola.

When Turnbull's marines first arrived in the Middle East the experts were inclined to scoff. Their attitude of condescension was abandoned when it was seen with what precision the newcomers handled their craft. In mid-June they went into Portolago Harbour, Leros, crossed two booms, sank the surviving destroyers with limpet charges and emerged without loss.

The way was now clear for Simi.

On 6th July Stewart Macbeth returned to base. He had made a personal reconnaissance of the island and pin-pointed the enemy dispositions. Two days later the striking force, under Brigadier Turnbull himself, comprising ten motor launches, two schooners, eighty-one members of the SBS and one hundred and thirty-nine from the Greek Sacred Squadron were concentrated in Penzik Bay, Turkey, under camouflage. Three parties were constituted: Main Force, under the Brigadier with Lapraik deputizing; West Force, under Captain Charles Clynes; and South Force, under Macbeth. On the night of July 13th the landings were made, and despite great enemy vigilance, passed everywhere unobserved. The only casualties suffered consisted of two Greek officers who fell into the water with heavy packs. They were drowned.

The approach marches were difficult but all three forces were lying up and overlooking their targets before dawn. At first light a barrage was opened upon Simi Castle—the main enemy stronghold—by mortars and multiple machine-guns. Two German 'Ems' barges which had left harbour a few minutes before zero hour now came scuttling back. They had sighted the force of five British launches which was coming in to bombard the castle. Both motor launches and the SBS opened fire on these ships. Presently, large white flags could be seen waving from their bridges before they ran ashore and were captured in good working order.

'Stud' Stellin was clearing Molo Point. He had taken his first objective without opposition. Ahead of him, Germans were running up the hill to man their machine-gun posts.

'I took a shot with my carbine,' said 'Stud', 'but misfired. I therefore called upon Private Whalen to give them the works. We strolled in with grenades, and I think that everybody went a little mad. Soon, all the enemy were either down and dead, or up and waving their hands.'

Stellin locked these prisoners in a church, left a sentry outside it and moved on to his next objective.

Clynes, scheduled to attack gun positions, gave them three minutes softening from his Brens and then ordered his Greeks to charge. 'All I can remember, then,' he said, 'is a general surge up the slope and two small and pathetic white handkerchiefs waving at the top of it. I ordered a "Cease fire" all round, and began to count my prisoners.'

By 0900 hours, Main Force Headquarters and the Vickers machine-gun and mortar troops had advanced to within 800 yards of the castle. Fire was intensified upon this target from all sides, mortar projectiles crashing on the battlements and nine-millimetre tracer searching every embrasure. The enemy reaction was spirited and indicated that they had by no means abandoned hope. Stellin, moving his patrol to clear some caïque yards, received most of the attention.

'The stuff started to whizz about. We had to cross a bridge. Somebody in the castle had a very accurate bead on that bridge. We doubled, but Lance-Corporal Roberts, Private Majury, and Marine Kinghorn became pinned down under a low parapet, the slightest movement causing fire to be brought upon them. I told them to stay there. . . .'

They did. They were not able to get up until the castle surrendered three hours later. Roberts, who attempted to while away the time by lighting a cigarette, raised his head an inch or two. He received a bullet graze from the temple to the neck.

Clynes had also been sent down to the caïque yard with orders to clear it. On the way he met Lieutenant Betts-Gray, who throughout the action did excellent liaison work. Betts-Gray was hugging the rocks, pursued by a hail of fire. Clynes and his patrol were presently pinned down in their turn. Private Bromley was hit in the arm, and Betts-Gray, who had had miraculous escapes all day, in the buttocks once, and in the back twice, was assisted into a house and put to bed.

To the south, Macbeth and Bury, with their forces, had assaulted a monastery position after considerable mortar preparation. The surviving enemy were driven down a promontory towards the extremity of the island, where Macbeth called upon them to surrender. The first demand written by Bob Bury, was rejected haughtily by the defenders as illegible. It was rewritten with the aid of a young Greek girl, who volunteered to carry it through the lines. This civilian armistice commission was successful and thirty-three more of the enemy laid down their arms.

Around the castle, the situation had developed into a stalemate, with mortar fire causing the garrison casualties and discomfort, but not sufficient in itself to bring about their surrender. Neither Brigadier Turnbull nor Lapraik considered that the position could be taken by direct assault. They decided to consolidate, make the maximum display of force at their disposal and institute surrender parleys.

Accordingly, Brigadier Turnbull sent a German petty-officer, commanding one of the 'Ems' barges, up under escort, with instructions to inform the enemy that they were completely surrounded, that the rest of the island was in British hands, and that further resistance on their part was as senseless as it was likely to prove costly.

The petty-officer returned an hour later. It appeared that the enemy were prepared to talk business. Lieutenant Kenneth Fox, a German speaker, now returned to the castle with the same man. A further hour elapsed during which the only incident was the emergence of a party of Italian *carabinieri* from the stronghold, weeping, and waving a Red Cross flag.

'I thought I recognized one of these fellows,' said Lapraik, 'and sure enough it was the old rascal who had given us so much trouble during our previous occupation of Simi. He grew very pale when he saw me . . . .'

Lieutenant-Commander Ramseyer, the naval liaison officer, was then sent up to expedite matters. He found Fox and the German Commander in agitated conference and himself in imminent danger from our mortar fire. At last, the capitulation was arranged and the garrison marched out. They had barely been collected and counted when three Messerschmitts flew over the port and dropped antipersonnel bombs.

'Too bad,' the German Commander is reported to have said, shaking his head. 'You see, that's what comes of being late. I thought they had forgotten about us. I radioed for them five hours ago.'

Prisoners taken in this action totalled 151, of whom seventeen were wounded. Twenty-one Germans and Italians had been killed. The SBS and Sacred Squadron losses were as usual microscopic, and, apart from the two Greek officers drowned, not a single man was killed. Six were wounded.

As soon as the Messerchmitts had disappeared, tea was taken by both armies in the caïque yards. Sausages were fried and an ox, provided by the delighted population, roasted on a bowsprit. As for the prisoners, they were so delighted to find themselves treated deferentially instead of being shot out of hand, that they revealed the existence of many a cache of wine in their living-quarters. Bottles were transferred to the SBS packs, to be drunk at base

Meanwhile, Lapraik, Macbeth, and Stellin, well known on the island, were borne to the town hall, where many speeches were made. The town jail was thrown open to the accompaniment of a furore which would have done credit to the storming of the Bastille. Unfortunately, only one prisoner was found inside and he, a Fascist, refused to be liberated.

'I admired these islanders,' said Lapraik, 'intensely; for they well knew that we could not remain and were rightly apprehensive of reprisals. But this did not diminish in any way their enthusiasm, though they were aware that hostile eyes were watching them, recording every incident. In the end, we caused them immense relief by taking the fifteen foremost quislings away with us.'

General demolitions were begun by Bill Cumper and installations as varied as 75-mm. gun emplacements, diesel fuel pumps and cable-heads, received generous charges. Ammunition and explosive dumps provided fireworks to suit the occasion. In the harbour, nineteen German caïques, some displacing as much as 150 tons, were sunk. At midnight the whole force sailed, the prisoners being crowded into the two 'Ems' barges. Stellin, with his patrol and Captain Pyke, Civil Affairs Officer, remained behind as rear party, with instructions to report subsequent events on Simi, and to distribute nearly thirty tons of food which had been brought in for the relief of the civilian population.

The German reaction was as expected, and followed the traditional pattern of attempted intimidation preceding assault. On the following morning the town was heavily bombed. Stellin and his men sat tight in their slit trenches. When it was all over they emerged to find, as they had hoped, that two enemy motor launches were attempting to enter the harbour. Such accurate fire was opened on these ships that they withdrew, blazing. So did Stellin, whose keen ear had detected the approach of more bombers, and who knew that this was the prelude to reoccupation of the island.

At three o'clock, from one of the more remote mountains, he watched the German flag hoisted over the citadel. But Stellin's adventures were not yet over; that night the launch re-embarking his party, encountered an 'E' boat on the return journey. So many and so various were Stellin's store of captured weapons that every man in his patrol was able to take a personal hand in the battle with a machine-gun. The 'E' boat was left in a sinking condition.

The great raid on Simi marked the end of SBS intervention in the Aegean. It had always been intended that the Sacred Squadron should take over this, their natural theatre of operations, as soon as they were fully trained and in a position to assume the heavy commitments involved. That happy state of affairs had now been achieved and Lapraik, instructed by Brigadier Turnbull, was able to write to the Greek Commander: 'Your group will operate in the Aegean until further notice. For the present, you will confine yourself to reconnaissance, but in September, raiding activities will be resumed upon a much larger scale. Sergeant Dale, SBS, will remain attached to you for Intelligence purposes.'

Lapraik, with his men, his prisoners, and his booty, withdrew to Castelrosso, and from Castelrosso to Beirut for a well-deserved holiday. Here they were met by the news that the SBS had been asked for in Italy for the purpose of attacking targets in Jugoslavia and Albania. Turkish waters would see them no more.

But it is not possible to leave those waters without some description of the extraordinary life led by all ranks there when not on operations.

Picture the deep, indented Gulf of Cos, with uninhabited shores and sullen, fir-covered mountains rising abruptly from the water's edge. In this two hundred miles of coastline it would not be easy for you to find the SBS, but if you were wise, you would look for some bay screened by small islands suitable for training purposes. Again, if you were wise, you would consult your map in search of one of the few streams from which drinkable water might be drawn.

Entering this bay, you would at first judge it to be empty.

Closer inspection would show you a large, squat, ugly schooner lying close to one shore, with her gang-plank down and a horde of dories, folboats, rubber dinghies, and rafts nuzzling one flank like kittens about the teats of their mother. Farther off, a full mile away, lie five or six motor launches and an MTB under camouflage, and within gin-and-lime distance of them a sleeker, trimmer, cleaner caïque, which is obviously naval property. In this area, too, are other subsidiary caïques. The intervening water is dotted with small boats from which men are fishing . . . mostly with grenades.

Let us approach the large and ugly schooner. She is the *Tewfik* of Port Said, the SBS depot ship. In her vast stern a naked figure is crouching, and whittling at something with a knife. It is Lassen, and he is making a bow with which to shoot pigs. Down below, in the murky cabin at the foot of the steep companion-way, David Sutherland, pipe in mouth, is writing an operational order. Beside him are rum bottles, magnums of champagne from Nisiros reserved for special occasions, and a neat list showing the casualties inflicted on the enemy during the current month . . . and our own.

'Blyth, Captain H. W., plus 4—OUT—4.4.44. Due in 12.4.44. Overdue. Target, CALCHI.'

Presently, Sutherland reaches a difficult point in his work. He takes the pipe from his mouth and shouts:

'Corporal Morris.'

A tall, angular, serious, and bespectacled figure comes bowling down the companion-way with a file in his hand. Curiously enough, it is the file which Sutherland wants, for Morris possesses second sight. Morris retires. His typewriter, seldom silent, begins clicking again in the distance.

Just forrard of the poop, Sergeant Jenkins, known colloquially as 'The Soldier's Friend' by reason of his claims to satisfy everyone, is trying to do three things at once. Sergeant Jenkins is accusing one SBS man of pinching a tin of sausage meat, endeavouring to prevent another from doing the same thing under his very nose, and issuing orders to the Greek cooks concerning dinner.

'Not octopus again,' he begs them. 'Not octopus, *please*.'

On the hatch beside him, Nobby Clarke, his magnificent moustache stained by indelible pencil marks, is endeavouring to write an operational report under difficult conditions. Two American war correspondents recline on the same hatch in deck-chairs. They are polishing recently acquired Lügers.

Farther forward, Guardsmen O'Reilly, Conby, and D'Arcy, mugs of rum and tea in their hands, are discussing the good old days in Libya. In the black hole behind them which is the main men's quarters, the severe and well-cropped head of Staff-Sergeant-Major John Riley can be seen. Riley, oblivious of the noisy and vulgar game of pontoon going on in his immediate neighbourhood, is playing bridge.

In the forepeak, German prisoners, poking their heads up inquisitively, are being given cigarettes by almsgivers.

Towards dusk, the scene becomes more animated, and the immense capacity of the British soldier for slumber less noticeable. The headquarter signallers are pursued, for they alone have news of what is going on in the latest raids. Perhaps a motor launch returns with the personnel from one of these raids . . . another is almost certainly setting out to continue them. Men who have been bathing, fishing, bartering with the local Turks, return, demanding supper loudly. Aft, Paddy Errett, Cumper's deputy, is cursing and producing perfectly packed explosive charges at two minutes' notice.

A motor boat chugs alongside, and Sutherland is whisked away to Levant Schooner 9, where Lieutenant-Commander Campbell, sherry glass in hand, is entertaining a couple of MTB skippers with the details of their coming patrol, which, to-night, will be north of Cos. 'E' boats are expected.

Sutherland and Campbell confer, confide, plot, send signals . . .

Keith Balsillie is zero-ing a German sniper's rifle found in Piscopi.

Marine Hughes is eating a tin of peaches . . . .

'Brown Body' Henderson is unable to find any volunteers for P.T.

South of Samos, Harold Chevalier, two days out from base, has just ordered a German caïque to heave-to.

STEPHEN CRANE
Marines Signalling Under Fire at Guantanamo

The Spanish–American War of 1898 had its beginning in the revolt of the Cubans against Spanish imperial rule, with the USA siding with the insurgents after the sinking of the USS Maine *in Havana harbour on 15 February 1898. Stephen Crane, the famous author of the American Civil War novel,* The Red Badge of Courage, *witnessed much of the fighting on Cuba as a newspaper reporter.* The Marblehead *mentioned at the start of the story is a USS cruiser.*

THEY WERE FOUR GUANTANAMO MARINES, officially known for the time as signalmen, and it was their duty to lie in the trenches of Camp McCalla, that faced the water, and, by day, signal the *Marblehead* with a flag and, by night, signal the *Marblehead* with lanterns. It was my good fortune—at that time I considered it my bad fortune, indeed—to be with them on two of the nights when a wild storm of fighting was pealing about the hill; and, of all the actions of the war, none were so hard on the nerves, none strained courage so near the panic point, as those swift nights in Camp McCalla. With a thousand rifles rattling; with the field-guns booming in your ears; with the diabolic Colt automatics clacking; with the roar of the *Marblehead* coming from the bay, and, last, with Mauser bullets sneering always in the air a few inches over one's head, and with this enduring from dusk to dawn, it is extremely doubtful if any one who was there will be able to forget it easily. The noise; the impenetrable darkness; the knowledge from the sound of the bullets that the enemy was on three sides of the camp; the infrequent bloody stumbling and death of some man with whom, perhaps, one had messed two hours previous; the weariness of the body, and the more terrible weariness of the mind, at the endlessness of the thing, made it wonderful that at least some of the men did not come out of it with their nerves hopelessly in shreds.

But, as this interesting ceremony proceeded in the darkness, it was necessary for the signal squad to coolly take and send messages. Captain McCalla always participated in the defence of the camp by raking the woods on two of its sides with the guns of the *Marblehead*. Moreover, he was the senior officer present, and he wanted to know what was happening. All night long the crews of the ships in the bay would stare sleeplessly into the blackness toward the roaring hill.

The signal squad had an old cracker-box placed on top of the trench. When not signalling they hid the lanterns in this box; but as soon as an order to send a message was received, it became necessary for one of the men to stand up and expose the lights. And then—oh, my eye, how the guerillas hidden in the gulf of night would turn loose at those yellow gleams!

Signalling in this way is done by letting one lantern remain stationary—on top of the cracker-box, in this case—and moving the other over to the left and right and so on in the regular gestures of the wig-wagging code. It is a very simple system of night communication, but one can see that it presents rare possibilities when used in front of an enemy who, a few hundred yards away, is overjoyed at sighting so definite a mark.

How, in the name of wonders, those four men at Camp McCalla were not riddled from head to foot and sent home more as repositories of Spanish ammunition than as marines is beyond all comprehension. To make a confession—when one of these men stood up to wave his lantern, I, lying in the trench, invariably rolled a little to the right or left, in order that, when he was shot, he might not fall on me. But the squad came off scatheless, despite the best efforts of the most formidable corps in the Spanish army—the Escuadra de Guantanamo. That it was the most formidable corps in the Spanish army of occupation has been told me by many Spanish officers and also by General Menocal and other insurgent officers. General Menocal was Garcia's chief of staff when the latter was operating busily in Santiago province. The regiment was composed solely of practicos, or guides, who knew every shrub and tree on the ground over which they moved.

Whenever the adjutant, Lieutenant Draper, came plunging along through the darkness with an order—such as: 'Ask the *Marblehead* to please shell the woods to the left'—my heart would come into my mouth, for I knew then that one of my pals was going to stand up behind the lanterns and have all Spain shoot at him.

The answer was always upon the instant: 'Yes, sir.'

Then the bullets began to snap, snap, snap, at his head, while all the woods began to crackle like burning straw. I could lie near and watch the face of the signalman, illumed as it was by the yellow shine of lantern-light, and the absence of excitement, fright, or any emotion at all on his countenance was something to astonish all theories out of one's mind. The face was in every instance merely that of a man intent upon his business, the business of wigwagging into the gulf of night where a light on the *Marblehead* was seen to move slowly.

These times on the hill resembled, in some ways, those terrible scenes on the stage—scenes of intense gloom, blinding lightning, with a cloaked devil or assassin or other appropriate character muttering deeply amid the awful roll of the thunder-drums. It was theatric beyond words: one felt like a leaf in this booming chaos, this prolonged tragedy of the night. Amid it all one could see from time to time the yellow light on the face of a preoccupied signalman.

Possibly no man who was there ever before understood the true eloquence of the breaking of the day. We would lie staring into the east, fairly ravenous for the dawn. Utterly worn to rags, with our nerves standing on end like so many bristles, we lay and watched the east—the unspeakably obdurate and slow east. It was a wonder that the eyes of some of us did not turn to glass balls from the fixity of our gaze.

Then there would come into the sky a patch of faint blue light. It was like a piece of moonshine. Some would say it was the beginning of daybreak; others would declare it was nothing of the kind. Men would get very disgusted with each other in these low-toned arguments held in the trenches. For my part, this development in the eastern sky destroyed many of my ideas and theories concerning the dawning of the day;

but then, I had never before had occasion to give it such solemn attention.

This patch widened and whitened in about the speed of a man's accomplishment if he should be in the way of painting Madison Square Garden with a camel's-hair brush. The guerillas always set out to whoop it up about this time, because they knew the occasion was approaching when it would be expedient for them to elope. I, at least, always grew furious with this wretched sunrise. I thought I could have walked around the world in the time required for the old thing to get up above the horizon.

One midnight, when an important message was to be sent to the *Marblehead*, Colonel Huntington came himself to the signal-place with Adjutant Draper and Captain McCauley, the quartermaster. When the man stood up to signal, the colonel stood beside him. At sight of the lights, the Spaniards performed as usual. They drove enough bullets into that immediate vicinity to kill all the marines in the corps.

Lieutenant Draper was agitated for his chief. 'Colonel, won't you step down, sir?'

'Why, I guess not,' said the grey old veteran in his slow, sad, always gentle way. 'I am in no more danger than the man.'

'But, sir—' began the adjutant.

'Oh, it's all right, Draper.'

So the colonel and the private stood side to side and took the heavy fire without either moving a muscle.

Day was always obliged to come at last, punctuated by a final exchange of scattering shots. And the light shone on the marines, the dumb guns, the flag. Grimy yellow face looked into grimy yellow face, and grinned with weary satisfaction. Coffee!

Usually it was impossible for many of the men to sleep at once. It always took me, for instance, some hours to get my nerves combed down. But then it was great joy to lie in the trench with the four signalmen, and understand thoroughly that that night was fully over at last, and that, although the future might have in store other bad nights, that one could never escape from the prison-house which we call the past.

II

At the wild little fight at Cusco there were some splendid exhibitions of wigwagging under fire. Action began when an advanced detachment of marines under Lieutenant Lucas, with the Cuban guides, had reached the summit of a ridge overlooking a small valley where there was a house, a well, and a thicket of some kind of shrub with great broad oily leaves. This thicket, which was perhaps an acre in extent, contained the guerillas. The valley was open to the sea. The distance from the top of the ridge to the thicket was barely two hundred yards.

The *Dolphin* had sailed up the coast in line with the marine advance, ready with her guns to assist in any action. Captain Elliott, who commanded the two hundred marines in this fight, suddenly called out for a signalman. He wanted a man to tell the *Dolphin* to open fire on the house and the thicket. It was a blazing, bitter hot day on top of the ridge with its shrivelled chaparral and its straight, tall cactus-plants. The sky was bare and blue, and hurt like brass. In two minutes the prostrate marines were red and sweating like so many hull-buried stokers in the tropics.

Captain Elliott called out: 'Where's a signalman? Who's a signalman here?'

A red-headed mick—I think his name was Clancy; at any rate, it will do to call him Clancy—twisted his head from where he lay on his stomach pumping his Lee, and, saluting, said that he was a signalman.

There was no regulation flag with the expedition, so Clancy was obliged to tie his blue polka-dot neckerchief on the end of his rifle. It did not make a very good flag. At first Clancy moved a way down the safe side of the ridge and wigwagged there very busily. But what with the flag being so poor for the purpose, and the background of ridge being so dark, those on the *Dolphin* did not see it. So Clancy had to return to the top of the ridge and outline himself and his flag against the sky.

The usual thing happened. As soon as the Spaniards caught sight of this silhouette, they let go like mad at it. To make things more comfortable for Clancy, the situation demanded that he face the sea and turn his back to the Spanish bullets. This was a hard game, mark you—to stand with the small of your back to volley firing. Clancy thought so. Everybody thought so. We all cleared out of his neighbourhood. If he wanted sole possession of any particular spot on that hill, he could have it for all we would interfere with him.

It cannot be denied that Clancy was in a hurry. I watched him. He was so occupied with the bullets that snarled close to his ears that he was obliged to repeat the letters of his message softly to himself. It seemed an intolerable time before the *Dolphin* answered the little signal. Meanwhile we gazed at him, marvelling every second that he had not yet pitched headlong. He swore at times.

Finally the *Dolphin* replied to his frantic gesticulation, and he delivered his message. As his part of the transaction was quite finished—whoop!—he dropped like a brick into thc firing line and began to shoot; began to get 'hunky' with all those people who had been plugging at him. The blue polka-dot neckerchief still fluttered from the barrel of his rifle. I am quite certain that he let it remain there until the end of the fight.

The shells of the *Dolphin* began to plough up the thicket, kicking the bushes, stones, and soil into the air as if somebody was blasting there.

Meanwhile, this force of two hundred marines and fifty Cubans and the force of—probably—six companies of Spanish guerillas were making such an awful din that the distant Camp McCalla was all alive with excitement. Colonel Huntington sent out strong parties to critical points on the road to facilitate, if necessary, a safe retreat, and also sent forty men under Lieutenant Magill to come up on the left flank of the two companies in action under Captain Elliott. Lieutenant Magill and his men had crowned a hill which covered entirely the flank of the fighting companies, but when the *Dolphin* opened fire, it happened that Magill was in the line of the shots. It became necessary to stop the *Dolphin* at once. Captain Elliott was not near Clancy at this time, and he called hurriedly for another signalman.

Sergeant Quick arose and announced that he was a signalman. He produced from somewhere a blue polka-dot neckerchief as large as a quilt. He tied it on a long, crooked stick. Then he went to the top of the ridge and, turning his back to the Spanish fire, began to signal to the *Dolphin*. Again we gave a man sole possession of a particular part of the ridge. We didn't want it. He could have it and welcome. If the young sergeant had had the smallpox, the cholera, and the yellow fever, we could not have slid out with more celerity.

As men have said often, it seemed as if there was in this war a God of Battles who held His mighty hand before the Americans. As I looked at Sergeant Quick wigwagging there against the sky, I would not have given a tin tobacco tag for his life. Escape for him seemed impossible. It seemed absurd to hope that he would not be hit; I only hoped that he would be hit just a little, little, in the arm, the shoulder, or the leg.

I watched his face, and it was as grave and serene as that of a man writing in his own library. He was the very embodiment of tranquillity in occupation. He stood there amid the animal-like babble of the Cubans, the crack of rifles, and the whistling snarl of the bullets, and wigwagged whatever he had to wigwag without heeding anything but his business. There was not a single trace of nervousness or haste.

To say the least, a fight at close range is absorbing as a spectacle. No man wants to take his eyes from it until that time comes when he makes up his mind to run away. To deliberately stand up and turn your back to a battle is in itself hard work. To deliberately stand up and turn your back to a battle and hear immediate evidences of the boundless enthusiasm with which a large company of the enemy shoot at you from an adjacent thicket is, to my mind at least, a very great feat. One need not dwell upon the detail of keeping the mind carefully upon a slow spelling of an important code message.

I saw Quick betray only one sign of emotion. As he swung his clumsy flag to and fro, an end of it once caught on a cactus pillar, and he looked sharply over his shoulder to see what had it. He gave the flag an impatient jerk. He looked annoyed.

J.E. JOHNSON
Dogfight Over Lille

In 1941, with the Battle of Britain over, much of the duty of Britain's fighter squadrons consisted in escorting bombing raids on German installations in France. Johnnie Johnson, who describes one such escort mission here, was Britain's leading Spitfire ace of WWII. The Bader referred to in the story is the famous RAF fighter commander, Douglas Bader, call-sign 'Dogsbody'.

HIGH SUMMER, AND THE AIR is heavy with the scent of white clover as we lounge in our deck-chairs watching a small tractor cut down the long clover and grass on our airfield. In some places it is almost a foot high, but it is not dangerous and we know that if we are skilful enough to stall our Spitfires just when the tips of the grasses caress the wheels then we shall pull off a perfect landing.

It is Sunday, and although it is not yet time for lunch we have already escorted some Stirlings to bomb an inland target. For some obscure reason the Luftwaffe seem to oppose our week-end penetrations with more than their usual ferocity, and now we are waiting for the second call which will surely come on this perfect day.

For once our chatter is not confined to Messerschmitts and guns and tactics. Yesterday afternoon Nip and I borrowed the Padre's car, a small family saloon, and drove to Brighton for dinner. Before the return journey we collected two pilots from 145 Squadron, and in the small hours, wedged together, began the journey back to Tangmere. Nip was driving, the rest of us asleep, and along the front at Hove he had a vague recollection of some confusion and shouting and a half-hearted barrier stretched across part of the road. He pressed on and thought little of the incident, but soon after the engine ran unevenly and became very hot. Somehow we coaxed the car home. Next morning a close inspection revealed a sinister hole just below the rear window. Shocked, we traced the path of the bullet, for it turned out that a sentry at Hove had challenged us and, not receiving a suitable reply, had opened fire. The bullet had passed between the two pilots on the back seat, had continued between Nip and me at shoulder height, drilled a neat hole through the dashboard, grazed the cylinder head and ploughed out through the radiator. Small wonder that the little car had barely struggled back to Tangmere! The Padre is more concerned with our lucky escape than the damage to his car, but Billy Burton is incensed that his pilots should have to run a gauntlet of fire at Hove. He is busy penning a letter to the military, but we keep out of his way, for we think that he is opening his attack from a very insecure base.

There is a fine haze and the soft bulk of the South Downs is barely discernible. We can just see the spire of Chichester cathedral, but above the haze the visibility is excellent and you can see Lille from fifty miles.

Lille! It lies seventy miles inland from Le Touquet and marks the absolute limit of our daylight penetrations over France. We often escort bombers to Lille, for it is a vital communications centre and contains important heavy industries. Not unnaturally the Luftwaffe are very sensitive about it. Their ground-control organisation has time to assess our intentions and bring up fighter reinforcements, and the run-up to the target is always strongly contested. We can be sure of a stiff fight when Lille is the target for the bombers.

The ops phone rings and the airman who answers it calls out to the CO; Billy Burton listens and replaces the receiver.

'That was the wing commander. Take-off at 13.25 with 610 and 145. We shall be target-support wing to the bombers. It's Lille again.'

Suddenly the dispersal hut is full of chatter and activity. We shall be the last Spitfires in the target area, for our job is to see that the beehive* leaves the area without interference. The sun will be almost directly overhead, and the Messerschmitts will be there, lurking and waiting in its strong glare. We shall fight today.

Highly coloured ribbons are pinned across the large map on the wall to represent the tracks of the beehive and the six

* *Beehive: a group of bombers protected by a swarm of fighters.*

supporting fighter wings, so that the map looks like one of those bold diagrams of London's Underground system. The two flight sergeants talk with their respective flight commanders about the serviceability of our Spitfires, and our names and the letters of our aircraft are chalked up on a blackboard which shows three sections of finger-fours.

It is fascinating to watch the reactions of the various pilots. They fall into two broad categories; those who are going out to shoot and those who secretly and desperately know they will be shot at, the hunters and the hunted. The majority of the pilots, once they have seen their names on the board, walk out to their Spitfires for a preflight check and for a word or two with their ground crews. They tie on their mae-wests, check their maps, study the weather forecast and have a last-minute chat with their leaders or wingmen. These are the hunters.

The hunted, that very small minority (although every squadron usually possessed at least one), turned to their escape kits and made quite sure that they were wearing the tunic with the silk maps sewn into a secret hiding-place; that they had at least one oilskin-covered packet of French francs, and two if possible; that they had a compass and a revolver and sometimes specially made clothes to assist their activities once they were shot down. When they went through these agonised preparations they reminded me of aged countrywomen meticulously checking their shopping-lists before catching the bus for the market town.

A car pulls up outside and our leader stumps into the dispersal hut, breezy and full of confidence. 'They'll be about today, Billy. We'll run into them over the target, if not before. Our job is to see the Stirlings get clear and cover any stragglers. Stick together. Who's flying in my section?'

'Smith, Cocky and Johnnie, sir,' answers Billy Burton.

'Good,' Bader grins at us. 'Hang on and get back into the abreast formation when I straighten out. O.K.?'

'O.K., sir,' we chorus together.

The wing commander makes phone calls to Stan Turner and Ken Holden. Brief orders followed by a time check. Ten minutes before we start engines, and we slip unobtrusively to our Spitfires, busy with our own private thoughts. I think of other Sunday afternoons not so very long ago when I was at school and walked the gentle slopes of Charnwood Forest clad in a stiff black suit.

Our house-master's greatest ambition was to catch us seniors red-handed smoking an illicit cigarette. And I think of my own father's deep-rooted objections to any form of strenuous activity on the Sabbath during the holidays at Melton Mowbray.

My ground crew have been with the squadron since it was formed and have seen its changing fortunes and many pilots come and go. They know that for me these last few moments on the ground are full of tension, and as they strap me in the cockpit they maintain an even pressure of chatter. Vaguely I hear that the engine is perfect, the guns oiled and checked and the faulty radio set changed and tested since the last flight. The usual cockpit smell, that strange mixture of dope, fine mineral oil, and high-grade fuel, assails the nostrils and is somehow vaguely comforting. I tighten my helmet strap, swing the rudder with my feet on the pedals, watch the movement of the ailerons when I waggle the stick and look at the instruments without seeing them, for my mind is racing on to Lille and the 109s.

Ken starts his engine on the other side of the field and the twelve Spitfires from 610 trundle awkwardly over the grass. Bader's propeller begins to turn, I nod to the ground crew and the engine coughs once or twice and I catch her with a flick of the throttle and she booms into a powerful bass until I cut her back to a fast tick-over. We taxi out to the take-off position, always swinging our high noses so that we can see the aircraft ahead. The solid rubber tail-wheels bump and jolt on the unyielding ground and we bounce up and down with our own backbones acting as shock absorbers.

We line our twelve Spitfires diagonally across one corner of the meadow. We wait until Ken's Squadron is more than half-way across the airfield and then Bader nods his head and we open out throttles together and the deep-throated roar of the engines thunders through the leather helmets and slams against our ear-drums. Air-borne, and the usual automatic drill. We take up a tight formation and I drop my seat a couple of notches and trim the Spitfire so that it flies with the least pressure from hands and feet.

One slow, easy turn on to the course which sends us climbing parallel to the coast. Ken drops his squadron neatly into position about half a mile away and Stan flanks us on the other side. Woodhall calls from the ops room to his wing leader to check radio contact:

'Dogsbody?'

'O.K., O.K.'

And that's all.

We slant into the clean sky. No movement in the cockpit except the slight trembling of the stick as though it is alive and not merely the focal point of a superb mechanical machine. Gone are the ugly tremors of apprehension which plagued us just before the take-off. Although we are sealed in our tiny cockpits and separated from each other, the static from our radios pours through the earphones of our tightly fitting helmets and fills our ears with reassuring crackles. When the leader speaks, his voice is warm and vital, and we know full well that once in the air like this we are bound together by a deeper intimacy than we can ever feel on the ground. Invisible threads of trust and comradeship hold us together and the mantle of Bader's leadership will sustain and protect us throughout the fight ahead. The Tangmere Wing is together.

We climb across Beachy Head, and over Pevensey Bay we swing to the starboard to cross the Channel and head towards the French coast. Some pilot has accidentally knocked on his radio transmitter and croons quietly to himself. He sounds happy and must be a Canadian, for he sings of 'The Chandler's Wife' and the 'North Atlantic Squadron'. He realises his error and we hear the sudden click of his transmitter, and again the only sound is the muted song of the engine.

Now Bader rocks his wings and we level out from the climb and slide out of our tight formation. We take up our finger-four positions with ourselves at 25,000 feet and Ken and Stan stacked up behind us. It is time to switch the gun button from 'safe' to 'fire' and to turn on the reflector sight, for we might want them both in a hurry.

'O.K., Ken?' from Bader.

'O.K., Dogsbody.'

'Stan?' from Bader again.

'You bet.'

The yellow sands of the coast are now plainly visible, and behind is a barren waste of sandhills and scrub. Well hidden in these sand-hills are the highly trained gunners who serve the 88 mm batteries. We breast the flak over Le Touquet. The black, evil flowers foul the sky and more than the usual amount of ironmongery is hurled up at us. Here and there are red marker bursts intended to reveal our position to the Messerschmitts. We twist and pirouette to climb above the bed of flak, and from his relatively safe position, high above, Stan sees our plight and utters a rude comment in the high-pitched voice he reserves for such occasions. The tension eases.

On across the Pas de Calais and over the battlefields of a half-forgotten war against the same foe. From the Tangmere ops room Woodhall breaks the silence:

'Dogsbody, from Beetle. The beehive is on time and is engaged.'

'O.K.'

'Fifty-plus about twenty miles ahead of you,' from Woodhall.

'Understood,' replies Bader.

'Thirty-plus climbing up from the south and another bunch behind them. Keep a sharp look-out,' advises the group captain.

'O.K., Woodie. That's enough,' answers the wing leader, and we twist our necks to search the boundless horizons.

'Looks like a pincer movement to me,' comments some wag. I suspect it is Roy Marple's voice, and again the tension slackens as we grin behind our oxygen masks. Woodhall speaks into his microphone with his last item of information.

'Dogsbody. The rear support wing is just leaving the English coast.' (This means we can count on some help should we have to fight our way out.) 'Course for Dover—310 degrees.' (This was a last-minute reminder of the course to steer for home.) Woodhall fades out, for he has done his utmost to paint a broad picture of the air situation. Now it is up to our leader.

'Dogsbody from blue one. Beehive at twelve o'clock below. About seven miles.'

'O.K. I see them,' and the wing leader eases his force to starboard and a better up-sun position.

The high-flying Messerschmitts have seen our wing and stab at Stan's top-cover squadron with savage attacks from either flank.

'Break port, Ken.' (From a pilot of 610.)

'Keep turning.'

'Tell me when to stop turning.'

'Keep turning. There's four behind!'

'Get in, red section.'

'We're stuck into some 109s behind you, Douglas.' (This quietly from Stan).

'O.K., Stan.'

'Baling out.'

'Try and make it, Mac. Not far to the coast.' (This urgently from a squadron commander.)

'No use. Temperatures off the clock. She'll burn any time. Look after my dog.'

'Keep turning, yellow section.'

So far the fight has remained well above us. We catch fleeting glimpses of high vapour trails and ducking, twisting fighters. Two-thirds of the wing are behind us holding off the 109s and we force on to the target area to carry out our assigned task. We can never reform into a wing again, and the pilots of 145 and 610 will make their way home in twos and fours. We head towards the distant beehive, well aware that there is now no covering force of Spitfires above us.

The Stirlings have dropped their heavy load of bombs and begin their return journey. We curve slowly over the outskirts of Lille to make sure the beehive is not harried from the rear. I look down at a pall of debris and black smoke rising from the target five miles below, and absurdly my memory flashes back to contrast the scene with those other schoolboy Sunday afternoons.

'Dogsbody from Smith. 109s above. Six o'clock. About twenty-five or thirty.'

'Well done. Watch 'em and tell me when to break.'

I can see them. High in the sun, and their presence only betrayed by the reflected sparkle from highly polished windscreens and cockpit covers.

'They're coming down, Dogsbody. Break left.' And round to port we go, with Smith sliding below Bader and Cocky and me above so that we cover each other in this steep turn. We curve round and catch a glimpse of four baffled 109s climbing back to join their companions, for they can't stay with us in a turn. The keen eyes of Smith saved us from a nasty smack that time.

'Keep turning, Dogsbody. More coming down,' from Cocky.

'O.K. We might get a squirt this time,' rejoins Bader. What a man, I think, what a man!

The turn tightens and in my extreme position on the starboard side I'm driving my Spitfire through a greater radius of curve than the others and falling behind. I kick on hard bottom rudder and skid inwards, down and behind the leader. More 109s hurtle down from above and a section of four angle in from the starboard flank. I look round for other Spitfires but there are none in sight. The four of us are alone over Lille.

'Keep turning. Keep turning.' (From Bader.) 'They can't stay with us.' And we keep turning, hot and frightened and a long way from home. We can't keep turning all bloody day, I think bitterly.

Cocky has not re-formed after one of our violent breaks. I take his place next to Bader and the three of us watch the Messerschmitts, time their dives and call the break into their attacks. The odds are heavily against us.

We turn across the sun and I am on the inside. The blinding light seems only two feet above Bader's cockpit and if I drop further below or he gains a little more height, I shall lose him. Already his Spitfire has losts its colour and is only a sharp, black silhouette, and now it has disappeared completely, swallowed up by the sun's fierce light. I come out of the turn and am stunned to find myself alone in the Lille sky.

The Messerschmitts come in close for the kill. At this range their camouflage looks dirty and oil-stained, and one brute has a startling black-and-white spinner. In a hot sweat of fear I keep turning and turning, and the fear is mingled with an abject humiliation that these bastards should single me out and chop me at their leisure. The radio is silent, or probably I don't hear it in the stress of trying to stay alive. I can't turn all day. Le Touquet is seventy hostile miles away; far better to fight back and take one with me.

Four Messerschmitts roar down from six o'clock. I see them in time and curve the shuddering, protesting Spitfire to meet them, for she is on the brink of a high-speed stall. They are so certain of my destruction that they are flying badly and I fasten on to tail-end Charlie and give him a long burst of fire. He is at the maximum range, and although my shooting has no apparent effect some of my despair and fear on this fateful afternoon seems to evaporate at the faint sound of the chattering machine guns. But perhaps my attack has its just reward, for Smith's voice comes loud and clear over the radio.

'One Spit behind, Dogsbody. A thousand yards. Looks like he's in trouble.'

Then I see them. Two aircraft with the lovely curving wings that can only belong to Spitfires. I take a long breath and in a deliberately calm voice:

'It's me, Dogsbody—Johnnie.'

'O.K., Johnnie. We'll orbit here for you. Drop in on my starboard. We'll get a couple of these—'

There is no longer any question of not getting home now that I am with Bader again. He will bring us safely back to Tangmere and I know he is enjoying this, for he sounds full of confidence over the radio. A dozen Messerschmitts still shadow our small formation. They are well up-sun and waiting to strike. Smith and I fly with our necks twisted right round, like the resting mallard ducks one sees in the London parks, and all our concentration focused on the glinting shoal of 109s.

'Two coming down from five o'clock, Dogsbody. Break right,' from me. And this time mine is the smallest turn so that I am the first to meet the attack. A 109 is very close and climbing away to port. Here is a chance. Time for a quick shot and no danger of losing the other two Spitfires if I don't get involved in a long tail chase. I line up my Spitfire behind the 109, clench the spade-grip handle of the stick with both hands and send short bursts into his belly at less than a hundred yards. The 109 bursts apart and the explosion looks exactly the same as a near burst of heavy flak, a vicious flower with a poisonous glowing centre and black swirling edges.

I re-form and the Messerschmitts come in again, and this time Bader calls the break. It is well judged and the wing leader fastens on to the last 109 and I cover his Spitfire as it appears to stand on its tail with wisps of smoke plummeting from the gun ports. The enemy aircraft starts to pour white smoke from its belly and thick black smoke from the engine. They merge together and look like a long, dirty banner against the faded blue of some high cirrus cloud.

'Bloody good shooting, sir.'

'We'll get some more.'

Woodhall—it seems an eternity since we last heard him—calls up to say that the rear support wing is over Abbeville. Unbelievably the Messerschmitts which have tailed us so long vanish and we are alone in the high spaces.

We pick up the English coast near Dover and turn to port for Sussex and Tangmere. We circle our airfield and land without any fuss or acrobatics, for we never know until we are on the ground whether or not a stray bullet has partially severed a control cable.

Woodhall meets us and listens to his wing leader's account of the fight. Bader has a tremendous ability to remember all the details and gives a graphic résumé of the show. The group captain listens carefully and says that he knew we were having a hard time because of the numerous plots of enemy formations on his operations table and our continuous radio chatter. So he had asked II Group to get the rear support wing over France earlier than planned, to lend a hand. Perhaps the shadowing Messerschmitts which sheered off so suddenly had seen the approach of this Spitfire wing.

Bader phones Ken and Stan while the solemn Gibbs pleads with us to sit down and write out our combat reports.

'Please do it now. It will only take two minutes.'

'Not likely, Gibbs. We want some tea and a shower and . . .'

'You write them and we'll sign them,' suggests a pilot.

Cocky walks in. He came back on the deck after losing us over Lille and landed at Hawkinge short of petrol.

'Dinner and a bottle at Bosham tonight, Johnnie?

'Right,' I answer at once.

'Count me in too,' says Nip.

The group captain is trying to make himself heard above the din.

'You chaps must watch your language. It's frightful. And the Waafs seem to be getting quite used to it. They don't bat an eyelid any more. But I'm sure you don't know how bad it sounds. I had it logged this afternoon.' And he waves a piece of paper in his hand.

Someone begins to read out from the record. We roar with laughter, slap each other on the back and collapse weakly into chairs, but this reaction is not all due to the slip of paper. Woodhall watches us and walks to the door hoping that we don't see the grin which is creasing his leathery countenance.

We clamber into our meagre transports, one small van per flight, and drive to Shopwhyke. We sit on the lawn and drink tea served by Waafs. These young girls wear overalls of flowered print and look far more attractive and feminine than in their usual masculine garb of collar and tie. One of our officers is a well-known concert pianist and he plays a movement from a Beethoven concerto, and the lovely melody fills the stately house and overflows into the garden.

PHILIP CHINNERY
The Evacuation of Kham Duc

The air evacuation of the allied Special Forces base at Kham Duc took place during the Vietnam War.

FOLLOWING THE LOSS OF LANG VEI in February 1968, the only remaining Special Forces border camp in I Corps was that at Kham Duc. Located ten miles from the Laotian border on the extreme western fringe of Quang Tin Province, the camp served as a base for allied reconnaissance teams and a training site for Vietnamese Civilian Irregular Defence Group troops. The first Special Forces A-detachment had moved into Kham Duc in September 1963 and found the outpost to be an ideal border surveillance site. It was, however, a difficult place to supply.

The border region south-west of Da Nang was among the most rugged in Vietnam and was nearly uninhabited except for the Vietnamese military dependants, camp followers and merchants living across the airstrip in Kham Duc village. The camp, village and airstrip were all situated in a mile-wide bowl, surrounded by jungle and hills which rose abruptly to heights of over 2,000 feet.

Although C-130 crews had been using the 6,000 foot asphalt runway for years, they detested the difficult landings made dangerous by the weather and the terrain, with the Ngok Peng Bum ridge to the west and the high Ngok Pe Xar mountain looming over Kham Duc to the east. It became even more difficult in April 1968 when the C-130s began frequent landings to bring in American engineers and construction materials to improve the runway. The stacks of equipment piled beside the runway and the considerable amount of enemy fire from the nearby high ground did little to improve matters.

In the early hours of 10 May, the forward operating base of Ngok Tavak, built around an old French fort five miles from Kham Duc, was attacked by a battalion of NVA troops. The outpost was defended by a 113-man Vietnamese Mobile Strike Force Company, together with eight Special Forces and three Australian advisers and 33 Marine artillerymen. They managed to hold out until noon, when the survivors were forced to abandon the fort and evade the enemy through the jungle, until they were extracted by helicopter during the evening.

At the same time that the attack on Ngok Tavak began, the camp at Kham Duc was blasted by heavy mortar and recoilless-rifle fire. This continued throughout the day as the 1st VC Regiment of the 2nd NVA Division moved into positions encircling the camp. At first light C-130s began to arrive with reinforcements from the Americal Division and, despite the communist shells falling on the runway, 900 Americans and 600 Vietnamese troops had arrived by nightfall.

As the enemy ground attack began during the early-morning darkness of 12 May, General Westmoreland reviewed the situation and determined that the camp lacked the importance and defensibility of Khe Sanh. He directed that the camp be abandoned and the defenders evacuated by air, despite the strong enemy presence.

By 1000 hours, three of the camp outposts were in enemy hands and company-size NVA assaults were taking place against three sides of the main perimeter. Army and Marine helicopters managed to extract some of the troops, but a Chinook was shot down, blocking the runway until engineers managed to drag it clear. A C-130 landed immediately and civilians, streaming from ditches alongside the runway, quickly filled the aircraft. As the pilot, Lieutenant Colonel Daryl D. Cole, began the take-off run down the cratered and shrapnel-littered strip, exploding mortar shells bracketed the aircraft and burst one of the tyres. Cole aborted the take-off and unloaded the passengers while the crew worked frantically to remove the ruined tyre.

Around 1100 hours Major Ray D. Shelton brought his C-123 in, and took 70 people on board, including 44 American engineers. Despite heavy automatic-weapons fire and a dozen mortar detonations near his ship, Shelton took off safely. He was soon followed by Cole's C-130, which took off with fuel streaming from holes in the wings. His only passengers now were three members of an Air Force combat control team, whose radio equipment had been destroyed. Cole landed on a foamed runway at Cam Ranh Bay and was later awarded the Mackay Trophy for 1968 for his efforts.

Heavy ground fire led to the orbiting C-130 command and control ship postponing any further evacuation attempts for the time being. At noon a massive NVA attack was launched against the main compound, but was stopped by ground support aircraft hurling napalm, cluster bomb units and 750-pound bombs into the final wire barriers. By the middle of the afternoon only 145 persons had been evacuated by the one C-123 and fifteen helicopter sorties. A dozen more transports were orbiting nearby, waiting their turn to go in, and, with time running out, another attempt was made at 1525 hours.

Major Bernard L. Bucher made a steep approach from the south in his C-130 and landed despite numerous hits. More than a hundred panicking civilian dependants crowded aboard and Bucher began his take-off run. He chose to take off towards the north, either unaware of, or disregarding, the concentration of enemy forces in that direction. As the aircraft cleared the northern boundary it was struck by enemy tracer fire, crashed and burned with no survivors. The Vietnamese troops amongst the Kham Duc defenders were, needless to say, shattered, having just watched their families die. It was not the first time, nor would it be the last, that the fighting performance of Vietnamese troops would be adversely affected by their concern over the presence of their dependants on the battlefield.

Landing behind Bucher was a C-130E flown by Lieutenant Colonel William Boyd Jr., who made an initial go-around just before touch-down. He loaded another hundred people aboard and took off to the south, banking after lift-off so that the aircraft would be masked by the rolling terrain. Boyd landed his Hercules safely at Chu Lai, despite numerous bullet holes and a smoke-filled interior. For this flight he was awarded the Air Force Cross.

Lieutenant Colonel John R. Delmore flew in next, spiralling down from directly overhead. As he neared the ground, bullets tore through the ship and, with all hydraulics gone and almost out of control, the Hercules smashed into the runway. The wrecked aircraft came to rest at the side of the strip and the fortunate crew scrambled out unhurt. They found some shelter and were soon picked up by a Marine helicopter.

The loss of two aircraft in a matter of minutes did nothing to inspire confidence in the remaining transport crews orbiting above. However, three more C-130s made it in and withdrew the last defenders. This final evacuation was made possible by close-in air strikes, with fighters laying a barrage down along both sides of the runway during the run in and while the transports loaded. Lieutenant Colonel Wallace crossed the field at right angles in his C-130E, and made a 270-degree turn at maximum rate of descent with power off and gear down. Touching down, he made a maximum-effort stop and was immediately swamped by a hundred panicking Vietnamese. The loadmaster had to rescue a woman and a baby trampled in the rush, as the civilians and the last few Americans dashed aboard. Wallace took off to the south and safety, just as a helicopter swooped down to take the Special Forces command group out of the camp.

As the advancing NVA infantry took over the camp, a near-tragedy occured. A C-130 flown by Lieutenant Colonel Jay Van Cleef was inexplicably instructed by the airborne control centre to land the three-man combat control team which had already been evacuated earlier in the day. Van Cleef protested that the camp was almost completely evacuated, but the control centre insisted that the team be returned and left.

Obediently Van Cleef landed his aircraft, and the three controllers ran from the ship towards the burning camp. He waited patiently for another two minutes for passengers expecting to be evacuated, and when none appeared he slammed the throttles open and took off. He duly notified the control ship that they had taken off empty, and was shocked to hear the control ship then report to General McLaughlin that the evacuation of Kham Duc was complete. His crew immediately and vehemently disabused the commander and pointed out that the camp was not evacuated, because they had, as ordered, just deposited a combat control team in the camp. There was a moment of stunned radio silence as the reality sank in: Kham Duc was now in enemy hands—except for three American combat controllers.

Meanwhile, Major John W. Gallagher Jr. and the other two controllers took shelter in a culvert next to the runway and started firing at the enemy in the camp with their M-16 rifles. The command post asked a C-123 to try to pick the men up, but as the aircraft touched down it came under fire from all directions. The pilot, Lieutenant Colonel Alfred J. Jeannotte Jr., could not see the team anywhere and jammed the throttles forward for take-off. Just before lift-off the crew spotted the three men, but it was now too late to stop. The C-123 took to the air and, low on fuel, turned for home. Jeannotte later received the Air Force Cross for his actions.

Technical Sergeant Mort Freedman described how he, Major Gallagher and Sergeant Jim Lundie reacted when the last Provider took off, leaving the three-man team behind. 'The pilot saw no one left on the ground, so he took off. We figured no one would come back and we had two choices: either be taken prisoner, or fight it out. There was no doubt about it. We had eleven magazines among us and were going to take as many of them with us as we could.'

The C-123 behind Jeannotte was being flown by Lieutenant Colonel Joe M. Jackson and Major Jesse W. Campbell. They had left Da Nang earlier in the day to haul some cargo, while Jackson went through the bi-annual check flight that is mandatory for all Air Force fliers. They had been recalled and sent to Kham Duc, arriving as the command ship requested that they make another pick-up attempt. Jesse Campbell radioed, 'Roger. Going in.'

Joe Jackson had been a fighter pilot for twenty years before being assigned to transport duty. He had flown 107 missions in Korea and had won the Distinguished Flying Cross. He knew that the enemy gunners would expect him to follow the same flight path as the other cargo planes and decided to call upon his fighterpilot experience and try a new tactic. At 9,000 feet, and rapidly approaching the landing area, he pointed the nose down in a steep dive. Side-slipping for maximum descent, and with power back and landing gear and flaps full down, the Provider dropped like a rock. Jackson recalls: 'The book said you didn't fly transports this way, but the guy who wrote the book had never been shot at. I had two problems, the second stemming from the first. One was to avoid reaching "blow up" speed, where the flaps, which were in full down position for the dive, are blown back up to neutral. If this happened, we would pick up even more speed, leading to problem two—the danger of overshooting the runway.'

Jackson pulled back on the control column and broke the Provider's descent just above the tree-tops, a quarter of a mile from the end of the runway. He barely had time to set up a landing attitude as the aircraft settled towards the threshold. The debris-strewn runway looked like an obstacle course, with a burning helicopter blocking the way a mere 2,200 feet from the touch-down point. Jackson knew that he would have to stop in a hurry, but decided against using the reverse thrust. Reversing the engines would automatically shut off the two jets that would be needed for a minimum-run take-off. He stood on the brakes and skidded to a halt just before reaching the gutted helicopter.

Thc thrcc controllers scrambled from the ditch and dived into the aircraft as the surprised enemy gunners opened fire. At the front of the aircraft Major Campbell spotted a 122mm rocket shell coming towards them, and both pilots watched in horror as it hit the ground just 25 feet in front of the nose. Luck was still on their side, however, and the deadly projectile did not explode. Jackson taxied around the shell and rammed the throttles to the firewall. 'We hadn't been out of that spot ten seconds when mortars started dropping directly on it,' he remembers. 'That was a real thriller. I figured they just got zeroed in on us, and that the time of flight of the mortar shells was about ten seconds longer than the time we sat there taking the men aboard.' Within seconds they were in the air again and one of the combat team recalled, 'We were dead, and all of a sudden we were alive!'

General McLaughlin, who had witnessed the event from overhead, approved nominations for the Medal of Honor for both pilots, who landed safely back at Da Nang to discover that their C-123 had not even taken one hit! In January 1969 Colonel Jackson received the Medal of Honor in a ceremony at the White House; Major Campbell received the Air Force Cross, and the rest of the crew were awarded Silver Stars.

Following the evacuation, air strikes demolished the rest of the camp. Out of the 1,800 military and civilians involved, 259 were lost, over half of these in the crash of Major Bucher's C-130. The US Army lost 25 men and two Chinooks, and two Marine CH-46s and two C-130s were destroyed. The battle had resulted in a total North Vietnamese victory, for the last Special Forces border surveillance camp on the north-western frontier of South Vietnam had been destroyed.

WILLIAM HOWARD RUSSELL
The Charge of the Light Brigade

The Charge of the Light Brigade took place during the Battle of Balaclava, 25 October 1854, the major engagement between the British and Russian armies in the Crimean War of 1854–1856. William Howard Russell was a journalist for the Times *newspaper of London.*

IF THE EXHIBITION OF THE most brilliant valour, of the excess of courage, and of a daring which would have reflected lustre on the best days of chivalry can afford full consolation for the disaster of today, we can have no reason to regret the melancholy loss which we sustained in a contest with a savage and barbarian enemy.

I shall proceed to describe, to the best of my power, what occurred under my own eyes, and to state the facts which I have heard from men whose veracity is unimpeachable, reserving to myself the exercise of the right of private judgement in making public and in suppressing the details of what occurred on this memorable day . . .

It will be remembered that in a letter sent by last mail from this place it was mentioned that eleven battalions of Russian infantry had crossed the Tchernaya, and that they threatened the rear of our position and our communication with Balaclava. Their bands could be heard playing at night by travellers along the Balaclava road to the camp, but they 'showed' but little during the day and kept up among the gorges and mountain passes through which the roads to Inkermann, Simpheropol, and the south-east of the Crimea wind towards the interior. It will be recollected also that the position we occupied in reference to Balaclava was supposed by most people to be very strong—even impregnable. Our lines were formed by natural mountain slopes in the rear, along which the French had made very formidable intrenchments. Below those intrenchments, and very nearly in a right line across the valley beneath, are four conical hillocks, one rising above the other as they recede from our lines. . . . On the top of each of these hills the Turks had thrown up earthen redoubts, defended by 250 men each, and armed with two or three guns—some heavy ship guns—lent by us to them, with one artilleryman in each redoubt to look after them. These hills cross the valley of Balaclava at the distance of about two and a half miles from the town. Supposing the spectator then to take his stand on one of the heights forming the rear of our camp before Sebastopol, he would see the town of Balaclava, with its scanty shipping, its narrow strip of water, and its old forts on his right hand; immediately below he would behold the valley and plain of coarse meadowland, occupied by our cavalry tents, and stretching from the base of the ridge on which he stood to the foot of the formidable heights on the other side; he would see the French trenches lined with Zouaves a few feet beneath, and distant from him, on the slope of the hill; a Turkish redoubt lower down, then another in the valley, then in a line with it some angular earthworks, then, in succession, the other two redoubts up Canrobert's Hill.

At the distance of two or two and a half miles across the valley there is an abrupt rocky mountain range of most irregular and picturesque formation, covered with scanty brushwood here and there, or rising into barren pinnacles and plateaux of rock. In outline and appearance, this position of the landscape is wonderfully like the Trossachs. A patch of blue sea is caught in between the overhanging cliffs of Balaclava as they close in the entrance to the harbour on the right. The camp of the Marines pitched on the hillsides more than one thousand feet above the level of the sea is opposite to you as your back is turned to Sebastopol and your right side towards Balaclava. On the road leading up the valley, close to the entrance of the town and beneath these hills, is the encampment of the 93rd Highlanders.

The cavalry lines are nearer to you below, and are some way in advance of the Highlanders, and nearer to the town than the Turkish redoubts. The valley is crossed here and there by small waves of land. On your left the hills and rocky mountain ranges gradually close in toward the course of the Tchernaya, till at three or four miles' distance from Balaclava the valley is swallowed up in a mountain gorge and deep ravines, above which rise tier after tier of desolate whitish rock garnished now and then by bits of scanty herbage, and spreading away towards the east and south, where they attain the alpine dimensions of Tschatir Dagh. It is very easy for an enemy at the Belbek, or in command of the road of Mackenzie's Farm, Inkermann, Simpheropol, or Bakhchisarai, to debouch through these gorges at any time upon this plain from the neck of the valley, or to march from Sebastopol by the Tchernaya and to advance along it towards Balaclava, till checked by the Turkish redoubts on the southern side or by the fire from the French works on the northern side, i.e., the side which in relation to the valley of Balaclava forms the rear of our position.

At half past seven o'clock this morning an orderly came galloping in to the headquarters camp from Balaclava, with the news that at dawn a strong corps of Russian horse supported by guns and battalions of infantry had marched into the valley, and had already nearly dispossessed the Turks of the redoubt No. 1 (that on Canrobert's Hill, which is farthest from our lines) and that they were opening fire on the redoubts Nos. 2, 3 and 4, which would speedily be in their hands unless the Turks offered a stouter resistance than they had done already.

Orders were dispatched to Sir George Cathcart and to HRH the Duke of Cambridge to put their respective divisions, the 4th and 1st, in motion for the scene of action, and intelligence of the advance of the Russians was also furnished to General Canrobert. Immediately on receipt of the news the General commanded General Bosquet to get the Third Division under arms, and sent a strong body of artillery and some 200 Chasseurs d'Afrique to assist us in holding the valley. Sir Colin Campbell, who was in command of Balaclava, had drawn up the 93rd Highlanders a little in front of the road to the town at the first news of the advance of the enemy. The marines on the heights got under arms; the seamen's batteries and marines' batteries on the heights close to the town were manned, and the French artillerymen and the Zouaves prepared for action along their lines. Lord Lucan's little camp was the scene of great excitement. The men had not had time to water their horses; they had not broken their fast from the evening of the day before, and had barely saddled at the first blast of the trumpet, when they were drawn up on the slope behind the redoubts in front of the camp to operate on the enemy's squadrons. It was soon evident that no reliance was to be placed on the Turkish infantrymen or artillerymen. All the stories we had heard about their bravery behind stone walls and earthworks proved how differently the same or similar people fight under different circumstances. When the Russians advanced the Turks fired a few rounds at them, got frightened at the distance of their supports in the rear, looked round, received a few shots and shell, and then 'bolted', and fled with an agility quite at variance with the commonplace notions of oriental deportment on the battlefield. But Turks on the Danube are very different beings from Turks in the Crimea, as it appears that the Russians of Sebastopol are not at all like the Russians of Silistria.

Soon after eight Lord Raglan and his staff turned out and cantered towards the rear of our position. The booming of artillery, the spattering roll of musketry, were heard rising from the valley, drowning the roar of the siege guns in front before Sebastopol. As I rode in the direction of the firing over the thistles and large stones which cover the undulating plain which stretches away towards Balaclava, on a level with the summit of the ridges above it, I observed a French light infantry regiment (the 27th, I think) advancing with admirable care and celerity from our right towards the ridge near the telegraph house, which was already lined with companies of French infantry, while mounted officers scampered along its broken outline in every direction.

General Bosquet, a stout soldierlike-looking man, who reminds one of the old *genre* of French generals as depicted at Versailles, followed, with his staff and small escort of Hussars, at a gallop. Faint white clouds rose here and there above the hill from the cannonade below. Never did the painter's eye rest upon a more beautiful scene than I beheld from the ridge. The fleecy vapours still hung around the mountain tops and mingled with the ascending volumes of smoke; the patch of sea sparkled freshly in the rays of the morning sun, but its light was eclipsed by the flashes which gleamed from the masses of armed men below.

Looking to the left towards the gorge we beheld six compact masses of Russian infantry which had just debouched from the mountain passes near the Tchernaya, and were slowly advancing with solemn stateliness up the valley. Immediately in their front was a regular line of artillery, of at least twenty pieces strong. Two batteries of light guns were already a mile in advance of them, and were playing with energy on the redoubts, from which feeble puffs of smoke came at long intervals. Behind the guns, in front of the infantry, were enormous bodies of cavalry. They were in six compact squares, three on each flank, moving down *en échelon* towards us, and the valley was lit up with the blaze of their sabres and lance points and gay accoutrements. In their front, and extending along the intervals between each battery of guns, were clouds of mounted skirmishers, wheeling and whirling in the front of their march like autumn leaves tossed by the wind. The Zouaves close to us were lying like tigers at the spring, with ready rifles in hand, hidden chin deep by the earthworks which run along the line of these ridges on our rear, but the quick-eyed Russians were manoeuvring on the other side of the valley, and did not expose their columns to attack. Below the Zouaves we could see the Turkish gunners in the redoubts, all in confusion as the shells burst over them. Just as I came up the Russians had carried No. 1 redoubt, the farthest and most elevated of all, and their horsemen were chasing the Turks across the interval which lay between it and redoubt No. 2. At that moment the cavalry, under Lord Lucan, were formed in glittering masses—the Light Brigade, under Lord Cardigan, in advance of the Heavy Brigade, under Brigadier–General Scarlett, in reserve. They were drawn up just in front of their encampment, and were concealed from the view of the enemy by a slight 'wave' in the plain. Considerably to the rear of their right, the 93rd Highlanders were drawn up in line, in front of the approach to Balaclava. Above and behind them on the heights, the marines were visible through the glass, drawn up under arms, and the gunners could be seen ready in the earthworks, in which were placed the heavy ships' guns. The 93rd had originally been advanced somewhat more into the plain, but the instant the Russians got possession of the first redoubt they opened fire on them from our own guns, which inflicted some injury, and Sir Colin Campbell 'retired' his men to a better position. Meantime the enemy advanced his cavalry rapidly. To our inexpressible disgust we saw the Turks in redoubt No. 2 fly at their approach. They ran in scattered groups across towards redoubt No. 3, and towards Balaclava, but the horse-hoof of the

Cossacks was too quick for them, and sword and lance were busily plied among the retreating band. The yells of the pursuers and pursued were plainly audible. As the Lancers and Light Cavalry of the Russians advanced they gathered up their skirmishers with great speed and in excellent order—the shifting trails of men, which played all over the valley like moonlight on water, contracted, gathered up, and the little *peloton* in a few moments became a solid column. Then up came their guns, in rushed their gunners to the abandoned redoubt, and the guns of No. 2 redoubt soon played with deadly effect upon the dispirited defenders of No. 3 redoubt. Two or three shots in return from the earthworks, and all is silent. The Turks swarm over the earthworks and run in confusion towards the town, firing their muskets at the enemy as they run. Again the solid column of cavalry opens like a fan, and resolves itself into the 'long spray' of skirmishers. It laps the flying Turks, steel flashes in the air, and down go the poor Muslim quivering on the plain, split through fez and musket-guard to the chin and breast-belt. There is no support for them. It is evident the Russians have been too quick for us. The Turks have been too quick also, for they have not held their redoubts long enough to enable us to bring them help. In vain the naval guns on the heights fire on the Russian cavalry; the distance is too great for shot or shell to reach. In vain the Turkish gunners in the earthen batteries which are placed along the French intrenchments strive to protect their flying countrymen; their shots fly wide and short of the swarming masses. The Turks betake themselves towards the Highlanders, where they check their flight and form into companies on the flanks of the Highlanders.

As the Russian cavalry on the left of their line crown the hill, across the valley they perceive the Highlanders drawn up at the distance of some half-mile, calmly awaiting their approach. They halt, and squadron after squadron flies up from the rear, till they have a body of some 1500 men along the ridge—Lancers and Dragoons and Hussars. Then they move *en échelon* in two bodies, with another in reserve. The cavalry who have been pursuing the Turks on the right are coming up the ridge beneath us, which conceals our cavalry from view. The heavy brigade in advance is drawn up in two columns. The first column consists of the Scots Greys and of their old companions in glory, the Enniskillens; the second of the 4th Royal Irish, of the 5th Dragoon Guards, and of the 1st Royal Dragoons. The Light Cavalry Brigade is on their left in two lines also. The silence is oppressive; between the cannon bursts, one can hear the champing of bits and the clink of sabres in the valley below. The Russians on their left drew breath for a moment, and then in one grand line dashed at the Highlanders. The ground flies beneath their horses' feet—gathering speed at every stride they dash on towards that thin red streak topped with a line of steel. The Turks fire a volley at 800 yards, and run. As the Russians come within 600 yards, down goes that line of steel in front, and out rings a rolling volley of Minié musketry. The distance is too great. The Russians are not checked, but still sweep onwards with the whole force of horse and man, through the smoke, here and there knocked over by the shot of our batteries above. With breathless suspense everyone awaits the bursting of the wave upon the line of Gaelic rock; but ere they came within 150 yards, another deadly volley flashes from the levelled rifles, and carries death and terror into the Russians. They wheel about, open files right and left, and fly back faster than they came.

'Bravo Highlanders! well done!' shout the excited spectators; but events thicken. The Highlanders and their splendid front are soon forgotten. Men scarcely have a moment to think of this fact that the 93rd never altered their formation to receive that tide of horsemen.

'No,' said Sir Colin Campbell, 'I did not think it worth while to form them even four deep!'

The ordinary British line, two deep, was quite sufficient to repel the attack of these Muscovite chevaliers. Our eyes were, however, turned in a moment on our own cavalry. We saw Brigadier General Scarlett ride along in front of his massive squadrons. The Russians—evidently *corps d'élite*— their light-blue jackets embroidered with silver lace, were advancing on their left at an easy gallop, towards the brow of the hill. A forest of lances glistened in their rear, and several squadrons of grey-coated dragoons moved up quickly to support them as they reached the summit. The instant they came in sight the trumpets of our cavalry gave out the warning blast which told us all that in another moment we would see the shock of battle beneath our very eyes. Lord Raglan, all his staff and escort, and groups of officers, the Zouaves, the French generals and officers, and bodies of French infantry on the height, were spectators of the scene as though they were looking on the stage from the boxes of a theatre. Nearly everyone dismounted and sat down, and not a word was said.

The Russians advanced down the hill at a slow canter, which they changed to a trot and at last nearly halted. The first line was at least double the length of ours—it was three times as deep. Behind them was a similar line, equally strong and compact. They evidently despised their insignificant-looking enemy, but their time was come.

The trumpets rang out through the valley, and the Greys and Enniskillens went right at the centre of the Russian cavalry. The space between them was only a few hundred yards; it was scarce enough to let the horses 'gather way', nor had the men quite space sufficient for the full play of their sword arms. The Russian line brings forward each wing as our cavalry advance and threaten to annihilate them as they pass on. Turning a little to their left, so as to meet the Russians' right, the Greys rush on with a cheer that thrills to every heart—the wild shout of the Enniskillens rises through the air at the same moment. As lightning flashes through a cloud the Greys and Enniskillens pierced through the dark masses of the Russians. The shock was but for a moment. There was a clash of steel and a light play of sword blades in the air, and then the Greys and the redcoats disappear in the midst of the shaken and quivering columns. In another moment we see them merging and dashing on with diminished numbers, and in broken order, against the second line, which is advancing against them to retrieve the fortune of the charge.

It was a terrible moment. 'God help them! They are lost!' was the exclamation of more than one man, and the thought of many. With unabated fire the noble hearts dashed at their enemy—it was a fight of heroes. The first line of Russians which had been smashed utterly by our charge, and had fled off at one flank and towards the centre, were coming back to swallow up our handful of men. By sheer steel and sheer courage Enniskillen and Scot were winning their desperate way right through the enemy's squadrons, and already grey horses and redcoats had appeared right at the rear of the second mass, when, with irresistible force, like one bolt from a bow, the 1st Royals, the

4th Dragoon Guards, and the 5th Dragoon Guards rushed at the remnants of the first line of the enemy, went through it as though it were madc of pasteboard, and dashing on the second body of Russians, as they were still disordered by the terrible assault of the Greys and their companions, put them to utter rout. This Russian horse in less than five minutes after it met our dragoons was flying with all its speed before a force certainly not half its strength.

A cheer burst from every lip—in the enthusiasm officers and men took off their caps and shouted with delight, and thus keeping up the scenic character of their position, they clapped their hands again and again . . .

And now occurred the melancholy catastrophe which fills us all with sorrow. It appears that the Quartermaster General, Brigadier Airey, thinking that the Light Cavalry had not gone far enough in front when the enemy's horse had fled, gave an order in writing to Captain Nolan, 15th Hussars, to take to Lord Lucan, directing His Lordship 'to advance' his cavalry nearer to the enemy. A braver soldier than Captain Nolan the army did not possess. He was known to all his arm of the service for his entire devotion to his profession, and his name must be familiar to all who take interest in our cavalry for his excellent work published a year ago on our drill and system of remount and breaking horses. I had the pleasure of his acquaintance, and I know he entertained the most exalted opinions respecting the capabilities of the English horse soldier. Properly led, the British Hussar and Dragoon could in his mind break square, take batteries, ride over columns of infantry, and pierce any other cavalry in the world, as if they were made of straw. He thought they had not had the opportunity of doing all that was in their power, and that they had missed even such chances as they had offered to them—that, in fact, they were in some measure disgraced. A matchless rider and a first-rate swordsman, he held in contempt, I am afraid, even grape and canister. He rode off with his orders to Lord Lucan. He is now dead and gone.

God forbid I should cast a shade on the brightness of his honour, but I am bound to state what I am told occurred when he reached His Lordship. I should premise that, as the Russian cavalry retired, their infantry fell back towards the head of the valley, leaving men in three of the redoubts they had taken and abandoning the fourth. They had also placed some guns on the heights over their position, on the left of the gorge. Their cavalry joined the reserves, and drew up in six solid divisions, in an oblique line, across the entrance to the gorge. Six battalions of infantry were placed behind them, and about thirty guns were drawn up along their line, while masses of infantry were also collected on the hills behind the redoubts on our right. Our cavalry had moved up to the ridge across the valley, on our left, as the ground was broken in front, and had halted in the order I have already mentioned.

When Lord Lucan received the order from Captain Nolan and had read it, he asked, we are told, 'Where are we to advance to?'

Captain Nolan pointed with his finger to the line of the Russians, and said, 'There are the enemy, and there are the guns, sir, before them. It is your duty to take them,' or words to that effect, according to the statements made since his death.

Lord Lucan with reluctance gave the order to Lord Cardigan to advance upon the guns, conceiving that his orders compelled him to do so. The noble Earl, though he did not shrink, also saw the fearful odds against him. Don Quixote in his tilt against the windmill was not near so rash and reckless as the gallant fellows who prepared without a thought to rush on almost certain death.

It is a maxim of war that 'cavalry never act without support', that 'infantry should be close at hand when cavalry carry guns, as the effect is only instantaneous', and that it is necessary to have on the flank of a line of cavalry some squadrons in column, the attack on the flank being most dangerous. The only support our Light Cavalry had was the reserve of Heavy Cavalry at a great distance behind them—the infantry and guns being far in the rear. There were no squadrons in column at all, and there was a plain to charge over before the enemy's guns were reached of a mile and a half in length.

At ten past eleven our Light Cavalry Brigade rushed to the front. They numbered as follows, as well as I could ascertain:

	MEN	
4th Light Dragoons	118	
8th Irish Hussars	104	
11th Prince Albert's Hussars	110	
13th Light Dragoons	130	
17th Lancers	145	
Total	607	sabres

The whole brigade scarcely made one effective regiment, according to the numbers of continental armies; and yet it was more than we could spare. As they passed towards the front, the Russians opened on them from the guns in the redoubts on the right, with volleys of musketry and rifles.

They swept proudly past, glittering in the morning sun in all the pride and splendour of war. We could hardly believe the evidence of our senses! Surely that handful of men were not going to charge an army in position? Alas! it was but too true—their desperate valour knew no bounds, and far indeed was it removed from its so-called better part—discretion. They advanced in two lines, quickening their pace as they closed towards the enemy. A more fearful spectacle was never witnessed than by those who, without the power to aid, beheld their heroic countrymen rushing to the arms of death. At the distance of 1200 yards the whole line of the enemy belched forth, from thirty iron mouths, a flood of smoke and flame, through which hissed the deadly balls. Their flight was marked by instant gaps in our ranks, by dead men and horses, by steeds flying wounded or riderless across the plain. The first line was broken—it was joined by the second, they never halted or checked their speed an instant. With diminished ranks, thinned by those thirty guns, which the Russians had laid with the most deadly accuracy, with a halo of flashing steel above their heads, and with a cheer which was many a noble fellow's death cry, they flew into the smoke of the batteries; but ere they were lost from view, the plain was strewed with their bodies and with the carcasses of horses. They were exposed to an oblique fire from the batteries on the hills on both sides, as well as to a direct fire of musketry.

Through the clouds of smoke we could see their sabres flashing as they rode up to the guns and dashed between them, cutting down the gunners as they stood. The blaze of their steel, as an officer standing near me said, was 'like the turn of a shoal of mackerel'. We saw them riding through the guns, as I have said; to our delight we saw them returning, after breaking through a column of Russian infantry, and scattering them like chaff, when the flank fire of the battery on the hill swept them down, scattered and broken as they were. Wounded men and dismounted troopers flying towards us told the sad tale—demigods could not have done what they had failed to do. At the very moment when they were about to retreat, an enormous mass of lancers was hurled upon their flank. Colonel Shewell, of the 8th Hussars, saw the danger, and rode his few men straight at them, cutting his way through with fearful loss. The other regiments turned and engaged in a desperate encounter. With courage too great almost for credence, they were breaking their way through the columns which enveloped them, when there took place an act of atrocity without parallel in the modern warfare of civilized nations. The Russian gunners, when the storm of cavalry passed, returned to their guns. They saw their own cavalry mingled with the troopers who had just ridden over them, and to the eternal disgrace of the Russian name the miscreants poured a murderous volley of grape and canister on the mass of struggling men and horses, mingling friend and foe in one common ruin. It was as much as our Heavy Cavalry Brigade could do to cover the retreat of the miserable remnants of that band of heroes as they returned to the place they had so lately quitted in all the pride of life.

At twenty-five to twelve not a British soldier, except the dead and dying, was left in front of these bloody Muscovite guns. Our loss, as far as it could be ascertained in killed, wounded, and missing at two o'clock today, was as follows:

	Went into Action Strong	Returned from Action	Loss
4th Light Dragoons	118	39	79
8th Hussars	104	38	66
11th Hussars	110	25	85
13th Light Dragoons	130	61	69
17th Lancers	145	35	110
	607	198	409

ANTHONY FARRAR-HOCKLEY
The Gloucesters at Imjin River

The communist regime of North Korea launched a major offensive in the Korean War on 22 April 1951, breaking through the line held by the United Nations west of Chungpyong Reservoir. The situation was saved only by the stand of the Gloucestershire Regiment at Imjin River against a much larger enemy force (consisting mostly of Chinese communist troops). Although the Gloucesters were defeated in the engagement, their action broke one arm of the North Korean advance. Anthony Farrar-Hockley, then a junior officer with the Gloucesters, describes the events of 23 April, the height of the fighting at Imjin River.

BELOW JOHN'S TRENCHES ON THE Castle Site, a tin can holding stones is rattling; another sounds close by. The watchers, listeners all, respond without a sound to this first warning. The barbed wire rattles, barb scrapes barb and locks; the tin can sound again. A whispered word and all safety catches are released. Here and there, the split pins of grenades are eased across the cast-iron shoulders.

A faint, incomprehensible sound is heard in the night; the air is ruffled lightly; an object falls near, by a slit trench, smoking. Less than two seconds pass in which the occupants regard it, understand its nature, duck and take cover as it explodes. This is the first grenade: the first of many.

Echoing now, the hill is lit with flame that flickers from above and below. Mortars begin to sound down near the Imjin and the call is taken up by those that lie to the south behind C Company. Slowly, like a fire, the flames spread east and west around Castle Hill; and east again across the village of Choksong, as the enemy from Gloster Crossing, tardily launched at last, meets and is repulsed by D Company.

Now, almost hand to hand, the Chinese and British soldiers meet. Figures leap up from the attacking force, run forward to new cover and resume their fire upon the men of the defence who, coolly enough, return their fire, as targets come to view, as the attackers close with them. Occasionally an individual climax may be reached in an encounter between two men when, only a few feet apart, each waits to catch the other unawares, sees a target, fires, and leaps across to follow his advantage.

And now, to the defenders' aid, the carefully planned defensive fire is summoned. The Vickers guns cut across the cliffs and slopes by which the Chinese forces climb to the attack. Long bursts of fire—ten, twenty, thirty, forty rounds—are fired and fired again: the water in the cooling jackets warms, the ground is littered with spent cases. The mortars and the gunners drop their high explosive in amongst the crowded ranks that press on to the hill slopes from the river crossings.

Such are the enemy's losses that now and then there is a brief respite for the defence as the attackers are withdrawn for reinforcement. The weight of defensive fire is so great that the enemy has realized he must concentrate his strength in one main thrust up to each hilltop. As the night wanes, fresh hundreds are committed to this task, and the tired defenders, much depleted, face yet one more assault.

Mike commands D Company—Lakri is fuming in Japan, moving heaven and earth to get a plane to bring him back from leave. Victors of their first encounters, D Company are sadly weakened by the ceaseless blows rained on them. One of Mike's platoons has been withdrawn right to the hilltop and they form a close defensive ring about the high ridge line which constitutes the vital ground of the position. Ever and again by weight of small-arms fire, by sorties, and as a result of many concentrations fired by mortars and guns, the assault waves are forced back. But still they reappear. For every casualty suffered by the enemy, two, three, four more Chinese will appear to take his place. Yet D Company is holding its ground.

From Castle Hill, the news is grave. John's platoon, now decimated, has been withdrawn by Pat before they are over-run completely. Their officer dead, so many others of their comrades dead or wounded, they go back to Phil's platoon position where they wait for dawn.

The Castle Site, the highest point of our defences forward, is taken after six hours fighting.

The dawn breaks. A pale, April sun is rising in the sky. Take any group of trenches here upon these two main hill positions looking north across the river. See, here, the weapon pits in which the defenders stand: unshaven, wind-burned faces streaked with black powder, filthy with sweat and dust from their exertions, look towards their enemy with eyes red from fatigue and sleeplessness; grim faces, yet not too grim that they refuse to smile when someone cracks a joke about the sunrise. Here, round the weapons smeared with burnt cordite, lie the few pathetic remnants of the wounded, since removed: cap comforters; a boot; some cigarettes half-soaked with blood; a photograph of two small girls; two keys; a broken pencil stub. The men lounge quietly in their positions, waiting for the brief respite to end.

'They're coming back, Ted.'

A shot is fired, a scattered burst follows it. The sergeant calls an order to the mortar group. Already they can hear the shouting and see, here and there, the figures moving out from behind cover as their machine-guns pour fire from the newly occupied Castle Site. Bullets fly back and forth; overhead, almost lazily, grenades are being exchanged on either side; man meets man; hand meets hand. This tiny corner of the battle that is raging along the whole front, blazes up and up into extreme heat, reaches a climax and dies away to nothingness—another little lull, another breathing space.

Phil is called to the telephone at this moment; Pat's voice sounds in his ear.

'Phil, at the present rate of casualties we can't hold on unless we get the Castle Site back. Their machine-guns up there completely dominate your platoon and most of Terry's. We shall never stop their advance until we hold that ground again.'

Phil looks over the edge of the trench at the Castle Site, two hundred yards away, as Pat continues talking, giving him the instructions for the counter attack. They talk for a minute or so; there is not much more to be said when an instruction is given to assault with a handful of tired men across open ground. Everyone knows it is vital: everyone knows it is appallingly dangerous. The only details to be fixed are the arrangements for supporting fire; and, though A Company's Gunners are dead, Ronnie will support them from D Company's hill. Behind, the machine-gunners will ensure that they are not engaged from the open, eastern flank. Phil gathers his tiny assault party together.

It is time; they rise from the ground and move forward up to the barbed wire that once protected the rear of John's platoon. Already two men are hit and Papworth, the Medical Corporal, is attending to them. They are through the wire safely—safely!—when the machine-gun in the bunker begins to fire. Phil is badly wounded: he drops to the ground. They drag him back through the wire somehow and seek what little cover there is as it creeps across their front. The machine-gun stops, content now it has driven them back; waiting for a better target when they move into the open again.

'It's all right, sir,' says someone to Phil. 'The Medical Corporal's been sent for. He'll be here any minute.'

Phil raises himself from the ground, rests on a friendly shoulder, then climbs by a great effort on to one knee.

'We must take the Castle Site,' he says; and gets up to take it.

The others beg him to wait until his wounds are tended. One man places a hand on his side.

'Just wait until Papworth has seen you, sir—'

But Phil has gone: gone to the wire, gone through the wire, gone towards the bunker. The others come out behind him, their eyes all on him. And suddenly it seems as if, for a few breathless moments, the whole of the remainder of that field of battle is still and silent, watching amazed, the lone figure that runs so painfully forward to the bunker holding the approach to the Castle Site: one tiny figure, throwing grenades, firing a pistol, set to take Castle Hill.

Perhaps he will make it—in spite of his wounds, in spite of the odds—perhaps this act of supreme gallantry may, by its sheer audacity, succeed. But the machine-gun in the bunker fires directly into him: he staggers, falls, is dead instantly; the grenade he threw a second before his death explodes after it in the mouth of the bunker. The machine-gun does not fire on three of Phil's platoon who run forward to pick him up; it does not fire again through the battle: it is destroyed; the muzzle blown away, the crew dead.

Before dawn, the Battalion Command Post had moved up the hill to the ridge between Guido's platoon and Paul's company head-quarters. From here, in a bunker constructed under R.S.M. Hobbs's supervision some days before, the Colonel could overlook the battle on the two hill positions north of us. The desperate nature of the struggle was manifest before the morning sun rose. By night, the calls for fire support, each fresh report from A or D Company Headquarters, and the Gunner wireless links had made it all too clear that this attack was in strength. If this was feinting, it was a costly, realistic feint!

Just after dawn, Walters, at his wireless, said that Pat wanted me on the set. I sat down on the reverse slope of the hill behind the bunker and spoke into the handset. Pat replied:

'I'm afraid we've lost Castle Site. I am mounting a counter-attack now but I want to know whether to expect to stay here indefinitely or not. If I am to stay on, I must be re-inforced as my numbers are getting very low.'

I told him to wait and went back into the bunker. The Colonel was standing in the Observation Post at the far end. I told him what Pat had said and asked what he intended to do. He looked through his glasses at D Company's hill and then said:

'I'll talk to him myself.'

We both went back to the wireless set. I stood watching the Colonel as he spoke to Pat, the distant crackle of rifle and light-machine-gun fire in my ears, and the long tack-tack-tack of the Vickers mingling with the hollow boom of the mortars firing from just below us. The Colonel had stopped talking; from the headset came the buzz of Pat's voice. Then the Colonel replied. He said:

'You will stay there at all costs until further notice.'

At all costs.

Pat knew what that order meant, and I knew—and the Colonel knew. As he got up I saw that he was pale and that his hand shook a little as he relit his pipe.

I watched the Colonel go back to the bunker as I put on the headset to speak to Pat again. The next half-hour would tell how the day would go for us.

There were two questions in the Colonel's mind as he stood at the open end of the bunker, viewing the action fought by his two forward companies: would the Chinese continue to press their attack in daylight with the threat of intervention by our aircraft; and, secondly, how long would it be before the Chinese discovered that both our flanks were completely open—that the ROKs were two and a half miles to the west, the Fifth Fusiliers two to the east—and encircle us? Yet, whatever the answer to these questions, his orders were to hold the road between Choksong and Solma-ri. Very well, the Battalion would hold it. And the Battalion would remain disposed as at present just as long as each sub-unit retained its integrity; for our present disposition was unquestionably well-suited to fighting an action designed to hold the road firmly.

I began talking to Pat again, discussing the prospect of reinforcements, and telling him that his ammunition replacement was already going forward in Oxford carriers under Henry's supervision. We spoke only very briefly and he ended by saying:

'Don't worry about us; we'll be all right.'

I said: 'Good luck.'

I did not speak to Pat again; he was killed a quarter of an hour later.

There were no planes that day; there were targets and more elsewhere. The Gunner Colonel spoke to me twice, and I knew from his voice how desperately he wanted to help us. So the Chinese were pushed unceasingly over the Gloster and Western Crossings. The guns and mortars fired all day but the Rifles and Fusiliers—to say nothing of the brave Belgians—needed support too. There were so many of them. Really, for a force reputedly bent on 'imperialist aggression' we must have seemed pathetically thin on the ground to the Chinese Commissars.

At about half past eight it became apparent that the positions of A and D Companies had become untenable; little by little they were being swamped by a tide of men. Each minute was widening the gaps between the little fighting groups—as yet still organized platoons and companies. The time had come when the advantage of holding the ground forward would be outweighed by the loss of much or all of two rifle-company groups. The order to withdraw was given over the wireless.

Watching from the Command Post, I saw the men withdrawing, step by step, down the reverse hill slopes: D Company and A Company leaving the ground they had fought for so well, that had cost the enemy such a price.

I went down the hill a little later and there, by the ford, the survivors of the night battle were coming in: a long, straggling line of men; for all were heavily laden with arms and ammunition. To me they looked cheerful, though tired—but something more than that: they looked surprised. I think, above all, it was a surprise to many of them that they had been withdrawn—grave though they had known their position to be, and dangerous their surroundings. Unquestionably, it was difficult for them to understand that, in holding their ground for so long, they had made a priceless contribution to the battle: but a soldier engaged in a fight that may be to the death has no time for the appreciation of such things. He is, to say the least, otherwise engaged.

Just north of the ford, along the roadsides, around the cookhouse and the Regimental Aid Post, they rested now, as Watkins issued tea as fast as he could make it, and all the bread, bacon and sausages he had to hand. Comrade passed mess tin to comrade, who drank and passed in turn to his next neighbour. Men lay back, without removing their haversacks, their heads resting in the ditches, smoking, talking quietly, resting. Yes, it had been a long night.

The Colonel came down the hill. He had just moved B Company back fifteen hundred yards to the very base of Kamak-San to conform with A and D Companies' withdrawal. He had now to fit the latter two into the revised defence disposition. With Mike and Jumbo he looked over the map and pointed out their new positions on the ground. Jumbo was to take the much-reduced A Company to man the key ridge to the west which Spike's Pioneers now held. Behind, looked down upon by this long feature—marked Hill 235—was a small, square, almost flat-topped hill, where Mike would deploy D Company. As Mike and Jumbo went outside again, Henry was marking the map afresh. The old, blue lines that circled Castle Hill, Choksong, the hill D Company had held, soon vanished from the shiny talc. Now two new rings marked their positions; the symbols were completed by the moving chinagraph. The operations map was fitted back into its place and Henry soon descended to correct his own in the Intelligence Office. I put out my hand to the telephone to tell the remainder of the Battalion how our new line stood, taking it from its rest without looking down. For I was looking at the tiny group of marks upon the talc; and as I looked I realized that this was what the Chinese would attack next—to-night!

When I recall that day, it rises in my memory as a series of incidents, clear in themselves, but joined by a very hazy thread of continuity.

I remember Colour-Sergeant Buxcey organising his Korean porters with mighty loads for the first of many ascents to their new positions. Nine, I think, he made. Nine times up the hill; and so, poor devils, nine times down a path at once precipitous and rough. On coming down, one wished for the easier journey of the upward climb; and upwards, sweating, breathless, weary, one envied those who went the opposite way.

When Buxcey's anxious face has left my mind, I can see Bob working at the Regimental Aid Post, one hand still wet with blood as he turns round, pausing for a moment to clean himself before he begins to minister to yet another wounded man. The ambulance cars are filled; the jeep that Bounden drives has been out time and again with the stretchers on its racks. Baxter, Brisland, Mills, the whole staff of the RAP, is hard at work with dressings, drugs, instruments. This is the reckoning they pay for basking in the sun down by the stream when times are quiet. It is a price they pay willingly and to the full.

I remember watching the slow, wind-tossed descent of a helicopter that came down for some casualties to whom the winding, bumpy road back south would have meant certain death. I saw Bob and the Padre standing back as the plane lifted, their hair blown wildly by the slipstream from the rotors as she lifted into the sky.

Shaw and Mr Evans, the Chief Clerk, went off to Seoul in my jeep. I watched them until they disappeared round the road-bend down by Graham's mortar pits. Richard was down by the ford, and Carl, the Counter-Mortar Officer.

'I'm sending my vehicles back, except for my jeep,' said Carl. 'I've decided I'll stay with you to make up your number of Forward Observation Officers. I've seen the Colonel.'

The lumbering half-tracks disappeared along the road and Carl settled down to chat to Guy on Gunner matters. I wondered what the Gunner Colonel was going to say on finding that his radar specialist had stayed with us. And I thanked God that the latter was a real Gunner as well as a boffin.

We were certainly going to discover that he had not forgotten how to shoot.

Donald, the Assistant Adjutant, came into the Command Vehicle. We had various things to discuss—welfare cases—two men had to go from the Battalion on a Field Hygiene course—there were messages from Freddie, who had thought of them as he rode back to B Echelon after his visit earlier in the day. Afterwards, we had some coffee and over it I told him that he had better stay forward to reinforce A Company, just for the time being. He went off happily to climb the slopes to Jumbo's Hill, as pleased as Punch that he could take command of a platoon—if only for the forthcoming engagement—before he was packed back to Rear H.Q. and his Assistant Adjutancy.

Jumbo had come forward that morning to find Pat and two of his platoon commanders, John and Philip, dead; only Terry left to lead fifty-seven fit men out of the original body nearly one hundred strong. The arrival of Donald would give him two platoon commanders. I put the phone back after telling him the news, and walked out on to the grass to get some sleep.

That morning the Padre said a funeral service for Pat, whose body had been sent back from Company Headquarters on the ammunition-laden Oxford Carrier which Henry had driven through a hail of fire descending on the pass to Choksong. Pat's body was the only one to which we could pay our last respects—but we did not forget the others. Three of us stood by while the solemn words were quietly said; then we saluted and walked away, each busy with his own thoughts.

Pat lay at rest beside the soft-voiced stream, quiet in the morning sunlight, the noise of last night's battle gone forever in the wind.

'The Second-in-Command is here, sir,' said Judkins, my batman. 'And are you going to have anything to eat?'

I opened my eyes to blue sky and huge white clouds. It was afternoon; I had slept for two hours. Judkins stood on the grass by the edge of my blanket, a mug and plate in one hand, a knife, fork, and spoon in the other.

I hated getting up; and I was a fool to refuse the hot stew Watkins had cooked. How little one learns by experience! I asked Judkins for some tea and had a cigarette with Digby, the Second-in-Command. He had come forward from Rear H.Q. some time before but had been unwilling to awaken me.

'The Colonel has told me to go back in view of this attack on Rear H.Q.,' he said. We settled a point or two before he got into his jeep and drove off with Bainbridge at the wheel, for all the world as if he was on his way to a dinner party. They were going to a party all right. Four hours before a sizeable force, which had circled us, had attacked Rear H.Q. The road was cut, and the route forward that might bring us relief or reinforcement was—at that very moment—closing.

It is dark, the moon obscured by cloud. Night is the time for their attack. Although we have had no planes during the day, our Gunners have inflicted too much damage to permit them to press their advance. Released from concern about our troops, hitherto so closely engaged on the hills forward, the Gunners delivered concentration after concentration on the almost endless series of targets before them before the enemy called a halt and went to ground.

But now it is dark. Already their stealthy infantry will have left the little holes in which they have kept hidden from the sun and our observers.

We sit in a battle Command Post. Walters is there at his wireless: nearby sit Richard, Henry, and Guy. Frank is laying a line from the Mortar Troop Headquarters where Sergeant-Major Askew keeps his solitary vigil; somewhere about is Smythe, the Signal Sergeant; Lucas, the Operations Clerk, is making yet another cup of coffee; the Colonel is sitting with his head against the earthen wall, taking advantage of the quiet to doze. I sit by Walters, and, in the glow of red light from the wireless, see that his eyelids are drooping, heavy with an unsatisfied need for sleep. My eyes are heavy, too. How marvellous, what luxury, to find oneself suddenly in a bed with nothing to wake up for until, say, breakfast on a silver tray, in thirty hours' time. Well, why ask a bed? A blanket on that grass outside. . . .

Frank is talking to me, and I realize that I have been dropping off into a doze. It is better that I get up and walk about outside for a little. Richard follows me as Frank departs for his Headquarters, a hundred yards away. We hear the stream rushing over the little waterfall; the light wind cools our cheeks, hot from the close atmosphere of the dug-out. The radiance of the moon is widening in the sky above us. Beneath our feet, the old year's grass rustles as we stroll up and down, talking.

Suddenly, Richard pauses in mid-sentence. We both look up, quickly, to the eastern end of C Company's ridge. The battle has started.

In the Command Post dug-out, the telephone is ringing.

In the original Battalion defensive layout, Denis's Company—B Company—were on the far right flank, holding the approaches to the great Kamak-San feature—itself too vast for us to hold—at the same time constituting the right rear base of the Battalion. Unlike C Company, they had never been absolutely in reserve, inasmuch as there had been nothing except the river between them and the enemy; although, of course, to their northwest, A and D Companies had been in closer proximity to an often evanescent foe. Now, with both A and D Companies withdrawn, their prospect of a major engagement became a certainty.

Whilst the battle had raged around Choksong village for the possession of A and D Companies' hills, B Company had been little more than spectators. A few Chinese patrols had bumped them during the hours of darkness, but they had held their fire, except at one post where a complete patrol of fifteen men was destroyed by an LMG of Geoff's platoon. Thus the Chinese did not know B Company's positions on the morning of the 23rd; for all they knew, their contact on the previous night might well have been with one of our patrols, instead of with a position in our main defences. Thus, expecting to renew the attack that night, they had sent a further series of patrols forward towards B Company during the morning; and these patrols were all in strength, designed to produce, at all costs, reaction from us.

Denis was determined not to reveal his positions unless absolutely compelled to; but, faced with a number of strong armed parties along his front, he realized that, sooner or later he would be forced to engage them. In these circumstances, he made up his mind to do so by sortie, by which means the enemy could not be certain either of the main position or—equally important—the strength of the force from which they had sprung.

Sergeant Petherick took out a force in this connection, expecting to engage, at most, twenty men: he returned after meeting two hundred. Backwards and forwards, all among the battle knolls that lay below the peak of Kamak-San, engagements flared up and died, only to be renewed elsewhere.

The daylight waned, the evening shadows deepened, merged and grew into one, to form the darkness of another night.

Below great Kamak-San, Denis's Company prepared themselves for what they knew the darkness would bring forth.

To the west, that night, the 1st ROK Division was to repulse, with great tenacity, a strong and vigorous attack by two divisions attempting to open up the road that ran from Munsan-Ni to Seoul—a part of the western highway that ran up from the south to the border on the Yalu River. Eastwards, the Fifth Fusiliers would fight desperately against attacks across the river in great strength; and beyond, the Belgians and the Rifles, Puerto Ricans, Turks, Americans would be engaged in increasing intensity.

Here, near Choksong, lay the centre of the attack upon the western sector; here ran the road which was, historically, the main route of invasion from the north.

Already one full day behind their time-plan for the advance, the Chinese now prepared to end the resistance once and for all, and surge along the road to Seoul through Uijong-bu, catching, perhaps, the whole left flank of the UN 3rd Division unawares.

Their problem now was, at what point should they attack? Last night's experience made it plain that one vast, human wave would never serve to overwhelm the sturdy wall of the defence. Further, the British left flank, on Hill 235, would not be easy to attack. They could not know of Jumbo's dangerous weakness on the ridge.

Then, too, attack upon the west might leave us time and opportunity to make a second withdrawal, on to Kamak-San, from which we should not easily be dislodged. The choice fell, therefore, upon the approaches to Kamak-San, and thus upon B Company and part of C, whose right flank lay across the western spur leading to the final, jagged crest.

I run into the dugout: Walters has answered the telephone, which he hands to me. Denis says:

'Well, we've started. They're attacking Beverly's platoon now—about a hundred and fifty, I should think.'

My torch is on the map; and I examine the exact location of the attack as the Colonel begins to talk to Denis. Nearby, I hear the heavier sound of shells exploding above the noisy small-arms fire and mortars. Recce is shooting along B Company's front.

Paul is on the other telephone; his news from C Company is the same: parties of enemy attempting to infiltrate, while others assault our positions in great strength, trying again to engulf us. Jack's platoon and David's are engaged; Guido's platoon is under machine-gun fire from D Company's former position.

It is ten minutes to twelve: the battle is warming.

Here they come again: a screaming mob of cotton-suited soldiers, their yellow faces gleaming in the light of the trip flares they have sprung and the mortar flares drifting slowly down beneath their parachutes.

An hour after midnight, the whole of B and C Companies are engaged; the guns, the mortars, the machine-guns once again deliver their supporting fire with all their might.

In character, the battle much resembles that of the previous night: wave after wave of men armed with grenades and burp-guns storm the positions under cover of mortar and machine-gun fire, are halted, engaged in a short desperate struggle, and driven back. A lull follows. Both sides reorganize. The attack recommences. The character of the battle is the same, too, in that these ceaseless blows, delivered in such strength, inevitably reduce our numbers speedily. Their casualties are high—much higher than ours; but in this battle of attrition they can afford them; we cannot.

It is in the nature of the ground that the battle differs; and the Chinese have made the mistake of attacking obliquely across our front—perhaps because they did not really know where B Company lay. Thus for the first two hours, much of the weight of their attack was spent fruitlessly. Only after great loss have they redirected their line of assault. Old Kamak-San looks down upon a ring of intermittent flame across his northern base. Last night the flames were further off. Now they are nearer; growing nearer, hour by hour.

It is three o'clock. In the Command Post we are drinking coffee and talking. The telephone is quiet for the moment but the noise of the battle reaches us clearly. As I sit talking to Richard, I wonder if he realizes how gravely we are situated: a vast body of the enemy pushing south; our flanks open; the road cut behind us. It is a great comfort to reflect that, though they can take Kamak-San without firing a shot—they have only to travel round our unguarded flanks, after all—it will do them no good. We hold the road; and we shall continue to hold it.

The telephone is ringing again: Paul is speaking:

'I'm afraid they've overrun my top position,' he says, 'and they're reinforcing hard. They're simply pouring chaps in up above us. Let me know what the Colonel wants me to do, will you?'

This is, immediately, disaster. The enemy has forced his way up on to Paul's highest defensive post by overwhelming his men with their numbers. The result of this is that the Chinese now command most of C Company's ground, have forced a wedge between C and B Company, and dominate the valley in which the mortars lie—heavy and medium—and the entire Headquarters. If we are not quick, we may be caught by the enemy who has only to fire over open sights straight down into us.

Already, however, the Colonel, who is listening, has made up his mind.

'Pack the Headquarters up,' he says, 'and get every one out of the valley up between D Company and the Anti-Tank Platoon position. I'm going to withdraw C Company in ten minutes; and I shall move B over to join us after first light.'

He picks up the telephone and starts to speak to Paul as I give Richard and Henry their instructions. They need but a few words: speed is the requirement here. Foolishly, I forget Frank has laid a line to the Command Post, and waste precious time going to his Headquarters. He is not there. I give a message to Sergeant-Major Askew and go on: Graham's mortars are warned—Sam's Headquarters—the Regimental Aid Post—the Regimental Sergeant-Major. Before I return to the Command Post, the first party of signallers is moving up the gorge towards D Company's hill.

Back at the Command Post I burn those papers that must *not* be taken. Lucas and I pick up Jennings, the Rear Link Wireless commander: together we smash the fixed radio-equipment. Again, I go around the area. Overhead, along the ridge C Company is holding, there is a sudden ominous quiet. I wonder if they are already mounting a machine-gun at the head of the valley; if they are already descending to the stream, crossing by the mortar pits which I am now approaching. It is no good wondering: I shall know soon enough what they are doing. The mortar pits stand silent, strangely deserted after the bustle of the earlier part of the night. Turning back along the road, I see a mug of steaming tea standing on a box at the entrance to Sam's HQ. The RAP has gone, too; Bob's jeep is in wild disorder; packages, web equipment, an old coffee tin are scattered across the seats, flung there in haste after he had removed the other contents. Everyone has gone.

Not quite everyone. There is a murmur of voices from the signals office; a metallic rasping catches my ear. As I step down from the bank on the edge of the road, two signallers appear. They have come back for space batteries, quite unaware that the sands in the hour-glass are fast running out. Indeed, I cannot be sure if there is even one grain left to fall: the Chinese have held the head of the valley for nearly forty minutes.

Anthony-Farrar Hockley was captured shortly afterwards by the North Vietnamese, and was interned in a POW camp.

JEFFREY ENGLISH
One for Every Sleeper

Jeffrey English was captured by the Japanese at the fall of Singapore, 1942. In May 1943 he was put to work on the Burma to Siam railway, where conditions caused the death of two out of every three POWs.

THE WORK HERE WAS AGAIN on a rock cutting, about a mile from the camp and reached through the usual little track of churned-up mud. The shifts changed over down at the cutting, not back at camp, and so the men were paraded at 7 a.m. to be counted, and then had to march down to commence work at 8 a.m. The party coming off duty had to march back to the camp, and did not arrive until some time after 8.30 a.m. But that did not mean ten and a half hours for food and sleep. On five days a week rations had to be collected from the river, which involved going out at 1.30 p.m. and getting back between 5 p.m. and 6 p.m.

At our previous camp the ration parties had been drawn from the semi-sick, but here *all* men not bedded down had to go on the working parties to the cutting, and so the afternoon ration parties had to be found from the now off-duty night shift. A man would work or be going to and from work for the best part of fourteen hours, do a four-hour ration fatigue, and have only six hours out of twenty-four for feeding, cleaning himself up, and sleeping.

For the first week or so, when we still had over 300 'fit' in the combined Anglo-Australian camp, each individual only got two ration fatigues a week. It would have been even less, but of course one half of our 300 were on the day shift, and only the other half were on the unhappy night shift.

On three pints of rice a day, all this, of course, was impossible and flesh and blood could not stand the strain; and in addition to the overwork we had dysentery and other diseases spreading at a frightening pace. As the numbers of 'fit' men dwindled, the burden carried by the remainder consequently grew, until after only a few weeks the fitter men were doing all five ration fatigues a week as well as working the night shift in the cutting, and only having two days a week of real rest. As they gradually cracked up, more unfortunates, just past the crisis of their exhaustion or illnesses but in no way fully recovered, would be forced out in their place, lasting in their turn perhaps three or four days before they themselves had to be replaced by yet others not quite so ill.

Just as this gruelling programme put that at our previous camp in the shade, so did the new Nip Engineers make the last lot look like gentlemen. There, they had generally beaten only those whom they caught flagging or had somehow provoked their precariously balanced ill-humour; but here they beat up indiscriminately, beating every man in a gang if they wanted it to go faster, and two of them in particular were simply blood-thirsty sadists.

They were known to us as 'Musso' and 'The Bull', and they seemed to compete amongst themselves as to who could cause the most hurt. They were both on the night shift, and both would come on duty with a rope's end strapped to the wrist. These they plied liberally, and they also carried a split-ended bamboo apiece, whilst Musso in particular would lash out with anything which came handy, such as a shovel. Every morning two or three men would come back to camp with blood clotted on their faces and shoulders or matted in their hair, whilst others would return with puffy scarlet faces but no eye lashes or eye brows, these having been burnt off where they'd had a naked acetylene flare waved slowly across the eyes—a favourite trick of another Nip known to us as 'Snowdrop'.

They drove the men on, not just to make them work, but as a cruel master drives a beast of burden to force it on to further efforts greater than it can manage; and one would see half a dozen men staggering along with an 18-foot tree trunk, or rolling an outsize boulder to the edge of the cutting, with the Nip running alongside lashing out at them or kicking their knees and shin and ankles to keep them going.

Frequently men fainted, and to make sure that they weren't shamming, the Nip would kick them in the stomach, ribs or groin. If the man still didn't move, the favourite trick was to roll him over face downwards, and then jump up and down on the backs of his knees, so as to grind the kneecaps themselves into the loose gravel. If he fell on his side, a variation was to stand on the side of his face and then wriggle about, grinding and tearing his undercheek in the gravel: and as a way of telling a faked faint from a real one, both of these methods are, believe me, highly efficacious.

On one occasion a man was beaten up so badly by the Nips that they thought he wouldn't live, and so they got four prisoners and told them to bury him under a heap of rocks. The prisoners observed that he wasn't yet dead, but the Nips indicated that that didn't matter—they could bury him alive. It was only after a great deal of persuasion by a spunky Australian officer (who naturally took a personal bashing for his trouble, but didn't let that deter him) that the Nips eventually changed their minds and let the man be carried back to camp. He was carried on a stretcher, and came round later, but the beating had sent him almost off his head; he disappeared into the jungle and we couldn't find him for two days. On the third day he crept in for food; but he was now quite mental and became a gibbering idiot at the mere sight of a Nip. Had we bedded him down in a hospital tent, he could very well have simply popped off again; and so we found him a job in the cook-house where he would be working with others, and he worked there for a shaky fortnight before he packed it in and died.

At the next camp up the road, at Hintok, whence we sometimes drew our rations, they literally beat one man to death. He was discovered resting in the bushes down at their cutting when he ought to have been working, and the Nips took him down to the cutting in front of all the other prisoners and gave him a terrific beating up. He fainted once or twice, and was brought round by the usual Nip methods; and they continued in this way until they could bring him round no more. He wasn't quite dead yet, and was carried back to camp: but although he regained consciousness he avoided going out again on the next shift by the simple device of dying.

The Hintok Nips were on much of a par with our own Musso and The Bull: and another pretty case arose from the familiar story of the Nips demanding a working party of 120 men when the most that Hintok could muster was 105. The Nips went into the hospital tent and brought out the first fifteen of those bedded down, all of whom were dysentery cases, some of them in a very bad way indeed. They were forced to join the parade, and they set off for the cutting. One man in particular was very, very bad, but no one was allowed to lag behind and help him get along, and after several collapses he at last could go no further.

He arrived back at the camp dragging himself through the mud on his hands and knees, and was put back into the hospital: but when the Nips returned that night they knew that they'd been one short all day. They dug him out from the hospital, supported by a man on either side as he could no longer stand by himself, and then with all the typical gallantry of the Japanese, they started in and beat him up. He lay writhing on the ground whilst they beat and kicked him senseless, and although they left him breathing he was dead within two hours.

In a similar case at our own camp, three men, all very sick, passed out on the way to work, and Musso sent the squad officer back to bring them down. They were rounded up and shepherded in, and Musso, as they approached, rushed forward and started beating them with a stout bamboo. He broke the first bamboo on one of them, seized another one and broke that one too, and then got a pick handle and used it as a two-handed club. He bashed them unmercifully, and then ordered them to pick up a length of rail from the light railway, and carry it over to the rock face. It being the night shift, there was no overhead scorching sun to add to their woes; but he ordered them to hold the length of rail above their heads.

No matter how he beat them, they couldn't get it above their heads, but at last they got it to chest level, and there he kept them holding it for the best part of twenty minutes. Every time they sagged he laid in with the pick-handle, and as they couldn't even ward off the blows with their hands they were in a horrible state by the time he let them go.

That same night Musso further distinguished himself. A fellow called 'B——' (I'll just call him that lest his widow might read this) had been holding a chisel and his mate missed with his sledgehammer and crushed B——'s hand. Musso blamed B——for not holding the chisel upright, and instead of knocking him off work and letting him have his broken fingers set, he put him onto the job of turning the big crank which worked one of the generators floodlighting the cutting. The handle was far too heavy for him to turn with his one good hand, so that he had to use the bleeding pulp of his crushed hand as well. Musso stood over him, and every time he flagged and the lights dimmed, he was beaten with a bamboo. He was kept at it for nearly an hour, during which time he twice fainted; but when he fainted for the third time he didn't come round. He was helped back to camp at the end of the shift, and he died a week later from cholera, from which he had probably already been sickening when Musso did his stuff on him.

Musso, mark you, was merely a private soldier—a private soldier under no restraint or the exercise of any control by his superiors. His was one of the few names which we managed to find out and retain—he was Superior Private Kanaga—and I must confess to having shed not a single tear when I learnt, after the war, that both he and The Bull were hanged after trial by the War Crimes Commission. What happened to Snowdrop I never learnt.

By the end of only three weeks at this new camp we were at the end of our tether. In our part of the camp alone we had fifty dead, 150 bedded down in hospital, and only fifty working; and the Australians had comparable figures but over double the size of ours.

Even the Nips realized that something had got to be done, for the men they still had were dropping of exhaustion: although they had tried to keep them going by sheer brutality alone, there comes a time when any amount of flogging seems preferable to more work.

The Nips had a bright idea. They explained that the fit working men needed more food than did those bedded down in hospital, which seemed eminently logical. The shine went off the ball, however, when they further explained that the way in which they would introduce the differential would be to keep the rations for the fit men exactly as they were—but would reduce the hospital to two meals a day.

T.E. LAWRENCE (LAWRENCE OF ARABIA) Torture

In November 1917, T.E. Lawrence was detained by the Turks whilst on an undercover reconnaissance of the desert town of Deraa in the Palestine, and subsequently tortured for refusing the homosexual advances of the local Turkish military governor.

PROPERLY TO ROUND OFF THIS spying of the hollow land of Hauran, it was necessary to visit Deraa, its chief town. We could cut it off on north and west and south, by destroying the three railways; but it would be more tidy to rush the junction first and work outwards. Talal, however, could not venture in with me since he was too well known in the place. So we parted from him with many thanks on both sides, and rode southward along the line until near Deraa. There we dismounted. The boy, Halim, took the ponies, and set off for Nisib, south of Deraa. My plan was to walk round the railway station and town with Faris, and reach Nisib after sunset. Faris was my best companion for the trip, because he was an insignificant peasant, old enough to be my father, and respectable.

The respectability seemed comparative as we tramped off in the watery sunlight, which was taking the place of the rain last night. The ground was muddy, we were barefoot, and our draggled clothes showed the stains of the foul weather to which we had been exposed. I was in Halim's wet things, with a torn Hurani jacket, and was yet limping from the broken foot acquired when we blew up Jemal's train. The slippery track made walking difficult, unless we spread out our toes widely and took hold of the ground with them: and doing this for mile after mile was exquisitely painful to me. Because pain hurt me so, I would not lay weight always on my pains in our revolt: yet hardly one day in Arabia passed without a physical ache to increase the corroding sense of my accessory deceitfulness towards the Arabs, and the legitimate fatigue of responsible command.

We mounted the curving bank of the Palestine Railway, and from its vantage surveyed Deraa Station: but the ground was too open to admit of surprise attack. We decided to walk down the east front of the defences: so we plodded on, noting German stores, barbed wire here and there, rudiments of trenches. Turkish troops were passing incuriously between the tents and their latrines dug out on our side.

At the corner of the aerodrome by the south end of the station we struck over towards the town. There were old Albatros machines in the sheds, and men lounging about. One of these, a Syrian soldier, began to question us about our villages, and if there was much 'government' where we lived. He was probably an intending deserter, fishing for a refuge. We shook him off at last and turned away. Someone called out in Turkish. We walked on deafly; but a sergeant came after, and took me roughly by the arm, saying 'The Bey wants you'. There were too many witnesses for fight or flight, so I went readily. He took no notice of Faris.

I was marched through the tall fence into a compound set about with many huts and a few buildings. We passed to a mud room, outside which was an earth platform, whereon sat a fleshy Turkish officer, one leg tucked under him. He hardly glanced at me when the sergeant brought me up and made a long report in Turkish. He asked my name: I told him Ahmed ibn Bagr, a Circassian from Kuneitra. 'A deserter?' 'But we Circassians have no military service.' He turned, stared at me, and said very slowly 'You are a liar. Enrol him in your section, Hassan Chowish, and do what is necessary till the Bey sends for him.'

They led me into a guard-room, mostly taken up by large wooden cribs, on which lay or sat a dozen men in untidy uniforms. They took away my belt, and my knife, made me wash myself carefully, and fed me. I passed the long day there. They would not let me go on any terms, but tried to reassure me. A soldier's life was not all bad. Tomorrow, perhaps, leave would be permitted, if I fulfilled the Bey's pleasure this evening. The

Bey seemed to be Nahi, the Governor. If he was angry, they said, I would be drafted for infantry training to the depot in Baalbek. I tried to look as though, to my mind, there was nothing worse in the world than that.

Soon after dark three men came for me. It had seemed a chance to get away, but one held me all the time. I cursed my littleness. Our march crossed the railway, where were six tracks, besides the sidings of the engine-shop. We went through a side gate, down a street, past a square, to a detached, two-storied house. There was a sentry outside, and a glimpse of others lolling in the dark entry. They took me upstairs to the Bey's room; or to his bedroom, rather. He was another bulky man, a Circassian himself, perhaps, and sat on the bed in a night-gown, trembling and sweating as though with fever. When I was pushed in he kept his head down, and waved the guard out. In a breathless voice he told me to sit on the floor in front of him, and after that was dumb; while I gazed at the top of his great head, on which the bristling hair stood up, no longer than the dark stubble on his cheeks and chin. At last he looked me over, and told me to stand up: then to turn round. I obeyed; he flung himself back on the bed, and dragged me down with him in his arms. When I saw what he wanted I twisted round and up again, glad to find myself equal to him, at any rate in wrestling.

He began to fawn on me, saying how white and fresh I was, how fine my hands and feet, and how he would let me off drills and duties, make me his orderly, even pay me wages, if I would love him.

I was obdurate, so he changed his tone, and sharply ordered me to take off my drawers. When I hesitated, he snatched at me; and I pushed him back. He clapped his hands for the sentry, who hurried in and pinioned me. The Bey cursed me with horrible threats: and made the man holding me tear my clothes away, bit by bit. His eyes rounded at the half-healed places where the bullets had flicked through my skin a little while ago. Finally he lumbered to his feet, with a glitter in his look, and began to paw me over. I bore it for a little, till he got too beastly; and then jerked my knee into him.

He staggered to his bed, squeezing himself together and groaning with pain, while the soldier shouted for the corporal and the other three men to grip me hand and foot. As soon as I was helpless the Governor regained courage, and spat at me, swearing he would make me ask pardon. He took off his slipper, and hit me repeatedly with it in the face, while the corporal braced my head back by the hair to receive the blows. He leaned forward, fixed his teeth in my neck and bit till the blood came. Then he kissed me. Afterwards he drew one of the men's bayonets. I thought he was going to kill me, and was sorry: but he only pulled up a fold of the flesh over my ribs, worked the point through, after considerable trouble, and gave the blade a half-turn. This hurt, and I winced, while the blood wavered down my side and dripped to the front of my thigh. He looked pleased and dabbled it over my stomach with his finger-tips.

In my despair I spoke. His face changed and he stood still, then controlled his voice with an effort, to say significantly, 'You must understand that I know: and it will be easier if you do as I wish.' I was dumbfounded, and we stared silently at one another, while the men who felt an inner meaning beyond their experience, shifted uncomfortably. But it was evidently a chance shot, by which he himself did not, or would not, mean what I feared. I could not again trust my twitching mouth, which faltered always in emergencies, so at last threw up my chin, which was the sign for 'No' in the East; then he sat down, and half-whispered to the corporal to take me out and teach me everything.

They kicked me to the head of the stairs, and stretched me over a guard-bench, pommelling me. Two knelt on my ankles, bearing down on the back of my knees, while two more twisted my wrists till they cracked, and then crushed them and my neck against the wood. The corporal had run downstairs; and now came back with a whip of the Circassian sort, a thong of supple black hide, rounded, and tapering from the thickness of a thumb at the grip (which was wrapped in silver) down to a hard point finer than a pencil.

He saw me shivering, partly I think, with cold, and made it whistle over my ear, taunting me that before his tenth cut I would howl for mercy, and at the twentieth beg for the caresses of the Bey; and then he began to lash me madly across and across with all his might, while I locked my teeth to endure this thing which lapped itself like flaming wire about my body.

To keep my mind in control I numbered the blows, but after twenty lost count, and could feel only the shapeless weight of pain, not tearing claws, for which I had prepared, but a gradual cracking apart of my whole being by some too-great force whose waves rolled up my spine till they were pent within my brain, to clash terribly together. Somewhere in the place a cheap clock ticked loudly, and it distressed me that their beating was not in its time. I writhed and twisted, but was held so tightly that my struggles were useless. After the corporal ceased, the men took up, very deliberately, giving me so many, and then an interval during which they would squabble for the next turn, ease themselves, and play unspeakably with me. This was repeated often, for what may have been no more than ten minutes. Always for the first of every new series, my head would be pulled round, to see how a hard white ridge, like a railway, darkening slowly into crimson, leaped over my skin at the instant of each stroke, with a bead of blood where two ridges crossed. As the punishment proceeded the whip fell more and more upon existing weals, biting blacker or more wet, till my flesh quivered with accumulated pain, and with terror of the next blow coming. They soon conquered my determination not to cry, but while my will ruled my lips I used only Arabic, and before the end a merciful sickness choked my utterance.

At last when I was completely broken they seemed satisfied. Somehow I found myself off the bench, lying on my back on the dirty floor, where I snuggled down, dazed, panting for breath, but vaguely comfortable. I had strung myself to learn all pain until I died, and no longer actor, but spectator, thought not to care how my body jerked and squealed. Yet I knew or imagined what passed about me.

I remembered the corporal kicking with his nailed boot to get me up; and this was true, for the next day my right side was dark and lacerated, and a damaged rib made each breath stab me sharply. I remembered smiling idly at him, for a delicious warmth, probably sexual, was swelling through me: and then that he flung up his arm and hacked with the full length of his whip into my groin. This doubled me half-over, screaming, or, rather, trying impotently to scream, only shuddering through my open mouth. One giggled with amusement. A voice cried, 'Shame, you've killed him.' Another slash followed. A roaring, and my eyes went black: while within me the core of life seemed to heave slowly up through the rending nerves, expelled from its body by this last indescribable pang.

By the bruises perhaps they beat me further: but I next knew that I was being dragged about by two men, each disputing over a leg as though to split me apart: while a third man rode me astride. It was momently better than more flogging. Then Nahi called. They splashed water in my face, wiped off some of the filth, and lifted me between them retching and sobbing for mercy, to where he lay: but he now rejected me in haste, as a thing too torn and bloody for his bed, blaming their excess of zeal which had spoilt me: whereas no doubt they had laid into me much as usual, and the fault rested mainly upon my indoor skin, which gave way more than an Arab's.

So the crestfallen corporal, as the youngest and best-looking of the guard, had to stay behind, while the others carried me down the narrow stair into the street. The coolness of the night on my burning flesh, and the unmoved shining of the stars after the horror of the past hour, made me cry again. The soldiers, now free to speak, warned me that men must suffer their officer's wishes or pay for it, as I had just done, with greater suffering.

They took me over an open space, deserted and dark, and behind the Government house to a lean-to wooden room, in which were many dusty quilts. An Armenian dresser appeared to wash and bandage me in sleepy haste. Then all went away, the last soldier delaying by my side a moment to whisper in his Druse accent that the door into the next room was not locked.

I lay there in a sick stupor, with my head aching very much, and growing slowly numb with cold, till the dawn light came shining through the cracks of the shed, and a locomotive whistled in the station. These and a draining thirst brought me to life, and I found I was in no pain. Pain of the slightest had been my obsession and secret terror, from a boy. Had I now been drugged with it, to bewilderment? Yet the first movement was anguish: in which I struggled nakedly to my feet, and rocked moaning in wonder that it was not a dream, and myself back five years ago, a timid recruit at Khalfati, where something, less staining, of the sort had happened.

The next room was a dispensary. On its door hung a suit of shoddy clothes. I put them on slowly and unhandily, because of my swollen wrists: and from the drugs chose corrosive sublimate, as safeguard against recapture. The window looked on a long blank wall. Stiffly I climbed out, and went shaking down the road towards the village, past the few people already astir. They took no notice; indeed there was nothing peculiar in my dark broadcloth, red fez and slippers: but it was only by the full urge of my tongue silently to myself that I refrained from being foolish out of sheer fright. Deraa felt inhuman with vice and cruelty, and it shocked me like cold water when a soldier laughed behind me in the street.

By the bridge were the wells, with men and women about them. A side trough was free. From its end I scooped up a little water in my hands, and rubbed it over my face; then drank, which was precious to me; and afterwards wandered along the bottom of the valley, towards the south, unobtrusively retreating out of sight. This valley provided the hidden road by which our projected raid could attain Deraa town secretly, and surprise the Turks. So, in escaping I solved, too late, the problem which had brought me to Deraa.

Further on, a Serdi, on his camel, overtook me hobbling up the road towards Nisib. I explained that I had business there, and was already footsore. He had pity and mounted me behind him on his bony animal, to which I clung the rest of the way, learning the feelings of my adopted name-saint on his gridiron. The tribe's tents were just in front of the village, where I found Faris and Halim anxious about me, and curious to learn how I had fared. Halim had been up to Deraa in the night, and knew by the lack of rumour that the truth had not been discovered. I told them a merry tale of bribery and trickery, which they promised to keep to themselves, laughing aloud at the simplicity of the Turks.

During the night I managed to see the great stone bridge by Nisib. Not that my maimed will now cared a hoot about the Arab Revolt (or about anything but mending itself); yet, since the war had been a hobby of mine, for custom's sake I would force myself to push it through. Afterwards we took horse, and rode gently and carefully towards Azrak, without incident, except that a raiding party of Wuld Ali let us and our horses go unplundered when they heard who we were. This was an unexpected generosity, the Wuld Ali being not yet of our fellowship. Their consideration (rendered at once, as if we had deserved men's homage) momently stayed me to carry the burden, whose certainty the passing days confirmed: how in Deraa that night the citadel of my integrity had been irrevocably lost.

TOM MOULSON
The Great Escaper

The breakout from Stalag Luft III in early 1944 was the biggest allied POW escape of the Second World War. The principal organiser of the breakout—the real event on which the film The Great Escape *is based—was the inveterate RAF escaper, Squadron Leader Roger Bushell. Bushell had been shot down over Dunkirk in 1939, where this account of his escaping career begins.*

THE FIRST PLACE TO WHICH they took him was Dulag Luft, a transit camp for aircrew prisoners near Frankfurt. After a period of solitary confinement, Bushell made a survey of the camp. In the playing field, and just outside the compound wiring, there was a goat in a kennel. If a hole were dug in the floor of the kennel and a trapdoor fitted to support the goat, a man could remain concealed from the sentries and stay outside the compound as the prisoners returned from the playing field after exercise. The hole was dug by relays of prisoners hiding in the kennel one by one, the sand being taken away in vessels used for feeding the goat. If the guards had counted the number of times the goat was fed their suspicions would have been aroused, but they did not. Bushell planned to hide in the kennel on the evening before a separate tunnel escape involving a number of prisoners; to climb the single wire surrounding the sports field as soon as it was dark, and thus to confuse his pursuers with the twenty-four hours' start over the tunnellers.

On the prospect of staying in the kennel until dark, someone asked him, 'What about the smell?' and Bushell replied, 'Oh, the goat won't mind that.'

It was an easy matter to falsify the roll call, and he got away smoothly. With his fluency in German and experience of the winter sports areas he set course for Switzerland, travelling by day in a civilian suit bought from one of the guards at Dulag Luft. He was able to engage safely in brief conversations, and navigating with the aid of guide books purchased from shops along the way he went to Tuttlingen by express train, and from there to Bonndorf by suburban line. His plan to throw the Germans at Dulag Luft off the scent was entirely successful, for none of the eighteen men who escaped by tunnel got farther than Hanover before being arrested, by which time he had out-distanced the radius of search.

From Bonndorf Bushell reached on foot the point he was making for, a few kilometres from the Swiss border. Things had gone almost too well and, being aware of his habitual over-confidence, he sat down for two hours and made himself generate caution for the last decisive stage. He had the alternatives of waiting for nightfall, with all its problems, or of bluffing it out by daylight. He chose the latter.

In the border village of Stühlingen he was halted by a guard. Pretending to be a drunken but amiable ski-ing instructor, Bushell was being conducted towards a check-point for an examination of his papers when he broke loose and bolted, dodging bullets, into a side street. The side street proved to be a cul-de-sac and he was run to earth within a minute. The officer to whom he was taken turned out to be a German he had known in his ski-ing days, and Bushell ventured to suggest that for old time's sake he be set free with a ten minutes' start. For once his persuasive charm had no effect, meeting only with a stony, Teutonic refusal.

Bushell served a punitive sentence in a Frankfurt gaol, intended to soften his morale; but he was made of firmer stuff and on being moved to Barth, near the Baltic coast, he escaped again with a Polish officer.

The two men separated, and Bushell was stumbling along a road near the concentration camp at Auschwitz on a dark night when he blundered into a sentry he had not seen, knocking him to the ground. With an instinctive courtesy he helped the soldier to his feet, handed him his rifle and said, 'Sorry!' The game was up once again.

It was decided to move this troublesome officer to a new camp, and he was herded into a cattle truck with several other prisoners and taken from Lübeck to Warburg. What pleasures awaited him there Bushell did not stay to see, and with five others prised open the truck's floorboards and dropped on to the track as the train was moving. One of the prisoners dropped on to the rail and lost both legs as a truck rolled over him.

With a Czech named Zafouk, Bushell reached Czechoslovakia where the Resistance boarded them with a courageous family in Prague. Bushell appreciated this limited freedom and would dress in civilian clothes and take daily walks around the city while waiting for the Resistance to complete arrangements for his transfer to Yugoslavia. But the assassination of the tyrant Heydrich activated a house-to-house search for students suspected of the crime. At the time, Bushell happened to be in a cinema with the daughter of the household where he was staying, and the audience was ordered to file out for a check on identity cards. As Bushell could not speak the language, his girl companion did the talking, but he was suspected and sent to a Gestapo prison in Berlin.

Bushell's cell was one of a number on either side of a corridor, and when they had locked his door and withdrawn he put his face to the grill and asked softly: 'Is anyone here British?' A voice four cells away in the direction of the latrines replied, 'Yes, Flight-Lieutenant Marshall, RAF.'

Marshall, who had known Bushell before the war, was also an escaper and had been captured in the same cinema and at the same time. Conversation between the two was restricted to furtive whisperings of a few seconds' duration whenever Bushell passed Marshall's cell. It took several days for Bushell to explain that he was refusing to admit his identity for fear of repercussions on the Prague family, which would be telling the same story as his. He was tormented by the thought of what would happen to them. One evening he whispered that he had left a note in the lavatory. When Marshall found it tucked behind the cistern it contained Bushell's service number, rank and full name. 'They are going to shoot me,' it stated; 'Please pass full particulars to the Red Cross.'

But Bushell learned that the Prague family had been executed and he admitted his identity. Until he did so he had consciously forfeited his right to protection by the Geneva Convention. Again a bona fide prisoner-of-war, he was sent to Stalag Luft III at the end of 1942, and it was here that he received his ultimatum: if he ever escaped again he would be shot.

Stalag Luft III, the large prison camp at Sagan, eighty miles east of Berlin, was a good camp and had only been opened the previous spring. The north compound to which Bushell was committed could almost have been a luxury camp; it held a thousand prisoners, was spacious and boasted private kitchens and washrooms with every barrack. There were excellent facilities for entertainment, and the commandant, Baron Von Lindeiner, hoped the British prisoners would enjoy their stay and even wish to remain in Germany after the war. His prisoners regretted that they had no desire to stay in Germany, war or no war, and bent their entire energies—diverted every useful item of food or material, subverted every sport or educational group, directed every imaginative talent—towards the predominant objective of escape.

The commandant and the senior British officer at Sagan both advised Bushell to take no further chances. 'I can't possibly stay here for long,' he replied; 'the winters are terrible.' But first he had a spell in 'The Cooler', the camp gaol, to undergo.

'The Cooler' was so overcrowded with delinquent prisoners that those assigned to it had to wait their turn until a cell was available. When Bushell was called he again found himself a few cells away from Marshall, and while the guards were not paying much attention they resumed their discussion. Bushell was obsessed by the prospect of being mysteriously liquidated, or of the circumstances surrounding his death being mis-represented. He was less afraid of dying, though he cherished life, than of being shot in cold blood on a false pretext such as resisting arrest, a thing he was far too sensible to do. 'If anything goes wrong,' he told Marshall, 'you'll know what to think.' He gave Marshall names and addresses of people to be informed in such an event.

Upon his release from 'The Cooler' Bushell flung himself with such intensity into the theory and practice of escape that, after playing minor roles in several escape bids, he rose rapidly through posts of ascending seniority in the Escape Organisation to Intelligence Officer, and finally to its top position—Chief Executive or 'Big X' of the North Compound. He studied case histories and learned from past mistakes; organised departments to take care of clothing, forged documents, rations, logistics, engineering and security, presiding over his cabinet like a prime minister. His nimble brain cut through to essentials quickly.

Three tunnels were to be constructed, and they were to be of such refinement that discovery of any one would lead to the belief that it must be the only one. To avoid danger of a security leak the word 'tunnel' was banned from all discussion. They were to be called 'Tom', 'Dick' and 'Harry'.

As 'Big X' Bushell introduced a new and important concept—that of collectivism, the abandonment of unco-ordinated private enterprise and concentration on a highly efficient and centralised organisation. As a corollary, there were to be no more inflexible timetables, and if for any reason the guards' (or 'ferrets') suspicions were aroused, all work was to cease immediately and not to be resumed until the security department gave the all-clear.

New arrivals at the compound were always impressed by their first encounter with Bushell, when he grilled them on what they had seen of the local area. His rather sinister appearance, with the gash over one eye, his forceful personality and well-developed powers of interrogation lent an awe-inspiring quality to the grim and clandestine surroundings of an improvised headquarters.

His intensity of purpose partially concealed a gentleness that was very real. 'Goon baiting'—playing practical jokes on the guards and undermining their morale—was an understood responsibility of the prisoner, not just a game. Despite his mastery of the art, Bushell sometimes expressed a compulsive remorse. 'It's not really fair,' he would say, 'some of these poor bastards are so simple they haven't a chance.'

'Tom' was discovered by sentries, and 'Dick' was then used solely as a repository for sand as work proceeded with 'Harry', now the only chance. Food and escape equipment was provided by the organisation for over two hundred escapers, considered the most optimistic estimate of the number which would get through the tunnel before it was discovered. If everything worked perfectly it would be possible for one man to go through every two minutes, making a total of two hundred and fifty during the eight hours of darkness. Long experience had taught, however, that there would always be hitches beyond the planners' control.

'Harry' was a miracle of planning and improvisation. With a length of 336 feet, 28 feet deep at the entrance in the north compound and 20 feet high at the exit among trees outside the double electrified wiring, it was furnished with electric lighting, manually operated air conditioning and relays of trolleys connecting three 'half-way houses' to carry prone escapers singly to the far end. 'Harry' had taken two hundred and fifty men working full time a year to dispose of the sand it displaced. A highly co-ordinated teamwork was devised to despatch the maximum number of men in the minimum time. Except for about forty priorities who were thought to have the best chance of reaching England, each man on the escape list got there by drawing from a hat. He had his belongings checked by the inspection committee to obviate jamming in the tunnel through the carrying of excessively bulky packages, was given an allotted time to arrive at Hut 104, which housed the entrance, and was thoroughly indoctrinated in his drill.

The organisation fixed the night of 24th March 1944 as the one for the break-out, twelve months after the commencement of work on 'Tom', 'Dick' and 'Harry'. Every known factor had been weighed: the weather would be suitable for travellers on foot ('walkers'); there would be no moon; a strong wind would disturb the adjacent pine forest and drown any sounds made by leaving the tunnel.

From mid-day the engineers finished off final details, connecting wiring and installing extra lights, while the forgery department filled in dates on the forged papers. A little after nine o'clock two engineers went to open the exit. Every man was in his place, and zero hour was nine-thirty. Then there occurred a train of mishaps: there was a delay in opening the shaft, and not until ten o'clock did those waiting down the shaft feel the gust of cool air which told them the surface had been broken. Word was then passed back that the exit, contrary to plan, was several yards short of the trees. As the papers were all date-stamped Bushell decided that the escape must continue, and hurriedly conferred with his colleagues on the escape committee to work out a revised method of control at the exit, necessary to avoid detection by the guards in their look-out posts. As the escapers moved forward on their trollies, further delays were caused by those who had broken the baggage regulations and got stuck in the tunnel with the bulkiness of their suitcases. The rate of departure dropped from two to twelve minutes per man. To add to these complications, an unexpected air raid on Berlin caused the camp electricity to be switched off, and with it the tunnel lighting. Over half an hour was lost as margarine lamps were substituted.

Bushell was noticed to be calm but more thoughtful than usual. Dressed as a businessman he had teamed up with Lieutenant Scheidhauer of the Free French Air Force, with whom he planned to travel by train to Alsace. Both were on the priority list and were among the first to leave. As the delays multiplied Bushell, in smart civilian suit and converted service overcoat, with astrakhan collar and felt hat, an efficient-looking briefcase in his hand, glanced at his watch and called down the shaft: 'Tell those devils to get a move on; I've got a train to catch.'

Bushell and Scheidhauer caught their train at Sagan station. Two days later, during the most extensive search the Reich had ever been forced to mount for escaped prisoners of war, they were recaptured at Saarbruecken railway station by security policeman and taken to Lerchesflur gaol. There they were interrogated by the Kriminal-polizei and admitted being escapers from Stalag Luft III.

When he learned of the escape, Hitler was incensed; he was angered at the tying-up of German resources in a time of great national stress and particularly afraid of an uprising among the foreign workers. At a stormy meeting with Goering, Himmler and Keitel, he gave instructions for the prisoners to be shot.

On orders received by teleprinter from Gestapo headquarters in Berlin, Bushell and Scheidhauer were handcuffed behind their backs and driven in a car along the autobahn leading to Kaiserslauten. The car was stopped after a few miles, the handcuffs removed, and the prisoners allowed to get out and relieve themselves. They must have known what was coming. Both were shot in the back, Scheidhauer dying instantly, Bushell after a few minutes. It was 28th March 1944.

Seventy-six prisoners escaped through the tunnel. Three made 'home runs', the rest were recaptured. Of these, the Gestapo shot fifty.

P.R. REID
Home Run from Colditz

Pat Reid was the British officer in charge of escape-planning at Schloss Colditz, the most impregnable of the German POW camps of World War II. This is the story of his own escape in 1942.

IT WAS OCTOBER 14TH. As evening approached, the four of us made final preparations. I said '*Au revoir* till tomorrow' to Van den Heuvel, and to Rupert, Harry, Peter Allan, and Kenneth and Dick. Rupert was to be our kitchen-window stooge. We donned our civilian clothing, and covered this with army trousers and greatcoats. Civilian overcoats were made into neat bundles.

In parenthesis, I should explain why we had to wear the military clothes over everything. At any time a wandering Goon might appear as we waited our moment to enter the kitchen, and there might even be delays. Further, we had to think of 'informers'—among the foreign orderlies, for example, who were always wandering about. If orderlies saw one of us leap through the kitchen window, it was just too bad—we might be after food—but it would be far worse if they saw a number of civilian-clothed officers in a staircase lobby—the orderlies' staircase as it happened—waiting, apparently, for their taxi to arrive!

Our suitcases were surrounded with blankets to muffle sound, and we carried enough sheets and blankets to make a fifty-foot descent, if necessary. Later we would wear balaclava helmets and gloves; no white skin was to be visible. Darkness and the shadows were to be our friends, we could not afford to offend them. Only our eyes and noses would be exposed. All light-coloured garments were excluded. We carried thick socks to put over our shoes. This is the most silent method of movement I know, barring removal of one's shoes—which we were to do for the crossing of the sentry's path.

Squadron-Leader MacColm was to accompany us into the kitchen in order to bend the window bar back into place and seal up the window after we had gone. He would have to conceal the military clothing we left behind in the kitchen and make his exit the next morning after the kitchen was unlocked. He could hide in one of the enormous cauldrons so long as he did not oversleep and have himself served up with the soup next day.

Immediately after the evening *Appell* we were ready and started on the first leg of our long journey. It was 6.30 p.m.

I was used to the drill of the entry window by now. At the nodded signal from Rupert, I acted automatically; a run, a leap to the sill, one arm through the cracked pane of glass, up with the window lever, withdraw arm carefully, open window—without noise—jump through, and close again softly. I was through. Only two had done it before at any one session. The question was, would five succeed? One after another they came. At least, they had not the window-lever latch to bother about.

The sentry was behaving himself. At regular intervals, as he turned his back, the signal was given. I could not see Rupert—but he was timing perfectly. I could see the sentry from behind the window throughout his beat.

Each time, as the sentry turned away, I heard a gentle scurry. I automatically opened the window, in jumped a body, and I closed the window again, breathing a heavy sigh. The drill was becoming automatic. It was taking as little as five seconds. Then, suddenly, just as the last of the five was due, I sensed—I do not know how—an uncertainty, a hesitation in the manner of the sentry as he turned away. I knew that he would behave oddly during this beat. My heart was in my mouth, for I expected to hear the scurry and anticipated a clash. But there was no scurry, and in the next instant the sentry stopped dead and turned around! It was nothing less than intuition on Rupert's part that saved us.

On the next turn of the sentry's beat, I heard the scurry, opened and closed again. At last all five of us were safe.

We removed our military clothing and handed it to MacColm.

I set about the window overlooking the German courtyard, and as darkness fell and the floodlights went on, I heaved on the bar until it was bent horizontal, and immediately attached to the unbent portion a long strip of black-painted cardboard resembling the bar. This hung downwards in the correct position and camouflaged the opening.

'All set!' I whispered to the others. 'I'm going out now. Hank! Wait until I'm hidden by the shadows of the large ventilator out there. Then join me as quickly as you can. Billie and Ronnie, remember not to follow until we have crossed the sentry's path safely.'

I squirmed through the hole in the bars on to the flat roof beyond. The roof joined the kitchen wall just below our window-sill. I crept quietly forward in a blaze of light. The eyes of a hundred windows glared down upon me.

The impression was appalling. 'Does nobody ever look out of a window at night?' I kept asking myself.

Happily there was shelter from the glare about halfway across the roof. The high square ventilator provided a deep shadow behind which I crawled. Hank soon followed. The sentry plied his beat not fifteen yards away.

For several days we had arranged music practices in the evenings in the senior officers' quarters (the theatre block). The music was to be used for signalling, and we had to accustom the sentry in front of us to a certain amount of noise. While Major Anderson (Andy) played the oboe, Colonel George Young played the concertina, and Douglas Bader, keeping watch from a window, acted as conductor. Their room was on the third floor, overlooking the German courtyard. Bader could see our sentry for the whole length of his beat. He was to start the practice at 7.30 p.m., when the traffic in the courtyard had died down. From 8 p.m. onwards he was to keep rigid control on the players so that they only stopped their music when the sentry was in a suitable position for us to cross his path. It was not imperative that they stopped playing every time the sentry turned his back, but when they stopped playing that meant we could move. We arranged this signalling system because, once on the ground, we would have little concealment, and what little there was, provided by an angle in the wall of the outbuildings, prevented us from seeing the sentry.

At 8 p.m. Hank and I crawled once more into the limelight and over the remainder of the roof, dropping to the ground over a loose, noisy gutter which gave me the jitters. In the dark angle of the wall, with our shoes around our necks and our suitcases under our arms, we waited for the music to stop. The players had been playing light jaunty airs—and then ran the gauntlet of our popular-song books. At 8 p.m. they changed to classical music; it gave them more excuse for stopping. Bader had seen us drop from the roof and would see us cross the sentry's path. The players were in the middle of Haydn's oboe concerto when they stopped.

'I shall make this a trial run,' I thought.

I advanced quickly five yards to the end of the wall concealing us, and regarded the sentry. He was fidgety and looked up at Bader's window twice during the five seconds' view I had of his back. Before me was the roadway, a cobbled surface seven yards wide. Beyond was the end of a shed and some friendly concealing shrubbery. As the sentry turned, the music started again. Our players had chosen a piece the Germans love. I only hoped the sentry would not be exasperated by their repeated interruptions. The next time they stopped we would go.

The music ceased abruptly and I ran—but it started again just as I reached the corner. I stopped dead and retired hurriedly. This happened twice. Then I heard German voices through the music. It was the duty officer on his rounds. He was questioning the sentry. He was suspicious. I heard gruff orders given.

Five minutes later I was caught napping—the music stopped while I was ruminating on the cause of the duty officer's interrogation and I was not on my toes. A late dash was worse than none. I stood still and waited. I waited a long time and the music did not begin again. A quarter of an hour passed and there was still no music. Obviously something had gone wrong upstairs. I decided therefore to wait an hour in order to let suspicions die down. We had the whole night before us, and I was not going to spoil the ship for a ha'p'orth o'tar.

All this time Hank was beside me—not a word passed his lips—not a murmur or comment to distract us from the job on hand.

In the angle of the wall where we hid, there was a door. We tried the handle and found it was open, so we entered in pitch-darkness and, passing through a second door, we took temporary refuge in a room which had a small window and contained, as far as we could see, only rubbish—wastepaper, empty bottles, and empty food-tins. Outside, in the angle of the wall, any Goon with extra-sharp eyesight, passing along the roadway, would spot us. The sentry himself was also liable to extend his beat without warning and take a look around the corner of the wall where we had been hiding. In the rubbish room we were much safer.

We had been in there five minutes when, suddenly, there was a rustling of paper, a crash of falling tins, and a jangling of overturned bottles—a noise fit to waken the dead. We froze with horror. A cat leaped out from among the refuse and tore out of the room as if the devil was after it.

'That's finished everything,' I exclaimed. 'The Jerries will be here in a moment to investigate.'

'The darn thing was after a mouse, I think,' said Hank. 'Let's make the best of things, anyway. They may only flash a torch round casually and we may get away with it if we try to look like a couple of sacks in the corner.'

'Quick, then,' I rejoined. 'Grab those piles of newspapers and let's spread them out a little over our heads. It's our only hope.'

We did so and waited, with our hearts thumping. Five minutes passed, and then ten, and still nobody came. We began to breathe again.

Soon our hour's vigil was over. It was 9.45 p.m. and I resolved to carry on. All was silent in the courtyard. I could now hear the sentry's footsteps clearly—approaching—and then receding. Choosing our moment, we advanced to the end of the wall as he turned on his beat. I peeped around the corner. He was ten yards off and marching away from us. The courtyard was empty. I tiptoed quickly across the roadway with Hank at my heels. Reaching the wall of the shed on the other side, we had just time to crouch behind the shrubbery before he turned. He had heard nothing. On his next receding beat we crept behind the shed, and hid in a small shrubbery, which bordered the main steps and veranda in front of the entrance to the *Kommandantur*.

The first leg of our escape was behind us. I dropped my suitcase and reconnoitred the next stage of our journey, which was to the 'pit'. Watching the sentry, I crept quickly along the narrow grass verge at the edge of the path leading away from the main steps. On one side was the path and on the other side was a long flower-bed; beyond that the balustrade of the *Kommandantur* veranda. I was in light shadow and had to crouch as I moved. Reaching the pit, about twenty-five yards away, before the sentry turned, I looked over the edge. There was a wooden trestle with steps. The pit was not deep. I dropped into it. A brick tunnel from the pit ran underneath the veranda and gave perfect concealment. That was enough. As I emerged again, I distinctly heard noises from the direction of the roofs over which we had climbed. Ronnie and Billie, who had witnessed our crossing of the roadway, were following. The sentry apparently heard nothing.

I began to creep back to the shrubbery where Hank was waiting. I was nearly halfway when, without warning, heavy footsteps sounded; a Goon was approaching quickly from the direction of the main Castle gateway and around the corner of the Castle building into sight. In a flash I was flat on my face on the grass verge, and lay rigid, just as he turned the corner and headed up the path straight towards me. He could not fail to see me. I waited for the end. He approached nearer and nearer with noisy footsteps crunching on the gravel. He was level with me. It was all over. I waited for his ejaculation at my discovery—for his warning shout to the sentry—for the familiar '*Hände hoch!*'—and the feel of his pistol in my back between the shoulder-blades.

The crunching footsteps continued past me and retreated. He mounted the steps and entered the *Kommandantur*.

After a moment's pause to recover, I crept the remainder of the distance to the shrubbery and, as I did so, Ronnie and Billie appeared from the other direction.

Before long we were all safe in the pit without further alarms, the second lap completed! We had time to relax for a moment.

I asked Billie: 'How did you get on crossing the sentry's beat?'

'We saw you two cross over and it looked as easy as pie. That gave us confidence. We made one trial, and then crossed the second time. Something went wrong with the music, didn't it?'

'Yes, that's why we held up proceedings so long,' I answered. 'We had a lucky break when they stopped for the last time. I thought it was the signal to move, but I was too late off the mark, thank God! I'd probably have run into the sentry's arms!'

'What do you think happened?' asked Ronnie.

'I heard the duty officer asking questions,' I explained. 'I think they suspected the music practice was phoney. They probably went upstairs and stopped it.'

Changing the subject, I said: 'I heard you coming over the roof. I was sure the sentry could have heard.'

'We made a noise at one point, I remember,' said Ronnie, 'but it wasn't anything to speak of. It's amazing what you can hear if your ears are expecting certain sounds. The sentry was probably thinking of his girl friend at that moment.'

'If it wasn't for girl friends,' I chimed in, 'we probably wouldn't be on this mad jaunt anyway, so it cuts both ways,' and I nudged Hank.

'It's time I got to work,' I added grimly.

My next job was to try to open the door of the building which I have described as the one from which our medium-sized officer escaped. The door was fifteen yards away; it was in deep shadow, though the area between the door and the pit was only in semi-darkness. Again watching the sentry, I crept carefully to the door, and then started work with a set of *passe-partout* keys I had brought with me. I had one unnerving interruption, when I heard Priem's voice in the distance returning from the town. I had just sufficient time to creep back to the pit and hide, before he came around the corner.

We laughed inwardly as he passed by us along the path talking loudly to another officer. I could not help thinking of the occasion when he stood outside Gephard's office and did not have the door unlocked!

Poor old Priem! He was not a bad type on the whole. He had a sense of humour which made him almost human.

It was 11 p.m. when Priem passed by. I worked for an hour on the door without success and finally gave up. We were checked, and would have to find another exit.

We felt our way along the tunnel leading from the pit under the veranda, and after eight yards came to a large cellar with a low arched ceiling supported on pillars. It had something to do with sewage, for Hank, at one point, stepped off solid ground and nearly fell into what might have been deep water! He must have disturbed a scum on top of the liquid because a dreadful stench arose. When I was well away from the entrance, I struck a match. There was a solitary wheelbarrow for furniture, and at the far end of the cavern-like cellar, a chimney flue. I had previously noticed a faint glimmer of light from this direction. Examining the flue, I found it was an air-vent which led vertically upwards from the ceiling of the cavern for about four feet, and then curved outwards towards the fresh air. Hank pushed me up the flue. In plan it was about nine inches by three feet. I managed to wriggle myself high enough to see around the curve. The flue ended at the vertical face of a wall two feet away from me as a barred opening shaped like a letter-box slot. The opening was at the level of the ground outside, and was situated on the far side of the building—the moat side for which we were heading, but it was a practical impossibility to negotiate this flue. There were bars, and in any case only a pigmy could have wriggled round the curve.

We held a conference.

'We seem to have struck a dead end,' I started; 'this place is a cul-de-sac and I can't manage the door either. I'm terribly sorry, but there we are!'

'Can anyone think of another way out?' asked Ronnie.

'The main gateway, I think, is out of the question,' I went on. 'Since Neave's escape nearly a year ago, they lock the inner gate this side of the bridge over the moat. That means we can't reach the side gate leading down into the moat.'

'Our only hope is through the *Kommandantur*,' suggested Billie. 'We can try it either now, and hope to get through unseen—or else try it early in the morning when there's a little traffic about and some doors may be unlocked.'

'Do you really think we'll ever pass scrutiny at that hour?' questioned Ronnie. 'If we must take that route, I think it's better to try it at about 3 a.m. when the whole camp is dead asleep.'

I was thinking how impossibly foolhardy was the idea of going through the *Kommandantur*. I remembered that other attempt—years ago now it seemed— when we had pumped men through the hole in the lavatory into the *Kommandantur*. I had considered then that the idea was mad. I thought aloud:

'There are only three known entrances to the *Kommandantur*: the main front door, the French windows behind, which open on to the grass patch right in front of a sentry, and the little door under the archway leading to the park. The archway gate is locked and the door is the wrong side of it.'

In desperation, I said: 'I'm going to have another look at the flue.'

This time I removed some of my clothing and found I could slide more easily up the shaft. I examined the bars closely and found one was loose in its mortar socket. As I did so, I heard footsteps outside the opening and a Goon patrol approached. The Goon had an Alsatian with him. A heavy pair of boots trampled past me. I could have touched them with my hand. The dog pattered behind and did not see me. I imagine the smell issuing from the flue obliterated my scent.

I succeeded in loosening one end of the bar and bent it nearly double. Slipping down into the cellar again, I whispered to the others: 'There's a vague chance we may be able to squeeze through the flue. Anyway, it's worth trying. We shall have to strip completely naked.'

'Hank and Billie will never make it,' said Ronnie. 'It's impossible; they're too big. You and I might manage it with help at both ends—with someone pushing below and someone else pulling from above.'

'I think I can make it,' I rejoined, 'If someone stands on the wheelbarrow and helps to push me through. Once I'm out, I can do the pulling. Hank had better come next. If he can make it, we all can.'

Hank was over six feet tall and Billie nearly six feet. Ronnie and I were smaller, and Ronnie was very thin.

'Neither Hank nor I,' intervened Billie, 'will ever squeeze around the curve on our tummies. Our knees are not double-jointed and our legs will stick. We'll have to come out on our backs.'

'Agreed,' I said. 'Then I go first, Hank next, then Billie and Ronnie last. Ronnie, you'll have no one to push you, but if two of us grab your arms and pull, we should manage it. Be careful undressing. Don't leave anything behind—we want to leave no traces. Hand your clothes to me in neat bundles, and your suitcases. I'll dispose of them temporarily outside.'

After a tremendous struggle, I succeeded in squeezing through the chimney and sallied forth naked on to the path outside. Bending down into the flue again, I could just reach Hank's hand as he passed me up my clothes and my suitcase, and then his own. I hid the kit in some bushes near the path and put on enough dark clothing to make me inconspicuous. Hank was stripped and struggling in the hole with his back towards me. I managed to grab one arm and heaved, while he was pushed from below. Inch by inch he advanced and at the end of twenty minutes, with a last wrench, I pulled him clear. He was bruised all over and streaming with perspiration. During all that time we were at the mercy of any passer-by. What a spectacle it must have been—a naked man being squeezed through a hole in the wall like toothpaste out of a tube! To the imaginative-minded in the eerie darkness, it must have looked as if the massive walls of the Castle were slowly descending upon the man's body while his comrade was engaged in a desperate tug-of-war to save his life!

Hank retired to the bushes to recover and dress himself.

Next came Billie's clothes and suitcase, and then Billie himself. I extracted him in about fifteen minutes. Then Ronnie's kit arrived. I gave him a sheet on which to pull in order to begin his climb. After that, two of us set about him, and he was out in about ten minutes. We all collapsed in the bushes for a breather. It was about 3.30 a.m. and we had completed the third leg of our marathon.

'What do you think of our chances now?' I asked Billie.

'I'm beyond thinking of chances,' was the reply, 'but I know I shall never forget this night as long as I live.'

'I hope you've got all your kit,' I said, smiling at him in the darkness.

'I should hate to have to push you back down the shaft to fetch it!'

'I'd give anything for a smoke,' sighed Billie.

'I see no reason why you shouldn't smoke as we walk past the barracks if you feel like it. What cigarettes have you got?'

'Gold Flake, I think.'

'Exactly! You'd better start chain-smoking, because you'll have to throw the rest away before you reach Leisnig. Had you thought of that?'

'But I've got fifty!'

'Too bad,' I replied. 'With luck you've got about three hours; that's seventeen cigarettes an hour. Can you do it?'

'I'll try,' said Billie ruefully.

A German was snoring loudly in a room with the window open, a few yards away. The flue through which we had just climbed gave on to a narrow path running along the top of the moat immediately under the main Castle walls. The bushes we hid in were on the very edge of the moat. The moat wall was luckily stepped into three successive descents.

The drops were about eighteen feet and the steps were about two yards wide, with odd shrubs and grass growing on them. A couple of sheets were made ready. After half an hour's rest, and fully clothed once more, we dropped down one by one. I went last and fell into the arms of those below me.

On the way down, Billie suddenly developed a tickle in his throat and started a cough which disturbed the dogs. They began barking in their kennels, which we saw for the first time, uncomfortably near the route we were to take. Billie in desperation ate a quantity of grass and earth, which seemed to stop the irritation in his throat. By the time we reached the bottom of the moat it was 4.30 a.m. The fourth leg was completed.

We tidied our clothes and adjusted the socks over our shoes. In a few moments we would have to pass underneath a lamp at the corner of the road leading to the German barracks. This was the road leading to the double gates in the outer wall around the Castle grounds. It was the road taken by Neave and by Van Doorninck.

The lamp was situated in full view of a sentry—luckily, some forty-five yards away—who would be able to contemplate our back silhouettes as we turned the corner and faded into the darkness beyond.

The dogs had ceased barking. Hank and I moved off first—over a small railing, on to a path, past the kennels, down some steps, round the corner under the light, and away into the darkness. We walked leisurely, side by side, as if we were inmates of the barracks returning after a night's carousal in the town.

Before passing the barracks I had one last duty to perform—to give those in the camp an idea as to what we had done, to indicate whether other escapers would be able to follow our route or not. I had half a dozen pieces of white cardboard cut into various shapes—a square, an oblong, a triangle, a circle, and so on. Dick Howe and I had arranged a code whereby each shape gave him some information. I threw certain of the cards down on to a small grass patch below the road, past which our exercise parade marched on their way to the park. With luck, if the parade was not cancelled for a week, Dick would see the cards. My message ran:

'Exit from pit. Moat easy; no traces left.'

Although I had pulled the bar of the flue exit back into place, we had, in truth, probably left minor traces. But as the alternative message was: 'Exit obvious to Goons'—which would have been the case, for instance, if we left fifty feet of sheet-rope dangling from a window—I preferred to encourage other escapers to have a shot at following us.

We continued another hundred yards past the barracks, where the garrison was peacefully sleeping, and arrived at our last obstacle—the outer wall. It was only ten feet high here, with coils of barbed wire stretched along the top. I was on the wall heaving Hank up, when, with a sudden pounding of my heart, I noticed the glow of a cigarette in the distance. It was approaching. Then I realised it was Billie. They had caught us up. We had arranged a discreet gap between us so that we did not look like a regiment passing under the corner lamp.

The barbed wire did not present a serious obstacle when tackled without hurry and with minute care. We were all eventually over the wall, but none too soon, because we had a long way to go in order to be safe before dawn. It was 5.15 in the morning, and the fifth leg of the marathon was over. The sixth and last stage—the long journey to Switzerland—lay ahead of us!

We shook hands all round and with '*Au revoir*—see you in Switzerland in a few days,' Hank and I set off along the road. Two hundred yards behind us, the other two followed. Soon they branched off on their route and we took to the fields.

As we trudged along, Hank fumbled for a long time in his pockets, and then uttered practically the first words he had spoken during the whole night. He said:

'I reckon, Pat, I must have left my pipe at the top of the moat.'

Hank and I walked fast. We intended to lie up for a day. Therefore, in order to be at all safe we had to put the longest distance possible between ourselves and the camp. We judged the German search would be concentrated in the direction of a village about five miles away, for which Ronnie and Billie headed and in which there was a railway station. The first train was shortly before morning *Appell*. Provided there was no alarm in the camp before then, and if the two of them could reach the station in time for the train (which now seemed probable), they would be in Leipzig before the real search started. This was the course Lulu Lawton had taken, but he had missed the train and had to hide up in a closely hunted area.

Hank and I chose a difficult route, calculated to put the hunters off the scent. We headed first south and then westwards in a big sweep in the direction of the River Mulde which ran due northwards towards the Elbe. In order to reach a railway station we had to trek about twenty miles and cross the river into the bargain. It was not a 'cushy' escape-route and we relied on the Germans thinking likewise.

We walked for about an hour and a half, and when it was almost daylight entered a wood and hid up in a thicket for the day. We must have been five miles away from the camp. Although we tried to sleep, our nerves were as taut as piano wires. I was on the alert the whole day.

'A wild animal must have magnificent nerves,' I said to Hank at one point.

'Wild animals have nerves just like you and I. That's why they are not captured easily,' was his comment.

Hank was not going to be easy to catch. His fiancée had been waiting for him since the night when he took off in his bomber in April 1940. It would plainly require more than a few tough Germans to recapture him. It gave me confidence to know he was beside me.

I mused for a long time over the queer twists that Fate gives to our lives. I had always assumed that Rupert and I would escape finally together. Yet it happened to be Hank's turn, and here we were. I had left old and tried friends behind me. Two years of constant companionship had cemented some of us together very closely. 'Rupert, Harry, Dick, Kenneth and Peter. Would I ever see them again?' Inside the camp the probability of early failure in the escape was so great that we brushed aside all serious thought of a long parting.

Here in the woods it was different. If I did my job properly from now on, it was probable that I would never see them again. We were not going back to Colditz; Hank was sure of that too. I was rather shaken by the thought, realising fully for the first time what these men meant to me. We had been through much together. I prayed that we might all survive the war and meet again.

As dusk fell we set off across the fields. Sometimes when roads led in our direction we used them, but we had to be very careful. On one occasion we only just left the road in time as we saw a light ahead (unusual in the blackout) and heard voices. A car approaching was stopped. As we by-passed the light by way of the fields, we saw an army motor-cyclist talking to a sentry. It was a control and they were after us. We passed within fifty yards of them!

It seemed a long way to the river. As the night wore on, I could hardly keep my eyes open. I stumbled and dozed as I walked, and finally gave up.

'Hank, I'll have to lie down for an hour and sleep. I've been sleep-walking as it is. I don't know where we're going.'

'OK. I'll stay on guard while you pass out on that bank over there under the tree,' said Hank, indicating a mound of grass looming ahead of us.

He woke me in an hour and we continued, eventually reaching the river. It was in a deep cutting, down which we climbed, and there was a road which ran along its bank. Towards our left, crossing the river and the cutting, was a high-level railway bridge. I decided to cross it. We had to reclimb the cutting. Sleep was overcoming me once more. The climb was steep and over huge rocks cut into steps like those of the pyramids. It was a nightmare climb in the pitch-darkness, as I repeatedly stumbled, fell down, and slept where I lay. Hank would tug at me, pull me over the next huge stone and set me on my feet without a word, only to have to repeat the performance again in a few moments. Halfway up the embankment we stopped to rest. I slept, but Hank was on the qui vive and, peering through the darkness, noticed a movement on the railway bridge. It needed a cat's eye to notice anything at all. He shook me and said:

'Pat, we're not going over that bridge; it's guarded.'

'How the hell do you know for certain?' I asked, 'and how are we going to cross the river, then?'

'I don't mind if we have to swim it, but I'm not crossing that bridge.'

I gave way, though it meant making a big half-circle, crossing the railway line and descending to the river again somewhere near a road bridge which we knew existed farther upstream.

Reaching the top of the railway-bridge embankment we crossed the lines, and as we did so we saw in the distance from the direction of the bridge the flash of a lighted match.

'Did you see that?' I whispered.

'Yes.'

'There's a sentry on the bridge, sure enough. You were right, Hank. Thank God you insisted.'

Gradually we edged down the hill again where the river cutting was less steep, and found that our bearings had not been too bad; for we saw the road bridge in the foreground. We inspected it carefully before crossing, listening for a long time for any sound of movement. It was unguarded. We crossed rapidly and took to the bushes on the far side, not a moment too soon; a motor-cycle came roaring round a bend, its headlights blazing, and crossed the bridge in the direction from which we had come.

We tramped wearily across country on a compass bearing until dawn. Near the village of Penig, where our railway station was situated, we spruced ourselves up, attempted a shave and polished our shoes. We entered the village—it was almost a small industrial town—and wended our way in the direction of the station. I was loth to ask our way at this time of the morning when few people were about. Instead, we wandered onwards past some coalyards where a tram-line started. The tracks ran alongside a large factory and then switched over to the other side of the road, passing under trees and beside a small river. We followed the lines, which eventually crossed a bridge and entered the town proper. I was sure the tram-lines would lead us to the station. The town was dingy, not at all like Colditz, which was of pleasing appearance. Upkeep had evidently gone to the dogs. Broken window-panes were filled with newspaper, ironwork was rusty, and the front doors of the houses, which opened directly on the street, badly needed a coat of paint.

We arrived at the railway station. It was on the far edge of the town and looked older and out of keeping with the buildings around it. It had a staid respectable atmosphere and belonged to a period before industry had come to Penig. We entered and looked up the trains. Our route was Munich via Zwickau. I saw we had a three-hour wait and then another long wait at Zwickau before the night express for Munich. Leaving the station, we walked out into the country again and settled down for a meal and a rest behind a barn near the road. It is dangerous to wait in railway stations or public parks and advisable to keep moving under any circumstances when in a town.

We returned to the station towards midday. I bought two third-class tickets to Munich and we caught the train comfortably. Our suitcases were a definite asset. My German accent was anything but perfect, but the brandishing of my suitcase on all occasions to emphasise whatever I happened to be saying worked like a soporific on the Germans.

In Zwickau, having another long wait, we boarded a tram. I tripped on the mounting-step and nearly knocked the conductress over. I apologised loudly.

'*Entschuldigen Sie mich! Bitte, entschuldigen, entschuldilgen! Ich bib ein Ausländer.*'

We sat down, and when the conductress came round I beamed at her and asked in broken German:

'*Gnädige Fräulein!* If you please, where is the nearest cinema? We have a long time to wait for our train and would like to see a film and the news pictures. We are foreigners and do not know this town.'

'The best cinema in Zwickau is five minutes from here. I shall tell you where to alight.'

'How much is the fare, please, *Fräulein*?'

'Twenty pfennigs each, if you please.'

'*Danke schön*,' I said, proffering the money.

After five minutes the tram stopped at a main thoroughfare junction and the conductress beckoned to us. As we alighted, one of the passengers pointed out to us with a voluble and, to me, incoherent stream of German exactly where the cinema was. I could gather that he was proud to meet foreigners who were working for the victory of 'Unser Reich'! He took off his moth-eaten hat as we parted and waved a courteous farewell.

Zwickau was just a greatly enlarged Penig as far as I could see. Dilapidation was visible everywhere. The inhabitants gave me an impression of impoverishment, and only the uniforms of officials, including the tram conductress, and those of the armed forces bore a semblance of smartness.

Hank and I spent a comfortable two hours in the cinema, which was no different from any other I have seen. German officers and troops were dotted about in seats all around us and made up ninety per cent of the audience. I dozed for a long time and I noticed Hank's head drooping too. After two hours I whispered to him:

'It's time to go. What did you think of the film?'

'What I saw of it was a washout,' Hank replied. 'I must have slept though, because I missed parts of it. It was incoherent.'

'This cinema seems to be nothing more than impromptu sleeping-quarters. Look around you,' and I nudged Hank. The German Army and Air Force were dozing in all sorts of postures around us!

'Let's go,' I said, and, yawning repeatedly, we rose and left the auditorium.

Returning to the station in good time, we boarded the express to Munich. It was crowded out, for which I was glad, and Hank and I spent the whole night standing in the corridor. Nobody paid any attention to us. We might as well have been in an express bound from London to the North. The lighting, however, was so bad that few passengers attempted to read. It was intensely stuffy owing to the overcrowding, the cold outside, and the blackout curtains on all windows. The hypnotic drumming and the swaying of the train pervaded all.

Our fellow-travellers were a mixed bag; a few army and air force other ranks, some workmen, and a majority of down-at-heel-looking business men or Government officials. There was not a personality among them; all were sheep ready to be slaughtered at the altar of Hitler. There was a police control in the early hours. I produced my much-soiled German leather wallet, which exposed my identity card or *Ausweis* behind a grimy scratched piece of celluloid. The police officer was curt:

'*Sie sind Auslander?*'

'*Jawohl.*'

'*Wo fahren Sie hin?*'

'*Nach München und Rottweil.*'

'*Warum?*'

'*Betonarbeit*' (that is, concrete work).

Hank was slow in producing his papers. I said:

'*Wir sind zusammen. Er ist mein Kamerad.*'

Hank proffered his papers as I added, taking the officer into my confidence:

'*Er ist etwas dumm, aber ein guter Kerl.*'

The control passed on and we relaxed into a fitful doze as we roared through the night towards Munich—and Switzerland.

We arrived in Munich in the cold grey of the morning—several hours late. There had been bombing and train diversions.

I queued up at the booking-office, telling Hank to stand by. When my turn came I asked for, '*Zweimal dritte Klasse, nach Rottweil.*' The woman behind the grill said:

'*Fünfundsechzig Mark, bitte.*'

I produced fifty-six marks, which almost drained me right out. The woman repeated:

'*Fünfundsechzig Mark, bitte—noch neun Mark.*'

I was confusing the German for fifty-six with sixty-five.

'*Karl*,' I shouted in Hank's direction, '*geben Sie mir noch zehn Mark.*'

Hank took the cue, and produced a ten-mark note which I handed to the woman.

'*Ausweis, bitte*,' she said.

I produced it.

'*Gut*,' and she handed my wallet back to me.

I was so relieved that as I left the queue, forgetting my part completely, I said in a loud voice:

'All right, Hank, I've got the tickets!'

I nearly froze in my tracks. As we hurried away I felt the baleful glare of a hundred eyes burning through my back. We were soon lost in the crowd, and what a crowd! Everybody seemed to be travelling. The station appeared to be untouched by bombing and traffic was obviously running at high pressure. We had another long wait for the train which would take us to Rottweil via Ulm and Tuttlingen. I noted with relief that the wait in Ulm was only ten minutes. Hyde-Thompson and his Dutch colleague, the second two officers of my theatre escape, had been trapped in Ulm station. The name carried foreboding and I prayed we would negotiate this junction safely. I also noticed with appreciation that there was a substantial wait at Tuttlingen for the train to Rottweil. It would give us an excuse for leaving the station.

In Munich I felt safe. The waiting-rooms were full to overflowing and along with other passengers we were even shepherded by station police to an underground bomb-proof waiting-room—signposted for the use of all persons having longer than half an hour to wait for a train.

Before descending to this waiting-room, however, I asked for the *Bahnhofswirtschaft* and roving along the counter I saw a notice '*Markenfreies Essen*', which meant 'coupon-free meals'! I promptly asked for two and also *Zwei Liter Pilsner*. They were duly served and Hank and I sat down at a table by ourselves to the best meal provided us by the Germans in two and a half years. The *Markenfreies Essen* consisted of a very generous helping of thick stew—mostly vegetable and potatoes, but some good-tasting sausage-meat was floating around as well. The beer seemed excellent to our parched gullets. We had not drunk anything since our repast on the outskirts of Penig when we had finished the water we carried with us.

We went to the underground waiting-room. We were controlled once in a cursory manner. I was blasé by now and smiled benignly at the burly representative of the *Sicherheitspolizei*—security police—as he passed by, hardly glancing at the wallets we pushed under his nose.

In good time we boarded the train for Ulm. Arriving there at midday, we changed platforms without incident and quickly boarded our next train. This did not go direct to Rottweil, but necessitated changing at Tuttlingen. Rottweil was thirty miles, but Tuttlingen only fifteen miles from the frontier! My intention was to walk out of the station at Tuttlingen with the excuse of waiting for the Rottweil train and never return.

This Hank and I duly did. As I walked off the station platform at Tuttlingen, through the barrier, we handed in our tickets. We had walked ten yards when I heard shouts behind us:

'*Kommen Sie her! Hier, kommen Sie zurück!*'

I turned round, fearing the worst, and saw the ticket-collector waving at us.

I returned to him and he said:

'*Sie haben Ihre Fahrkarten abgegeben, aber Sie fahren nach Rottweil. Die müssen Sie noch behalten.*'

With almost visible relief I accepted the tickets once more. In my anxiety I had forgotten that we were ostensibly due to return to catch the Rottweil train and, of course, still needed our tickets.

From the station we promptly took the wrong road; there were no signposts. It was late afternoon and a Saturday (October 17th). The weather was fine. We walked for a long time along a road which refused to turn in the direction in which we thought it ought to turn! It was maddening. We passed a superbly camouflaged factory and sidings. There must have been an area of ten acres completely covered with a false flat roof of what appeared to be rush matting. Even at the low elevation at which we found ourselves looking down upon it, the whole site looked like farmland. If the camouflage was actually rush matting, I do not know how they provided against fire risks.

We were gradually being driven into a valley heading due south, whereas we wished to travel westwards. Leaving the road as soon as possible without creating suspicion, we tried to make a short-cut across country to another highway which we knew headed west. As a short-cut it misfired, taking us over hilly country which prolonged our journey considerably. Evening was drawing in by the time we reached the correct road. We walked along this for several miles, and when it was dark, took to the woods to lie up for the night.

We passed a freezing, uncomfortable night on beds of leaves in the forest and were glad to warm ourselves with a sharp walk early the next morning, which was Sunday. I was thankful it was a Sunday because it gave us a good excuse to be out walking in the country.

We now headed along roads leading south-west, until at 8 a.m. we retired again to the friendly shelter of the woods to eat our breakfast, consuming most of what was left of our German bread, sugar, and margarine.

We had almost finished our repast when we were disturbed by a farmer who approached and eyed us curiously for a long time. He wore close-fitting breeches and gaiters like a typical English gamekeeper. I did not like his attitude at all. He came close to us and demanded what we were doing. I said:

'*Wir essen. Können Sie das nicht sehen?*'

'*Warum sind Sie hier*?' he asked, to which I answered:

'*Wir gehen spazieren; es ist Sonntag, nicht wahr*?'

At this he retired. I watched him carefully. As soon as he was out of the wood and about fifty yards away, I saw him turn along a hedge and change his gait into a trot.

This was enough for me. In less than a minute we were packed and trotting fast in the opposite direction, which happened to be southward! We did not touch the road again for some time, but kept to the woods and lanes. Gradually, however, the countryside became open and cultivated and we were forced once more to the road. We passed a German soldier, who was smartly turned out in his Sunday best, with a friendly '*Heil Hitler!*' Church bells were ringing out from steeples which rose head and shoulders above the roofs of several villages dotted here and there in the rolling country around us.

We walked through one of the villages as the people were coming out of church. I was terrified of the children, who ran out of the church shouting and laughing. They gambolled around us and eyed us curiously, although their elders took no notice of us at all. I was relieved, none the less, when we left the village behind us. Soon afterwards, the country again became wooded and hilly, and we disappeared amongst the trees, heading now due south.

As the afternoon wore on I picked up our bearings more accurately, and we aimed at the exact location of the frontier crossing. A little too soon—I thought—we reached the frontier road, running east and west. I could not be sure, so we continued eastwards along it to where it entered some woods. We passed a fork where a forest track, which I recognised, joined it. I knew then that we were indeed on the frontier road and that we had gone too far eastwards. At that moment there were people following us, and we could not break off into the woods without looking suspicious. We walked onward casually and at the end of the wooded portion of the road we heard suddenly:

'*Halt! Wer da!*' and then, more deliberately, '*Wo gehen Sie hin?*'

A sentry-box stood back from the road in a clump of trees and from it stepped forth a frontier guard.

'*Wir gehen nach Singen*,' I said. '*Wir sind Ausländer.*'

'*Ihren Ausweis, bitte.*'

We produced our papers, including the special permit allowing us to travel near the frontier. We were close to him. His rifle was slung over his shoulder. The people who had been following us had turned down a lane towards a cottage. We were alone with the sentry.

I chatted on, gesticulating with my suitcase brazenly conspicuous.

'We are Flemish workmen. This evening we take the train to Rottweil, where there is much construction work. We must be there in the morning. Today we can rest and we like your woods and countryside.'

He eyed us for a moment; handed us back our papers and let us go. As we walked on I dreaded to hear another 'Halt!' I imagined that if the sentry were not satisfied with us he would, for his own safety, move us off a few yards so that he could unsling his rifle. But no command was given and we continued our 'Sunday afternoon stroll'. As we moved out of earshot Hank said to me:

'If he'd reached for his gun when he was close to us just then, I would have knocked him to Kingdom come.'

I would not have relished being knocked to Kingdom come by Hank and I often wonder if the sentry did not notice a look in Hank's eye and think that discretion was perhaps the better part of valour! A lonely sentry is not all-powerful against two enemies, even with his gun levelled. Our story may have had a vague ring of truth, but none the less, we were foreigners within half a mile of the Swiss frontier!

Soon we were able to leave the road and we started to double back across country to our frontier crossing-point. Just as we came to a railway line and climbed a small embankment, we nearly jumped out of our skins with fright as a figure darted from a bush in front of us and ran for his life into a thicket and disappeared. I could have assured him, if only he had stopped, that he gave us just as big a fright as we gave him!

By dusk we had found our exact location and waited in deep pine woods for darkness to descend. The frontier was scarcely a mile away. We ate a last meal nervously and without appetite. Our suitcases would not be required any more, so they were buried. When it was pitch-dark, we pulled on socks over our shoes, and set off. We had to negotiate the frontier-crossing in inky blackness, entirely from memory of the maps studied in Colditz. We crossed over more railway lines and then continued, skirting the edge of a wood. We encountered a minor road, which foxed me for a while because it should not have been there according to my memory, but we carried on. Hearing a motor-cycle pass along a road in front of us, a road running close to and parallel with the frontier, warned us of the proximity of our 'take-off' point. We entered the woods to our left and proceeded parallel with the road eastwards for about a hundred yards and then approached it cautiously. Almost as we stumbled into it, I suddenly recognised the outline of a sentry-box hidden among the trees straight in front of us!

We were within five yards of it when I recognised its angular roof. My hair stood on end. It was impossible to move without breaking twigs under our feet. They made noises like pistol shots and we could be heard easily. We retreated with as much care as we could, but even the crackle of a dried leaf caused me to perspire freely.

To compensate for this unnerving encounter, however, I now knew exactly where we were, for the sentry-box was marked on our Colditz map and provided me with a check bearing. We moved off seventy yards and approached the road again. Peering across it, we could discern fields and low hedges. In the distance was our goal: a wooded hill looming blacker than the darkness around it, with the woods ending abruptly halfway down its eastern slopes, towards our left. This end of the woods was our 'pointer'. There was no 'blackout' in Switzerland, and beyond the hill was the faintest haze of light, indicating the existence of a Swiss village.

At 7.30 p.m. we moved off. Crouching low, and at the double, we crossed the road and headed for our 'pointer'. Without stopping for breath we ran—through hedges—across ditches—wading through mud—and then on again. Dreading barbed wire which we could never have seen, we ran, panting with excitement as much as with breathlessness, across fields newly ploughed, meadows and marshland, till at last we rounded the corner of the woods. Here, for a moment, we halted for breath.

I felt that if I could not have a drink of water soon I would die. My throat was parched and swollen and my tongue was choking me. My heart was pounding like a sledge-hammer. I was gasping for breath. I had lived for two and a half years, both awake and in sleep, with the vision of this race before me and every nerve in my body was taut to breaking-pitch.

We were not yet 'home'. We had done about half a mile and could see the lights of the Swiss village ahead. Great care was now necessary, for we could easily recross the frontier into Germany without knowing it, and stumble on a guard-post. From the corner of the wood we had to continue in a sweeping curve, first towards our right, and then left again towards the village. Where we stood we were actually in Switzerland, but in a direct line between us and the Swiss village lay Germany.

Why had we run instead of creeping forward warily? The answer is that instinct dictated it and, I think in this case, instinct was right. Escapers' experience has borne out that the psychological reaction of a fleeing man to a shouted command, such as 'Halt', varies. If a man is walking or creeping the reaction is to stop. If he is running the reaction is to run faster. It is in the split seconds of such instinctive decisions that success or failure may be determined.

We continued on our way at a rapid walk, over grass and boggy land, crouching low at every sound. It was important to avoid even Swiss frontier-posts. We had heard curious rumours of escapers being returned to the Germans by unfriendly Swiss guards. However untrue, we were taking no risks.

We saw occasional shadowy forms and circled widely around them and at last, at 8.30 p.m., approached the village along a sandy path.

We were about a thousand yards inside the Swiss frontier. We had completed the four-hundred-mile journey from Colditz in less than four days.

Under the first lamp-post of the village street, Hank and I shook hands in silence . . .

We beat Ronnie and Billie by twenty-six hours. At 10.30 p.m. the following evening they crossed the frontier safely!

RALPH BARKER
Mediterranean Hijack

The crew of a Beaufort bomber from Britain's airbase in Malta achieved, in 1942, one of the boldest escapes of the Second World War. Shot down and captured by the Italian airforce, the Beaufort's crew was taken to an Italian airbase off the coast of Greece, where this account of their escape begins.

'TOMORROW BAD, TONIGHT GOOD,' said the Italians. They realised even more fully what was meant when they were taken to bed. Four of the Italians had given up their two double rooms so that their prisoners should pass a comfortable night.

Strever paired off with Dunsmore, and the two New Zealanders shared the second room. Guards were posted in the passage and outside the windows. They began to feel at last that they were prisoners, and found the realisation disturbingly and surprisingly unpleasant. Their captors' words echoed in their minds. Tomorrow bad.

On the wall of the New Zealanders' room was a map of the Adriatic Sea and the Grecian coast. Brown and Wilkinson turned towards it eagerly. Somewhere on that map was the spot in which they were spending the night. They plotted the approximate position of the Axis convoy, and then looked for land some two hours' flying in a northerly direction.

'We're somewhere here,' said Wilkinson, tapping the map. 'Levkas—or perhaps as far south as Corfu. It's a hundred to one we're somewhere in that area.'

'There's Taranto!' said Brown. 'Should be about an hour and a half's flying.'

Wilkinson did not speak again for some time. When he did eventually break the silence, Brown was nearly asleep.

'I'm going to get out of this mess if I can,' he said.

They were awakened at seven o'clock next morning, and breakfasted well on eggs (the first they'd seen for many weeks), bacon, tomatoes, toast and coffee. While they were at breakfast they were left alone for a few moments. Instantly they began to discuss the possibility of escape.

'I've worked out where we are,' said Wilkinson. 'Either Levkas or Corfu. Taranto can't be more than about 200 miles. If we don't do something quickly we'll be in a POW camp by lunch-time.'

'Not a hope here,' said Dunsmore. 'We've as much chance of eluding them here as a bunch of film stars at a world première. Better wait till we get to Taranto.'

'You know what they say,' said Strever. 'The best chances come immediately after capture. Once they get us to Taranto there'll be no more of this being fêted like transatlantic flyers. Life'll start to get rough then.'

'Has anyone thought of trying to capture the aircraft and fly it to Malta? Malta's about 350 miles, I reckon.'

'I've thought of it, Wilkie,' said Strever. 'I thought of it yesterday. We probably had a better chance then than we'll get today. They're bound to mount a guard on us now. Still, we'll keep our eyes open.'

'Look out,' said Brown. The guards had arrived to escort them to the jetty. They had no further chance to discuss escape.

The whole Italian headquarters staff seemed to have preceded them to the jetty to see them off. Everyone wanted to shake hands with them and take pictures, and as they boarded another Cant floatplane—not the same one as the previous day, and a different crew—a battery of cameras clicked into action. Strever could not help contrasting the carefree atmosphere here with the grim bitterness of life at Malta. Life here was leisurely and luxurious and food and drink plentiful. Life at Malta was hectic and austere. It was hard to believe that their two countries were locked in a desperate battle for survival. Strever tried hard to recapture the bitter enmity of the fighting, but the gaiety of his captors disarmed him. Resenting the feeling of goodwill that abounded, he stepped quickly into the plane.

The Cant crew consisted of pilot, second pilot, engineer, wireless operator/observer, and a corporal acting as escort, armed with a .45 revolver that looked as though it had been rescued from a museum. Strever and his crew entered the plane first, followed by the guard. Then came the Italian crew, in high spirits, each carrying two or more large cases, which they dumped in the fuselage. They were going home on leave. The flight was part and parcel of the party, and the holiday spirit was already abroad.

The Italian pilot introduced himself. 'Captain Gatetama Mastrodrasa, at your service.' He grinned, showing a set of incredibly white, even teeth. 'We go to Italy on leave. I see my bambino'—he rocked an imaginary baby in his arms—'for the first time. For you, it is bad.' He shrugged his shoulders and opened the palms of his hands, then turned on his heel and went forward to his pilot's seat.

Space was restricted in the crew compartment of the Cant and the nine men were in close proximity of each other. Pilot and second pilot sat in the front of the perspex cockpit, with the corporal escort standing behind and between them, facing backwards. Next came the wireless operator, and flight engineer. In the back of the elongated crew compartment Strever and his crew squatted on the floor.

They were airborne at 0940. That meant that they ought to reach Taranto about 1110, barring accidents. They sat quietly and tried to look relaxed and resigned. Nevertheless the corporal's belt and holster fascinated them. How quick would he be on the draw? What firearms might the other members of the crew have ready to hand? And if they could turn the tables on the Italians, what then? Could they effectively subdue the whole crew and at the same time fly an unfamiliar aircraft and navigate it from an unknown point to a tiny island notoriously hard to find, without radio and perhaps without maps?

Well, it might be worth a try.

Staggering along under an overload of men and luggage, unable to climb above 1,000 feet, where the air was sickeningly bumpy and unbearably hot, the Cant made slow and unsteady progress towards the heel of Italy. Four men faced the prospect of years of imprisonment. Four men were going on leave. Poised between the two parties, a kind of neutral umpire, stood the corporal guard.

The corporal sat down behind the pilot. It was a bad day for a non-flyer; a wretched day for a ground type with a queasy stomach. The corporal felt the sweat pouring from his forehead. Yet he felt cold. He longed to set foot on the sure earth again. How long had they said? Ninety minutes? They could hardly be half way yet. He found himself swallowing incessantly. His head ached intolerably and he longed to lie down. Up-currents and down-draughts played battledore and shuttlecock with his stomach. He gritted his teeth fiercely, determined not to be sick. His eyeballs felt like roundshot. His jowls drooped. His energy was spent and he felt an overwhelming apathy. If only the plane would crash or something. Anything to get down on the deck.

Wilkinson sat facing the wireless operator/observer, whose log sheets were strewn on the navigation table between them. Behind the observer sat the corporal, his face a ghastly parchment. Wilkinson looked at his watch. 1025. They must be about half way. They daren't leave it much longer. Perhaps a fighter escort might be sent to meet them. Soon they would be picked up by the Italian coastal radar. It was now or never.

Somehow he had to distract the observer's attention and get his hands firmly planted on the airsick corporal's gun.

The only trick he knew was a schoolboy affair. You pointed suddenly out of the window and while your victim turned his head away you had him momentarily at your mercy. Schoolboys were used to the trick and didn't always buy it. He would have to take a chance with this fellow.

'Look!'

The observer turned his head, and instantly the window clouded into an opaque blackness and then splintered into stars as Wilkinson's fist sank into his jaw. There was no recoil. Wilkinson allowed the impetus of the punch to carry him past the table; then he jumped over the observer's slouched body and snatched the corporal's revolver. His hands closed over it greedily and he tore at it with all his strength. Next moment the pistol was in his hands, and as the corporal fell back into the pilot's lap he handed the pistol to Strever, who had quickly backed him up, leaving Dunsmore and Brown to attend to the observer and flight engineer. The corporal fell between the pilot and the control column, and as he struggled to free himself he fouled the controls and sent the floatplane into a steep dive. Wilkinson, flung forward like a piece of loose cargo, caught the corporal by the scruff of the neck and with a Herculean effort lifted him clear.

By this time Strever was pointing the gun coolly in the pilot's ribs, believing the day had been won, unaware that the second pilot was in the act of turning a Luger on him.

Brown, holding down the stunned observer, saw the Italian second pilot swing triumphantly round with the Luger. Another second and their dreams of capturing the aircraft would be over. The nearest missile to hand was a seat cover. He gathered it and hurled it with one movement, like the throw of a classic coverpoint. The seat cover flew through the air unerringly, striking the Luger and knocking it from the second pilot's grasp. Instantly there was a free-for-all as the two crews struggled for possession of the Luger. Strever kept the pilot covered while Dunsmore hooked the Luger out of the scrum back to Wilkinson. The morale of the Italian crewmen was broken.

But Captain Mastrodrasa was not done with yet. He kept the Cant in a steep dive, determined to foil the Beaufort crew's escape by landing the Cant on the sea.

Strever brandished the revolver before his eyes, and then raised it as though he would smash in the Italian's skull. The horizon came down from above them like a blind as the Cant floatplane slowly levelled out.

Meanwhile Dunsmore and Brown were busy tying up the rest of the crew with a length of mooring hawser. Dunsmore tied them up while Brown seized a monkey-wrench from the tool-kit and stood poised above them.

'One move out of you lot and I'll dong you,' he shouted, swinging the wrench. The Italians understood the gesture—and the onomatopoeia. The Italian captain, too, was hustled back to be tied up, but every time Dunsmore thought he had them firmly secured, the Italians shook their heads and wriggled their wrists to show that they could still free themselves. Eventually Dunsmore tied them up with their trouser-belts.

Strever took over the controls and turned the floatplane ninety degrees to port of their previous track in the rough direction of Malta. For one glorious moment they relaxed, breathless and dishevelled, flushed and exultant, revelling in a sense of freedom and power, undisputed masters of the plane in which they had been travelling to Italy two minutes earlier as prisoners of war.

CHARLES FOLEY
The Rescue of Benito Mussolini from Gran Sasso

The rescue of Mussolini from a mountain prison by Major Otto Skorzeny, the SS Chief of Germany's Special Forces, was one of the most daring exploits of WWII. In July 1943 the Italian dictator had been overthrown in a coup d'état by forces which wanted armistice with the Allies, and was interned on the Gran Sasso, the highest peak in the Apennines. Hitler, who retained a deep friendship for Mussolini, ordered Skorzeny to secure the Duce's release. Any conventional operation was ruled out by the impregnability of the terrain, the size of the Italian guard and the fact that such an operation would inevitably give the guard time to kill their captive before it reached a conclusion. Consequently, Skorzeny determined on a glider landing of his Special Forces on the mountain ledge in front of the building in which Mussolini was held. Charles Foley's account of Skorzeny's mission of 12 September 1943 is based on interviews with Skorzeny himself.

IT WAS BRIGHT AND WINDLESS, that September morning which the knot of men waiting at the airfield knew must be the last for quite a few of them. Great banks of white cloud lying athwart their north-easterly course might help to get them on their way unhindered; and the still, transparent morning would have softened the trials of their landing—if only they could have taken off as planned.

The start had been set for dawn—when they might hope to float down unperceived by a sleepy enemy—but the gliders were held up on their journey from the Riviera; they could not arrive before 11 a.m. at the earliest.

That meant, by Student's reckoning, twenty-four hours' delay—but there were not twenty-four hours to spare. They would simply have to accept the further risk of approaching in daylight and, moreover, at an hour when they would be the sport of warm air currents which might whisk the gliders from their path like so many paper darts.

Certainly, Skorzeny thought, since nobody in his senses would expect a glider operation at high noon, an added measure of surprise, if they lived to exploit it, might be achieved. So he went cheerfully among his men, distributing boxes of fresh fruit that he had bought to lend a picnic touch to the expedition. They were to take off at exactly 1 p.m., which would give them a landing time of about two o'clock.

The delay allowed Radl to follow a fancy of his own; he hurried into Rome, where uneasy truce still reigned, and returned with an otherwise unimportant Italian, General Soletti, who had shown much favour to the Germans. Soletti was told his help was needed in 'an important enterprise', it being Radl's hope that the sight of an Italian among the attackers might help to upset the garrison on the Gran Sasso.

The expedition, twelve gliders with their towing planes, was to be led to the dropping zone by the pilot who had taken Skorzeny and Radl on their numbing reconnaissance flight. Ten men in the first two gliders would cover the landing of the third with Skorzeny and Warger aboard; Radl was to follow in a fourth.

By half-past twelve the aircraft were drawn up, ready for the men to board them—and at that instant the sirens wailed. By the time they were all in shelter, Allied bombs were bursting all over the place—one of those jests of Providence as cruel as the rainstorm which wrecks the family outing. Yet when the all-clear sounded, Skorzeny found his gliders were untouched; the damage, as far as their interest went, was confined to craters on the runway.

Skorzeny followed his men into his glider and pulled Soletti after him into the front seat. With this extra passenger between his knees he signalled: the armada began to leave.

They took off dead on time. Skorzeny did not know till later that two machines behind him ran into bomb-holes and never left the ground. What he did see, once they had emerged from the bank of white cloud and had risen to 12,000 feet, was that his two leading gliders had vanished. They had lost their guide, and also the covering party. So much the worse; since they would soon be approaching the Gran Sasso area Skorzeny would have to tax his memory of the photographic trip to lead the way in. But wedged in his seat he could not see where he was going.

He pulled out a knife and began to hack at the canvas deck and bulkheads. As they gave way, he blessed the flimsy fabric. Cool air rushed into the overheated shell, crammed as it was with men and weapons, and, peering through the rents, he could see the granite mountains below.

The Gran Sasso came into view. Soon they were a-top of it: there was the hotel again, and on that dizzy perch alongside, the triangular ledge on which they would alight.

'Let go!' he told the pilot. The tow-rope parted and they were swooping freely, with no sound but the gush of the wind on their wings. Then the pilot was jabbing with his finger at the triangle below while he turned his goggled face toward Skorzeny. By no flight of hyperbole could the space be called a landing-field: it was a sloping shelf, for all the world like a ski-jump; and as they lost more height they saw it to be studded with outcrop rock.

General Student had provided against such a contingency. At a final briefing he had categorically laid down that unless they could make a smooth landing they must abandon the attack and glide to safety in the valley. Those were his unquestioned orders; in a spasm of defiance Skorzeny elected to disobey. He shouted to the pilot: 'Dive—crashland! As near the hotel as you can.'

They hurtled towards the mountain, the parachute brake whipping from their tail. In another instant the glider was jolting and pitching over the boulders like a dinghy flung upon a reef. A shuddering crash, then it was still.

He was alive, was Skorzeny's first thought; his second: *three minutes*.

He burst out of the wrecked glider; before him, like a cliff-face twenty yards ahead, was the wall of the hotel. An Italian carabinier was standing there, rooted to the spot; he was stupefied by this apparition which had fallen almost at his feet out of the silent sky.

Skorzeny plunged past him to the first doorway: inside was a signalman tapping at a transmitter. A kick sent the chair from under him; Skorzeny's gun smashed the radio. But the room led nowhere.

Out again and full-tilt round a corner; he heard his men pounding behind him. A ten-foot terrace—they hoisted him up to it. From there, at an upper window, he spotted an unmistakeable shorn head. 'Get back!' he yelled to Mussolini. 'Get back from the window.' And dashed off round the terrace.

At last: the main entrance, flanked by two sentry posts. The guards wore a look of wild amazement; before they could get their breath, Skorzeny's men had booted their machine-guns off the supports and scrambled through the door. A voice far behind was shouting in Italian; Soletti was adding to the confusion.

Skorzeny butted his way through a press of soldiers in the lobby; they were at too-close quarters to shoot, even had they known what had come on them. He took a flight of stairs, turned a corner and flung open a door. The first thing he saw—Mussolini, with two Italian officers.

One of Skorzeny's brawniest subalterns, Lieutenant Schwerdt, panted into the room after him. And just then two shining faces bobbed through the window: a couple of his men had swarmed up the lightning conductor to be with him. They overcame the Italian officers and dragged them from the room. Schwerdt took over as Mussolini's bodyguard.

From the window Skorzeny saw how other friends were faring. Radl was in sight, bounding towards the hotel; his glider had made a tolerable landing. Skorzeny hailed him with a shout: 'We've got him here. All well so far. You look after the ground floor for me.'

Three more gliders crash-landed, and men poured out. A fourth, landing some distance away, was smashed to pieces—no one moved from the wreckage. He could not hope for much more strength, so he turned back across the room, threw open the door and shouted in his bad Italian: 'I want the commander. He must come at once.' Some bewildered shouting—an Italian colonel appeared.

'I ask your immediate surrender,' Skorzeny said in French.

'Mussolini is already in our hands. We hold the building. If you want to avert senseless bloodshed you have sixty seconds to go and reflect.'

Before the anxious minute was up the colonel came back. This time he carried a goblet brimming with red wine. 'To a gallant victor,' he bowed. Skorzeny thanked him and drained the beaker—he was thirsty. Cheers arose from the Germans below as a white sheet was flung from the window.

And now Skorzeny could spare time for Mussolini, who had been put into a corner of the room and there shielded by the bulk of Lieutenant Schwerdt. He came forward: a stocky man looking older than his portraits showed him, in a blue suit that was too large. He wore a stubble of beard; his pate sprouted grey bristle. But his eyes were black, ardent and excited.

It was a moment for history—the thought crossed Skorzeny's mind. He spoke in German: 'Duce, I have been sent by the Leader to set you free.' And Mussolini, who always considered his public, replied for posterity: 'I knew my friend Adolf Hitler would not abandon me. I embrace my liberator.'

Skorzeny went to see to the disarming of the Italian garrison and discovered he had captured an important personage from Rome—none other than the General Cueli who was responsible for keeping Mussolini sealed up and shut away. Having, through his intercepted code message, unwittingly put Skorzeny on the scent leading to the Gran Sasso, he was further unfortunate in choosing this day for a visit to his charge. Skorzeny was delighted to see him.

But now for a more urgent matter: the get-away. Both ends of the funicular were in German hands; a telephone call from the valley station said the paratroops had carried out their part. Since Mussolini could never hope to reach Rome by road once the alarm was given, it had been arranged that paratroopers should capture the nearby airfield at Aquila and hold it briefly while Mussolini was taken off by three Heinkel planes. But now Skorzeny's luckless radio operator could not get through to signal the rescue planes to set out from Rome. The alternative plan worked out in advance called for a single light aircraft to land in the valley: this had been done, but in coming down its landing gear was damaged. There remained a third, desperate choice: Captain Gerlach, Student's personal pilot, might try to land a tiny Stork spotter plane alongside the hotel itself and pick up Mussolini from the mountain ledge—an operation so hair-raising that Skorzeny and Radl had to put it to General Student as only the most theoretical of possibilities.

Now it was their only hope.

Skorzeny glanced heavenwards, and there, sure enough, the Stork was circling. Well, there was nothing for it. It had been said that Gerlach could do miracles in the air—let him perform one now.

Skorzeny got his troops, helped by some prisoners, to move the biggest boulders from a strip of the landing ledge and at a signal Gerlach came delicately down on it. Gerlach was ready for anything until he heard what was actually wanted. Then he recoiled. To weigh down his frail craft with the united loads, each in its own right substantial, of Mussolini and Skorzeny! It was mad: he refused point-blank to consider it.

Skorzeny took him aside. He told how Hitler had personally commanded him, Skorzeny, to deliver Mussolini: now Gerlach had in his hands the only means through which that mission could be fulfilled; if he should stand aloof he would be defying Hitler's wishes. And what would there be left to them to do if they failed the Leader? Blow their brains out; that was all.

At last Gerlach gave in: 'Have it your own way. If it's neck or nothing anyway we had better be on the move.'

Squads hurriedly set to work again on the strip; even Mussolini lent a hand in rolling one or two boulders.

They squashed into the plane; Mussolini behind the pilot, Skorzeny behind Mussolini. With the engine turning, twelve men clung to the Stork, digging their heels in for a tug-of-war. Gerlach held a hand aloft until the engine's pitch rose in a crescendo; as he dropped his hand the men let go and the plane catapulted across the scree.

Skorzeny grasped the steel spars on either side of him, throwing his weight from side to side against the swaying motion as one wheel or the other was lifted by a rock. Suddenly a crevasse yawned before them; the plane shot over it and continued its career beyond, with the port wheel buckled. Then it went hurtling over the edge of the ravine.

In the group of Germans standing on the Gran Sasso, there was suddenly a gap. Radl had collapsed; he had fainted.

Gerlach brought off his miracle. With consummate skill he lifted the Stork gently from its nose-dive to flatten out a few hundred feet above the valley floor.

The rest seemed smooth sailing; even the glissade at Rome on starboard and rear wheels. And there, immaculate on the dusty airfield, forewarned by that instinct for an Occasion that animates aides-de-camp and diplomatic vice-marshals, there waited General Student's ADC, standing stiffly at the salute while the three crumpled figures stepped on to friendly soil.

QUENTIN REYNOLDS
The Amazing Colonel Doolittle

The bombing attack on Tokyo led by US Army Air Force Colonel James Doolittle in April 1942 was an act of American defiance in the face of Japanese advance in the Pacific theatre. It was also a feat of airmanship, since it involved flying B-25 bombers off an aircraft carrier (the USS Hornet*), something widely considered to be aeronautically impossible due to the relative shortness of a carrier's flight deck.*

THE BIG *HORNET* WAS TWENTY-FOUR HOURS out of San Francisco when Doolittle gathered his men in an empty ward room to brief them on the mission.

At least ten thousand men had in one way or another contributed to the whole organization of this project. High-ranking Naval and Air Force officers, air field personnel at Wright Field, at Eglin and at Sacramento had helped prepare the planes. Naval commanders of the escorting ships and their crews had all been part of the huge jigsaw which Duncan had so skillfully assembled, yet at this moment only eight men knew the complete details of the operation—King, Duncan, Low, Arnold, Nimitz, Halsey, Mitscher, and Doolittle. Now the time had come to reveal everything to the pilots and crews of the B-25s.

Doolittle looked at these men with satisfaction. They could do things with this medium bomber that the designer of the airplane had never envisioned. Each man in this group had demonstrated his capability during the training at Eglin. It was a magnificent group, Doolittle felt. He had gotten to know many of them well by now, and those he wasn't close to, Jack Hilger vouched for.

Hilger was proving himself to be a magnificent executive officer. Like Doolittle, his approach to the difficulties of the operation was completely cerebral. He was calm, quiet, and like Doolittle, had the knack of inspiring great confidence in the other men.

'Well, here it is,' Doolittle said to them when they were assembled. 'For the benefit of those of you who don't know, here are your targets. We're going to bomb Tokyo, Yokohama, Osaka, Kobe and Nagoya. The Navy is going to take us in as close as possible, and then we'll take off from the deck. It's going to be a tight squeeze, but it's all been worked out. The Chinese government will cooperate with us. After we hit our targets we'll land at small Chinese airports not far inland and tank up there—the gas is waiting for us. Then we'll fly to Chungking. We're going to be on this carrier a long time, but we've got plenty of work to do. Above all, keep your planes in perfect condition. Any questions?' There were none. Then Doolittle continued.

'We've just got some unexpected news. We had hoped to be able to go on to Vladivostok after leaving our targets, but the Russians have turned us down flat. They are not at war with the Japs and they figure that if we went on to one of their Russian bases after bombing Japan, it might be construed as an unfriendly gesture. So Vladivostok is out. Let me repeat. Under no circumstances are you to head for Vladivostok. One more thing, and this is important. At all costs, avoid hitting the Temple of Heaven.'

'What in hell is that?' one of the pilots asked, puzzled.

'That's the Emperor's palace; stay clear of it.'

He explained that the present plans called for the take-off to be in the late afternoon of April 18, unless the task force was previously intercepted; then take-off would be immediate.

There were still no questions. Everyone felt great; the speculation, the uncertainty of the past weeks was gone. Now they were face to face with a tangible flying problem. Once brought out into the open it lost some of its terrifying aspects. Now it was a question of rechecking gas consumption and of how to meet the various emergencies that might arise. This is what they'd been trained for. Now they could study the operational problems involved, and best of all, they could discuss them openly. There was no need for further secrecy.

'No questions?' Jimmy grinned. 'Okay. There's just one thing more. When we get to Chungking, I'm going to throw the biggest damned party you guys ever saw.'

The Navy's preliminary organizing had been so complete that they even had two Naval officers on board who were familiar with the location of Japanese factories, machine shops, ammunition centers, shipyards and other prospective targets. They were Lieutenant Commander Stephen Jurika and Commander Appolo Soucek. The two Naval officers knew Japan thoroughly, and they not only gave the men a pretty good idea of how to recognize their targets but they supplemented this with a few lessons in Chinese. They made the raiders repeat again and again the all-important phrase, *'Lushu hoo megwa fugi'* (I am an American), which would be useful in case crews had to bail out over Chinese territory—a contingency far from remote. Doolittle put Davey Jones in charge of a map room, and pilots and navigators spent hours each day studying the targets.

In the midst of these preparations Doolittle found time to chuckle over a note he had sent to his old friend Roscoe Turner, the great speed flyer. Turner had written to Doolittle suggesting that he and a group of the famous racing pilots be organized into a special combat group. 'After all,' Turner had said, quite truthfully, 'we have all forgotten more about flying than these kids will ever know. All they have is youth. We have the experience.' Doolittle, then on the eve of leaving for Sacramento, had written, 'Dear Roscoe, let's face it—you and I are too old for combat flying. Leave that to the kids, old-timer.' Now he, Doolittle, was to lead one of the most hazardous combat raids ever attempted. When the news came out, Roscoe Turner would explode.

The *Hornet* was five hundred miles out of San Francisco when Doolittle said to Mitscher, 'I guess it's time we sent that sixteenth plane back to San Francisco.'

'I guess it is,' the skipper said.

'Seems an awful waste of a good airplane,' Doolittle said dolefully. 'Pity we can't take it along and aim it at Tokyo.'

Mitscher looked at Doolittle and sighed. 'Okay, Jim, okay. Take it along.'

Mitscher turned the *Hornet* flag headquarters over to Doolittle, and every night Jack Hilger, Dave Jones, Major Harry Johnson, the administrative officer, Ski York and Ross Greening had dinner together. They discussed nothing but the technical aspects of the raid.

By now Doolittle had impressed upon them all the fact that the Navy was boss until they were air-borne. If the task force was attacked or even spotted, Pete Mitscher (he was known as Marc Mitscher only in the Naval records) would be the complete boss. The one eventuality they all hoped would not arise would be to be spotted before closing in within range of Japan. Doolittle had convinced Hilger, Jones, York and Greening that this was no suicide operation; his calculations gave everyone a fifty-fifty chance of survival. The word had been passed along. A fifty-fifty chance sounded good to the men. By now they knew their Doolittle. He didn't play guessing games. When he said 'fifty-fifty,' that figure had come off a drawing board. It had been the result of cold, hard calculation.

'Hell,' calm Bill Bower smiled, 'you take a fifty-fifty chance every time you cross Market Street in San Francisco.'

The fifty-fifty chance, however, did not apply if the desperate alternative of having to take off fifteen hundred miles from their targets eventualized. The pilots tried not to think of that. But occasionally they discussed it among themselves. Jack Hilger brought this up with Doolittle one night at dinner.

'Some of the boys feel they would be better off going right on in,' he said, 'instead of risking capture by the Japs. How do you feel about that, Colonel?'

'I'm an old man,' Doolittle grinned. 'I'll be damned if I am going to spend the rest of my life in some Jap jail. But tell the men to get any ideas like that out of their heads. They are all young, they are all healthy, and even if they are captured or forced down in the China Sea they still have a chance.'

The task force steamed on steadily. Doolittle kept the men busy. He knew that this was no time for them to be brooding. The *Hornet* let out kites behind the ship to give the crews some badly needed shooting practice. The crew of the *Hornet* and the Navy pilots aboard had great respect for the men whom they now called Doolittle's Raiders. Everyone from Pete Mitscher down to the galley boys did everything possible to make life pleasant for these sea-borne Air Force crews.

It was inevitable that the Army pilots should become friendly with the Naval pilots aboard. Doolittle's men spent a lot of time with the pilots and crews of Torpedo Squadron Eight. (A month later, in the Battle of Midway, this whole squadron, with the exception of Ensign Gay, would be wiped out attempting to torpedo Jap carriers.)

One day a rumor spread through the ship that Tokyo had been bombed by four-engined land-based American planes. It was a disheartening shock to the men who had been so intent about getting there first. Because radio silence was now the rule on the *Hornet* and her sister ships, it was impossible to radio for details. But then came the happy news that the rumor was merely a garbled version of the raid General Royce had made on the Philippines.

Doolittle had worked out every detail of the strike. He decided that he would take off about four in the afternoon of April 18, carrying four clusters of incendiary bombs. That would bring him over Tokyo just before nightfall. The two thousand pounds of incendiarics could be expected to start some beautiful fires. After setting his fires he would head for the coast, cross the China Sea and try to find a Chinese airfield called Chu Chow, and land there in darkness. The other fifteen planes would take off from the *Hornet* just before dusk. They would reach Tokyo during the night. The fires set by his incendiaries should act as beacons to guide them to their targets.

Doolittle felt that the safety factor could be immeasurably increased if the other fifteen planes could hit their targets at night. To begin with, it had been established that as yet the Jap air force had virtually no night fighters. If the B-25's went in at fifteen hundred feet, they would be above effective machine-gun and small-arms fire range, and below the altitude where the heavier antiaircraft guns operated most efficiently. In addition, they would have the great advantage of approaching the China coast around dawn and being able to locate Chinese airfields in daylight. He felt that he himself and his crew would probably have to bail out unless they were favored with really good weather, but that was a calculated risk that must be taken.

'I have something that may amuse your boys,' Mitscher told Doolittle one afternoon, producing a handful of Japanese medals. They had been presented to Mitscher and other officers some years before on a visit to Japan.

'It's time we sent these medals back where they came from,'

he grinned. 'Suppose we tie them to the bombs you are going to drop.'

Mitscher and Doolittle made quite a ceremony out of it. The task force plunged deeper and deeper into Japanese-controlled waters. Tension mounted among the crew as the *Hornet*, bucking strong winds and heavy seas, roared into the home stretch at full speed. The eight destroyers and two tankers were left far behind.

Not one of these men had ever been in combat. They didn't know then what nearly every combat man eventually learns; fear is something that usually creeps into a man's heart before the danger has been encountered, leaves, and then returns when the danger is past. During the last week most of them were haunted by dreams, and at night many found themselves lying tensely in bed wide-awake with sweat on their foreheads. Fear is the enemy of sleep. They were to leap off into the unknown, and none knew what awaited them. Doolittle had dreams of a different nature. He, Hilger, Greening and Jones were men who thought rather than felt. Their dreams were filled with the hundred and one technical aspects of the operation. The very take-off haunted them. The weather was turning rough. Their take-off calculations had been predicated on the fact that the planes would be able to take off from a level flight deck. Could they take off from a carrier that was rolling dizzily and pitching horribly? These four just had no time for fear and very little capacity for feeling it. Doolittle was the engineer, thinking in terms of the mechanical and navigational problems involved; Hilger, the executive, had the burden of caring for every minute detail; Greening was constantly testing his guns and his bombsights; Davey Jones spent most of his time going over his maps with the pilots and navigators.

At 6:30 A.M. Saturday, April 18, the siren gave the signal 'General Quarters,' which meant that there was trouble afoot. Doolittle hurried to the bridge to stand behind the grim-faced Mitscher. Almost on the horizon Doolittle could see what looked like a tiny ship, and then it was hidden in dark, black smoke.

A Japanese patrol ship had been spotted and the cruiser *Northampton* had been ordered to destroy it. Now it was up to Halsey. The task force was 823 miles off the Japanese coast. If it could stay on its present course another nine or ten hours, Doolittle felt that the hazards of the raid would not be exceptional. But if Halsey insisted that they take off now, the risks would be increased enormously. A man on the bridge of the *Enterprise* began wigwagging furiously. A signal officer standing close to Captain Mitscher wrote down the message and handed it to him. Halsey had decided. Mitscher turned to Doolittle and shrugged his shoulders.

'You know the score, Jimmy,' he said quietly.

Doolittle nodded. That small Japanese ship had seen the task force long before it had been spotted itself. If it had radio or wireless on board, by now Tokyo knew that a group of American ships was headed for the Japanese coast. Within a matter of minutes Japanese airfields with airplanes ready and pilots eager might have been alerted.

'We'll get off as soon as possible, Pete,' he said, and then gave the signal that called all of his crews into the briefing room. He walked in with Mitscher. The *Hornet* was rolling slightly but pitching heavily.

'This is it, men,' Doolittle told his crews. 'You all know exactly what to do. We have to take off about twelve hours ahead of schedule. This task force has to get the hell out of here fast. I have got just three additional things to tell you. The pitching of this ship presents a problem which we will solve this way. Watch the way I take off and do exactly as I do. If we take off when the bow of the ship is at the height of its pitch, it means we will be taking off uphill, and we may not have enough power to clear the deck. If we take off when the flight deck has its nose in the sea, we will end up in the drink. Here's how we'll do it. As the bow, after reaching its lowest point, begins to come up, give it the gun. You'll have the advantage of travelling for two seconds downhill. By the time you reach the end of the flight deck the nose of the ship should be just ship level and your take-off should be easy. This way we will be able to take advantage of the pitching of the ship. Any questions?'

The men sat there quietly, listening intently to his crisp but still rather casual voice. There were no questions.

'We will have to travel a little further than we figured on,' Doolittle continued. 'I've had ten additional five-gallon cans of gasoline put in each aircraft. As soon as the gas tanks back by the rear gun mount start to empty, crew chiefs will refuel them from the five-gallon cans. Don't jettison the cans as you use them or we'll leave a perfect trail for the Japs back to the task force. Wait until you empty all of the cans and then dump them all at once.

'One thing more.' Doolittle turned to Pete Mitscher. 'Captain, you have been wonderful to us. So was your whole crew. I have got to ask you just one more favor. After we have taken off, can you maintain a straight course for a few moments?'

Mitscher nodded.

'All the metal on this ship has affected some of our compasses. We all know you are headed exactly due west now. As each plane takes off it will circle and then fly directly over the length of the *Hornet*. In that way each of us can get an exact compass check. If there are no questions, let's get going. But fast.' Then Doolittle added, 'One more word—watch those suicide fighters of theirs. They'll be glad to swap one pilot and a forty-thousand-dollar Zero for five of us and a two-hundred-thousand-dollar bomber.'

During the brief time that had elapsed between the sighting of the Jap ship and Doolittle's briefing, the *Hornet* crew had pulled the B-25's into position. Lieutenant White, the medical officer, had prescribed one pint of whiskey for each man, and those were put into the planes. Quickly, efficiently, without a bit of lost motion, crewmen 'topped' the gas tanks of each B-25. The gauges already read full, but this was to take care of any evaporation or spillage that might have taken place. The wind had increased now to gale proportions (27 knots). Doolittle walked to his plane. There were no dramatics. He didn't go from plane to plane wishing the pilots and crews luck. That was for amateurs—these were professionals. Every minute counted now. Doolittle climbed into the pilot seat, warmed, then idled his engines. A Navy flight officer stood at the bow of the ship to the left with a checkered flag in his hand. Doolittle and his pilots had learned the carrier customs well. When the man with the flag started swinging it in a circle faster and faster, Doolittle knew it meant to give your engine more throttle. Doolittle turned toward Dick Cole with a question in his eyes. Cole had gone through his check list.

'Everything okay, Colonel,' he said laconically.

Doolittle called through his intercom to crew chief Sergeant Paul Leonard sitting in the back of the plane. 'Everything all right, Paul?' he asked, and 'Everything okay, Colonel,' came the calm answer.

Doolittle turned his eyes back to the man with the checkered flag. He gave the engine more throttle. The flag dropped, he released the brakes, and 31,000 pounds of airplane, bombs and men began to roar down the flight deck. With full flaps and engines roaring at full throttle, the plane lunged down the deck into the teeth of the gale. Every other pilot was watching the take-off. If Doolittle couldn't do it, they couldn't. Just as the *Hornet* lifted itself to a level position, Doolittle took off with a hundred feet to spare. He hung the ship almost straight up on its props, leveled off, and came around in a tight circle. He had made it look incredibly easy, and every pilot now felt better. Doolittle completed his turn and watched the number two ship take off. Travis Hoover was the pilot. The *Hornet's* deck came up after its pitch unexpectedly fast, and Hoover's plane had to scramble uphill. It took off and dropped abruptly, and Doolittle, watching, tried to pray it up. Just before the wheels were about to hit the water, Hoover managed to lift its nose up. Brick Holstrom's plane, Bob Gray's plane, Davey Jones' plane, Dean Hallmark's plane, Ted Lawson's plane, all took off beautifully. But by now Doolittle was headed for Tokyo. He kept the plane almost on the deck, less than two hundred feet above the sea. Two hours out, he turned the controls over to Cole and checked with navigator Henry Potter. Everything appeared to be going on schedule, although strong head winds meant added fuel consumption. Doolittle took over the controls again. About five hours after they had left the *Hornet* they saw the Japanese coast.

Doolittle turned to Potter. 'We're either fifty miles north of Tokyo or fifty miles south of it, that's the way I figure it.'

'I think we're about thirty miles north,' Potter said calmly.

Doolittle nodded.

'We've got company, Colonel,' Cole laughed, and Doolittle, looking out to the left, saw a B-25 dipping its wings in a friendly gesture. This was Travis Hoover's plane—right on schedule. They would go in together.

Now they were over the land, and to his left Doolittle saw a large lake. Potter had been right. The map said that this was just about thirty miles north of Tokyo. He turned south, flying at almost treetop level, and then suddenly, dead ahead of him but a thousand feet above, were five Jap fighters. Doolittle wasn't sure that the fighters had spotted him. There was only one way to find out. He turned to the left, and the five Jap planes turned also. It seemed obvious now to Doolittle that the ship which had intercepted them had carried a radio and had sent out a warning. The whole operation promised to be more difficult than he had anticipated, and the fifty-fifty chances of survival he had announced with such confidence didn't look so good now. In a few moments, Doolittle felt, the Jap planes would peel off and dive at him. He had to think and act quickly.

He straightened out, heading toward Tokyo again, and the five fighters followed suit. Then to the left he saw two hills. He might be able to play hide-and-seek with these Jap fighters. He made another sharp left turn to streak along the valley formed by the hills. The Jap planes turned too, but not quite fast enough. He was through the valley, and a sharp right turn brought him back on his course toward Tokyo. The hill had hidden him from the five fighters for a matter of a few seconds, but that was enough. Evidently thinking that he had continued on his course paralleling the valley, they shot off to the east. All of Doolittle's B-25's had been camouflaged, and the olive drab of the wings melted beautifully into the green of the Japanese countryside.

Doolittle kept his eyes straight ahead, and there suddenly was Tokyo. His target was a munitions factory.

Doolittle lifted the plane to fifteen hundred feet. 'Approaching target,' he told Sergeant Fred Braemer, the bombardier.

And Braemer called back cheerfully, 'All ready, Colonel.'

The bomb bay was opened and Doolittle made his run. It was up to bombardier Braemer now. A small red light blinked on the instrument board and Doolittle knew that the first five-hundred-pound incendiary cluster had gone. In quick succession the red light blinked three more times, and the airplane, relieved of two thousand pounds, seemed to leap into the air. Up to now he had been too intent upon finding the target to notice whether the antiaircraft guns had been firing. He swung the plane toward the coast. Now, looking around, he saw that the sky was pockmarked with black puffs. Through the intercom he called to Sergeant Leonard, 'Everything okay back there, Paul?'

'Everything fine,' Leonard said cheerfully.

'They're missing us a mile, Paul,' Doolittle told him.

Just then a blast rocked the ship and peppered it with bomb fragments. A shell had burst some hundred feet to the left.

'Colonel, that was no mile,' Paul Leonard laughed.

'We're getting out of here,' Doolittle said, giving the engines full throttle and shooting down to the relative safety of a hundred feet. Ahead Jimmy saw an aircraft factory with some thirty brand-new Jap training planes standing temptingly on line. Sergeant Braemer saw it too.

'Colonel, can't we burn up some of those Jap planes?' he yelled through his intercom.

Doolittle resisted the temptation. 'No, Fred,' he said sadly. 'It would only alert them down there, and this would give them a chance to raise hell with any of the boys coming after us.'

At full speed the ship approached the coast. Doolittle was flying directly over what appeared to be a fine concrete highway.

The alert Braemer called, 'Colonel, there is either a tank or armored car up ahead. Can't I let it have a burst?'

'Relax, Fred,' Doolittle called back. 'They probably think we are a friendly aircraft. Let them keep on thinking that. And knocking off one tank isn't going to win this war.'

They crossed the coast and headed southwest, skirting Shikoku and Kyushu. The weather had been fine on this stretch, with a twenty-five-mile tail wind helping. They passed Yaku Shima. Potter was doing a beautiful job of navigation. Now they were over the East China Sea and the weather changed. It became overcast and presently a heavy rain began to fall. The wind changed and Doolittle, calculating the distance left to go against the remaining gasoline supply, came to the unhappy conclusion that he couldn't make the China coast. He told the crew to be prepared to ditch.

'See that the raft is ready, Fred,' he called to Braemer. He then told Leonard to make certain of hanging on to the emergency rations.

'We'll keep going until we're dry,' he added.

Then, unaccountably, the wind died down and the rain stopped. Doolittle, checking his fuel again, decided he might make the coast after all.

Every member of the crew had his eyes glued straight ahead, hoping to catch sight of land. Now a favoring tail wind appeared.

Land, even if it was occupied by the Japs, seemed more inviting than did the cold East China Sea beneath them.

'There it is,' Paul Leonard yelled. 'Damned if I don't feel like Columbus.' He had seen a small offshore island. The islands and the hills in back of the coast were shrouded with low clouds. Darkness was falling. China did not look very hospitable, but then Doolittle hadn't expected China to welcome him with open arms. He knew that when the State Department had informed Chiang Kai-shek of the raid, the Generalissimo had protested vigorously. He feared that if Tokyo were bombed the Japs would retaliate viciously against his own forces. When his discouraging refusal of cooperation had arrived, Hap Arnold told him that it was too late to do anything about it; the task force which carried the raiders was already in Japanese waters and radio silence was being observed. Admiral Halsey had relayed all this information to Doolittle on the *Hornet*.

Actually, the only cooperation Doolittle had wanted from the Chinese was radio help in reaching Chinese airfields. Arnold had sent a message to Doolittle saying that a 'Homer' would be flown from Chungking to Chu Chow by an American crew, and that this should give Doolittle and his men a radio fix that should make it possible for them to find the Chinese field. But there was one thing that Doolittle did not know. He did not know that the plane flying the radio equipment from Chungking to Chu Chow had crashed in the hills surrounding the Chinese airfield. The crew had been killed and all of the radio equipment destroyed.

Doolittle learned afterwards that Chinese airfields had picked up his frantic plea for a 'fix,' but they had thought the message had been sent by Jap planes and had ordered an immediate radio blackout. A few hours before, Chungking had sent a message alerting Chinese airfields to be ready for a friendly American group of planes, but the message had been garbled in transmission and not one air base commander in China knew that Doolittle and his raiders were on the way. These were risks which no amount of careful planning could foresee.

As he crossed the coast he climbed up to nine thousand feet and put the plane on automatic pilot. Then he sent out the prearranged code signal and waited for word from the Homer that would bring him to Chu Chow. There was no answer. He tried again and again, but there was nothing but complete silence. He figured he was about fifty miles from the airport, and now he knew that if he was to reach it at all it would have to be on his own instruments.

Doolittle knew that Chu Chow was in a hollow framed by a four-thousand-foot mountain range. He knew that he was close to it, but the darkness and the bad weather kept him from determining exactly where they were.

'We don't dare go down; we can't live under this stuff,' he muttered to Cole, so they remained at nine thousand feet, far above the mountains. He agreed with Potter that they were approximately over Chu Chow.

'In this weather, we can't get a better fix than we've got now,' he said to the crew. 'If we keep on going in any direction, we'll just be getting further away from Chu Chow. I'm going to circle as long as we have any gas left. If the weather breaks, we'll go down and take a better look. If it doesn't, we'll have to jump.'

Fifteen minutes later it was obvious that the overcast was not going to break. If anything it had thickened, and finally, although the engines kept roaring, the gas gauge showed empty.

'We'll have to bail out,' Doolittle said calmly through his intercom. 'Leonard first, then Braemer, then Potter, then Cole. Got it?'

'Got it, Colonel,' Leonard called back laconically.

He circled twice more, put the plane on gyro-pilot, and then the starboard motor began to cough. 'Get going,' he cried, and in rapid succession Leonard, Braemer and Potter leaped from the ship.

He turned to copilot Cole. 'Be seeing you in a few minutes, Dick,' he said.

Cole smiled and tried to rise from his seat. Doolittle saw that the straps of his parachute somehow had become entangled with the back of the pilot's seat. He untangled them and slapped Cole on the shoulder. Cole disappeared through the escape hatch. Doolittle shut off the gasoline and dove into the black night.

His descent was smooth. He was worried only about one thing. If he landed on hard ground, it was quite possible he would re-break the two ankles which had been fractured in South America back in the 1920's. He decided that instead of making the conventional paratrooper's landing, he would try to touch the ground lightly with his feet, and with knees bent take the full shock of the landing on his rump. But he landed in one of the softest, wettest rice paddies in China. He sank to his knees, sat down to his waist and then scrambled out of the rice paddy, soaking wet and bitter cold.

Doolittle was promoted to Brigadier-General and awarded the Medal of Honor for his part in the Tokyo Mission.

GUY GIBSON VC
Dambusting

The now famous attack on the Ruhr Valley dams by RAF 617 Squadron took place on 16 May 1943. The purpose of the raid, which was the culmination of considerable scientific experiment and air training, was to disrupt production in Germany's industrial heartland. Nineteen Lancaster bombers, led by Wing Commander Guy Gibson, took part in the action, eight of which were lost. The Möhne and Eder dams, were, however, destroyed. (A third dam, the Sorpe, survived the bouncing-bomb that hit it.) Here Guy Gibson describes the attack on the Möhne dam. He was killed in action a year later.

THE MINUTES PASSED SLOWLY as we all sweated on this summer's night, sweated at working the controls and sweated with fear as we flew on. Every railway train, every hamlet and every bridge we passed was a potential danger, for our Lancasters were sitting targets at that height and speed. We fought our way past Dortmund, past Hamm—the well-known Hamm which has been bombed so many times; we could see it quite clearly now, its tall chimneys, factories and balloons capped by its umbrella of flak like a Christmas tree about five miles to our right; then we began turning to the right in between Hamm and the little town of Soest, where I nearly got shot down in 1940. Soest was sleepy now and did not open up, and out of the haze ahead appeared the Ruhr hills.

'We're there,' said Spam.

'Thank God,' said I, feelingly.

As we came over the hill, we saw the Möhne Lake. Then we saw the dam itself. In that light it looked squat and heavy and unconquerable; it looked grey and solid in the moonlight, as though it were part of the countryside itself and just as immovable. A structure like a battleship was showering out flak all along its length, but some came from the powerhouse below it and nearby. There were no searchlights. It was light flak, mostly green, yellow and red, and the colours of the tracer reflected upon the face of the water in the lake. The reflections on the dead calm of the black water made it seem there was twice as much as there really was.

'Did you say these gunners were out of practice?' asked Spam, sarcastically.

'They certainly seem awake now,' said Terry.

They were awake all right. No matter what people say, the Germans certainly have a good warning system. I scowled to myself as I remembered telling the boys an hour or so ago that they would probably only be the German equivalent of the Home Guard and in bed by the time we arrived.

It was hard to say exactly how many guns there were, but tracers seemed to be coming from about five positions, probably making twelve guns in all. It was hard at first to tell the calibre of the shells, but after one of the boys had been hit, we were informed over the RT that they were either 20-mm type or 37-mm, which, as everyone knows, are nasty little things.

We circled around stealthily, picking up the various landmarks upon which we had planned our method of attack, making use of some and avoiding others; every time we came within range of those bloody-minded flak-gunners they let us have it.

'Bit aggressive, aren't they?' said Trevor.

'Too right they are.'

I said to Terry, 'God, this light flak gives me the creeps.'

'Me, too,' someone answered.

For a time there was a general blind on the subject of light flak, and the only man who didn't say anything was Hutch, because he could not see it and because he never said anything about flak, anyway. But this was not the time for talking. I called up each member of our formation and found, to my relief, that they had all arrived, except, of course, Bill Astell. Away to the south, Joe McCarthy had just begun his diversionary attack on the Sorpe. But not all of them had been able to get there; both Byers and Barlow had been shot down by light flak after crossing the coast;

these had been replaced by other aircraft of the rear formation. Bad luck, this being shot down after crossing the coast, because it could have happened to anybody; they must have been a mile or so off track and had got the hammer. This is the way things are in flying; you are either lucky or you aren't. We, too, had crossed the coast at the wrong place and had got away with it. We were lucky.

Down below, the Möhne Lake was silent and black and deep, and I spoke to my crew.

'Well, boys, I suppose we had better start the ball rolling.' This with no enthusiasm whatsoever. 'Hello, all Cooler aircraft. I am going to attack. Stand by to come in to attack in your order when I tell you.'

Then to Hoppy: 'Hello, "M Mother". Stand by to take over if anything happens.'

Hoppy's clear and casual voice came back. 'OK, Leader. Good luck.'

Then the boys dispersed to the pre-arranged hiding-spots in the hills, so that they should not be seen either from the ground or from the air, and we began to get into position for our approach. We circled wide and came around down moon, over the high hills at the eastern end of the lake. On straightening up we began to dive towards the flat, ominous water two miles away. Over the front turret was the dam silhouetted against the haze of the Ruhr Valley. We could see the towers. We could see the sluices. We could see everything. Spam, the bomb-aimer, said, 'Good show. This is wizard.' He had been a bit worried, as all bomb-aimers are, in case they cannot see their aiming points, but as we came in over the tall fir trees his voice came up again rather quickly. 'You're going to hit them. You're going to hit those trees.'

'That's all right, Spam. I'm just getting my height.'

To Terry: 'Check height, Terry.'

To Pulford: 'Speed control, Flight-Engineer.'

To Trevor: 'All guns ready, gunners.'

To Spam: 'Coming up, Spam.'

Terry turned on the spotlights and began giving directions—'Down—down—down. Steady—steady.' We were then exactly sixty feet.

Pulford began working the speed; first he put on a little flap to slow us down, then he opened the throttles to get the air-speed indicator exactly against the red mark. Spam began lining up his sights against the towers. He had turned the fusing switch to the 'ON' position. I began flying.

The gunners had seen us coming. They could see us coming with our spotlights on for over two miles away. Now they opened up and the tracers began swirling towards us; some were even bouncing off the smooth surface of the lake. This was a horrible moment: we were being dragged along at four miles a minute, almost against our will, towards the things we were going to destroy. I think at that moment the boys did not want to go. I know I did not want to go. I thought to myself, 'In another minute we shall all be dead—so what?' I thought again, 'This is terrible—this feeling of fear—if it is fear.' By now we were a few hundred yards away, and I said quickly to Pulford, under my breath, 'Better leave the throttles open now and stand by to pull me out of the seat if I get hit.' As I glanced at him I thought he looked a little glum on hearing this.

The Lancaster was really moving and I began looking through the special sight on my windscreen. Spam had his eyes glued to the bombsight in front, his hand on his button; a special mechanism on board had already begun to work so that the mine would drop (we hoped) in the right spot. Terry was still checking the height. Joe and Trev began to raise their guns. The flak could see us quite clearly now. It was not exactly inferno. I have been through far worse flak fire than that; but we were very low. There was something sinister and slightly unnerving about the whole operation. My aircraft was so small and the dam was so large; it was thick and solid, and now it was angry. My aircraft was very small. We skimmed along the surface of the lake, and as we went my gunner was firing into the defences, and the defences were firing back with vigour, their shells whistling past us. For some reason, we were not being hit.

Spam said, 'Left—little more left—steady—steady—steady—coming up.' Of the next few seconds I remember only a series of kaleidoscopic incidents.

The chatter from Joe's front guns pushing out tracers which bounced off the left-hand flak tower.

Pulford crouching beside me.

The smell of burnt cordite.

The cold sweat underneath my oxygen mask.

The tracers flashing past the windows—they all seemed the same colour now—and the inaccuracy of the gun positions near the power-station; they were firing in the wrong direction.

The closeness of the dam wall.

Spam's exultant, 'Mine gone'.

Hutch's red Very lights to blind the flak-gunners.

The speed of the whole thing.

Someone was saying over the RT, 'Good show, leader. Nice work.'

Then it was all over, and at last we were out of range, and there came over us all, I think, an immense feeling of relief and confidence.

Trevor said, 'I will get those bastards,' and he began to spray the dam with bullets until at last he, too, was out of range. As we circled round we could see a great 1000-feet column of whiteness still hanging in the air where our mine had exploded. We could see with satisfaction that Spam had been good, and it had gone off in the right position. Then, as we came closer, we could see that the explosion of the mine had caused a great disturbance upon the surface of the lake and the water had become broken and furious, as though it were being lashed by a gale. At first we thought that the dam itself had broken, because great sheets of water were slopping over the top of the wall like a gigantic basin. This caused some delay, because our mines could only be dropped in calm water, and we would have to wait until all became still again.

We waited.

We waited about ten minutes, but it seemed hours to us. It must have seemed even longer to Hoppy, who was the next to attack. Meanwhile, all the fighters had now collected over our target. They knew our game by now, but we were flying too low for them; they could not see us and there were no attacks.

At last—'Hello, "M Mother". You may attack now. Good luck.'

'OK. Attacking.'

Hoppy, the Englishman, casual, but very efficient, keen now on only one thing, which was war. He began his attack.

He began going down over the trees where I had come from a few moments before. We could see his spotlights quite clearly, slowly closing together as he ran across the water. We saw him approach. The flak, by now, had got an idea from which direction the attack was coming, and they let him have it. When he was about 100 yards away someone said, hoarsely, over the RT: 'Hell! He has been hit.'

'M Mother' was on fire; an unlucky shot had got him in one of the inboard petrol tanks and a long jet of flame was beginning to stream out. I saw him drop his mine, but his bomb-aimer must have been wounded, because it fell straight on to the power-house on the other side of the dam. But Hoppy staggered on, trying to gain altitude so that his crew could bale out. When he had got to about 500 feet there was a vivid flash in the sky and one wing fell off; his aircraft disintegrated and fell to the ground in cascading, flaming fragments. There it began to burn quite gently and rather sinisterly in a field some three miles beyond the dam.

Someone said, 'Poor old Hoppy!'

Another said, 'We'll get those bastards for this.'

A furious rage surged up inside my own crew, and Trevor said, 'Let's go in and murder those gunners.' As he spoke, Hoppy's mine went up. It went up behind the power-house with a tremendous yellow explosion and left in the air a great ball of black smoke; again there was a long wait while we watched for this to clear. There was so little wind that it took a long time.

Many minutes later I told Mickey to attack; he seemed quite confident, and we ran in beside him and a little in front; as we turned, Trevor did his best to get those gunners as he had promised.

Bob Hay, Mickey's bomb-aimer, did a good job, and his mine dropped in exactly the right place. There was again a gigantic explosion as the whole surface of the lake shook, then spewed forth its cascade of white water. Mickey was all right; he got through. But he had been hit several times and one wing-tank lost all its petrol. I could see the vicious tracer from his rear-gunner giving one gun position a hail of bullets as he swept over. Then he called up, 'OK. Attack completed.' It was then that I thought that the dam wall had moved. Of course we could not see anything, but if Jeff's theory had been correct, it should have cracked by now. If only we could go on pushing it by dropping more successful mines, it would surely move back on its axis and collapse.

Once again we watched for the water to calm down. Then in

came Melvyn Young in 'D Dog'. I yelled to him, 'Be careful of the flak. It's pretty hot.'

He said, 'OK.'

I yelled again, 'Trevor's going to beat them up on the other side. He'll take most of it off you.'

Melvyn's voice again. 'OK. Thanks.' And so as 'D Dog' ran in we stayed at a fairly safe distance on the other side, firing with all guns at the defences, and the defences, like the stooges they were, firing back at us. We were both out of range of each other, but the ruse seemed to work, and we flicked on our identification lights to let them see us even more clearly. Melvyn's mine went in, again in exactly the right spot, and this time a colossal wall of water swept right over the dam and kept on going. Melvyn said, 'I think I've done it. I've broken it.' But we were in a better position to see than he, and it had not rolled down yet. We were all getting pretty excited by now, and I screamed like a schoolboy over the RT: 'Wizard show, Melvyn. I think it'll go on the next one.'

Now we had been over the Möhne for quite a long time, and all the while I had been in contact with Scampton Base. We were in close contact with the Air Officer Commanding and the Commander-in-Chief of Bomber Command, and with the scientist, observing his own greatest scientific experiment in Damology. He was sitting in the operations room, his head in his hands, listening to the reports as one after another the aircraft attacked. On the other side of the room the Commander-in-Chief paced up and down. In a way their job of waiting was worse than mine. The only difference was that they did not know that the structure was shifting as I knew, even though I could not see anything clearly.

When at last the water had all subsided I called up No 5—David Maltby—and told him to attack. He came in fast, and I saw his mine fall within feet of the right spot; once again the flak, the explosion and wall of water. But this time we were on the wrong side of the wall and could see what had happened. We watched for about five minutes, and it was rather hard to see anything, for by now the air was full of spray from these explosions, which had settled like mist on our windscreens. Time was getting short, so I called up Dave Shannon and told him to come in.

As he turned I got close to the dam wall and then saw what had happened. It had rolled over, but I could not believe my eyes. I heard someone shout, 'I think she has gone!' Other voices took up the cry and quickly I said, 'Stand by until I make a recco.' I remembered that Dave was going in to attack and told him to turn away and not to approach the target. We had a closer look. Now there was no doubt about it; there was a great breach 100 yards across, and the water, looking like stirred porridge in the moonlight, was gushing out and rolling into the Ruhr Valley towards the industrial centres of Germany's Third Reich.

Nearly all the flak had now stopped, and the other boys came down from the hills to have a closer look to see what had been done. There was no doubt about it at all—the Möhne Dam had been breached and the gunners on top of the dam, except for one man, had all run for their lives towards the safety of solid ground; this remaining gunner was a brave man, but one of the boys quickly extinguished his flak with a burst of well-aimed tracer. Now it was all quiet, except for the roar of the water which steamed and hissed its way from its 150-foot head. Then we began to shout and scream and act like madmen over the RT, for this was a tremendous sight, a sight which probably no man will ever see again.

Quickly I told Hutch to tap out the message, 'Nigger', to my station, and when this was handed to the Air Officer Commanding there was (I heard afterwards) great excitement in the operations room. The scientist jumped up and danced round the room.

Then I looked again at the dam and at the water, while all around me the boys were doing the same. It was the most amazing sight. The whole valley was beginning to fill with fog from the steam of the gushing water, and down in the foggy valley we saw cars speeding along the roads in front of this great wave of water, which was chasing them and going faster than they could ever hope to go. I saw their headlights burning and I saw water overtake them, wave by wave, and then the colour of the headlights underneath the water changing from light blue to green from green to dark purple, until there was no longer anything except the water bouncing down in great waves. The floods raced on, carrying with them as they went—viaducts, railways, bridges and everything that stood in their path. Three miles beyond the dam the remains of Hoppy's aircraft were still burning gently, a dull red glow on the ground. Hoppy had been avenged.

Then I felt a little remote and unreal sitting up there in the warm cockpit of my Lancaster, watching this mighty power which we had unleashed; then glad, because I knew that this was the heart of Germany, and the heart of her industries, the place which itself had unleashed so much misery upon the whole world.

We knew, as we watched, that this flood-water would not win the war; it would not do anything like that, but it was a catastrophe for Germany.

I circled round for about three minutes, then called up all aircraft and told Mickey and David Maltby to go home and the rest to follow me to Eder, where we would try to repeat the performance.

JAMES McPHERSON
The *Merrimack* and the *Monitor*

The American Civil War saw the dawn of a new age in naval warfare, when the Confederate Merrimack *(also known as the* Virginia*) clashed with the Northern* Monitor *in 1862 in the first battle between two ironclads.*

HAVING NO TRADITIONS AND FEW old-navy prejudices to overcome, the rebels got a head start into the new era of ironclad warships. In July 1861 they began grafting an armor-plated casemate onto the salvaged hull of the frigate *Merrimack*. Work began in July. The capacity of the Tredegar Iron Works was stretched to the limit to construct two layers of two-inch iron plate sufficient to protect a superstructure 178 feet long and 24 feet high above the waterline and one-inch plate covering the 264-foot hull down to three feet below the waterline. The superstructure sloped at an angle of 36° to give added protection by causing enemy shots to ricochet. The strange appearance of this craft, rechristened the *Virginia*, reminded observers of a barn floating with only its roof above water. The *Virginia* was armed with ten guns: four on each broadside plus fore and aft seven-inch pivot rifles. Attached to her prow was an iron ram to stave in the hulls of wooden warships. The principal defects of this otherwise formidable vessel were its unreliable engines and deep draft. Unable to build new engines of adequate horsepower, the rebels reconditioned the two old *Merrimack* engines that had been condemned by the prewar navy and slated for replacement. The weight of the *Virginia*'s armor gave her a draft of twenty-two feet. This prevented operations in shallow water while her unseaworthiness prevented her from venturing into the open sea. The weak engines and ungainly design limited her speed to four or five knots and made her so unmaneuverable that a 180-degree turn took half an hour. Some of these problems would not become apparent until the *Virginia* was launched; in the meantime she inspired hope in the South and fear in the North.

This fear was the main factor in overcoming northern inertia on the ironclad question. With a conventional navy superior to anything the Confederates could construct, and preoccupied with the need to build up the blockade fleet, Secretary of the Navy Welles did not at first want to experiment with newfangled notions. But rumors of rebel activities caused Congress to force his hand with a law of August 3, 1861, directing the construction of three prototype ironclads. Welles set up a naval board to assess the dozens of proposals submitted by shipbuilders. The board accepted two, which resulted in the building of the *Galena* and the *New Ironsides*, ships of conventional design overlaid by iron plating.

No bid came from John Ericsson, the irascible genius of marine engineering who had contributed the screw propeller and several other innovations to ship design. Bitter about earlier feuds with the navy, Ericsson sulked in his New York office until a shipbuilder persuaded him to submit his radical design to the Navy Department. Ericsson's proposal incorporated several novel features. A wooden hull sheathed with thin iron plate would be overlaid by a flat deck 172 feet long with perpendicular sides extending below the waterline and protected by 4.5 inch armor plating. The propeller, anchor, and all vital machinery would be protected by this shell, which was designed to float with less than two feet of freeboard, giving the craft the appearance of a raft—and also presenting a small target to enemy fire. Sitting on the deck was Ericsson's most important innovation: a revolving turret encased in eight inches of armor and containing two eleven-inch guns. This turret, along with the shallow draft (11 feet), light displacement (1,200 tons, about one-fourth of the *Virginia*'s displacement), and eight-knot speed would give Ericsson's ship maneuverability and versatility. She could almost literally dance around a heavier enemy and fire in any direction.

Lincoln and Welles were impressed by Ericsson's design. But would it float? More specifically, would it stay afloat in a heavy sea? Some members of the naval board were skeptical. They had never seen anything like this cheesebox on a raft. Ericsson appeared before the board and overcame their doubts with a bravura performance. They awarded him a contract, but ridicule of 'Ericsson's folly' by senior navy officers caused Welles to hedge his bet: the ship must prove a 'complete success' (whatever that meant) or its builders must refund every penny of the $275,000 the government agreed to pay for it. Ericsson was not concerned; he had confidence in his creation. He subcontracted the work to several firms to save time, and supervised almost every detail personally. Starting three months later than the South, northern industry launched Ericsson's ironclad on January 30, 1862, two weeks before the Confederates launched the *Virginia*. Doubters present at each launching predicted that these crazy craft would never float, but cheered the disproof of their predictions. Several more weeks were required to finish the fittings of both ships. Ericsson named his vessel *Monitor* (one who admonishes and corrects wrongdoers). There was no time for test runs to determine whether she fulfilled the terms of the contract; the *Monitor*'s test would be trial by combat.

On March 8 the *Virginia* steamed out from Norfolk on what her crew assumed was a test run. But this too was to be the real thing. Five Union ships mounting a total of 219 guns guarded the mouth of the James River at Hampton Roads: the *Minnesota*, *Roanoke*, *St Lawrence*, *Congress*, and *Cumberland*. The last three were sailing ships—pride of the navy in the 1840s but already made obsolescent by steam. The first two were steam frigates (the *Roanoke* was disabled by a broken shaft), pride of the navy in 1862. But the fighting this day would make them obsolescent as well. Rumors that the *Merrimack* (as the Federals continued to call the *Virginia*) was coming out had circulated for weeks. Today she came, heading first for the twenty-four-gun *Cumberland*, sending several shells into her side before ramming and tearing a seven-foot hole in her hull that sent her to the bottom. While this was happening, the *Cumberland* and *Congress* fired numerous broadsides at the *Virginia*, which 'struck and glanced off,' in the words of a northern observer, 'having no more effect than peas from a pop-gun.' This was not quite accurate; before the day was over two of the *Virginia*'s guns were knocked out, every fitting on deck and part of her smokestack were shot away, her ram was wrenched off by the collision with the *Cumberland*, two of her crew were killed and several were wounded. But none of the ninety-eight shots that struck her penetrated the armor or did any disabling damage.

After sinking the *Cumberland*, the *Virginia* went after the fifty-gun *Congress*, raking the helpless vessel with broadsides which started fires that eventually reached the powder magazine and blew her up. The *Minnesota* having run aground in an effort to help her sister ships, the *Virginia* turned her attention to this flagship of the fleet that had captured Hatteras Inlet the previous August. But the *Virginia*'s deep draft prevented her from closing with the *Minnesota* as night came on. The rebels left the *Minnesota* and the other ships for the morrow, and called it a day.

And what a day—the worst in the eighty-six-year history of the U. S. navy. The *Virginia* sank two proud ships within a few hours—a feat no other enemy would accomplish until 1941. At least 240 bluejackets had been killed, including the captain of the *Congress*—more than the navy suffered on any other day of the war. The whole Union fleet at Hampton Roads—still the main blockade base—was threatened with destruction. A taste of panic flavored the telegrams to Washington that night. The cabinet met in emergency session next morning. Secretary of the Navy Welles tried to calm Secretary of War Stanton's nerves with news that the *Monitor* was on its way from Brooklyn to Hampton Roads to confront the *Virginia*. But would she get there in time? And even if she did, was this two-gun 'tin can on a shingle' any match for the rebel monster?

She did, and she was. The *Monitor* had arrived alongside the *Minnesota* the night before, her crew exhausted from fighting a storm that had almost sunk them on the way from Brooklyn. The prospect of fighting the *Virginia*, however, started their adrenalin pulsing again. When the Confederate ship steamed out on the morning of March 9 to finish off the Federal fleet, her crew spied a strange craft next to the *Minnesota*. 'We thought at first it was a raft on which one of the *Minnesota*'s boilers was being taken to shore for repairs,' said a *Virginia* midshipman. But the boiler ran out a gun and fired. A *Monitor* crewman described the *Virginia*'s response: 'You can see surprise in a ship just as you can see it in a man, and there was surprise all over the Merrimac.' The rebels turned their attention from the stranded *Minnesota* to this strange vessel that began circling the sluggish *Virginia* 'like a fice dog' and hurling 175-pound shot from her eleven-inch guns. For two hours the ironclads slugged it out. Neither could punch through the other's armor, though the *Monitor*'s heavy shot cracked the

Virginia's outside plate at several places. At one point the southern ship grounded. As the shallower-draft *Monitor* closed in, many aboard the *Virginia* thought they were finished. But she broke loose and continued the fight, trying without success to ram the *Monitor*. By this time the *Virginia*'s wheezy engines were barely functioning, and one of her lieutenants found her 'as unwieldy as Noah's Ark.' The *Monitor* in turn tried to ram the *Virginia*'s stern to disable her rudder or propeller, but just missed. Soon after this a shell from the *Virginia* struck the *Monitor*'s pilot house, wounding her captain. The Union ship stopped fighting briefly; the *Virginia*, in danger of running aground again, steamed back toward Norfolk. Each crew thought they had won the battle, but in truth it was a draw. The exhausted men on both sides ceased fighting—almost, it seemed, by mutual consent.

This day saw the completion of a revolution in naval warfare begun a generation earlier by the application of steam power to warships. Doomed were the graceful frigates and powerful line-of-battle ships with their towering masts and sturdy oak timbers. When the news of the *Monitor-Virginia* duel reached England, the London *Times* commented: 'Whereas we had available for immediate purposes one hundred and forty-nine first-class warships, we have now two, these two being the *Warrior* and her sister *Ironside* [Britain's experimental ironclads]. There is not now a ship in the English navy apart from these two that it would not be madness to trust to an engagement with that little *Monitor*.'

Of more immediate interest in Washington, the Union fleet at Hampton Roads was saved. For the next two months the *Monitor* and *Virginia* eyed each other warily but did not fight. With no ironclads in reserve, neither side could risk losing its indispensable weapon. When McClellan's army invaded the Virginia peninsula and forced the Confederates back toward Richmond in May 1862, Norfolk fell to the Federals and the *Virginia* was stranded. Too unseaworthy to fight her way into open water and too deep-drafted to retreat up the James River, the plucky ironclad was blown up by her crew on May 11, less than three months after she had been launched. The *Monitor* also failed to live until her first birthday. On the last day of 1862 she sank in a gale off Cape Hatteras while being towed south for a blockade assignment.

BARRETT TILLMAN
The Last Corsair to Bring down a MiG

The Corsair F4U piston-engined fighter was obsolete by the time of the Korean War, and technically no match for the North Vietnamese's MiG-15 jet. This, however, did not stop one US Corsair pilot, Marine Captain Jesse G. Folmar, from downing a MiG fighter in the third year of the war.

IN THE FALL OF 1952 a new menace threatened carrier-based fighter bombers. MiG-15 jets made some of their deepest penetrations yet into Korean airspace. Royal Navy pilots off the *HMS Ocean* fought back-to back combats with the enemy jets on 9 and 10 August. The Hawker Sea Furies claimed one kill, a probable, and three damaged in exchange for one loss and one damaged. The Russian jets were not employed effectively, but the implication was clear: MiGs could bounce the Corsairs at any time.

MAG-12, now under George Axtell, laid plans. Tactics for fighting the faster, better-climbing MiGs were formulated and pilots briefed accordingly. It appeared their new tactics would be put to the test on 7 September during a recon north of Taedong Estuary. 'Postcard,' the advanced radar station on Cho-do Island, informed a flight of F4Us that hostiles were high overhead. Subsequent reports indicated the enemy jets splitting to either side, obviously intending to bracket the Corsairs. The Marines initiated a defensive weave at 2,500 feet, waiting for the Reds to pounce. But nothing happened. Apparently the MiGs preferred less wary opponents.

Two days later the Marines made contact. Two flights of VMA-312 (redesignated from VMF) off the *Sicily* had expended their ordnance on Communist shipping near Chinnampo, southwest of Pyongyang. Thus, the Corsairs were in their best maneuvering configuration when four MiGs appeared from the northwest, over the Yellow Sea.

The MiGs attacked by sections. As the first two began a run, two Corsairs turned into them, forcing a nose-to-nose confrontation. Rather than trade gunfire, the jets climbed upsun. The Marines dived for the deck and headed west, keeping a close watch on their assailants. The MiGs separated, going for both flanks as they had on the 7th. But by the time the F4Us were over Cho-do they had descended through 1,000 feet and the jets turned north.

Next day, 10 September, VMA-312 again tangled with MiGs near Chinnampo. And this time the Communists were more aggressive. Captain Jesse G. Folmar and First Lieutenant Willie L. Daniels launched at 1610 on a two-plane strike against some 300 North Korean troops reported on the south shore of the Taedong River. A TarCap flight was also dispatched, with all Corsairs guarding the same radio frequency in case of trouble.

Coasting in at 10,000 feet, Folmar test-fired his four 20-millimeters and Daniels his six .50 calibers. They located the target area and broke away to explore the estuary before attacking. Three miles east of U.S. occupied Sock to island, Folmar began a turn in his weave. Then he saw two MiGs in loose echelon, heading for the Corsairs. In the next few seconds several things happened. Folmar called, 'Tally ho, bandits!' He went to combat power, jettisoned his ordnance and belly tank, and hollered over the guard channel that he was engaged. At the same time he turned towards the threat, telling Daniels to stay close.

Four hundred yards to port, Daniels shot a look over his right shoulder. A MiG was diving in astern of Folmar. Daniels broke into it and traded gunfire in a brief head-on pass. The MiG turned left and disengaged, allowing Daniels to reverse his turn and complete the weave off Folmar's starboard beam. Daniels glanced at his airspeed indicator and saw he had only 140 knots on the dial.

While Daniels swapped gunfire with his MiG, Folmar saw two more. They closed rapidly from eight o'clock, and Folmar desperately turned left, trying to bring his guns to bear before the bandits opened fire. But the deflection angle was too great, the closing speed too fast. Tracers passed ahead of the 4B; the Reds had over-deflected.

Apparently one MiG passed between Folmar and Daniels. Folmar rolled into a right-hand bank and found the jet in a climbing left turn. The MiG was temporarily vulnerable.'I pulled up, got him in my gunsight, gave him about twenty mils lead, and held a five-second burst,' Folmar reported. 'I could tell I had him boresighted by the blinking flashes along the left side of the fuselage.'

The MiG emitted a gray stream of smoke which turned black in seconds. As it pitched down slightly and decelerated, the pilot ejected in a tumbling ball of smoke. When the parachute opened, Folmar and Daniels passed close enough to see the MiG driver's G-suit was afire. The flaming jet went vertically into the water from 7,000 feet.

As the two Corsairs resumed their weave, four more MiGs approached in loose column. Three or four remained overhead, making ineffective high side passes, but others pressed the attack. A MiG came down on Folmar from six o'clock high. 'There's one on your tail,' screamed Daniels, who weaved towards the jet and fired a quick burst. The bandit passed ahead of the F4Us, out of range.

The odds were now seven against two. Folmar decided that was all the advantage he wanted to concede, and called, 'Break hard left, down.' The two Marines dived for the water at about 35 degrees, Daniels weaving to the right, when another MiG attacked. 'There's another one on your tail,' Daniels told his leader, but Folmar already knew.

The 33-year-old captain had just begun accelerating in his dive when he saw tracers passing to his left. He felt a severe explosion in the port wing, which shuddered violently. The wing had taken 37-mm hits which gutted it to the inboard gun. Knocking off the aileron and four feet of the tip. Folmar had trouble holding the Corsair level; it wanted to roll to port. Yet another MiG began a pass, but Daniels turned towards it and the jet shied away.

Folmar had applied full right stick but the F4U was becoming uncontrollable. He knew he'd never land it in this condition. He transmitted the distress signal, gave his position, and prepared to jump. Between 2,5000 and 3,000 feet he rolled out the right side of the cockpit, fell clear, and pulled his ripcord. 'I heard an earsplitting cracking sound and I saw another MiG fly by me at very close range, his guns blazing at the tight-spinning Corsair,'

Folmar recalled. American antiaircraft guns on nearby Sock-to Island opened fire and the seven MiGs withdrew to the northeast. Folmar dropped into the water only a quarter-mile offshore.

Daniels circled, noting a landing craft and amphibian speeding towards his leader, and headed for the ship. En route, Daniels called the rescue plane and learned Folmar was aboard, in good shape except for an injured arm. The combat had lasted less than eight minutes, and Folmar was rescued in a similar time.

After losing one of their valuable jets to Corsairs, the Communists were not so aggressive for the next few weeks. 'Bandit tracks' were seen high over Pyongyang, but not until 29 September did they become belligerent again. A 312 division was heading west out of Chinnampo when four MiGs surprised the Corsairs by attacking out of the sun. They were spotted just as they opened fire, and the Marines broke hard right to evade the attack. Before the Reds completed their pass, the F4Us dived behind the cover of a mountain range. They waited until the jets withdrew to the north. After that, MiG attacks became increasingly rare.

Jesse Folmar and Willie Daniels's one-sided combat demonstrated the elements of success in fighting jets. A sharp lookout, teamwork, flying skill, and radio discipline defeated the tremendous advantage held by the MiGs. Folmar's victim was the last enemy jet to fall to a piston-engined aircraft during the war.

ERIC SCHMITT
Scud Hunting

The Scud missile was the most potent weapon in the Iraqi armoury during the Persian Gulf War of 1991. New York Times *journalist Eric Schmitt describes the efforts of US Air Force Strike Eagle crews to destroy Scud missile launchers and other Iraqi targets during Operation Desert Storm.*

IN SAUDI ARABIA, FEB. 23—Preparations for an allied ground offensive have brought no respite for the men who fly the Air Force's F-15E Strike Eagle jets. For them, the air war remains a deadly race of dodging spitting anti-aircraft guns and streaking rockets over targets they have christened Scudville, Samstown, AAA Alley and Rat a Tat Tat.

In the crater-pocked landscape they stalk their quarry: tanks, bridges and the main targets, long-range Scud missiles.

The search is carried out in a cramped cockpit for up to eight hours, with fliers peering into the darkness and then down to the surreal glow of an infrared radar screen that turns night into day on the ground below.

The two-man F-15E crews on Scud patrol do not talk openly about death or fatigue, their two greatest worries. They busy themselves with routine tasks to crowd out fears of exploding surface-to-air missiles. They speak of 'spanking' a 60-ton Iraqi tank they blast into a burning metal carcass with a laser-guided 2,000-pound bomb.

'You're trained to hit targets, not people, so you never have to see anyone eye to eye,' said First Lieut. Glenn G. Watson, a 24-year-old weapons officer from Austin, Tex. 'But at night, you sit alone in bed knowing there are people out there and you're bombing them.'

At a sprawling air base in central Saudi Arabia, two squadrons of the pointy-nosed, twin-tailed Strike Eagles from North Carolina roar off every night to the north, usually in pairs, to run carefully planned raids. Some nights the jets bomb tanks; on others they seek out Scud missiles and launchers and whatever else lies in their 'kill box,' an area defined by grid coordinates.

Bristling with precision-guided bombs, air-to-air missiles and a 20-millimeter cannon, the dark-gray, all-weather F-15E is designed to use its heavy firepower and night-fighting sensors to attack targets that are more easily defended in daylight.

The F-15E pilots and back-seat weapons officers, who aim the bombs, have been flying one mission a night—usually three to five hours—six nights a week since the war began. That tempo far surpasses normal peacetime training, and the fliers have had to cope with much higher stress and fatigue.

'There are so many things going on around you in the pitch dark,' said Capt. John Hoff Jr., 28, of Boonville, Mo., the pilot who flies with Lieutenant Watson. 'You're watching where other aircraft are, where people are shooting from, where your target is, and all the while the plane is moving at 500 miles an hour.'

Flight surgeons assigned to the F-15E units, the 335th and the 336th Tactical Fighter Squadrons, prescribed amphetamines with the kick of 20 cups of coffee to keep crews awake during the hectic first week of the war. Sedatives were distributed to help them sleep.

Even when fliers adjust their internal clocks to working at night and sleeping in the day, night flying has other burdens. The crews have few outside visual references once they turn out their running lights when they cross the border into Kuwait or Iraq. They face the danger of losing their bearings, even judging which way is up and down.

In recent weeks, the flight schedule for the night fighters has eased a bit and drugs are rarely used anymore.

Fliers have also adapted to the missions and know better the type of enemy fire to expect.

Physicians who monitor the crews daily for signs of fatigue nonetheless worry that a prolonged war, with continued bombing, could push fliers to their physical and psychological limits.

'I'm extremely concerned about them,' said Capt. Jack Ingari, a flight surgeon with the F-15E squadrons, who flies periodic missions to understand the strains of night flying. 'These are untested waters. We've never been in such a high-technology, prolonged air war.'

For Captain Hoff and Lieutenant Watson, and most of the F-15E crews here, work begins around 4 P.M. after eight hours' rest in tents segregated from the rest of this base.

In a tent along the flight line that serves as squadron headquarters, the two young fliers meet Lieut. Col. Mike DeCuir, 40, and Maj. Larry Coleman, 37, an experienced pilot and weapons officer team who make up the other half of the two-plane patrol.

Working side-by-side for weeks, even months, the partners come to know each other's tiniest habits and idiosyncrasies—crucial nuances during combat missions when radio chatter is limited and decisions are made in split seconds.

The two teams pore over their assigned target, a communications complex, assessing the route, the attack strategy, the appropriate bombs to drop and the enemy antiaircraft fire anticipated.

Like batters scouting a new pitcher, the partners have already discussed weather, ground artillery threats and targets with counterparts who flew earlier missions.

More than a month into the war, the two teams, with 25 to 30 missions each, plan carefully, but an air of quiet confidence has replaced the tense anxiety that filled the squadron room in the war's early days.

'You slowly work your way up to the mission, whereas 30 days ago, emotionally, we were up immediately,' said Colonel DeCuir. 'We've learned to pace ourselves a bit.'

What took five or six hours to plan when the Iraqi Air Force was still a threat and ground-fire batteries were unknown, is now finished in about 60 minutes.

The first few days of war were the roughest, mentally and physically, the fliers said. The strain from the sudden surge in the frequency and duration of missions was intense.

'You would think, "How am I going to perform? Am I going to screw up?"' said Major Coleman, who lives in the Cumberland Gap area of eastern Tennessee.

The fliers wear one-piece olive-green flight suits made of flame-retardant fabric. They strap on a parachute harness and a G-suit, which, when it is plugged to a hose in the cockpit, inflates during combat maneuvers to keep the blood from rushing from a flier's head, causing blackouts. Finally, there are lucky charms.

'There's no fighter pilot who's superstitious, but everyone carries a charm,' said Lieutenant Watson, grinning, but declining to reveal his talisman.

Slung over a flier's shoulder are dark-green survival bags holding a steel-gray fiberglass helmet, checklists, radios, flight manuals and a handgun, either .38 caliber or 9 millimeter.

For the younger men, there have been many long, private talks to prepare for the likelihood of killing and the possibility of dying.

'You get into little groups and talk about everything: being scared about getting shot at, watching someone else go down and working together,' Lieutenant Watson said.

The patrol's mission tonight was quick and uneventful, meaning no antiaircraft fire. The two jets dropped their laser-guided, 500-pound bombs in 18 minutes, destroying several buildings and vehicles, and quickly headed home.

Even on the best-scouted missions, though, there is always the fear of SAM's, surface-to-air missiles: a sudden white flash on the ground and then a 'red ball of fire' rocketing toward you, Captain Hoff said.

'It's a completely new experience having someone on the ground trying to kill you as hard as they can,' Captain Ingari said.

For the crews, survival depends on split-second midair gyrations—'shucking and jiving' in fighter-pilot lingo—to shake a missile.

'You hear a lot of chatter on the radio,' Major Coleman said. 'You shouldn't hear any explosions. If you hear an explosion, it's too close.'

In the first three days of the mission, however, the F-15E squadrons had two planes shot down. Two crew members were captured; two are still listed as missing.

'It's a bad feeling talking to someone on the radio and suddenly they're not there,' Major Coleman said.

The fliers say they are containing their grief, but flight surgeons said the bottled-up emotions will be reckoned with.

JOHN SIMPSON
The Bombing of Baghdad

John Simpson, the Foreign Affairs Editor of the British Broadcasting Corporation, was in Baghdad when Operation Desert Storm 1991 began. This is his account of the allied bombardment of the Iraqi capital.

Thursday
17 January

IT HAD TAKEN US MUCH too long to get our gear together. I was angry with myself as we ran across the marble floor of the hotel lobby, scattering the security men and Ministry of Information minders.

A voice wailed after us in the darkness: 'But where are you going?' 'There's a driver here somewhere,' said Anthony Wood, the freelance cameraman we had just hired. When I saw which driver it was, I swore. He was the most cowardly of them all. The calmer, more rational voice of Eamonn Matthews, our producer, cut in: 'We'll have to use him. There's no one else.' It was true. The other drivers knew there was going to be an attack, and had vanished.

We had no idea where we wanted to go. There was no high ground, to give us a good shot of the city. We argued as the car screeched out of the hotel gate and down into the underpass. 'No bridges,' I said. 'He's heading for 14th July Bridge. If they bomb that we'll never get back.'

The driver swerved alarmingly, tyres squealing. At that moment, all round us, the anti-aircraft guns started up. Brilliant red and white tracer arched into the sky, then died and fell away.

There was the ugly rumble of bombs. I looked at my watch: 2.37 a.m. The bombing of Baghdad had begun 23 minutes earlier than we had been told to expect. For us, those minutes would have made all the difference.

The sweat shone on the driver's face in the light of the flashes. 'Where's he going now?' He did a wild U-turn, just as the sirens started their belated wailing. Anthony wrestled with the unaccustomed camera. 'I'm getting this,' he grunted. The lens was pointing at a ludicrous angle into the sky as another immense burst of fireworks went off beside us. It was hard not to flinch at the noise.

'The bloody idiot—he's heading straight back to the hotel.' The driver had had enough. He shot in through the gates and stopped. We had failed ignominiously in our effort to escape the control of the authorities and now we were back.

I had become obsessed with getting out of the Al Rasheed Hotel. It smelled of decay, and it lay between five major targets the presidential palace, the television station, an airfield, several Ministries. I had no desire to be trapped with 300 people in the underground shelters there, and I wanted to get away from the government watchers. Television requires freedom of action, and yet we were trapped again.

In the darkness of the lobby angry hands grabbed us and pushed us downstairs into the shelter. The smell of frightened people in a confined space was already starting to take over. Anthony held the camera over his head to get past the sobbing women who ran against us in the corridor. Children cried. Then the lights went out, and there was more screaming until the emergency power took over. Most of the Western journalists, were hanging round the big shelter. I was surprised to see one of the cameramen there: he had a reputation for courage and independence, but now he was just looking at the waves of frightened people with empty red eyes. Anthony, by contrast was neither worried nor elated. He was mostly worried about getting his equipment together.

Not that it *was* his equipment. Anthony had stepped in to help us because our own cameramen had to leave. It had been a difficult evening. As more and more warnings came in from New York, Paris and London, about the likelihood of an attack, almost every news organisation with people in Baghdad was instructing them to leave. The personal warnings President Bush had given to American editors suggested that the coming onslaught would be the worst since the Second World War.

I remembered my grandfather's stories of men going mad under the bombardment at the Somme and Passchendaele. This would be the first high-tech war in history and most newspapers and television companies were reluctant to expose their employees to it. The BBC, too, had ordered us out. Some wanted to; others didn't. In the end it came to a four-three split: Bob Simpson, the radio correspondent and a good friend of mine for years, decided to stay; so did Eamonn Matthews. I was the third. In our cases the BBC, that most civilised of British institutions, came up with a sensible formula: it was instructing us to leave, but promised to take no action against us if we refused.

We still needed a cameraman. But by now there were several people whose colleagues had decided to move out, but who were determined to stay themselves. We found two who were prepared to work with us: Nick Della Casa and Anthony Wood.

There seemed to be no getting out of the shelter. Guards, some of them armed with Kalashnikovs, stood at each of the exits from the basement. They had orders to stop anyone leaving. The main shelter was now almost too full to sit or lie down. Some people seemed cheerful enough, and clapped and sang or watched Iraqi television. Children were crying, and guests and hotel staff were still arriving all the time from the upper floors.

In the general panic, the normal patterns of behaviour were forgotten. A woman in her thirties arrived in a coat and bath towel, and slowly undressed and put on more clothes in front of everyone. Nobody paid her the slightest attention. The heavy metal doors with their rubber linings and the wheel for opening and closing them, as in a submarine, stayed open.

Even so, I felt pretty bad. From time to time it seemed to me that the structure of the hotel swayed a little as if bombs were landing around us. Perhaps it was my imagination. To be stuck here, unable to film anything except a group of anxious people, was the worst thing I could imagine. Anthony and I got through the submarine door and tried to work our way up the staircase that led to the outside world. A guard tried to stop us, but I waited till the next latecomer arrived and forced my way through. Anthony followed.

The upper floors were in darkness. We laboured along the corridor, trying to work out by feel which was our office. Listening at one door, I heard the murmur of voices and we were let in. The sky was lit up by red, yellow and white flashes, and there was no need for us to light torches or candles. Every explosion had us cowering and ducking. I wandered round a little and asked a friendly cameraman to film what's called in the trade 'a piece to camera' for me.

Despite the crash and the whine of bombs and artillery outside we whispered to each other. By now, though, I was acclimatising to the conditions, and sorted out the words in my head before I started. You are not popular with cameramen if you need too many takes under such circumstances.

Back in the corridor there was a flash from a torch, and an Iraqi called out my name. A security man had followed me up from the shelter. In order to protect the others I walked down towards him in the yellow torchlight. I had no idea what I was going to do, but I saw a partly open door to my left and slipped inside. I was lucky. The vivid flashes through the window showed I was in a suite of rooms which someone was using as an office.

I worked my way past the furniture and locked myself in the bedroom at the end. Lying on the floor, I could see the handle turning slowly in the light from the battle outside. When the security man found the door was locked he started banging on it and calling out my name, but these doors were built to withstand rocket attacks; a mere security man had no chance.

Close by, a 2,000-pound penetration bomb landed, but contrary to the gossip in the hotel neither my eyeballs nor the fillings in my teeth came out. I switched on the radio I found by the bed and listened to President Bush explaining what was going on. It was 5.45, and I was soon asleep.

At nine o'clock there was more banging on the door, and more calling of my name. It was Eamonn, who had tracked me down to tell me he had got our satellite telephone to work. Smuggling the equipment through the airport two weeks before had been a smart piece of work, and in a city without power and without communications we now had both a generator and the means to broadcast to the outside world.

Eamonn moved the delicate white parasol of the dish around until it locked on to the satellite. It was hard to think that something so complex could be achieved so easily. We dialled up the BBC and spoke to the pleasant, cool voice of the traffic manager. It was just as if we were somewhere sensible, and not sheltering against a brick wall from the air raids. I gave a brief account to the interviewer at the other end about the damage that the raids had caused in the night: the telecommunications tower damaged, power stations destroyed. I had less idea what was happening on the streets. Directly the broadcast was over. I headed out with Anthony for a drive around. 'Not good take picture now, Mr John,' said the driver. He was an elderly crook but I had an affection for him all the same. 'Got to work, I'm afraid, Ali.' He groaned.

It was extraordinary: the city was in the process of being deprived of power and communications, and yet the only sign of damage I could see was a broken window at the Ministry of Trade. The streets were almost empty, except for soldiers trying to hitch a lift. 'Going Kuwait, Basra,' said Ali. Some were slightly wounded, and their faces seemed completely empty.

Iraqis are normally animated and sociable, but there was no talking now, even in the bigger groups. A woman dragged her child along by its arm. A few old men squatted with a pile of oranges or a few boxes of cigarettes in front of them. An occasional food shop or a tea-house was open; that was all.

'Allah.' A white car was following us. 'He see you take picture.' I told Ali to take a sudden right turn, but he lacked the courage. The security policeman waved us down. 'Just looking round,' I said, as disarmingly as I could. 'He say you come with him.' 'Maybe,' said Anthony.

We got back into the car, and followed the white car for a little. The Al Rasheed Hotel was in the distance. 'Go there,' I said loudly, and Ali for once obeyed. The policeman waved and shouted, but by now the sirens were wailing again and the Ministry of Defence, on the left bank of the river, went up in a column of brown and grey smoke.

Ali put his foot down, and made it to the hotel. The policeman in his white car arrived 30 seconds after us, but obediently searched for a place in the public car park while the three of us ran into the hotel and lost ourselves in the crowd which filled the lobby.

In a windowless side office, where our minders sat for safety,

I spotted a face I knew: Jana Schneider, an American war photographer, completely fearless. Throughout the night she had wandered through Baghdad filming the falling missiles. Near the Sheraton she had watched a 'smart' bomb take out a Security Ministry building while leaving the houses on either side of it undamaged.

I found it hard to believe, and yet it tied in with my own observation. This extraordinary precision was something new in warfare. As the day wore on, Baghdad seemed to me to be suffering from an arteriosclerosis—it appeared unchanged, and yet its vital functions were atrophying with each new air raid. It was without water, power and communication.

I was putting together an edited report for our departing colleagues to smuggle out when someone shouted that a cruise missile had just passed the window. Following the line of the main road beside the hotel and travelling from south-west to north-east, it flashed across at 500 miles an hour, making little noise and leaving no exhaust. It was 20 feet long, and was a good hundred yards from our window. It undulated a little as it went, following the contours of the road. It was like the sighting of a UFO.

Another air raid began, and I ran down the darkened corridor to report over our satellite phone. Lacking the navigational sophistication of the cruise missile, I slammed into a heavy mahogany desk where the hotel security staff sometimes stationed themselves. I took the corner in the lower ribs and lay there for a little.

When I reported soon after that I was the only known casualty of the day's attacks among the Al Rasheed's population and explained that I had cracked a couple of ribs, this was taken in London to be a coded message that I had been beaten up.

I was deeply embarrassed. Having long disliked the journalist-as-hero school of reporting, I found myself a mild celebrity for something which emphatically hadn't taken place. An entire country's economic and military power was being dismantled, its people were dying, and I was broadcasting about cracked ribs. Each time they hurt I felt it was a punishment for breaking the basic rule: don't talk about yourself.

In the coffee shop, a neat but exhausted figure was reading from a thick sheaf of papers. Naji Al-Hadithi was a figure of power for the foreign journalists in Baghdad, since he was Director-General of the Information Ministry. Some found him sinister: a *New York Times* reporter took refuge in the US embassy for four nights after talking to him. I thought he was splendid company, a considerable Anglophile, and possessed of an excellent sense of humour. Once I took a colleague of mine to see him, and he asked where we'd been. 'We went to Babylon, to see what the whole country will look like in a fortnight's time,' I said. For a moment I thought I'd gone much too far, then I saw Al-Hadithi was rocking with silent laughter.

Now he looked close to exhaustion, and his clothes were rumpled. He read out some communiqués and a long, scarcely coherent letter from Saddam Hussein to President Bush. Afterwards we talked about the censorship the Ministry planned to impose. In the darkened lobby of the hotel, with the candlelight glinting on glasses and rings and the buttons of jackets, we argued amicably about the new rules. It seemed to me that it was the Security Ministry, not his own, that was insisting on them.

That evening Brent Sadler, the ITN correspondent, rang me. CNN had warned him that our hotel was to be a target that evening. I told the others. No one wanted to go down to the shelter. We decided instead to do what Jana Schneider had done the previous night, and roam the streets.

I cleared out my safety deposit box, and gathered the necessities of my new life: identification in case of arrest, money for bribes, a hairbrush in case I had to appear on television, a notebook and pen. No razor, since without water shaving was impossible. But we were unlucky again. The sirens wailed early, at eight o'clock, and the automatic doors of the hotel were jammed shut. Once again, we were taken down into the shelter.

The whole cast of characters who inhabited our strange new world was there: Sadoun Jenabi, Al-Hadithi's deputy, a large, easy-going man who had spent years in Britain and stayed in the shelter most of the time now; and English peace compaigner, Edward Poore, who was a genuine eccentric, carried a cricket bat everywhere and had knotted a Romanian flag round his neck to remind himself of the time he spent there in the revolution; most of our minders and security men; just about all the journalists; and a large number of the hotel staff and their families, settling down nervously for the night. It was cold. I put a flak-jacket over me for warmth and used my bag as a pillow.

Friday 18 January

Anthony woke me at three o'clock by treading on me. He was filming in the semi-dark, and the building was vibrating as missiles dropped around us. 'I'm getting out,' he said. He tried to persuade a guard that he was suffering an epileptic fit, but it didn't work. Next he spotted a guard who had fallen asleep, and crept past him.

It was a profitable night for Anthony; another cruise missile passed him, heading down the same road, and he filmed it, the exhaust a dot of brilliance in the blackness.

The missile strikes, which we felt as faint quiverings in the shelter, were spectacular explosions from the fifth floor. The hotel wasn't hit, but it was in the centre of the action.

When the rest of us made our way upstairs at seven, we realised what we had missed. From that evening onwards, directly the sirens went, there was a stampede of journalists heading for the staircase which led to the upper floors. And although the security men patrolled the corridors most nights, and sometimes broke down doors, we always managed to avoid them.

In mid-afternoon there was a sudden call to go and see the Information Minister, Latif Jassim. There was little warning. By the time he joined us at the Ministry it was almost too dark to film. We had to stand him under the only light in the entire ground floor of the building. Al-Hadithi looked more tired than ever, but Jassim was chipper enough, and claimed a victory because Iraq hadn't been defeated in the first two days, as some American analysts had suggested.

It was the first mention of a theme which was to echo round the entire Arab world. Standing up to the Americans itself constituted a victory. He spoke of having captured British and American pilots, and in his quiet voice it didn't sound like just a propaganda claim. He ended by thanking us for staying on in Baghdad in spite of the pressure from our governments and our organisations.

Eamonn was having trouble locking the dish on to the satellite when we got back. The reason seemed to be the jamming waves put out by American Awacs aircraft, which were accompanying an attack by B-52 bombers.

The security people and the minders started to panic, shouting at us to get inside fast. The bombing started, a rumble that shook the ground and rippled the water in the stagnant pool of sewage that had formed 20 yards from where we had set up the phone. The magnificent red beard of an Irish-Australian reporter appeared at an upstairs window 'The power station! The power station's gone up!' There was a rush to see it and film it.

Annoyed by the nervousness of the minders, I stayed by the satellite phone, finishing off my script. 'Keep calm,' I called out. 'It's perfectly safe.' There was a thick whistling sound beside my head, and a heavy machine-gun bullet, near the end of its flight, flattened itself on the step in front of me. A minder picked it up and waved it in my face. 'You see? You see? And you say it's safe!' I made a grab for the bullet, but missed. At least it didn't hit us, I thought.

The minder was preoccupied by the affair later. When the raid was over and he was supposed to be censoring what I said, he scarcely seemed to notice when I broke the rules and started answering questions from David Dimbleby in London. All I was allowed to do was to read over my written report, as passed by the censors; but the minder kept playing with the bullet that had just missed my head, and looked up at the darkening sky.

The security people guarded us as best they could but Eamonn became adept at getting the satellite phone going every time there was a raid and the minders vanished. He kept watch when I was broadcasting. Once I had to interrupt myself halfway through a reply and pretend to be fiddling with the controls. The security man obligingly knelt down and tried to help me. As for the minders, I had the impression many of them disliked the role of censor and tried to ignore as much as possible of what we were doing.

I always refused to enter into any agreements about what I would and wouldn't do. 'You are prevaricating again, Mr John,' said Sadoun Jenabi, the number two at the Information Ministry, that evening. 'I know you. You are refusing to give me any undertakings.' His face was covered by three days' growth of beard now, and his eyes were red. 'It's my duty to broadcast, that's all. I'm not going to promise not to broadcast.' I had come to like Jenabi, and I didn't want to give him cause to say I had deceived him.

That night Anthony camped out in the hotel grounds. I eluded the security man in the darkness and found him lurking near the swimming pool. I gave him a hip-flask of Laphroaig and helped him settle on a bench from which he could film the night's attacks. As I walked away I could see the faint glimmer of his torch.

The sirens had already gone and the raids were beginning. The hits were still a long way off, and lit up the horizon like sheet lightning, flaring up and fading suddenly across great areas of night sky. Then the yellow surface-to-air missiles went up with a roar, and red tracer bullets chased each other through the air. Near us an artist was firing in delicate patterns, weaving his shots in and out skilfully.

The fighting came closer, and the missiles began exploding close too. But I was too tired to worry. I made it up to the fifth floor, ribs aching, took off my dirty clothes for the first time since the war began, arranged the necessary equipment in case my room took a hit (pain-killers, field dressings, torch) and read a little Evelyn Waugh by candlelight. The crump of a missile made the flame flicker, but I blew it out and fell asleep.

VERE HODGSON
Doodlebugs in July

In 1944 V1 flying-bombs, or 'Doodlebugs', began landing on Southern England. Vere Hodgson's diary from July of that year records her experiences dodging Doodlebugs in London.

T*UESDAY, 18TH* SLEPT SOUNDLY IN my lowly bed—but there were explosions. It was a lively night from all accounts. One night I shall awake to find myself in the next world! Onc fell in De Vere Gardens. News does not pour in as in the Big Blitz days. Everyone keeps close to their own Rabbit Hole, ready to bolt down it immediately. I do not go out to see the damage, but try to snatch a little sleep after a bad night.

Had a bit of Camembert cheese today! Miss Jones' sister, a nurse, brought it back from France. Both historic and appetizing.

Wednesday, 19th Started at 1 a.m. and ceased neither by night nor by day! Woke wearily at 7.30 a.m. and trailed up the road. We lost count during the day. Mr Hillyard had one in the City. Various shops in Notting Hill are taking a prolonged holiday.

Auntie tried to cross the Park to Church on Sunday, but turned back on hearing a Warning. She hurried to the local Church only to find the vicar had ordered all the congregation to move under the galleries. How we adapt ourselves!

Thursday, 20th Night began badly. Composed my soul for the end twice! One barely scraped our roof—but everyone else thought the same. It fell at Shepherd's Bush. Could not find my torch—all the time the thing was coming nearer and nearer. Bumped my head in the dark. It is almost necessary to sleep with a torch in one's hand.

While Miss M. was dictating letters I made her move outside her room away from the glass. She stops up her ears, afraid of the blast sending her deaf.

An article on Count Ciano's diary. Evidently Edda has it, and has had copies made and sent to seven different places. She will publish later to vindicate her husband. It tells of Mussolini's paroxysms of rage. . . .

Friday, 21st Far from good. Slept on and off for about five hours. Thuds on London all day. But at 8 a.m. the voice of the announcer was full of suppressed excitement, as he stated: the news is sensational. It was to the effect that some of the military chiefs had revolted against Hitler. The plot had been put down. Hitler had convinced the German people that he was alive by speaking to them round midnight.

All day we have waited for news. When men do such desperate deeds I can't think why they don't make sure they will succeed. Germany has cut herself off from Sweden and Switzerland.

People at Paddington and Kings Cross are having nerve-racking experiences waiting in queues. After an hour of standing there is the announcement: 'Take cover. Flying Bomb approaching.' What does one do? Stick it, or sacrifice that hard-won place in the queue!

Saturday, 22nd The Pig Breeder's son is fed up. He says Hounslow has had more than its share. They sleep in a surface shelter. He saw one the other night at tree-top height. Doubted it would clear the Shelter, but it glided on before the explosion. These bombs seem to make another war impossible. The finest Air Force in the world is no protection against them. By another 30 years they will have mastered the art of sending them to New York, and if we are too high-minded to use them we shall certainly be wiped out in a short space of time by enormous pantechnicons screaming through the air. It would be a matter of a week to wipe out London. The English will never be safe again. This will profoundly affect our lives after the war. Until this we did feel that behind a Cloud of Spitfires we could dwell serene. But this hope has gone.

I have not much further real hope for our poor old civilization. The brain of man has gone so far beyond his morals that the only thing to do is to scrap him and start again.

It is 11 p.m. as I write this. One has just passed over this house, much closer than I like. Been temporarily under the table. It has now dashed on to fall on some unfortunate folk.

Tuesday, 25th Not much authentic news from Germany. It

would seem that Hitler will triumph over his Generals. But from neutral sources it is said they are not all caught—but are in communication with those of like mind on the Fighting Fronts. The Russians will go surging in on a thousand marching feet and give the Germans a taste of their own medicine. This is intended to sound vindictive. As the London taxi-driver said: 'Hitler should be killed by a Fly Bomb.' One rumour says the bomb blew off Hitler's trousers—a new pair had to be found to greet Mussolini! As Mr Churchill says—the Germans at this moment are killing one another. He has been to Normandy.

In the night a great explosion, caused by a Spitfire following it from goodness knows where, and exploding it over Hammersmith. The grandfather clock in this office never disturbs us in the day, but in the Dead of Night it is loud, and seems to give a terrible cough before it strikes midnight.

Don't like the sound of these rockets they are preparing for us. We are nearing Firenze—our soldiers are betting to be there before Saturday. I hope so. How thrilled they will be with those cobbled streets. Bernard Shaw is 88. I fear he is lingering too long. Why worry about money at his age? He cannot need it.

Saturday, 29th A spot of excitement. No sooner had I reached my little flat than a Doodle came close in our direction. Roar grew louder. We sat on the stairs. It was losing height—but it passed over us. We took breath—heard the engine stop—and then the explosion. We understood it had cleared Campden Hill and dropped on that unfortunate Kensington High St. The next moment another came roaring over. Believe it or not—in the space of four minutes, four of those beastly things crossed our roof.

Had lunch and went out shopping, and to see where they had dropped. Milkman thought it was Phillimore Gardens. Later we heard opposite Pontings. They were commandeering buses for ambulances. Then out came the truth—it was at the end of Holland Walk, had devastated Lyons Restaurant at corner of Earls Court Road . . . crowded with people for lunch. Went to look—shop unrecognizable. I make these full records, because people are undergoing a great test here. Some friends have just written me from the country that they had been rescued from the débris of their house in Westminster.

Crowds at Paddington today were the largest in living memory. They had to close it for 2 hours, and admit people in batches. Ban is lifted from Devon and Cornwall, and people are going there. I don't blame them. Just going to bed down. Trust to see the night through!

Smell of the lime trees in our drive is exquisite. Auntie Nell is convinced she will not live to see the end of the war. The end is hope deferred . . . we are always near, but it is not yet. [Note: She did not live to see the end.]

End of July Auntie has had a ring from East Ham Vicarage saying it has been blasted. They were all sleeping in the cellar. As the curate was in the drawing-room and they heard all the glass go, they rushed upstairs to see if he was alive . . . all this in the middle of the night.

JOHN COMER
Mission to Bremen

John Comer was a top turret gunner on a US Air Force B-17 bomber flying missions from England in WWII.

October 8—Bremen (Germany)

'OK! WAKE UP. LET'S GO! Listen to the roster: Comer, Counce, Balmore, Legg, and Harkness flyin' 755 with Gleichauf. . .'

'Wait! You mean 765,' I said.

'No! 755 like I said.'

'But 765 is our ship,' I replied.

'Not today. Some other crew is flyin' it. Good luck.'

Reese was gone before I could say anything else.

Jim exploded. 'Damn those clerks at Operations! Giving our ship to some other crew an' makin' us fly one we've never seen before.'

'It's an error in typing but too late to do anything about it. George, how about you standing by the Briefing Room door while Jim and I get to the aircraft early? I don't remember aircraft 755.'

The aircraft was in excellent condition. An hour later I said to Jim, 'Things are going too well this mornin'—not normal. We must be overlooking something.'

George came out on the next truck. 'Didn't sound too bad. I'd say medium tough.'

'You think we need more ammunition?'

'Don't think so.'

A Jeep pulled up and the Flight Surgeon stepped out. 'Rub some of this salve on your face where the mask does not cover it. I hope it'll cut down on frostbite.' Captain Ralston was a good one. He never succeeded in finding an ointment to prevent frostbite but he kept trying.

The crew chief drew me aside. 'How long you fellows been here?'

'Since July.'

The chief looked relieved. 'Who is your pilot?'

'Gleichauf.'

'Oh, good man.'

Paul was well known to the veteran crew chiefs. They took pride in the condition of the aircraft assigned to them. When necessary the ground crews put in long hours. They became upset when an inexperienced crew abused an airplane. The chiefs, of course, expected battle damage, but they were incensed when planes returned with unnecessary wear on brakes and engines caused by pilots who did not have enough experience or did not care. Gleichauf had a reputation for respecting an aircraft and the men who kept them in good condition.

When the pilot arrived, I started sounding off about some other crew assigned to our airplane but Gleichauf cut it short. 'Some clerk made an error. Forget the bitching and let's get ready to start engines.' He waited for the rest of the men to gather around him. 'We're goin' to Bremen today. The fighter opposition is not expected to be too rough. There are two hundred and fifty flak guns—very accurate. There are two hundred fighters in the area, so it could turn out rougher than expected. P-47's will go with us nearly to the I.P. The target is submarine installations.'

As we approached the enemy coast I went into my regular ritual. 'Oh, God, be with me today and keep me from danger . . .' Instantly my brain received a message as clear as if it had come routinely over the intercom system, except it was not audible. 'German pilots rising up to meet you are asking the same thing. How can you be so misguided, understand so little?' Where did the message come from? I put small credence in prayer in the sense of physical phenomena. It had always been for me more of a ritual or historical practice of Christianity than a direct communication with a higher power. I had never really expected a positive response. My mind reeled from the impact of a new dimension with which it was unprepared to cope.

'Navigator to crew, fighters nine o'clock. It's the escort right on time.'

'Waist to Turret.'

'Waist to Turret—come in.'

I recovered when I realized that someone was calling my position. 'This is the Turret—go ahead.'

'Number four engine is vibrating too much—could be detonation.'

'Turret to Copilot, what's the temperature of number four?'

'Two fifteen.'

'That oughta be OK if the gauge is accurate. You can try two things: switch to automatic rich or open the flaps and drop it down to about two hundred.'

I saw the cowl flaps open slightly and in a few minutes Jim called again, 'Number four looks OK now.' I made a mental note to tell the crew chief to check the cylinder head temperature gauge for number four engine.

We crossed over the edge of the Low Countries and entered the air above Germany. The P-47's dipped their wings and turned back toward England. What went through the minds of the men who flew the P-47's when they had to break off and leave us alone to face the fury of Goering's vicious fighters?

'Tail to crew! Fighters at six o'clock. More fighters low and coming up.'

'Copilot to Tail, let us know what they're up to back there.'

'Tail to crew—four fighters closing fast at six o'clock high.'

'Radio to crew, I think they're gonna come on in.'

'Turret to Copilot, watch forward an' call me if anything shows up—I'm goin' to help the Tail.'

'OK, Turret.'

When I spun around I could hardly believe what I saw. Four fighters were flying so close together they looked like one enormous four-engine aircraft. Surely they did not intend to attack us that way! The greenest German pilot should have known better, but they kept coming. At six hundred yards I saw the first flash of cannon fire which was the signal for the formation gunners to let go with a furious assault. Every fifth round was what we called a tracer. It was a projectile with a magnesium insert in the rear, which would ignite and glow brightly as it flew through the air. Immediately the sky was ablaze with tracers. Almost all top turrets, some balls and all tails poured a heavy barrage at those four unfortunate fighters. The enormous mass of fifty caliber slugs was so devastating that there were four puffs of black smoke and a sky filled with debris that erased four poorly-trained German pilots. They made two horrendous mistakes: one, flying so close together that they gave us a single target; and two, choosing the worst possible angle of attack where they would have to face the maximum fire power a B-17 formation could bring to bear.

'Tail to Turret, they were crazy. They didn't have a chance.'

'A good way to commit suicide.'

A curious thought ran through my mind. 'Perhaps in their twisted teutonic thinking they were reaching for Valhalla—if so, I hoped they found it.'

'Navigator to crew, fighters—nine o'clock level—eleven o'clock level.'

They came at us from four directions. A Jerry defence commander must have stirred them up and they were breathing fire—mean and rough. It might have been what they saw us do to those four green pilots. For the next fifteen minutes it was a savage fight as intense as I can remember.

We were in the low location, called 'purple heart corner'. On the first heavy fire the turret clutch kicked out of position, stopping the action. I jumped out, removed the cumbersome gloves from one hand, reached high up into the maze of cables and reset the clutch. The turret was quickly back in operation. The next burst of prolonged firing kicked the clutch out again.

'Turret to Copilot, the damn clutch keeps jumping out! Must be a weak spring. I've got to try to wire it in position.'

'Hurry it up. If the turret is out of action too long, the fighters will notice it.'

As fast as possible, I re-engaged the clutch and wrapped copper wire around it to hold it in position—I hoped. As I climbed back into the turret, a fighter zoomed by spraying us with machine gun fire. A slug knocked out my intercom phones. I did manage to repair the mike, but the ear phone system was dead.

As we approached the target the enormous field of flak ahead was unbelievable. And frightening! My thoughts were 'Good God! Can anything fly through that?' I knew how accurate the flak was over Bremen. The German gunners had excellent radar control. Intense anti-aircraft fire was far less dangerous than fighter attacks, but more scary: there was no way to fight back at bursting shells.

WHAM! The heavy crashing noise came from below me. I dropped down to survey the damage. My first fear was that one or both pilots might be seriously injured, but as far as I could see with a quick look, both were OK.

'Turret to Copilot, over.'

'Go ahead.'

'Are either of you hurt? My earphones are dead, so give me some sign.'

I leaned down enough to see him and he shook his head, which told me there was nothing too serious. Several fighters were circling high and to my left and I was watching them closely. I turned to the right for a quick look and was petrified! A huge rectangular mass the size of a large car was flying alongside, not far from me, glistening in the bright sunlight like a thousand diamonds. 'What is that monstrous thing?' I said to myself. 'Some fantastic new weapon the Germans are throwing at us? If that mass explodes it could blow us out of the sky.' I hid on the opposite side of the computing sight to take the small amount of cover available, and peeked around it at the terrifying apparition. It began to lose speed and broke up into shimmering reflections that fanned out behind into a luminous cloud of particles. How could that huge mass have gotten twenty-five thousand feet up in the sky? What was it?

Fighters were streaking in straight ahead too low for me to get any shots. We caught a direct hit on number three engine and it began to vibrate heavily. I heard a loud smash underneath and suddenly my intercom was working. (Like a radio that you kick and it resumes playing.)

'Copilot to Ball.'

'Go ahead.'

'Can you see any oil leaking from number three engine?'

'It's throwin' oil real bad.'

'Pilot to Copilot—feather number three.'

The engine slowed down and eventually stopped.

'Copilot to Ball—is number three still leakin'?'

'It's about stopped.'

I felt the bombs fall out and soon we were clear of that awful flak! I looked back and the sky was a solid mass of boiling black smoke. How in the hell did any of us get through it?

There was a loud bang from number two engine. It must have

taken a hard smash from a cannon shell or a big piece of flak. I waited for smoke or heavy vibrations but when, after thirty seconds, it was still running smoothly, I relaxed. Had we lost another engine it would have been extremely hazardous for us alone among all of those snarling fighters. We could not have kept up with the formation on two engines.

Another attack came and I heard something strike the radio room with a sound of tearing metal.

'Copilot to Radio—Copilot to Radio—come in.'

'Copilot to Waist, can you see Radio?'

'I can see him. Got some equipment damage, and he's rubbing his ass like he may have been zipped there, but don't think it is too serious.'

'Go check out Radio an' call me back.'

'He's OK now, Copilot, he's motioning that his intercom is knocked out.'

'Waist to Copilot.'

'Go ahead Wilson.'

'765 has been hit—looks bad—don't think she can keep up with us.'

I watched 765 fall back with mounting apprehension. Soon she was out of my range of vision.

'Ball to crew—765 is gone! No chutes. Damn!'

After a few minutes the Ball continued, 'Six fighters tore her apart. Looked to me like they had time to jump.'

Our faithful old aerial warhorse was finished! As she rolled back within my sight far below, I felt stabs of anguish. It was like losing an old friend with whom I had shared both escapades and harrowing experiences.

A fighter zoomed up from below and cut loose at us with cannon fire.

'Tail to Copilot, a twenty millimeter shell damn near got me. Knocked off one of my boots an' crashed on through without exploding.'

Aircraft Tinker Toy moved into the space that 765 had been holding.

'Tail to crew, look at Tinker Toy. She's riddled from the ball to the tail.'

'That's Tinker Toy doing her special thing,' said the Bombardier.

'Copilot to crew, two fighters comin' in eleven o'clock high. Let 'em have it Turret! Hey, Navigator, blast the bastards.'

They were going for Tinker Toy and hit her dead center of the cockpit. I saw a small explosion.

Counce called, 'They got the pilot! Copilot is hit, too. The engineer is trying to move the pilot's body so he can get in his seat.'

'Turret to Copilot, I think I just saw the engineer put Tinker Toy on auto pilot until he can try to get control.'

Kels motioned for Gleichauf to switch over to intercom.

'What is it?'

'Keep your eye on Tinker Toy. Pilot is dead. Engineer put her on auto pilot. He's trying to move the pilot's body. The copilot is slumped in his seat—can't tell how bad he's wounded.'

'We'll watch her—don't want a collision with Tinker Toy.'

The fighters kept striking her. One wing was badly torn and an engine cowling knocked off. But she flew on. In my imagination I could hear her taunting the fighters: 'Yah! Yah! You kraut pimps! You can't knock me down. Go ahead! Try it! You square-headed bastards ain't good enough to get me. Yah! Yah! Yah! Go ahead and try to shoot me down! Yah! Yah!'

The wounded copilot raised up in his seat momentarily and helped the engineer with a control then collapsed again. How could the two men in the cockpit withstand that awful blast of super frigid wind blowing squarely in their faces without windshields?

Suddenly I realized my left hand was so cold it was becoming numb. That was normally a sign that the electric glove had burned out. I looked down at the hand. It was bare except for a thin silk glove. Where was the electric glove? Oh! I had removed it to wire the turret clutch in place. At thirty-five below, I was handling the metal gun controls with a hand covered only with the light silk glove normally worn under the electric outer glove. Impossible! My hand would have frozen solidly in a very few minutes. Yet, I was looking at the numb hand and the electric glove was resting where I took it off much earlier—before we reached the target. There was only one explanation: in the excitement of the action my blood pressure had gone sky high, pushing a large quantity of warm blood to the hands which replaced some of the lost heat.

When the fighter attacks finally faded out my relief was quickly punctured by the antics of number three engine. It suddenly unfeathered and began to revolve out of control. It required engine oil pressure to hold a propellor in a feathered position with the blades flat to the wind. If the oil pressure failed, the blades would shift to an angle, and the strong wind would rotate them. That was called windmilling, and with no means of control, the propellor revolutions would rev up to fantastic speeds. With no lubrication the engine would get hotter and hotter until it became red hot. The danger was that it might tear off of the aircraft with severe damage. The engine revved up and up beyond the twenty-five hundred R.P.M. red line limit. I watched with a sinking feeling as it shot up to three thousand. Then, to my immense relief, and for no reason that I could think of at the moment, it began to level off, then started slowing down. Eventually it stopped and resumed a feathered position again.

'Turret to Ball.'

'Go ahead, Turret.'

'Check number three again for an oil leak.'

'No oil leak from number three engine.'

'Pilot to Turret. What's wrong with number three prop?'

'Not sure. Could be a fracture in the oil pressure system in the prop hub that opens and closes. Ball says no oil leak down below so far. If it starts squirting out oil we'll have a runaway prop.'

'Turret to Waist. Jim, how does this sound to you?'

'Don't see how it could be anything but a pressure leak.'

Five minutes later the process repeated. All of the way back to Ridgewell that propellor would race up to three thousand revolutions and, having made its point, return to zero. Each time the speed zoomed upward my blood pressure went up with it.

We could have caught fighters again, but fortunately nothing else happened. Tinker Toy had serious landing problems but ended with nothing worse than slipping off the runway into sticky mud. A crowd gathered quickly to see what new horrors she had thrown at her crew. And again the question: was she really a jinx ship? For the men who flew combat raids in her it was more than a wartime superstition. It was a series of nightmares! That day her nose was blown off, both windshields were wiped out, one wing was battered, and she was heavily damaged from the radio to the tail. The cockpit was splattered with blood, bits of flesh and hair—a horrible sight to see.

When I climbed out of 755 the crew chief was waiting. 'You had better put in a call for some sheet metal men, you will probably need two new engines, the radio is shattered, you will need two windshields, and one wing flap. The tail is also damaged. I think all of the main fuel tanks will have to be replaced because they are bound to be perforated . . .'

The 381st sent out twenty-one ships and lost seven. The 100th had another bad day and lost eight. The total loss for the raid was thirty-seven Forts. Of the returning aircraft, seventy-five percent were damaged.

As soon as we were on the ground, I asked Gleichauf and Purus about the huge mass of shining particles I saw near the Target. It turned out to be a new way to confuse the enemy radar by dumping out bales of thin aluminium foil fragments. The light pieces floating in the air confused the enemy radar by appearing to be aircraft. What I saw was a compressed bale of foil that had not yet begun to break up. Later on it was thrown in bulk from several aircraft regularly and was called 'chaff'.

After the mission I hit the sack, weary, exhausted and in a state of confusion. What did the message I received on the way to Bremen mean and where did it come from? I never expected to get an answer to a prayer, if indeed, that is what had happened. There was absolutely no doubt but that I did get a communication. The question was, 'Where did it come from?' A simplistic answer would have been straight from God. I could have accepted that except it seemed too simple—too easy to draw such a conclusion as fact. I tried to think about it in rational channels, although I realized that at some point any religion steps beyond logic or reason into mystical or metaphysical phenomena. The danger faced each mission made me ready to turn to any spiritual assistance that was readily available, but I needed to separate the real from the dross that had accumulated in my mind.

MARTIN PÖPPEL
Diary of a German Paratrooper on the Eastern Front, Winter 1942

Leutnant Martin Pöppel served with the German Parachute Army from September 1939 to April 1945 (when he was captured by the allies in the battle for the Rhineland), and fought in most of the Wehrmacht's major campaigns. Below he writes of his experiences on the central sector of the Russian front in the winter of 1942.

THIS TIME WE'RE TO BE sent to the Welisz-Surasz-Demidorff region, which means that we aren't to make a drop but are to act as mobile 'fire brigade' again. We regard ourselves as a unit of elite troops, but they are apparently determined to send us to the slaughter in infantry operations. Oh yes, the news has certainly spread that when the paratroopers arrive, the front holds.

From 4 Regiment, Leutnant Stahl of 3 Company is put under our command, along with Obergefreites Nagel, Fuchs, Wald and Fried from the communication section. On 7 November we move into position on the Szappszo Lake. In my platoon, calm and reliable Feldwebel Sulima is leading 1 Group and Feldwebel Gaerte 2 Group, but he's soon transferred to headquarters personnel as an officer candidate. My platoon headquarters leader is Unteroffizier Hein.

The first weeks are spent building bunkers, communication trenches, camouflaged machine gun positions, the installation of sledge paths for supplies etc. Up above in the Company

Command Post, they're even building a sauna. Our tireless old organiser Hauptmann Laun is really in his element. After a long time, I've at last got decent skis under my feet again, enabling me to travel cross-country to Kiselli and the supply train.

These are quiet days, with only a few salvoes of rifle and machine-gun fire from the Russians on the islands over on the other side. Perhaps because of this, an incomprehensible laxity has made its appearance in the Company. Protected by the lake, the men reckon that they are quite safe here. When I return from a patrol of our positions, the sentry fails to notice me until I'm within three metres of him. If I'd been the enemy, he'd be dead. At another of our positions, nicknamed 'Cape Horn', both sentries have made themselves comfortable: Gefreite Stöger is lying fast asleep, in the full light of day. Maybe he already guessed that on 10 December he'd be seriously wounded by a bullet through the head.

Our embrasures are too widely spaced and have to be altered. I've got the power to grant leave for three men, but wonder seriously whether I shouldn't refuse to let them go, since the attitude of the men in general has been so unsatisfactory. But then, we're so far from home, and our loved ones are waiting for us.

On 14 December we come under heavy mortar fire and, despite our excellent positions, Gefreite Zweig receives a serious head wound, Obergerfreite Langer is shot through the upper arm shortly afterwards, and Gefreite Beckert is hit by shell splinters. Yet despite these casualties, the men will only work when I arrive on the scene and make them. They must know how important for their own safety it is to build secure positions, but they're as stubborn as mules, totally pigheaded. There are excellent fellows among them, but many are revealing their bad sides. This criticism includes our NCOs, the Unteroffiziere, as well. What infuriates me most is that they've suddenly forgotten how to improvise, so that everything has to be decided for them and orders given before they'll do anything. The most reliable man is still Feldwebel Sulima.

In mid-December it gets dreadfully wet and cold, snow and rain together. The Russians will soon have to withdraw from the furthermost islands, so they won't be so close. But we're in mire up to our knees!

And then suddenly there's a cloudless, starlit night, a wonderful blue morning sky. Unfortunately, along with it comes the onset of the most appalling, biting cold. At least we're better equipped for this second Russian winter, with thick overcoats, felt boots, earflaps, parkas. We content ourselves with providing intermittent but effective concentrations of fire, particularly with our mortars and 3.7 cm anti-tank guns. Otherwise it stays quiet. Von Pretzmann celebrates with us, in no uncertain manner, the birth of his second daughter—not a dry eye in the house. An amazing drunken session, followed by a hangover of equally enormous proportions. Then post arrives from home and, naturally enough, the mood of the men improves. My fiancée encloses a photograph and my batman carves a lovely frame for it out of beechwood.

We're preparing our wartime Christmas and are rewarded with a heavy fall of snow. In the early morning the area roundabout has become like something out of a fairytale. The branches are bending under the weight of the snow, and glittering like sugar-covered Christmas cakes. Quickly off with the skis and off for a general clean-up in the sauna, down 'to the last louse'. A fantastic bath, leaving me feeling wonderfully fit and well. But then another piece of bad luck. We've scarcely finished celebrating the arrival of Obergefreite Demitter when our gunner Krin is wounded. We still have hardly enough men to post proper sentries so men have to be sent to us from the train—at least they're good paratroop drivers.

Naturally enough, the whole place is in chaos on the 24 December. For days the men have been making attractive decorations and ornaments such as lamps, ashtrays, and picture frames, and have been putting up Christmas trees and decorating them with silver foil from our cigarette packets. In the morning Ivan leaves us in peace, but he spends the afternoon shooting aimlessly throughout the whole area. It's clear that the Commissars want to spoil our Christmas celebrations if they can. Unchristian of them, and doomed to be unsuccessful.

Early in the evening I take a detachment from the platoon to the Commander. Each base has made a little present for him—for instance the 'Cape of Good Hope' has made a beautiful lamp and 'Cape Arcona' a litter basket. The Commander is very enthusiastic about these gifts and spends a short time celebrating the festive season with us. For Christmas each officer receives some spirits, twenty cigars, forty cigarettes etc., and the men get similar gifts. We return to the bunker with a sledge crammed with letters and presents for the men. From far away we can hear them singing Christmas carols, the harsh deep voices of the older men and the light tones of the youngest soldiers, our newest recruits. We're greeted joyously, and deliveries are taken to all the sentries and to every base. A real festive mood takes hold.

It's my first real wartime Christmas. I'm up again very early on Christmas morning, first of all to attend to my duties, collating and evaluating the reports. But then I can attend to my own parcels, stuffed with cigarettes, delicious biscuits, pralines and chocolate. Although the sausage has somehow got mixed up with the apples and pralines, it's still the best I've ever tasted. Each letter is read over and over again, each man alone with his feelings. Of course, Ivan sends his own special Christmas greetings in the form of 12 cm shells and little 7.62 'cigars', but the bunkers we worked so arduously to build prove themselves strong and secure, and the Russians can't spoil our good humour.

On the 26 December—when I'm still at Company HQ with two of my men—we spot a red alarm signal from below. Red alert! We race pell-mell back to base. More signals—white this time—illuminate the night sky, sub-machine guns crack, we can hear rifle and the more gentle pop of pistols. Within twenty minutes, we reach our little peninsula. The Russians have made their way over the ice with a raiding party of about twenty men and have attacked our island. Yet again, the sentries didn't see them until too late. But my men were on their toes this time and responded so effectively that I almost missed the action altogether.

We scour the entire base, shooting at the Russians in their white parkas as they try to escape on foot and on skis. Between 10 and 15 of them are lying some twenty to fifty metres away, not moving, apparently dead. But when one of my men goes closer, he's shot (though fortunately only wounded slightly). To avoid any further casualties on our side, I make several calls for the Russians to surrender; when they don't, I order the men to fire on each and every one. Only then do we approach them. There are no Commissars among them. They're carrying sludgy bread in their haversacks, also millet, and are mostly Asiatics, well-nourished and wearing practical winter clothing.

After that things are quiet for a time, but then from 18.30 until 19.15 hours the Russians bombard the entire sector with machine-gun and mortar fire, at least three barrels of 7.62 artillery. Gefreite Horn is wounded by a shell splinter in the thigh. Our own artillery returns the fire, managing to silence the enemy guns. Our telephone lines have been cut, so the line-layers have to brave the cold night to retrieve the situation.

Until New Year everything stays nice and peaceful, with only a Russian field gun giving us cause to scuttle hither and thither. Ivan brings this into the front line before daybreak, fires a couple of times and then disappears again. The Russians have an impressive superiority over us in heavy guns and are damned impressive at finding the range. Back in officer training school we'd been told about the superb Russian artillery skills and the fact that they had entire battalions of the stuff. Why didn't our side take account of it and set up heavy artillery battalions of our own? What we have is nowhere near enough.

New Year's Eve (This is what I wrote at the time):

The men are sitting at the tables, recounting stories about the year gone by, talking about the action we've seen and the many friends we've lost. Although there's plenty of punch and grog the mood remains quiet. Five minutes before midnight each man lifts his glass, and we drink quietly and calmly to the New Year. What will it bring us? Our thoughts and conversations turn towards home, to our loved ones, our Führer and our Fatherland.

We're not afraid to cry as we stand to remember our Führer and our fallen comrades. It's like an oath binding us together, making us grit our teeth and carry on until victory.

What is life worth to us? It's true that our joy in living and lust for life are stronger now than they've ever been, but each of us is ready to sacrifice his life for the holy Fatherland. This Fatherland is my faith, and my only hope. All the best feelings in my heart are directed towards it.

At home, they'll be sitting under the Christmas tree as well. I can see my brave old Dad, see him stand and drink with reddened eyes to the soldiers. And my courageous mother, she'll certainly be crying a bit, and my little sister too. But one day there'll be another New Year when we can all be together, happily reunited after a victorious end to the mass slaughter of the nations. That superior spirit which moves the young people must lead us to victory: there is no alternative. To win through or to die in battle—those are my thoughts at 01.00 hours on the first day of 1943.

Now, forty years later, as I sit and look at these notes I wrote then, I can only shake my head in wonder at the way our young people were so inspired, but so very much misled. And I want to shout, to cry out to the youngsters of today: Never, never let yourselves be persuaded into fighting for anyone or anything. Yet still I must admit to doubts, to the feeling that under certain circumstances it might be necessary to risk one's life to protect freedom.

But then—what is freedom?

We toil and labour at our bunkers and defensive positions, for it seems certain that the Russian's big attack won't be delayed much longer and they'll certainly attempt to blow us all to pieces beforehand. On 7 January Gefreite Timm is hit in the lower body, and Erken has a dangerous stomach wound. Then Rochlitz accidentally shoots himself, in the head, whilst cleaning his pistol. The men are drilled over and over again, and instructed to take extra care when cleaning their weapons, but these things still happen. Fate.

On 11 January I order my men to cease fire—maybe it'll make Ivan a little nervous about our intentions.

We're still desperately short of men, enough to make us celebrate the arrival of every replacement. On 12 January Gefreite Dietrich arrives, fresh from Gardelegen. This damned work and the continuous watchfulness are really playing on our nerves. But only a couple of hours later, Obergefreite Wilfert is brought in with a head wound. The irregular Russian zone fire continues to claim its victims, and we're powerless against it despite taking every precaution.

On 14 January there's another large delivery of post, which cheers everyone up no end. Although the days remain quiet, at night the Russians have started sending over large numbers of reconnaissance planes. Something's definitely in the air. Horn arrives from the military hospital, and we're sent Gefreites Balz and Hansen from the train. A bit of breathing space at last. Then my old platoon headquarters leader, Unteroffizier Dewitz, arrives back from officer candidate school. Oberleutnant Hölters has been killed in action and I go on my skis to his funeral. But then I get an unexpected pleasure when I meet up with my old gunner from Dietl gun, Max Grübl, and he's got the most enormous parcel for me. My sweet innocent parents have given it him to bring for me—they obviously think that you can travel right up to the front line by train.

Old 'Iron Gustav' is still circling around, we see it almost every day on its reconnaissance flights. We've no anti-aircraft guns so it goes its way unhindered. Obergefreite Götz has been wounded. But we're managing to harass the Russians too, from our strongly built and well-camouflaged defensive positions, with fixed fire from our machine-guns. We already know where they are and can adjust our fire accordingly. I manage to get someone from a range of 1400 metres.

One afternoon I narrowly escaped a flight of my own. Quite unsuspectingly, I was standing near an explosive charge unaware that it was about to be detonated. A sudden shout of 'Get down!' and I fell flat just as the whole lot went up. Fortunately for them, the shock made me completely forget to shoot the idiots on guard.

Since 1 February we've been in a state of increased alert: according to information from Russian deserters, the big offensive will begin on my right flank. There are also rumours that we're to be relieved—many even purport to know the exact date. But such stories leave the veterans amongst us cold, we're immune to latrine rumours by now.

Unteroffizier Idzykowski is firing at a Russian sentry post using the telescopic sight, observed by Obergefriete Fuchs and myself. Suddenly there's a hail of fire from the other side. When Fuchs grabs himself around the heart I'm sure that he's done for and start to drag him to the trenches. But he manages to hobble to the bunker under his own steam—I can hardly believe my eyes—and removes a 14 milimetre antitank rifle bullet from his shoe! We're both stunned at his incredible luck. At 11.00 hours Obergerfeite Waldfried is hit at the entrance to the bunker. Though I get to him straight away, there's nothing anyone can do to save him. At least his death means that he was spared a court-martial for his serious misconduct and dereliction of duty during his sentry duties. Unfortunately, incidents such as those are greatly on the increase at the moment. I catch Obergefreite Kluwe with a woollen scarf wrapped round both ears during sentry duty, having got within two metres of him. I'd really like to give him a good military thrashing. This negligence, it's enough to make you puke!

5 February. Stalingrad is on everybody's lips. We try to imagine what the soldiers there must be enduring, and marvel at their heroic dedication to duty. Surely their conduct will strengthen our whole people—a nation which has such men can never be defeated.

In the middle of February the thaw sets in—and how! Now we can clearly see the enemy's trenches and bunkers, and they can see ours just as plainly. Water is dripping and running everywhere; the mud is knee-deep in the trenches and has to be shovelled out; clothes and weapons are all filthy.

19 February. It's 02.00 hours. I can't get the Goebbels speech calling for total war out of my mind. The speech was so tremendous and fantastic that I feel I have to write home with my own response. Everyone was carried away by his words, all of us were under his spell. He spoke to us from the heart. Total War at last—yes of course, but why not earlier? He calls for the utmost effort from each and every one of us, for each one to do his duty in service to the Fatherland. Only in this way—we all agree—can we win the war. For us, Stalingrad was a signal, calling us to make a sacred commitment.

20 February. One of my best men, Max Grübl, has been killed in a place where hardly any other shots were fired, by a bullet through the collar bone which pierced a blood vessel. His young, strong life has been snuffed out. A fine lad, through and through. He would have been the first to be granted leave, in recognition of his guts in the counter-attack on 'Cape Horn'.—We're going to miss him, our Max.

Yesterday I came back from a tour round the Front. I made an enormous cross-country ski trip via Kiselli-Sabolotze-Klimati to Oberleutnant Ruthe's 'game park'. They're living in feudal conditions there, in the best of senses, in a giant 'bungalow' made of birchwood with an open chimney and chairs of birch. Misloviky, Eugen Scherer, the 'Cap'n' and all the old Feldwebels were there, so we got drunk on memories and current happenings as well as on vast quantities of alcohol. After long abstinence I was so totally plastered that I took days to get over it. Those were two wonderful days, unforgettable. I met up with Kay Umbach again, a man I remembered from the old days. A nice chap and very much on the ball when things needed organising, he had important connections. Once he was told to acquire wine in the Rhineland and was given six days to do it. Without informing anybody, he took twelve days before appearing with large quantities of wine, and simply said that it couldn't be done any quicker. Whenever he went and did something wrong, he just called his uncle in the Reich Air Ministry in Berlin, General Christiansen, and everything was hunky-dory. He had an excellent relationship with Oberleutnant Ruthe. This gentleman was a young huntsman and Kay managed to organise many a fine hunt for them both. I was astonished at the superb supplies and the vast quantities of schnapps they'd acquired. A few weeks later, however, I discovered that he and Ruthe had definitely gone too far. As it was described to me, a rations supply bunker had already been set up in no man's land for a future advance. Kay managed to track it down, with the approval of Ruthe, and they were living in the land of milk and honey on the contents. It was obvious that they had things that we could only dream about—we hadn't had any stuff like that for ages. But then the whole thing was discovered and this time even Kay had to take at least some of the blame. Both men were transferred.

25 February. Slowly but surely, life is changing. Most of the winter clothing has been withdrawn. Gefreite Haas, wounded two weeks ago by a bullet in the leg, comes back to us. Sadly for him, he hadn't got a nice 'blighty' one this time.

A variety show at the train in Sachoti. A Ukrainian troupe in attractive national costume puts on a really excellent performance, wonderful folk-dances to Russian music. It was well worth the hour-long march to get there. Things are still quiet, with only our 'Knallmax' gun firing to great effect at the Russian bunkers. In the evening we visit the Commander to discuss the general situation, and also to talk lightheartedly about job training. Fred Kröger suggests that we should build a house together, me as manager and him as cook. (He reminded me about the conversation years later, and we had a good laugh over it).

On 10 March I order the platoon to fire at will—six heavy machine guns, two light machine guns and a number of mortars.

A superb piece of theatre as the tracer trajectories cut through the night sky, it really cheered the men up. Five Russian Martin bombers fly overhead, but fortunately they drop their cargo well behind us. Since yesterday there has been no firing at all from the islands opposite. Has Ivan evacuated the area, or is he just trying to make us think so? The footbridge to my command post, fifty metres long and one metre fifty wide, is finished, well-camouflaged and only waiting for its official opening. Now I've been promoted to 'Prince of the Szappszo Lake' and anyone who passes by has to pay tribute. The days are becoming more beautiful, warmer, the nights are clearer and we don't need to post as many sentries.

On 20 March the great battle begins. From 05.15 hours the Russian artillery has been firing in our left sector. Within a few minutes at least two hundred shells from twelve gun barrels have been counted, along with 7.62, 10.5 and 12 cm mortars. A sinister rolling barrage across the Front. Nine Ratas fly over Tinovka, and at the same time the Russian artillery is firing smoke grenades in the direction of Akti, certainly as a signal. My Idzykowski recce patrol arrives back and runs into Oberleutnant Leonhardt, who's taking his platoon to reinforce the Gustmann's Hill. But no enemy movement can be seen, at least not where we are. Close by on our left, though, we hear that seven or eight tanks have broken through, and two assaults by Russian infantry have been beaten off. Along the entire enemy line we can hear loud voices, the barking of dogs, the noise of lorries and tanks. On the next day there's another heavy barrage, this time up to 18 cm calibre, four 'Stalin organs' (Katyusha multi-barrelled rocket projectors) with them: these have little effect but their eerie whistling stretches the nerves to breaking point. The fire is getting too close and I order the reserve group to get ready, Feldwebel Sulima with fourteen men. The bombardment continues to increase, but at last our own artillery is returning fire. At 10.45 hours the news comes in that Maklakova has been retaken in a counter-attack. Eventually, things quieten down. The Russians haven't achieved the breakthrough. They were facing 4 Regiment over there, commanded by the excellent Commander Walter, a man I know from Narvik.

Nothing happens after all, so on 25 March the old rumours about a transfer return start circulating again. Where will we be sent? Damn it, at least let's get away from here. We're attack troops, not defenders.

There was a lot of action last night. At 22.00 hours our own artillery began a bombardment of the 'Knobloch' base, to such effect that windows here rattled and the sand trickled through the joists. For two solid hours they bombarded the positions in order to soften them up. At 04.00 hours the base was seized back from the Russians with very few casualties on our side.

The rumours that we're about to be relieved have proved to be well-founded. At 16.00 hours officers from the relief unit come through the positions. The 'Murderers Division'—we don't know why they're called that—is relieving us, excellent infantrymen. Two of their Hauptmanns with the Gold Cross are discussing the situation with us. Then on 28 March it actually happens. At 02.30 hours the sentry suddenly shouts in delight: 'The relief is here!' You had better believe how happy we are. Our base is taken over by a Leutnant with a heavy machine-gun squad, its Unteroffizier a fine East Prussian and an excellent marksman.

There's no question of sleep now so we chat until morning. Then it's time to guide the new men round our positions, hand over sketches and situation maps, count ammunition and hand it over, and finally make our departure. 'Cape Horn' and 'Pigheaded Bunker' have been our home for six months, half a year full of happenings. The long nights of entrenchment, the work, the watching—they're all over now. I think of our many wounded and of our dead comrades Max Grübl, Zweig and Waldfried, men we must leave in this place.

ERWIN ROMMEL
Retreat from El Alamein

The Battle of El Alamein, October–November 1942, was the turning point of the Second World War in North Africa. The engagement resulted in a decisive victory for the British 8th Army, led by Montgomery, over Rommel's Afrika Corps. Here General (later Field Marshall) Rommel gives his view of the battle. At the beginning of the engagement he was in Germany, where he had been sent to recover his health, and General Stumme was deputising for him in Africa.

On the afternoon of the 24th, I was rung up on the Semmering by Field Marshal Keitel, who told me that the British had been attacking at Alamein with powerful artillery and bomber support since the previous evening. General Stumme was missing. He asked whether I would be well enough to return to Africa and take over command again. I said I would. Keitel then said that he would keep me informed of developments, and would let me know in due course whether I was to return to my command. I spent the next few hours in a state of acute anxiety, until the evening, when I received a telephone call from Hitler himself. He said that Stumme was still missing—either captured or killed—and asked whether I could start for Africa immediately. I was to telephone him again before I actually took off, because he did not want me to interrupt my treatment unless the British attack assumed dangerous proportions. I ordered my aircraft for seven o'clock next morning and drove immediately to Wiener Neustadt. Finally, shortly after midnight, a call came through from the Fuehrer. In view of developments at Alamein he found himself obliged to ask me to fly back to Africa and resume my command. I took off next morning. I knew there were no more laurels to be earned in Africa, for I had been told in the reports I had received from my officers that supplies had fallen far short of my minimum demands. But just how bad the supply situation really was I had yet to learn.

On arriving at Rome at about 11.00 hours (25th October) I was met at the airport by General von Rintelen, Military Attaché and German General attached to the Italian forces. He informed me of the latest events in the African theatre. After heavy artillery preparation, the enemy had taken part of our line south of Hill 31; several battalions of 164th Division and of Italians had been completely wiped out. The British attack was still in progress and General Stumme still missing. General von Rintelen also informed me that only three issues of petrol remained in the African theatre; it had been impossible to send any more across in the last weeks, partly because the Italian Navy had not provided the shipping and partly because of the British sinkings. This was sheer disaster, for with only 300 kilometres worth of petrol per vehicle between Tripoli and the front, and that calculated over good driving country, a prolonged resistance could not be expected; we would be completely prevented from taking the correct tactical decisions and would thus suffer a tremendous limitation in our freedom of action. I was bitterly angry, because when I left there had been at least eight issues for the Army in Egypt and Libya, and even this had been absurdly little in comparison with the minimum essential of thirty issues. Experience had shown that one issue of petrol was required for each day of battle; without it, the army was crippled and could not react to the enemy's moves. General von Rintelen regretted the situation, but said that he had unfortunately been on leave and had consequently been unable to give sufficient attention to the supply question.

Feeling that we would fight this battle with but small hope of success, I crossed the Mediterranean in my Storch and reached headquarters at dusk (25th October). Meanwhile, General Stumme's body had been found at midday and taken to Derna. He had apparently been driving to the battlefield along the Alarm track when he had suddenly been fired on in the region of Hill 21 by British infantry using anti-tank and machine-guns. Colonel Buechting had received a mortal wound in the head. The driver, Corporal Wolf, had immediately swung the car round, and

General Stumme had leapt out and hung on to the outside of it, while the driver drove at top speed out of the enemy fire. General Stumme must have suddenly had a heart attack and fallen off the car. The driver had noticed nothing. On Sunday morning the General had been found dead beside the Alarm track. General Stumme had been known to suffer from high blood-pressure and had not really been fit for tropical service.

We all deeply regretted the sudden death of Stumme. He had spared no pains to command the army well and had been day and night at the front. Just before setting off on his last journey on the 24th of October, he had told the acting Chief of Staff that he thought it would be wise to ask for my return, since with his short experience of the African theatre, and in view of the enormous British strength and the disastrous supply situation, he felt far from certain that he would be able to fight the battle to a successful conclusion. I, for my part, did not feel any more optimistic.

General von Thoma and Colonel Westphal reported to me that evening on the course of the battle to date, mentioning particularly that General Stumme had forbidden the bombardment of the enemy assembly positions on the first night of the attack, on account of the ammunition shortage. As a result the enemy had been able to take possession of part of our minefield and to overcome the occupying troops with comparatively small losses to himself. The petrol situation made any major movement impossible and permitted only local counter-attacks by the armour deployed behind the particular sector which was in danger. Units of the 15th Panzer Division had counter-attacked several times on the 24th and 25th October, but had suffered frightful losses in the terrible British artillery fire and non-stop R.A.F. bombing attacks. By the evening of the 25th, only 31 of their 119 tanks remained serviceable.

There were now only very small stocks of petrol left in North Africa and a crisis was threatening. I had already—on my way through Rome—demanded the immediate employment of all available Italian submarines and warships for the transport of petrol and ammunition. Our own air force was still unable to prevent the British bombing attacks, or to shoot down any major number of British aircraft. The R.A.F.'s new fighter-bombers were particularly in evidence, as is shown by the fact that every one of the captured tanks belonging to the *Kampfstaffel* had been shot up by this new type of aircraft.

Our aim for the next few days was to throw the enemy out of our main defence line at all costs and to reoccupy our old positions, in order to avoid having a westward bulge in our front.

That night our line again came under a heavy artillery barrage, which soon developed into one long roll of fire. I slept only a few hours and was back in my command vehicle again at 05.00 hours [*26th October*], where I learnt that the British had spent the whole night assaulting our front under cover of their artillery, which in some places had fired as many as five hundred rounds for every one of ours. Strong forces of the panzer divisions were already committed in the front line. British night-bombers had been over our units continuously. Shortly before midnight the enemy had succeeded in taking Hill 28, an important position in the northern sector.*[1] He had then brought up reinforcements to this point ready to continue the attack in the morning with the object of extending his bridge-head west of the minefields.

Attacks were now launched on Hill 28 by elements of the 15th Panzer Division, the Littorio and a Bersaglieri Battalion, supported by the concentrated fire of all the local artillery and A.A. Unfortunately, the attack gained ground very slowly. The British resisted desperately. Rivers of blood were poured out over miserable strips of land which, in normal times, not even the poorest Arab would have bothered his head about. Tremendous British artillery fire pounded the area of the attack. In the evening part of the Bersaglieri Battalion succeeded in occupying the eastern and western edges of the hill. The hill itself remained in British hands and later became the base for many enemy operations.

I myself observed the attack that day from the north. Load after load of bombs cascaded down among my troops. British strength round Hill 28 was increasing steadily. I gave orders to the artillery to break up the British movement north-east of Hill 28 by concentrated fire, but we had too little ammunition to do it successfully. During the day I brought up the 90th Light

1

* Called by the British 'Kidney Ridge'—from the shape of the ring contour on the map.

Division and the *Kampfstaffel*, in order to press home the attack on Hill 28. The British were continually feeding fresh forces into their attack from Hill 28 and it was clear that they wanted to win through to the area between El Daba and Sidi Abd el Rahman. I therefore moved the Trieste into the area east of El Daba. Late in the afternoon German and Italian dive-bomber formations made a self-immolating attempt to break up the British lorry columns moving towards the north-west. Some 60 British fighters pounced on these slow machines and forced the Italians to jettison their bombs over their own lines, while the German pilots pressed home their attack with very heavy losses. Never before in Africa had we seen such a density of anti-aircraft fire. Hundreds of British tracer shells criss-crossed the sky and the air became an absolute inferno of fire.

British attacks supported by tanks tried again and again to break out to the west through our line south of Hill 28. Finally, in the afternoon, a thrust by 160 tanks succeeded in wiping out an already severely mauled battalion of the 164th Infantry Division and penetrated into our line towards the south-west. Violent fighting followed in which the remaining German and Italian tanks managed to force the enemy back. Tank casualties so far, counting in that day's, were 61 in the 15th Panzer Division and 56 in the Littorio, all totally destroyed.

Following on their non-stop night attacks, the R.A.F. sent over formations of 18 to 20 bombers at hourly intervals throughout the day, which not only caused considerable casualties, but also began to produce serious signs of fatigue and a sense of inferiority among our troops.

The supply situation was now approaching disaster. The tanker *Proserpina*, which we had hoped would bring some relief in the petrol situation, had been bombed and sunk outside Tobruk. There was only enough petrol left to keep supply traffic going between Tripoli and the front for another two or three days, and that without counting the needs of the motorised forces, which had to be met out of the same stocks. What we should really have done now was to assemble all our motorised units in the north in order to fling the British back to the main defence line in a concentrated and planned counter-attack. But we had not the petrol to do it. So we were compelled to allow the armoured formations in the northern part of our line to assault the British salient piecemeal.

Since the enemy was operating with astonishing hesitancy and caution, a concentrated attack by the whole of our armour could have been successful, although such an assembly of armour would of course have been met by the heaviest possible British artillery fire and air bombardment. However, we could have made the action more fluid by withdrawing a few miles to the west and could then have attacked the British in an all-out charge and defeated them in open country. The British artillery and air force could not easily have intervened with their usual weight in a tank battle of this kind, for their own forces would have been endangered.

But a decision to take forces from the southern front was unthinkable with the petrol situation so bad. Not only could we not have kept a mobile battle going for more than a day or two, but our armour could never have returned to the south if the British had attacked there. I did, however, decide to bring the whole of the 21st Panzer Division up north, although I fully realised that the petrol shortage would not allow it to return. In addition, since it was now obvious that the enemy would make his main effort in the north during the next few days and try for a decision there, half the Army artillery was drawn off from the southern front. At the same time I reported to the Fuehrer's H.Q. that we would lose the battle unless there was an immediate improvement in the supply situation. Judging by previous experience, there was very little hope of this happening.

Relays of British bombers continued their attack throughout the night of the 26th. At about 02.00 hours a furious British barrage by guns of every calibre suddenly began in the northern sector. Soon it was impossible to distinguish between gun-fire and exploding shells and the sky grew bright with the glare of muzzle-flashes and shell-bursts. Continuous bombing attacks seriously delayed the approach march of the 21st Panzer Division and a third of the Ariete. By dawn the 90th Light Division and the Trieste had taken up position round the southern side of Sidi Abd el Rahman.

That morning [*27th October*] I gave orders to all formations to pin down the British assault forces during their approach by all-out fire from every gun they could bring to bear.

The tactics which the British were using followed from their apparently inexhaustible stocks of ammunition. Their new tank, the General Sherman, which came into action for the first time during this battle, showed itself to be far superior to any of ours.

Attacks against our line were preceded by extremely heavy artillery barrages lasting for several hours. The attacking infantry then pushed forward behind a curtain of fire and artificial fog, clearing mines and removing obstacles. Where a difficult patch was struck they frequently switched the direction of their attack under cover of smoke. Once the infantry had cleared lanes in the minefields, heavy tanks moved forward, closely followed by infantry. Particular skill was shown in carrying out this manœuvre at night and a great deal of hard training must have been done before the offensive.

In contact engagements the heavily gunned British tanks approached to a range of between 2,000 and 2,700 yards and then opened concentrated fire on our anti-tank and anti-aircraft guns and tanks, which were unable to penetrate the British armour at that range. The enormous quantities of ammunition which the enemy tanks used—sometimes they fired over 30 rounds at one target—were constantly replenished by armoured ammunition carriers. The British artillery fire was directed by observers who accompanied the attack in tanks.

In the early hours of the 27th of October, the British attacked again towards the south-west at their old break-in point south of Hill 28. At about 10 a.m. I went off to Telegraph Track. Two enemy bomber formations, each of 18 aircraft, dropped their bombs inside ten minutes into our defence positions. The whole front continued to lie under a devastating British barrage.

Local counter-attacks were due to be launched that afternoon by the 90th Light Division on Hill 28 and by the 15th and 21st Panzer Divisions, the Littorio and a part of the Ariete, against the British positions between minefields L and I.

At 14.30 hours I drove to Telegraph Track again, accompanied by Major Ziegler. Three times within a quarter of an hour units of the 90th Light Division, which had deployed and were standing in the open in preparation for the attack, were bombed by formations of eighteen aircraft. At 15.00 hours our dive-bombers swooped down on the British lines. Every artillery and anti-aircraft gun which we had in the northern sector concentrated a violent fire on the point of the intended attack. Then the armour moved forward. A murderous British fire struck into our ranks and our attack was soon brought to a halt by an immensely powerful anti-tank defence, mainly from dug-in anti-tank guns and a large number of tanks. We suffered considerable losses and were obliged to withdraw. There is, in general, little chance of success in a tank attack over country where the enemy has been able to take up defensive positions; but there was nothing else we could do. The 90th Light Division's attack was also broken up by heavy British artillery fire and a hail of bombs from British aircraft. A report from the division that they had taken Hill 28 unfortunately turned out to be untrue.

That evening further strong detachments of the panzer divisions had to be committed in the front to close the gaps. Several of the 90th Light Division's units also went into the line. Only 70 tons of petrol had been flown across by the Luftwaffe that day, with the result that the army could only refuel for a short distance, for there was no knowing when petrol would arrive in any quantity and how long the divisions would have to get along with the few tons we could issue to them. The watchword 'as little movement as possible' applied more than ever.

In the evening we again sent S O S s to Rome and the Fuehrer's H.Q. But there was now no longer any hope of an improvement in the situation. It was obvious that from now on the British would destroy us bit by bit, since we were virtually unable to move on the battlefield. As yet, Montgomery had only thrown half his striking force into the battle.

LUDOVIC KENNEDY
The Sinking of HMS *Hood*

The great German battleship Bismarck *was sunk in May 1941, after a naval action which ranged from the Baltic to the Bay of Biscay. The engagement also saw the loss of the British battle-cruiser HMS* Hood; *of her crew of 1400 all but three perished. Ludovic Kennedy took part in the pursuit of the* Bismarck *as an officer on HMS* Tartar.

AND SO THE TWO ADMIRALS, Lütjens and Holland, riding on their great chargers, came at each other like knights of old, with guns for lances and armoured bridges for visors and pennants streaming in the wind. And beneath their feet, on the airy decks and in the warm bellies of their mounts, were their six thousand young seconds, half on either side, who felt no personal ill will towards each other at all, who in different circumstances might have played and laughed and sung together, kissed each other's sisters, visited each other's homes, but now, because of this time and place, were at each other's throats, concentrating as never before to ensure that they killed first, that their knights' lances toppled the other in the tourney.

In the gun turrets of the four ships, the first shells and cartridges and silken bags of cordite had been sent up from shell rooms and magazines far below, were even now rammed home in the barrels of each gun, the breeches had been closed and locked, the gun ready lamps were burning: the guns of *Hood* and *Bismarck* were over twenty yards long, weighed 100 tons apiece. The range-finding ratings leaned heads forward on rubber eye-cushions: the German range-finders were stereoscopic, which meant centring the little yellow *Wandermark* on the base of the enemy's superstructure; British range-finders were co-incidental, presenting an enemy vessel in two images which required merging into one. The British Navy had considered stereoscopic equipment after the first war, for it was deadly accurate, especially at initial ranges; but it required special aptitudes and a cool head which might be lost in the heat of the battle, so in the end they rejected it. The ranges both visual and radar were fed by electrical circuits to computers in transmitting stations deep below each bridge, along with own course and speed, enemy's course and speed, wind velocity, air density, rate of range-change, and, thus programmed, the computers fed to the gun-turrets an ever changing stream of directions for the training and elevation of the guns. In four gunnery control positions above each bridge, the four gunnery control officers—Schneider, McMullen, Moultrie and Jasper saw the gun ready lamps burn in front of them, stood by to open fire.

For a few moments then, as the two squadrons raced towards each other in that cold, pale dawn, with the eastern sky pink and violet on the low cirrus and a hazy blue above, there was in all the ships a silence made more striking by the knowledge of the thunder that was to come. Men's voices and hands had done all they could by way of preparation: the only sounds now were sea sounds, bows slicing the water, whistling wind and spray.

On *Hood*'s bridge a man with headphones on his ears began singing out softly the closing ranges as given from the gunnery control position, like the conductor of a Dutch auction. And at about the same time as Admiral Holland's Chief Yeoman of Signals was hoisting the preparatory signal to open fire to *Prince of Wales*, Admiral Lütjens was ordering his Chief Yeoman to hoist JD, the signal to open fire to *Prinz Eugen*. When the range was down to thirteen miles, Admiral Holland said, 'Execute.' The Chief Yeoman shouted to the flag deck, 'Down Flag 5', Captain Kerr said, 'Open fire' and in the control tower the gunnery officer said 'Shoot!'

There came the tiny, tinkly, ridiculous ding-ding of the fire gong, like an overture scored for triangle, for a moment the world stood still, then the guns spoke with their terrible great roar, the blast knocked one almost senseless, thick clouds of cordite smoke, black and bitter-smelling, clutched at the throat, blinded the vision, and four shells weighing a ton apiece went rocketing out of the muzzles at over 1,600 miles an hour. To Busch in the *Prinz Eugen, Hood*'s gun flashes appeared as 'great, fiery rings like suns', and Jasper beside him called out 'Damn it, those aren't cruiser's guns, they're battleships', just as *Bismarck*'s second gunnery officer Lieutenant Albrecht was telling Schneider the same. Now it was *Prince of Wales*'s turn, Esmond Knight in his air defence position was deafened by the crash of the forward turrets, felt the breath squeezed from his body, was unable to see for the smoke. As it cleared, he saw an orange ripple of fire run down the length, first of *Bismarck*, then *Prinz Eugen*.

In the tightly-shut armoured control position on *Bismarck's* bridge Lütjens and his staff rocked to the roar of *Bismarck's* opening salvo. This battle was not of his choosing, for his instructions were to shun any engagement with enemy forces not escorting a convoy, and he had delayed permission to open fire so long that there were some in *Bismarck* and *Prinz Eugen* who thought he was hoping to avoid it. But with the ice to the west of him, the two cruisers to the north, and Holland's force to the east, there was no escape; and in that situation his orders were to fight all out.

Now the shells were in the air, like flights of arrows, and men on either side, counting the seconds until their arrival, asked themselves anxiously where they would fall. Some believed they were directed to them personally, had their name on them as the saying went, felt the first stirrings of panic. 'He's fired,' came the agitated voice of a petty officer on *Prinz Eugen's* bridge, and Captain Brinkmann said quietly, 'Keep calm, man. Of course he's fired. Now let's see what comes of it.' With a shriek and a roar the shells fell, great geysers of water leapt in the air, high as Hiltons, white as Daz. *Hood's* shells landed in the vicinity of *Prinz Eugen*, but not dangerously so, *Prince of Wales's* were a thousand yards short of *Bismarck*; but the shells of *Bismarck* and *Prinz Eugen* were deadly accurate, they enveloped *Hood* in a curtain of splashes, the men of *Prince of Wales* saw it with horror and relief.

If Admiral Holland's plan of the night before had worked, and he had come upon Lütjens unseen, he might already have won a great victory. But now everything had gone sour on him, he had the worst of every world. By steering at this angle he was denying his own force the maximum of fire-power and yet giving the enemy more to aim at than necessary. He had reduced his initial superiority in heavy guns of eighteen against eight to ten against eight, which was about to be reduced to nine against eight, as one of the *Prince of Wales's* forward guns had a defect which would render it inoperative after the first salvo. Further, while the British fire was divided between *Bismarck* and *Prinz Eugen*, the German fire was concentrated on *Hood*. It would have helped if *Norfolk* and *Suffolk* had closed up on *Bismarck*, worried her from the rear, drawn the fire from her after turrets: this was Holland's intention, and orders to Müllenheim-Rechberg in *Bismarck's* after control to keep his eyes fixed on the two cruisers show that Lütjens was expecting it. But Holland had failed to give Wake-Walker the necessary orders; the opportunity was lost.

There were other handicaps. The Germans had what sailors call the weather gauge, which meant the British ships were steaming into wind, the spray drenching the lenses of the forward turrets' two thirty-foot range-finders, necessitating use of the small range-finders in the control tower instead. And by keeping *Prince of Wales* close to him, making her conform to his movements rather than let her vary her course and speed, Holland was making it easier for the Germans to range-find, more difficult for the British ships to observe each other's fall of shot.

The shells went to and fro, east and west. One from *Hood* landed just ahead of *Prinze Eugen*, the water rose in a tall, white column and, falling, drenched fo'c'sle and upperworks, smeared the lenses of periscopes and telescopes that jutted out from the armoured control position on the bridge. Other splashes rose on the port bow, and Captain Brinkmann ordered the helmsman to steer towards them, knowing that salvoes never land in the same place twice. Then he opened the heavy door, went outside with Friebe to see through dry binoculars. *Prinze Eugen's* first salvo had been a little short, now she was firing her second. Twenty seconds went by, Brinkmann saw the white fountains shoot up, some short, some over—a straddle—and then a flame leapt up on *Hood's* boatdeck amidships. 'It's a hit,' shouted one of Jasper's crew excitedly, 'the enemy's on fire.' Busch saw the fire as 'a glaring blood-red rectangle which began to emit thick fumes', Captain Leach in *Prince of Wales* as 'a vast blow-lamp', Captain Phillips in *Norfolk* as 'a glow that pulsated like the appearance of a setting, tropical sun'.

On *Hood's* bridge the fire was reported by the torpedo officer as being caused by a shell-burst among the 4-inch anti-aircraft ammunition. Able Seaman Tilburn, one of the 4-inch guns' crews, was ordered with others to put the fire out, was about to do so when ammunition in the ready-use locker started exploding, so they all lay flat on the deck. Then another shell, or perhaps two, hit *Hood*, killing many of the gun crews now sheltering in the aircraft-hangar; and part of a body, falling from aloft, struck Able Seaman Tilburn on the legs.

Now Holland decided, whatever the risks to *Hood*, that he could no longer afford to keep half his gun-power out of action. He had already made one small alteration back to port, and to bring the after turrets of both ships to bear, he hoisted the signal for another. While some on *Prince of Wales's* bridge were looking at the fire in *Hood*, and others had their eyes fixed on the enemy, one man's telescope had never wavered, despite the smoke and confusion of battle, from the flagship's yardarm. 'From *Hood*, sir,' shouted the Chief Yeoman of Signals as the flags went up. 'Two Blue. Turn twenty degrees to port together.' Captain Leach and Lieutenant-Commander McMullen heard the news with joy: now at last the four-gun after turret with its frustrated crew would be brought into action.

The executive signal came down, the two ships began to turn. Then the incredible happened. When Schneider in *Bismarck* saw the fire on *Hood's* boatdeck, he ordered an immediate broadside, and presently, and for the fifth time in four minutes, *Hood* was hidden by a curtain of shell splashes. But at least one shell of that broadside made no splash: it came plunging down like a rocket, hit the old ship fair and square between centre and stern, sliced its way through steel and wood, pierced the deck that should have been strengthened and never was, penetrated to the ship's vitals deep below the water-line, exploded, touched off the 4-inch magazine which in turn touched off the after 15-inch magazine. Before the eyes of the horrified British and incredulous Germans a huge column of flame leapt up from *Hood's* centre. One witness in *Norfolk* said it was four times the height of the mainmast, another that it 'nearly touched the sky'. Busch saw it as a red and white funnel-shaped glow, Esmond Knight as a long, pale red tongue, Lieut-Commander Havers in *Suffolk* as a stick of red rhubarb, Lieutenant Schmitz, the war artist in *Prinz Eugen*, as in the shape of a sinister fir-tree. It was followed by a thick mushroom-shaped cloud of smoke which to Lieut-Commander Towell in *Prince of Wales* had the appearance of steam, but which Esmond Knight described as 'dark yellow, like the smoke from a gorse fire'. One of the oddest things about the explosion was that it made no noise. On *Hood's* bridge Midshipman Dundas and Signalman Briggs heard nothing unusual, and Esmond Knight said, 'I remember listening for it and thinking it would be a most tremendous explosion, but I don't remember hearing an explosion at all.' As the smoke welled upwards and outwards bits and pieces of *Hood* could be seen flying through the air—part of a 15-inch gun turret, the mainmast, the main derrick. Captain Brinkmann noticed the ship's shells exploding high up in the smoke, bursting like white stars. To Esmond Knight it seemed the most famous warship in the world was blowing up like a huge Chinese Christmas cracker.

In all disasters, however unexpected and dramatic, there is often a moment, maybe no longer than a fraction of a second, when those about to die comprehend dimly that something unusual has happened, that things are not as they should be. On *Hood's* bridge, after the great flame had shot up, there was time for Signalman Briggs to hear the officer of the watch report the compass had gone, the quartermaster to report the steering had gone, the captain to order a switch to emergency steering: then the ship fell sideways like a collapsing house. On the boat-deck Able Seaman Tilburn was conscious of a most extraordinary vibration. He saw a man beside him killed, another's side ripped open by a splinter and the guts coming out, went over to the side to be sick, found the deck level with the water. And elsewhere in the ship there were others calmly watching dials or adjusting levers who suddenly were aware that something very strange was happening to them, who, as they were lifted off their feet, and plates and bulkheads collapsed around them, sensed for one terrible, brief moment, no longer than it takes a flash of lightning, that death had come to fetch them.

In *Prince of Wales, Bismarck* and *Prinz Eugen* only a handful of men saw *Hood's* end with their own eyes: the vast majority were below decks and to them the incredible news came on inter-com and by telephone, second hand. Some simply did not believe it. *Prinz Eugen's* executive officer, Commander Stoos, on duty in the lower command post, hearing his captain's voice announcing the news, said quietly, 'Some poor fellow up there has gone off his head.' In *Bismarck's* after transmitting station Leading Seaman Eich heard Commander Schneider's joyous shout, 'She's blowing *up*,' and would remember the long drawn out '*uuup*' for the rest of his life. In the after director tower Müllenheim-Rechberg heard it too, and despite orders to stick to the two cruisers, couldn't resist swinging round to see for himself. The smoke was clearing to show *Hood* with a broken back, in two pieces, bow and stern pointing towards the sky. As he watched, he saw the two forward turrets of *Hood* suddenly spit out a final salvo: it was an accident, the circuits must have been closed at the moment she was struck, but to her enemies it seemed a last defiant and courageous gesture.

Now *Prince of Wales*, turning to port to obey Holland's orders, had to go hard a-starboard to avoid the wreckage ahead, and Jasper, through *Prinz Eugen's* main range-finder, saw on the far side of *Prince of Wales* a weird thing—the whole forward section of *Hood*, rearing up from the water like the spire of a cathedral, towering above the upper deck of *Prince of Wales*, as she steamed by. Inside this foresection were several hundred men, trapped topsy-turvy in the darkness of shell-room and magazine. Then *Prince of Wales* passed, both parts of *Hood* slid quickly beneath the waves, taking with them more than 1,400 men, leaving only a wreath of smoke on the surface. 'Poor devils, poor devils!' said Jasper aloud, echoing the thoughts of those around him; for as sailors they had just proved what sailors do not care to prove, that no ship, not even *Hood*, is unsinkable, and that went for *Bismarck* and *Prinz Eugen* too.

SAMUEL ELIOT MORISON
The Naval Battle of Guadalcanal

On 7 August 1942, the US First Marine division established a bridgehead on the Japanese-occupied island of Guadalcanal. Initially, Japanese opposition was light but soon rapidly intensified. The Japanese sent in troop reinforcements by sea and set up a naval bombardment of the US airstrip, Henderson Field. A naval battle between the US and Japan at Guadalcanal thus became inevitable.

IT WAS NOW FRIDAY THE Thirteenth [November 1942], last day of life for eight ships and many hundred sailors, including two American admirals.

Early in the midwatch a *Helena* radar operator detected a suspicious 'blip' on his scope. Then appeared two traces that were neither friendly ships nor neutral land masses. The report went out at 0124: 'Contacts bearing 312 and 310, distant 27,000 and 32,000 yards.' Obviously one was a group of ships screening another 5000 yards behind it.

Three minutes after this first contact, Admiral Callaghan ordered his 13-ship column to change course two points to starboard, to course 310°. Apparently he desired a head-on clash rather than the more subtle run-around accompanied by torpedo launchings from the flanks. At 0130 *Helena* informed all ships that the enemy disposition was on their port bow distant 14,500 yards, steaming at speed 23 knots on course 105°. Opposing forces were closing at a rate of over 40 knots, and as the range decreased the initial American advantage of radar vanished. Fire control men, intent on the complicated controls of rangekeepers, watched the relentless spinning of the range dials, heard the drone of the range talker's voice, 'Range one three O double O—range one two O double O,' wondering why no word came to let fly 'fish' or commence gunfire. For ten long minutes their questions remained unanswered. Course was changed to due north, speed upped to 20 knots. On board *San Francisco* Admiral Callaghan, blind for want of adequate radar, was continually and urgently calling on his seeing-eye dogs, *Helena* and *O'Bannon*, for vital ranges, bearings, courses and composition. Yet this same voice radio (TBS) channel was the tactical control circuit; imperative directions for course, speed and gunfire had to be sandwiched between information requests. The outlets of the 'squawk box' (voice radio) on the ships' bridges delivered a confused medley that baffled listeners and fast typists alike.

The fast-approaching Japanese did not listen in on this circuit; they were unaware of an enemy in the Sound. But they were not to be caught with defences down. In anticipation of the scheduled shore bombardment, stocky gunners waited in their turrets while torpedomen, secondary battery gun crews, and searchlight operators stood alert at battle stations. Without radar, Admiral Abe realized that any surface action would be quick, close and decisive.

Inexorably the range closed. Commander Stokes of Desdiv 10, embarked in van destroyer *Cushing*, suddenly sighted Japanese destroyers crossing ahead, port to starboard, at the uncomfortably close range of 3000 yards. A flash radio report was passed down the line as *Cushing's* skipper, Lieutenant Commander Parker, turned left from a northerly heading at 0141 in order to unmask his torpedo batteries. His quick turn avoided collision with the enemy but resulted in a pile-up of the van, in which every ship struggled to keep station while swinging to the new course 315°. *Atlanta*, heavier than the destroyers, had to swing hard left. 'What are you doing?' asked Callaghan over voice radio. 'Avoiding our own destroyers,' answered Captain Jenkins.

The ships seen by Stokes were destroyers *Yudachi* and *Harusame*, whose skippers may have been startled but were certainly not asleep. By 0142, a minute after first sighting, the entire Japanese force knew of the contact, surprise was lost, and the American delay in opening fire gave Admiral Abe's ships six whole minutes to prepare for action.

The United States ships were doubly confused by the sudden left turn and the resulting press of voice radio transmissions. Nobody could be certain whether reported target bearings were true or relative to the reporting ships. Nobody knew which target to take under fire, or when. Commander Stokes could stand it no longer. 'Shall I let them have a couple of fish?' he asked. Permission was granted, but by this time the enemy destroyers had scudded into the darkness. Finally, at 0145, Admiral Callaghan gave the word, 'Stand By to Open Fire!'

The prologue was now over and the principals in place; Americans confused, Nipponese surprised. Through the darkness Japanese night glasses picked up the loom of ships almost within their own formation, *Atlanta's* high superstructure standing above the low destroyer silhouettes. At 0150 Japanese searchlight shutters clicked open; beams shot out, feeling right and left; one probably from *Akatsuki* quickly came to the rest on the port wing of *Atlanta's* bridge, bathing the whole superstructure with the kind of light that sailors rightly fear. The cruiser's gunnery officer shouted two orders, 'Commence Firing! Counter-illuminate!' The range was a scant 1600 yards, with solution already set on the range keeper; the cruiser's 5-inch guns spewed forth a stream of shells which extinguished the offending light, but not quickly enough. While *Atlanta* sent salvo after salvo crashing into the Nips on both bows, they and their sister ships concentrated on her. Enemy shells crunched into the misnamed 'Lucky A'. One of them killed Admiral Scott, all but one of his staff, and others on the bridge. Simultaneously, from *San Francisco* came the long-awaited order: 'Odd ships commence fire to starboard, even ships to port.'

Atlanta's participation in the battle was brief. Japanese destroyers, ever ready to exploit torpedo opportunities, dispatched several salvos at the confused American column. One, perhaps two, hit *Atlanta*. Their explosion lifted her bodily from the water, then set her down shuddering and crippled. In the plotting room, fire control men watched the needle on the pitometer log (the ship's speed indicator) slide down the scale until it rested against zero. *Atlanta* was dead in the water, and the battle scarce begun. The ship's mascot terrier, misnamed 'Lucky,' whimpered pitifully in a corner of the damage control station, while the officer in charge telephoned vainly for reports from damaged areas.

From now on, Japanese and American ships mingled like minnows in a bucket. It is impossible to reconstruct their tracks; we can only relate what happened to each. Van destroyer *Cushing* sent several salvos screaming after a destroyer to starboard, but within two minutes received shell hits amidships which severed all power lines and slowed her down. Her bow was pointing almost due north when her skipper sighted *Hiei* on his port beam, on a collision course. Using hand steering control and what little way remained, he swung *Cushing* right and, by local control, fired six 'fish' at the enemy battlewagon less than half a mile distant. None hit *Hiei*, which was also the target of destroyer and cruiser gunfire; but she didn't like it and turned slowly away to the westward. *Cushing* had only a few moments to exult like David. A probing searchlight beam picked her out and enemy gunfire reduced her to a sinking wreck in short order.

Laffey, directly astern of *Cushing*, also entered a disastrous argument with *Hiei*, passing so close that collision was barely averted. Her torpedoes, launched at too short a range, failed to arm and bounced harmlessly off the battleship's sides. Topside machine-gunners sprayed the pagoda-like bridge with 20-mm and 1.1 bullets as *Hiei* passed, shooting. Then two large-caliber gun salvos and a torpedo in the fantail put *Laffey* out of action for all time. She was promptly abandoned, the third to go. Many swimming survivors were killed when the burning hull exploded.

Destroyers *Sterett* and *O'Bannon*, respectively third and fourth in column, had better luck. The former, as an odd-numbered ship, ordered Action Starboard and took an enemy vessel under rapid fire at 4000 yards' range. Although the *Hiei* fracas on her port had rendered visual fire control difficult, radar and early fire-igniting hits on the target solved the problem. Three minutes after *Sterett* had opened fire, an enemy salvo found its mark in her port side aft, disabling her steering gear. This was followed by a hit on her foremast which destroyed the radar. But *Sterett* and her wiry little skipper, Commander Jesse G. Coward, were still full of fight. Maneuvering her with the engines, Coward turned his attention to *Hiei* and pumped out four torpedoes at 2000 yards' range. Simultaneously *O'Bannon* was getting in a few licks; she had opened fire when the first searchlight burst out and so continued throughout the battle. The illuminating Jap took a pummeling from her guns before *O'Bannon* turned on *Hiei*, then some 1200 yards on her port bow. Commander Wilkinson, in the midst of a maneuver to avoid collision with *Sterett*, ordered fire on the big battleship.

At that moment came a puzzling order from Admiral Callaghan: 'Cease firing own ships!' *O'Bannon's* skipper checked fire momentarily and then launched two carefully aimed torpedoes at *Hiei*. He thought they had scored, but actually they either failed to hit or did not explode. The range was so short that the battleship was unable to depress her guns sufficiently to hit back. As her 14-inch salvos shrieked harmlessly over their heads, *O'Bannon's* sailors had the pleasure of seeing this enemy ship of the line completely enveloped in sheets of incandescent flame. A moment later, *O'Bannon* sheered left to avoid the sinking *Laffey's* bow, and tossed life jackets to survivors as she passed. Torpedo wakes crossed her bow. Suddenly an enormous underwater explosion jolted the ship, disrupting light and power and rattling the teeth of all on board. This quake may have been *Laffey's* explosive death rattle or it may have been an enemy torpedo exploding at the end of its run.

Admiral Abe had already disposed of a light cruiser and two destroyers; but his position on the flag bridge of *Hiei*, cynosure of American gunfire, blinded him to the actual progress of the battle and he ordered a change of course in order to get clear. The American column had actually penetrated the center of his formation between his van destroyers, and between his two battleships. This was not according to book, and the Admiral did not like it. While *Hiei* was bearing the brunt of American fury, her sister battleship *Kirishima*, about 800 yards on the flagship's quarter, was dishing out 14-inch punishment but receiving only near-misses in return. She was nicked but once during the entire engagement, by an 8-inch shell. Both battleships turned left in compliance with the retirement order; *Hiei* so slowly that she was rapidly left behind, but she had not yet been torpedoed and was in not too bad a shape.

Flagship *San Francisco*, sixth in the American column and astern of *Atlanta*, had entered the fray promptly, taking under fire an enemy vessel on her starboard beam less than two miles distant. For illumination she used 5-inch star shell, fired to burst above and beyond the target. The unblinking beam of a searchlight, originating on her starboard quarter, wavered and then settled on her; and the illumination of American ships astern served to silhouette her to the enemy. After delivering seven hefty salvos, *San Francisco* shifted to a target described as a 'small cruiser or a large destroyer.' Two full main-battery salvos were pumped into the vessel, 'setting her on fire throughout her length.' It will be recalled that *Atlanta* was now dead in the water and ahead of *San Francisco*; the crew of *Atlanta* believe that she was the victim. How else can one explain Admiral Callaghan's order to cease fire? Before he gave that order, however, the flagship's main-battery control officer had sighted *Hiei* and contributed some well-placed salvos toward the devastation of that ship. When the Cease Firing order took effect, *San Francisco* was the first to suffer. *Kirishima* on her starboard hand dealt out heavy blows; another enemy ship on her starboard quarter employed searchlight illumination and gunfire to good effect; a destroyer darting down her port side raked the superstructure. Steering and engine control were temporarily lost, and as she slowed down, an avalanche of shellfire from three different ships snuffed out the lives of Admiral Callaghan and his staff, of Captain Cassin Young and of nearly every man on the bridge.

At this juncture, cruisers astern of *San Francisco* rallied to her support. *Portland*, seventh in line, had closed firing keys when the enemy illuminated. Her shells located a starboard-hand target whose return fire registered but one hit, which wounded the executive officer. Five minutes after the battle's start, Captain Laurance DuBose received the Cease Firing order but disregarded it except for an incredulous inquiry addressed to the flagship: 'What's the dope, did you want to cease fire?' Callaghan had time to answer 'Affirmative', and to order a course change to the northward. *Portland* checked fire briefly while turning, then picked up a target three miles to starboard and commenced gnawing away at it with her turret guns. A Japanese torpedo tore through the water toward her. A terrific wallop rocked the cruiser as the explosion ripped a huge chunk from her stern, bending the structure so that projecting hull plates acted as an unwanted auxiliary rudder and she made an involuntary complete circle. As she came out of it *Hiei* loomed up in her sights, range 4000 yards, and *Portland* let her have it from both forward turrets. This concluded the evening's main-battery performance for the 'Sweet Pea,' as her crew called this happy ship.

Helena, next astern, was favored by fortune. Opening fire at the same instant as the ships ahead of her, she directed her tracers at the inquisitive searchlight on her port beam some two miles away. Enemy shell splashes reared up in ugly gouts astern but *Helena* received only minor superstructure damage. During the next few minutes Captain Hoover made strenuous efforts to avoid the damaged ships ahead while his guns shifted from target to target. Almost simultaneously his 6-inch main battery lashed out at a ship that was pummeling *San Francisco*, his 5-inchers went after a destroyer on the starboard quarter, and his heavy machine guns worked over a ship of unfriendly contour only 3000 yards distant, probably *Nagara*. When the enemy's retirement opened the range, bullets from 'Helen' hastened him on his way.

Juneau, last cruiser in column, fired along with the rest of the task force during the hectic quarter-hour between 0148 and 0203. In common with other ships, she had difficulty in identifying targets; Callaghan's Cease Firing order belayed a brief spraying of *Helena*. An enemy torpedo sundered *Juneau's* forward fireroom with a shock which put the ship completely out of action, dead in the water and probably with a broken keel. From that moment her main concern was to clear out and keep afloat.

Bringing up the rear, and thus late for the initial slugfest, were destroyers *Aaron Ward, Barton, Monssen* and *Fletcher*. Captain Robert G. Tobin, the squadron commander who flew his pennant in the first-named, was handicapped by lack of orders and an ineffective radar. His opening ranges were considerably greater than the side-scraping distances at which the van destroyers fought, and the jumbled state of the column rendered target selection and station-keeping almost impossible. *Aaron Ward* opened up on a target 7000 yards on her starboard bow, discharged 10 salvos and then checked fire because friendly cruisers fouled her range. Commander Gregor was forced to stop and back engines to avoid collision with a ship ahead—probably *Helena*. Ten minutes elapsed before he could feel certain that an enemy target was in the optics, and then *San Francisco* charged into his line of sight. A target showing unfamiliar recognition lights sharp on the starboard bow was next taken under fire at a mile-and-a-half range, and firing continued until the ship appeared to explode and sink. *Aaron Ward* then used enemy searchlights as points of aim. She received one hit in the director which occasioned a shift to local control of gun batteries.

Destroyer *Barton*, commissioned as recently as 29 May, had a total combat life of exactly seven minutes. She opened fire, launched four torpedoes to port, stopped to avoid collision and, when almost dead in the water, received a torpedo in the forward fireroom which was followed almost instantly by another in the forward engine room. She broke in two and sank in a matter of seconds, taking with her all but a handful of the crew.

Monssen, her conning party eagerly listening to the jabber of the voice radio, trailed *Barton*. She had lost the use of her fire control radar during the afternoon air fight and was forced to rely on radio information and optics. Her knowledge of the situation was slight but her interest was great, particularly after a torpedo passed directly under her keel. *Monssen* fired a 5-torpedo salvo at a battleship on her starboard bow, then turned her attention to another vessel two miles on the starboard beam, launching a spread of five more torpedoes. The 5-inch guns meanwhile went after targets on the port side while the 20-mm guns raised havoc on the topside of a destroyer a quarter of a mile to starboard. Star shell began to burst over and around *Monssen*, lighting up the ship like a night-club floor show. Lieutenant Commander McCombs, believing the star shell to be friendly, switched on his fighting lights; and the click of that light switch was the death knell of his ship. Two blinding tentacles of light grasped her, a deluge of explosives followed, torpedoes hissed by. Some 37 shell hits reduced *Monssen* to a burning hulk.

Destroyer *Fletcher*, despite her station in the very rear of the column, had excellent information from a superior search radar. When the enemy first illuminated *Atlanta*, Commander Cole triggered his firing keys at the offending ship, then some 5500 yards on his port bow. Next, observing that many other ships had chosen the same target, *Fletcher* shifted to a more distant target and had the satisfaction of starting some bright blazes. The order Cease Firing caused her to check momentarily and then resume firing at a third target still farther back in the enemy formation. Eight minutes after the first shot, *Fletcher* sailors witnessed the sudden disintegration of *Barton* and the riddling of *Monssen*. Now that the column was in complete disorder, Commander Cole decided to leave this cluttered area, make another evaluation and return to launch his yet unused torpedoes. Aided by a constant flow of information from the radar room, he threaded his way through the maelstrom of friends and foes, turned south, bent on 35 knots and rounded up to a firing position ahead of the enemy. Torpedo wakes swirled under and around her, gun salvos bracketed her, but *Fletcher* had a charmed life; she emerged without even her paint work scratched.

Four bells of this sinister midwatch had struck during these fifteen minutes of raw hell. A literally infernal scene presented itself to the participants. The struggle had deteriorated into a wild and desperate mêlée. The greenish light of suspended star shell dimmed the stars overhead. Elongated red and white trails of shell tracers arched and crisscrossed, magazines exploded in blinding bouquets of white flame, oil-fed conflagrations sent up twisted yellow columns. Dotting the horizon were the dull red glows of smoldering hulls, now obscured by dense masses of smoke, now blazing up when uncontrolled fires reached new combustibles. The sea itself, fouled with oil and flotsam, tortured by underwater upheavals, rose in geysers from shell explosions.

By 0200 November 13, the main issue had been decided by Admiral Abe's order to *Hiei* and *Kirishima* to turn left and steam north. Henderson Field and its precious planes were safe for that night at least, but nobody on the American side knew it.

Fighting continued with little respite after the battlewagons retired, *Hiei* to the south of Savo, *Kirishima* to the north. A short lull gave *Cushing* opportunity to fight fires on board, but just as they were brought under control several enemy salvos came her way. The flames then took charge and finally, at 0315, with magazines in volcanic action, the skipper ordered Abandon Ship. *Laffey* was already on the iron bottom. *Sterett*, with steering gear disabled, encountered an enemy destroyer 1000 yards on her starboard bow at 0220 and launched two torpedoes which appeared to hit and sink her; but, shortly after, *Sterett* was peppered with 5-inch shells and forced to retire southeastward, slowing down periodically to reduce the windage on the flames.

Commander Wilkinson in *O'Bannon* decided, since the scene was utterly confused, to haul off to the southeastward in an effort to locate friend or foe. At 0215 he sighted a smoking vessel on the port bow but wisely withheld torpedo fire on what later proved to be

San Francisco. Thinking that enemy transports might have entered the Sound, *O'Bannon* turned south and investigated the shoreline. Saint Christopher, Saint Barbara and the luck of the Irish must have been with plucky *O'Bannon* on this fearful night.

Atlanta's fighting men by 0200 were mere spectators, a status which they had neither time nor inclination to enjoy. Their ship was ravaged by more than *50* large-caliber shell hits, holed by torpedoes and consumed by fire. Survivors found devastation behind every bulkhead and in almost every compartment. Below decks men groped in complete darkness through acrid smoke and sloshed heavily in oily waters on flooded decks. Cursing and coughing, they labored to seal hull ruptures, succor the many wounded and bring fires under control. The main deck was a charnel house. Burned and eviscerated corpses, severed limbs and chunks of flesh mixed with steel debris, littered it from stem to stern. Blood, oil and sea water made a nasty, slippery slush through which one could move only on hands and knees. The 'spud locker' amidships had burst open, strewing the decks with potatoes; no joke to groaning men who slipped on the treacherous tubers. Muzzles of useless guns drooped silent over the motionless dead. Seven out of the eight 5-inch turrets had been hit, all but four of the machine guns were smashed. Flames ate greedily into the superstructure, belching out as burning ammunition detonated. Shadowy figures, the only living part of this macabre setting, moved perilously back and forth as bucket brigades or to jettison the cumbersome weights which threatened to capsize the ship, or to carry the wounded to improvised dressing stations. Admiral Scott was dead but Captain Jenkins and his executive officer, Commander Campbell D. Emory, were spared serious injury. They were able gradually to establish communications with the little knots of survivors around the ship and to direct a coördinated effort to save *Atlanta*. Gasoline handybillys were rigged to fight fire, a damage control party worked to get one fireroom back into operation, the remaining guns were manned, the injured were taken to comparative safety aft.

As the battle drew to a close, *San Francisco's* topsides were in almost as bad shape as *Atlanta's*, but three circumstances saved the flagship from annihilation. The close range had prevented the enemy from depressing his guns sufficiently to score hits below the waterline; thin-skinned bombardment shells, fatal to human lives and damaging to superstructure, had been deflected by armor; she had suffered no torpedo hits. On the navigation bridge Lieutenant Commander Bruce McCandless, communications officer, found himself the only able-bodied survivor. In central station, Lieutenant Commander H. E. Schonland, acting first lieutenant, learned that he had succeeded to command. Realizing that his knowledge of damage control was vital to the ship's survival, he elected to lead the fight against the twenty-five fires then raging, and ordered McCandless to conn the ship out of harm's way. That he did very well, skirting the coast of Guadalcanal.

Portland, with her warped stern, continued to steam in tight circles for the remainder of the night. Captain DuBose at one time counted nine burning vessels in the Sound. *Helena* ceased firing at 0216 and, except for brief searchlight scrutiny, received no more attention from the enemy. Captain Hoover, unable to contact either Scott or Callaghan and believing his to be the senior undamaged command, called all ships (only two answered) and at 0226 ordered them to follow him and retire via Sealark Channel. *Juneau* got way on by the end of the midwatch and moved toward Indispensable Strait.

Meantime, Captain Tobin's three remaining destroyers of the rear were acting individually. *Aaron Ward* with guns in local control lashed out at enemy searchlights that were guiding salvos her way. She cleared out after being pierced by nine medium-caliber shells. The damage was cumulative and progressive, so that by 0235 she lay dead in the water with a flooded engine room, and spent the rest of the night in efforts to get way on. *Monssen* burned and exploded with such fury that she was hastily abandoned. The crew, clinging to life rafts, watched their ship flame and erupt throughout the remaining hours of darkness.

Fletcher, the apparently untouchable Shadrach of the American task force, was now in an excellent position to reenter the contest with torpedoes. A large target was selected and radar commenced tracking as the ship stalked her prey. The enemy vessel, on an easterly course, was shooting to the northward, probably at her friends, when *Fletcher* dispatched ten 'fish' on a three-and-a-half-mile run at 36 knots. Having shot her bolt, *Fletcher* retired in the general direction of Sealark Channel.

On the enemy side, it is probable that most torpedo tubes were emptied during the first ten minutes. At any rate, after

0200 the Martian display diminished rapidly. *Hiei* steered an erratic north westerly course, limping from damage to steering and communication systems and loss of fire power. She had taken over *50* topside hits. Destroyer *Akatsuki*, one of the forward screening vessels, had gone down. *Yudachi* of the advanced flank, emerging from a penetration run through the American forces, underwent a severe explosion at 0220 which stopped her dead some five miles south of Savo Island. Three destroyers had been hit but not stopped: *Ikazuchi*, forecastle gun damaged; *Murasame*, forward boiler room out; *Amatsukaze*, minor scars. These three retired to the north in company with undamaged ships, *Samidare* took off *Yudachi* survivors and followed them later, and the Patrol Unit of three destroyers stood by the stricken battleship.

A glassy, metallic sea, stippled by the floating litter of death and destruction, reflected the sun's first rays. The mountains of Guadalcanal turned from black to purple and then to lush green. Sailors on crippled warships of both nations stood by their damaged guns, grimly aware that between ship and ship no quarter would be given. Early birdmen could see eight crippled ships scattered without order between Savo Island and Guadalcanal. Five were American: unsteerable *Portland*, shattered *Atlanta*, immobile *Aaron Ward*, burning and abandoned *Cushing* and *Monssen*. The Rising Sun was still flying on rudderless *Hiei* and her loyal protectors and on flaming and abandoned *Yudachi*. It was inevitable that more compliments would be exchanged.

Portland, still churning in circles, embraced *Yudachi* 12,500 yards distant, with six salvos. Enough of these 36 projectiles hit to produce a magazine explosion which completely erased the destroyer, a cheering sight to many a swimming American. *Hiei* sent four 2-gun salvos careering down the 13-mile range to *Aaron Ward*; the third straddled but did not hit. Fortunately, the Marine Corps aircraft which promptly appeared on the scene proved so interesting to *Hiei* that she laid off the destroyer until tugs could tow her out of range, eventually to an anchorage in Tulagi Harbor.

On board *Atlanta* all efforts were concentrated on saving the ship. Captain Jenkins, wounded painfully in the foot, urged his bedraggled seamen to superhuman efforts. First, it was necessary to get the pumps going to counteract the continual seepage of water. Apprehensive of beaching off the enemy-held shore of Guadalcanal, the Captain ordered the port anchor walked out and issued small arms to all hands. Wounded and nonessential ratings were sent ashore in Higgins boats hastily provided by the Lunga base. Even after 0939, when tug *Bobolink* had taken her in tow, *Atlanta* shot at a Japanese 'Betty' which ventured too close; the seamen of *Bobolink*, rendered bloodthirsty by previous experiences, machine-gunned every dark head they saw afloat until Captain Jenkins begged them to desist lest mistakes be made. By 1400 the cruiser was anchored off Kukum, but she could not be kept afloat. No salvage facilities were available, she was listing heavily to port and the enemy was expected again that night. So the crew was ordered to scuttle the old girl with a demolition charge. *Atlanta* went down three miles off Lunga Point shortly after dark on Friday evening, the Bloody Thirteenth.

Cushing and *Monssen* continued to burn but did not sink until late in the afternoon. The water around them was blanketed with debris. At daylight three gallant sailors boarded burning *Monssen* to rescue eight helpless wounded and place them in a life raft. Rescue craft from Guadalcanal plowed through wreckage and oil, picked up friends and were evaded by foes who had been indoctrinated not to accept rescue.

All day *Portland* continued her efforts to recover steering control. A score of Higgins boats nosed her bow, huffing and puffing in a vain struggle to offset the torque of the bent stern. Every conceivable maneuver and gadget were tried. Sea-anchors improvised of canvas and garbage cans were streamed. Finally *Bobolink*, after leaving *Atlanta*, pushed *Portland's* starboard bow so vigorously that she was able to crawl along on a steady course. 'Sweet Pea' finally anchored in Tulagi Harbor at 0100 November 14.

The American vessels which had retired from the hot spot around Savo found themselves at dawn in a formation proceeding southeasterly down Indispensable Strait. Captain Hoover of *Helena*, now senior officer present, took charge of *San Francisco*, *Juneau*, *O'Bannon*, *Sterett* and *Fletcher*—three of them lame ducks. Zigzagging through a smooth sea at 18 knots, they set course for the New Hebrides. In order to provide anti-submarine protection, *Fletcher* and *Sterett* were placed 4000 yards ahead of the heavy ships. As *O'Bannon's* sound gear had been damaged by the previous night's underwater explosion, she was sent ahead to transmit a radio message to Admiral Halsey. At 0950 *Sterett* made a sound contact and delivered an urgent depth-charge attack with indeterminate results.

An hour later, this task force touched the nadir of its fortune. *Helena* was steaming 1000 yards ahead of *San Francisco; Juneau* was 1000 yards on the latter's starboard beam. Submarine I–*26*, cruising at periscope depth, drew a bead and fired a spread of torpedoes. Two of them shot past *San Francisco* but she, with no means of rapid communication left, could not broadcast the alarm. Straight and true, one enemy torpedo traveled toward *Juneau*, and at 1101 detonated against her port side under the bridge. Horrified sailors in *San Francisco* saw the light cruiser disintegrate instantaneously and completely, sinking with apparently no trace except a tall pillar of smoke and a little debris. Nobody waited to look for survivors. A Flying Fortress, attracted thither by the force of the explosion, was informed of the disaster and asked to relay a rescue request to Admiral Halsey's headquarters.

Unfortunately this message never got through. Of more than a hundred men who miraculously survived the eruption and who clung pitifully to the flotsam that marked their ship's end, all but ten perished. Three paddled their raft to a small island where friendly natives and a European trader brought them back to life, and a Catalina carried them home. Another PBY rescued six; *Ballard* picking up the sole survivor of one raft on 20 November. Almost 700 men, including the five Sullivan brothers, went down with *Juneau* or died in life rafts.

So ended the wildest, most desperate sea fight since Jutland, one that recalls the Anglo–Dutch battles of the seventeenth century. Ship losses were fairly well balanced; two light cruisers and four destroyers as against two destroyers and a battleship so badly damaged that airmen could sink her next day. Casualties on the American side were many times those of the enemy. But the Japanese bombardment mission was completely frustrated—Yamamoto admitted as much by relieving Abe and depriving him of any further sea command. Callaghan, on the other hand, completed his mission; he saved Henderson Field from a bombardment which might well have been more serious than 'the' bombardment of mid-October, and certainly would have stopped the American air operations, which next day disposed of eleven troopladen transports.

Thus, in the end, all mistakes were canceled out by valor. While the shells that were to strike him down were being loaded into enemy gun breeches, Admiral Callaghan called out over voice radio, 'We want the big ones!'—meaning Japanese battleship. His men stopped one; on the following night Admiral Lee consigned another to the iron bottom. Let none deny praise, glory and honor to those who fell on Friday the Bloody Thirteenth with two great seamen and gallant gentlemen, Daniel O'Callaghan and Norman Scott.

ERNEST HEMINGWAY
Voyage to Victory

The novelist Ernest 'Papa' Hemingway worked for many years as a newspaper correspondent, and reported both the Spanish Civil War and World War Two. 'Voyage to Victory' is his account of D-Day 1944, the invasion of Normandy, as witnessed from a US landing craft.

OUT A WAY, ROLLING IN the sea, was a Landing Craft Infantry, and as we came alongside of her I saw a ragged shell hole through the steel plates forward of her pilot-house where an 88-mm. German shell had punched through. Blood was dripping from the shiny edges of the hole into the sea with each roll of the LCI. Her rails and hull had been befouled by seasick men, and her dead were laid forward of her pilot-house. Our lieutenant had some conversation with another officer while we rose and fell in the surge alongside the black iron hull, and then we pulled away.

Andy* went forward and talked to him, then came aft again, and we sat up on the stern and watched two destroyers coming along toward us from the eastern beaches, their guns pounding away at targets on the headlands and sloping fields behind the beaches.

'He says they don't want him to go in yet; to wait,' Andy said.

'Let's get of the way of this destroyer.'

'How long is he going to wait?'

'He says they have no business in there now. People that should

* Lieutenant (jg) Robert 'Andy' Anderson, the officer in charge of Hemingway's landing craft.

have been ahead of them haven't gone in yet. They told him to wait.'

'Let's get in where we can keep track of it,' I said. 'Take the glasses and look at that beach, but don't tell them forward what you see.'

Andy looked. He handed the glasses back to me and shook his head.

'Let's cruise along it to the right and see how it is up at that end,' I said. 'I'm pretty sure we can get in there when he wants to get in. You're sure they told him he shouldn't go in?'

'That's what he says.'

'Talk to him and get it straight.'

Andy came back. 'He says they shouldn't go in now. They're supposed to clear the mines away, so the tanks can go, and he says nothing is in there to go yet awhile.'

The destroyer was firing point blank at the concrete pillbox that had fired at us on the first trip into the beach, and as the guns fired you heard the bursts and saw the earth jump almost at the same time as the empty brass cases clanged back on to the steel deck. The five-inch guns of the destroyer were smashing at the ruined house at the edge of the little valley where the other machine gun had fired from.

'Let's move in now that the can has gone by and see if we can't find a good place,' Andy said.

'That can punched out what was holding them up there, and you can see some infantry working up that draw now,' I said to Andy. 'Here, take the glasses.'

Slowly, laboriously, as though they were Atlas carrying the world on their shoulders, men were working up the valley on our right. They were not firing. They were just moving slowly up the valley like a tired pack train at the end of the day, going the other way from home.

'The infantry has pushed up to the top of the ridge at the end of that valley,' I shouted to the lieutenant.

'They don't want us yet,' he said. 'They told me clear they didn't want us yet.'

'Let me take the glasses—or Hemingway,' Andy said. Then he handed them back. 'In there, there's somebody signalling with a yellow flag, and there's a boat in there in trouble, it looks like. Coxswain, take her straight in.'

We moved in toward the beach at full speed, and Ed Banker looked around and said, 'Mr Anderson, the other boats are coming, too.'

'Get them back!' Andy said. '*Get them back*!'

Banker turned around and waved the boats away. He had difficulty making them understand, but finally the wide waves they were throwing subsided and they dropped astern.

'Did you get them back?' Andy asked, without looking away from the beach where we could see a half-sunken LCV(P) foundered in the mined stakes.

'Yes, sir,' Ed Banker said.

An LCI was headed straight towards us, pulling away from the beach after having circled to go in. As it passed, a man shouted with a megaphone, 'There are wounded on that boat and she is sinking.'

'Can you get in to her?'

The only words we heard clearly from the megaphone as the wind snatched the voice away were 'machine-gun nest'.

'Did they say there was or there wasn't a machine-gun nest?' Andy said.

'I couldn't hear.'

'Run alongside of her again, coxswain,' he said. 'Run close alongside.'

'Did you say there was a machine-gun nest?' he shouted.

An officer leaned over with the megaphone. 'A machine-gun nest has been firing on them. They are sinking.'

'Take her straight in, coxswain,' Andy said.

It was difficult to make our way through the stakes that had been sunk as obstructions, because there were contact mines fastened to them that looked like large double pie plates fastened face to face. They looked as though they had been spiked to the pilings and then assembled. They were the ugly, neutral grey-yellow colour that almost everything is in war.

We did not know what other stakes with mines were under us, but the ones that we could see we fended off by hand and worked our way to the sinking boat.

It was not easy to bring on board the man who had been shot through the lower abdomen, because there was no room to let the ramp down the way we were jammed in the stakes with the cross sea.

I do not know why the Germans did not fire on us unless the destroyer had knocked the machine-gun pillbox out. Or maybe they were waiting for us to blow up with the mines. Certainly the mines had been a great amount of trouble to lay and the Germans might well have wanted to see them work. We were in the range of the antitank gun that had fired on us before, and all the time we were manoeuvring and working in the stakes I was waiting for it to fire.

As we lowered the ramp the first time, while we were crowded in against the other LCV(P), but before she sank, I saw three tanks coming along the beach, barely moving, they were advancing so slowly. The Germans let them cross the open space where the valley opened on to the beach, and it was absolutely flat with a perfect field of fire. Then I saw a little fountain of water jut up, just over and beyond the lead tank. Then smoke broke out of the leading tank on the side away from us, and I saw two men dive out of the turret and land on their hands and knees on the stones of the beach. They were close enough so that I could see their faces, but no more men came out as the tank started to blaze up and burn fiercely.

By then, we had the wounded man and the survivors on board, the ramp back up, and were feeling our way out through the stakes. As we cleared the last of the stakes, and Currier opened up the engine wide as we pulled out to sea, another tank was beginning to burn.

We took the wounded boy out to the destroyer. They hoisted him aboard it in one of those metal baskets and took on the survivors. Meantime, the destroyers had run in almost to the beach and were blowing every pillbox out of the ground with their five-inch guns. I saw a piece of German about three feet long with an arm on it sail high up into the air in the fountaining of one shellburst. It reminded me of a scene in Petrouchka.

The infantry had now worked up the valley on our left and had gone on over that ridge. There was no reason for anyone to stay out now. We ran in to a good spot we had picked on the beach and put our troops and their TNT and their bazookas and their lieutenant ashore, and that was that.

The Germans were still shooting with their anti-tank guns, shifting them around in the valley, holding their fire until they had a target they wanted. Their mortars were still laying a plunging fire along the beaches. They had left people behind to snipe at the beaches, and when we left, finally, all these people who were firing were evidently going to stay until dark at least.

The heavily loaded ducks that had formerly sunk in the waves on their way in were now making the beach steadily. The famous thirty-minute clearing of the channels through the mined obstacles was still a myth, and now, with the high tide, it was a tough trip in with the stakes submerged.

We had six craft missing, finally, out of the twenty-four LCV(P)s that went in from the *Dix*, but many of the crews could have been picked up and might be on other vessels. It had been a frontal assault in broad daylight, against a mined beach defended by all the obstacles military ingenuity could devise. The beach had been defended as stubbornly and as intelligently as any troops could defend it. But every boat from the *Dix* had landed her troops and cargo. No boat was lost through bad seamanship. All that were lost were lost by enemy action. And we had taken the beach.

There is much that I have not written. You could write for a week and not give everyone credit for what he did on a front of 1135 yards. Real war is never like paper war, nor do accounts of it read much the way it looks. But if you want to know how it was in an LCV(P) on D-Day when we took Fox Green beach and Easy Red beach on the sixth of June, 1944, then this is as near as I can come to it.

MARTHA GELLHORN
The Battle of the Bulge

In December 1944, facing defeat, Hitler tried a desperate last gamble of an offensive on the Western front. The result was the Battle of the Bulge.

January 1945

THEY ALL SAID IT WAS wonderful Kraut-killing country. What it looked like was scenery for a Christmas card: smooth white snow hills and bands of dark forest and villages that actually nestled. The snow made everything serene, from a distance. At sunrise and sunset the snow was pink and the forests grew smoky and soft. During the day the sky was covered with ski tracks, the vapor trails of planes, and the roads were dangerous iced strips, crowded with all the usual vehicles of war, and the artillery made a great deal of noise, as did the bombs from the Thunderbolts. The nestling villages, upon closer view, were mainly rubble and there were indeed plenty of dead Krauts. This was during the German counteroffensive which drove through Luxembourg and Belgium and is now driven back. At this time the Germans were being 'contained', as the communiqué said. The situation was 'fluid'—again the communiqué. For the sake of the record, here is a little of what containing a fluid situation in Kraut-killing country looks like.

The road to Bastogne had been worked over by the Ninth Air Force Thunderbolts before the Third Army tanks finally cleared the way. A narrow alley was free now, and two or three secondary roads leading from Bastogne back to our lines. 'Lines' is a most inaccurate word and one should really say 'leading back through where the Germans weren't to where the Americans were scattered about the snowscape.' The Germans remained on both sides of this alley and from time to time attempted to push inward and again cut off Bastogne.

A colleague and I drove up to Bastogne on a secondary road through breath-taking scenery. The Thunderbolts had created this scenery. You can say the words 'death and destruction' and they don't mean anything. But they are awful words when you are looking at what they mean. There were some German staff cars along the side of the road; they had not merely been hit by machine-gun bullets, they had been mashed into the ground. There were half-tracks and tanks literally wrenched apart, and a gun position directly hit by bombs. All around these lacerated or flattened objects of steel there was the usual riffraff: papers, tin cans, cartridge belts, helmets, an odd shoe, clothing. There were also, ignored and completely inhuman, the hard-frozen corpses of Germans. Then there was a clump of houses, burned and gutted, with only a few walls standing, and around them the enormous bloated bodies of cattle.

The road passed through a curtain of pine forest and came out on a flat, rolling snow field. In this field the sprawled or bunched bodies of Germans lay thick, like some dark shapeless vegetable.

We had watched the Thunderbolts working for several days. They flew in small packs and streaked in to the attack in single file. They passed quickly through the sky and when they dived you held your breath and waited; it seemed impossible that the plane would be able to pull itself up to safety. They were diving to within sixty feet of the ground. The snub-nosed Thunderbolt is more feared by the German troops than any other plane.

You have seen Bastogne and a thousand other Bastognes in the newsreels. These dead towns and villages spread over Europe and one forgets the human misery and fear and despair that the cracked and caved-in buildings represent. Bastogne was a German job of death and destruction and it was beautifully thorough. The 101st Airborne Division, which held Bastogne, was still there, though the day before the wounded had been taken out as soon as the first road was open. The survivors of the 101st Airborne Division, after being entirely surrounded, uninterruptedly shelled and bombed, after having fought off four times their strength in Germans, look—for some unknown reason—cheerful and lively. A young lieutenant remarked, 'The tactical situation was always good.' He was very surprised when we shouted with laughter. The front, north of Bastogne, was just up the road and the peril was far from past.

At Warnach, on the other side of the main Bastogne road, some soldiers who had taken, lost and retaken this miserable village were now sightseeing the battlefield. They were also inspecting the blown-out equipment of two German tanks and a German self-propelled gun which had been destroyed here. Warnach smelled of the dead; in subzero weather the smell of death has an acrid burning odor. The soldiers poked through the German equipment to see if there was anything useful or desirable. They unearthed a pair of good bedroom slippers alongside the tank, but as no one in the infantry has any chance to wear bedroom slippers these were left. There was a German Bible but no one could read German. Someone had found a German machine pistol in working order and rapidly salted it away; they hoped to find other equally valuable loot.

The American dead had been moved inside the smashed houses and covered over; the dead horses and cows lay where they were, as did a few dead Germans. An old civilian was hopelessly shovelling grain from some burned and burst sacks into a wheelbarrow; and farther down the ruined street a woman was talking French in a high angry voice to the chaplain, who was trying to pacify her. We moved down this way to watch the goings-on. Her house was in fairly good shape; that is to say, it had no windows or door and there was a shell hole through the second-floor wall, but it was standing and the roof looked rainproof. Outside her parlor window were some German mines, marked with a white tape. She stood in her front hall and said bitterly that it was a terrible thing, she had left her house for a few moments that morning, and upon returning she found her sheets had been stolen.

'What's she saying?' asked an enormous soldier with red-rimmed blue eyes and a stubble of red beard. Everyone seems about the same age, as if weariness and strain and the unceasing cold leveled all life. I translated the woman's complaint.

Another soldier said, 'What does a sheet look like?'

The huge red-bearded man drawled out, 'My goodness,' a delicious expression coming from that face in that street. 'If she'd of been here when the fighting was going on, she'd act different.'

Farther down the street a command car dragged a trailer; the bodies of Germans were piled on the trailer like so much ghastly firewood.

We had come up this main road two days before. First there had been a quick tempestuous scene in a battalion headquarters when two planes strafed us, roaring in to attack three times and putting machine-gun bullets neatly through the second-story windows of the house. The official attitude has always been that no Germans were flying reclaimed Thunderbolts, so that is that. No one was wounded or killed during this brief muck-up. One of the battalion machine-gunners, who had been firing at the Thunderbolts, said, 'For God's sake, which side are those guys fighting on?' We jumped into our jeep and drove up nearer the front, feeling that the front was probably safer.

A solitary tank was parked close to a bombed house near the main road. The crew sat on top of the tank, watching a village just over the hill which was being shelled, as well as bombed by the Thunderbolts. The village was burning and the smoke made a close package of fog around it, but the flames shot up and reddened the snow in the foreground. The armed forces on this piece of front consisted, at the moment, of this tank, and out ahead a few more tanks, and somewhere invisibly to the left a squadron of tanks. We did not know where our infantry was. (This is what a fluid situation means.) The attacked village would soon be entered by the tanks, including the solitary watchdog now guarding this road.

We inquired of the tank crew how everything went. 'The war's over,' said one of the soldiers, sitting on the turret. 'Don't you know that? I heard it on the radio, a week ago. The Germans haven't any gasoline. They haven't any planes. Their tanks are no good. They haven't any shells for their guns. Hell, it's all over. I ask myself what I'm doing here,' the tankist went on. 'I say to myself, boy, you're crazy, sitting out here in the snow. Those ain't Germans, I say to myself, didn't they tell you on the radio the Germans are finished?'

As for the situation, someone else on the tank said that they would gratefully appreciate it if we could tell them what was going on.

'The wood's full of dead Krauts,' said another, pointing across the road. 'We came up here and sprayed it just in case there was any around and seems the place was full of them, so it's a good thing we sprayed it all right. But where they are right now, I wouldn't know.'

'How's your hen?' asked the Captain, who had come from Battalion HQ to show us the way. 'He's got a hen,' the Captain explained. 'He's been sweating that hen out for three days, running around after it with his helmet.'

'My hen's worthless,' said a soldier. 'Finished, no good, got no fight in her.'

'Just like the Germans,' said the one who listened to the radio.

Now two days later the road was open much farther and there was even a rumor that it was open all the way to Bastogne. That would mean avoiding the secondary roads, a quicker journey, but it seemed a good idea to inquire at a blasted German gun position. At this spot there were ten Americans, two sergeants and eight enlisted men; also two smashed German bodies, two dead cows and a gutted house.

'I wouldn't go up that road if I was you,' one of the sergeants said. 'It's cut with small-arms fire about a quarter of a mile farther on. We took about seventeen Heinies out of there just a while back, but some others must of got in.'

That seemed to settle the road.

'Anyhow,' the sergeant went on, 'They're making a counter-attack. They got about thirty tanks, we heard, coming this way.'

The situation was getting very fluid again.

'What are you going to do?' I said.

'Stay here,' said one of the soldiers.

'We got a gun,' said another.

War is lonely and individual work; it is hard to realize how small it can get. Finally it can boil down to ten unshaven gaunt-looking young men, from anywhere in America, stationed on a vital road with German tanks coming in.

'You better take that side road if you're going to Bastogne,' the second sergeant said.

It seemed shameful to leave them. 'Good luck,' I said, not knowing what to say.

'Sure, sure,' they said soothingly. And later on they got a tank and the road was never cut and now if they are still alive they are somewhere in Germany doing the same work, as undramatically and casually—just any ten young men from anywhere in America.

About a mile from this place, and therefore about a mile and a half from the oncoming German tanks, the General in command of this tank outfit had his headquarters in a farmhouse. You could not easily enter his office through the front door, because a dead horse with spattered entrails blocked the way. A shell had landed in the farmyard a few minutes before and killed one cow and wounded a second, which was making sad sounds in a passageway between the house and the barn.

The air-ground-support officer was here with his van, checking up on the Thunderbolts who were attacking the oncoming German tanks. 'Argue Leader,' he said, calling on the radio-phone to the flight leader. 'Beagle here. Did you do any good on that one?'

'Can't say yet,' answered the voice from the air.

Then over the loud-speaker a new voice came from the air, talking clearly and loudly and calmly. 'Three Tigers down there with people around them.'

Also from the air the voice of Argue Leader replied rather peevishly, 'Go in and get them. Don't stand there talking about it.' They were both moving at an approximate speed of three hundred miles an hour.

From the radio in another van came the voice of the Colonel commanding the forward tank unit, which was stopping this counterattack on the ground. 'We got ten and two more coming,' said the Colonel's voice. 'Just wanted to keep you posted on the German tanks burning up here. It's a beautiful sight, a beautiful sight, over.'

'What a lovely headquarters,' said a solider who was making himself a toasted cheese sandwich over a small fire that served everyone for warmth and cookstove. He had opened the cheese can in his K ration and was doing an excellent job, using a German bayonet as a kitchen utensil.

'Furthermore,' said a lieutenant, 'they're attacking on the other side. They got about thirty tanks coming in from the west too.'

'See if I care,' remarked the soldier, turning his bread carefully so as to toast it both ways. A shell landed, but it was farther up the road. There had been a vaguely sketched general ducking, a quick reflex action, but no one of course remarked it.

Then Argue Leader's voice came exultantly from the air. 'Got those three. Going home now. Over.'

'Good boys,' said the ground officer. 'Best there is. My squadron.'

'Listen to him,' said an artillery officer who had come over to report. 'You'd think the Thunderbolts did everything. Well, I got to get back to work.'

The cow went on moaning softly in the passageway. Our driver, who had made no previous comment during the day, said bitterly, 'What I hate to see is a bunch of livestock all beat up this way. Goddammit, what they got to do with it? It's not their fault.'

Christmas had passed almost unnoticed. All those who could, and that would mean no farther forward than Battalion Headquarters, had shaved and eaten turkey. The others did not shave and ate cold K rations. That was Christmas. There was little celebration on New Year's Eve, because everyone was occupied, and there was nothing to drink. Now on New Year's Day we were going up to visit the front, east of Luxembourg City. The front was quiet in the early afternoon, except for artillery, and a beautiful fat-flaked snowstorm had started. We decided, like millions of other people, that we were most heartily sick of war; what we really wanted to do was borrow a sled and go coasting. We borrowed a homemade wooden sled from an obliging little boy and found a steep slick hill near an abandoned stone quarry. It was evidently a well-known hill, because a dozen Luxembourg children were already there, with unsteerable sleds like ours. The sky had cleared and the ever present Thunderbolts returned and were working over the front less than four kilometers away. They made a lot of noise, and the artillery was pounding away too. The children paid no attention to this; they did not watch the Thunderbolts, or listen to the artillery. Screaming with joy, fear, and good spirits, they continued to slide down the hill.

Our soldier driver stood with me at the top of the hill and watched the children. 'Children aren't so dumb,' he said. I said nothing. 'Children are pretty smart,' he said. I said nothing again. 'What I mean is, children got the right idea. What people ought to do is go coasting.'

When he dropped us that night he said, 'I sure got to thank you folks. I haven't had so much fun since I left home.'

On the night of New Year's Day, I thought of a wonderful New Year's resolution for the men who run the world: get to know the people who only live in it.

There were many dead and many wounded, but the survivors contained the fluid situation and slowly turned it into a retreat, and finally, as the communiqué said, the bulge was ironed out. This was not done fast or easily; and it was not done by those anonymous things, armies, divisions, regiments. It was done by men, one by one—your men.

RUSSELL F. WEIGLEY
Nuts

The following incident occurred during the German offensive in the Battle of the Bulge, 1944.

IT IS NOT SURPRISING THAT the enemy detected in the westerly battles a scarcity of American infantry grievous enough to warrant a surrender demand. About noon on December 22, four Germans under a flag of truce entered the lines of Company F of the 327th. A major, a captain, and two enlisted men, they described themselves as 'parlementaires'. The commander of the 327th could not immediately be found, so it was the regimental operations officer who received from the Germans a written note from 'The German Commander', which he delivered to division headquarters. The note referred to the progress of German spearheads farther west toward the Meuse as evidence of the futility of holding out at Bastogne, which adds perspective to the importance of the battles concurrently being fought by the 2nd and 3rd Armored and 84th Infantry Divisions in front of the Meuse crossings. Thus suggesting that the German tide was irresistible anyway, the note demanded the surrender of the encircled town within two hours, on pain of annihilation of 'the U.S.A. troops in and near Bastogne'.

[Brigadier-General Anthony C.] McAuliffe received this demand just as he was about to leave headquarters to congratulate the defenders of a roadblock who had given an especially good account of themselves. He dropped the message on the floor, said 'Nuts', and left.

When he returned his staff reminded him of the message, and for the first time he gave it serious enough thought to ask what he should say in reply. His G-3 suggested, 'That first remark of yours would be hard to beat.'

'What did I say?' asked McAuliffe, and he was told. So the formal reply, typed on bond paper and delivered to the officer parlementaires at the F Company command post by Colonel Joseph H. Harper of the 327th, read:

To the German Commander:
Nuts!
The American Commander

Harper naturally found the parlementaires uncertain about the translation. He also found them apparently assuming their surrender demand would be met. Settling at first for advising them that the reply was decidedly not affirmative, by the time he had escorted the German officers back to the Company F outpost line, where they picked up the two enlisted men, Harper had pondered long enough on what he took to be their arrogance to send them off with: 'If you don't understand what "Nuts" means, in plain English it is the same as "Go to hell". I will tell you something else—if you continue to attack, we will kill every goddamn German that tries to break into this city.'

J.F.C. FULLER
Stalingrad

The Battle of Stalingrad, 1942, was the decisive battle of the Second World War on the Eastern front.

THE BATTLE PROPER FOR STALINGRAD opened on September 15, and after a week's desperate fighting the Germans penetrated to the centre of the city. On the 26th and 27th they broke into the factory district and seized the 'Iron Heights', but on the 29th they were ejected. Reinforcements were then brought up and on October 4, supported by large numbers of tanks and bomber aircraft, the attack was renewed. For 10 days the attack was pressed with the utmost ferocity, street by street, house by house, both day and night, until the attackers were physically and morally exhausted. Stalingrad had become a second Verdun.

Hitler ordered a change of tactics; storming was to cease and the city systematically to be devastated by artillery fire and bombing. This was a senseless operation because it substituted rubble heaps for houses, and the former are the more easily defensible. The battle became one of prestige; Stalin was determined to hold the city which bore his name, and because of its name Hitler was equally determined to wrest it from his adversary. Yard by yard, over ground and under ground, the attackers fought their way through the ruins in what became known as the *Rattenkrieg* ('rat war'). On November 9 Hitler announced that 'not one square yard of ground will be given up.' The battle continued until November 12, when in the last German general assault the Volga was reached in the south of the city.

By mid-November the German situation was as follows:

The Fourth Panzer Army, considerably reduced in strength and which on November 10 had been withdrawn to refit, was in the Kotelnikovo area.

The Sixth Army was in and around Stalingrad, and also held the gap between the Volga and Don as well as the Don between Kachalinskaya and Kletskaya, with the exception of a small bridgehead the Russians had established at Kremenskaya.

West of Kletskaya to Veshenskaya stood the Third Rumanian Army, and since November 2 the Fourth Rumanian Army—part of Manstein's Eleventh Army—had been brought up to hold the Ergeni Hills south of the Volga elbow in order to cover the right flank and the Novorossisk-Stalingrad railway. The rest of Manstein's army was ordered to the Leningrad front.

In the Caucasus the head of Army Group A was still about Mozdok, and a weak Rumanian force held Elista.

North of the Third Rumanian Army lay the Eighth Italian Army on the Don between Veshenskaya to west of Pavlovsk, and to its north stood the Second Hungarian Army as far as Korotoyak, where it contacted the right of the Second German Army in the Voronezh area.

It was early November and Hitler's attention was suddenly attracted to events in North Africa. The battle of El Alamein had been fought and won by Montgomery on November 5, and Morocco and Algeria invaded by Eisenhower on November 8. To counter this extension of the war in the south, German reinforcements were not sent east, but were sent west into France and to Tunisia. The moment was propitious for a Russian counter-offensive.

It was no sudden inspiration on the part of the Russians, for since early July they had prepared a counter-offensive, and by November, when winter would favour them, they had concentrated powerful forces in the forests north of the Don. Further, in preparation of their counterstroke, while their enemy pressed into the Caucasus and closed in on Stalingrad, they had carried out a series of violent attacks in the Voronezh area in order to pin down the German Second Army, and had also made many local attacks along the Don. They had seized a number of fords along the Don and had established several bridgeheads, including one at Serafimovitch. On October 25 a report was received at headquarters O.K.W. that the Russians had started bridging, and on November 2 this was confirmed by air reconnaissance. Two days later German agents reported that in the near future the Kremlin had decided to launch a powerful offensive, either over the Don or against Army Group Centre. They intended to do both.

These counter-offensives were planned and organized by Marshal Zhukov and his Chief of Staff, General Vassilevski. The attack over the Don was to be carried out in three phases by three armies north of the river in cooperation with an attack south of Stalingrad. The three northern armies were commanded by General Rokossovski, General Vatutin, and General Gorlikov, and respectively were deployed on the fronts Volga-Serafimovitch, Serafimovitch-Veshenskaya, and Veshenskaya to south of Voronezh. Approximately they faced the left wing of the German Sixth Army and the Third Rumanian Army, the Italian Eighth Army, and the Second Hungarian Army. The southern attack was to be made by General Yeremenko's army against the Fourth Rumanian Army on the Ergeni Hills. The second counter-offensive was to be launched against the German central sector between Vielikye-Luki and Rzhev, so as to impede reinforcements to the Don front; the attack began on November 25, and does not concern us.

The aim of the Don counter-offensive was to pinch out the German Sixth Army by a concentric attack on Kalach by the armies of Rokossovski and Yeremenko, and in which Vatutin's left wing was to protect Rokossovski's right flank. Once it was under way Vatutin was to break through the Eighth Italian Army and advance on Likhaya on the Stalino–Stalingrad railway, and thence on Rostov, the bottleneck of German communications. Gorlikov was to follow Vatutin and break through the Second Hungarian Army, force the German Second Army westward of Voronezh, and then advance south-westward on Bielgorod and Kharkov.

On November 19 the offensive was opened by Rokossovski. With three armoured corps and four cavalry corps in first line and 21 infantry divisions in second line, he debouched from bridgeheads between Serafimovitch and Kletskaya; broke through the right of the Third Rumanian Army, and while his right wing, in cooperation with Vatutin's left, pressed the enemy in rout toward the Chir river, with his centre he advanced on Kalach. Immediately after this attack his left wing moved against the Don-Volga gap, but was repulsed by the Sixth Army.

On the following day, Yeremenko, with two armoured corps

and nine infantry divisions, broke through the Fourth Rumanian Army on the Ergeni Hills; then, while his left wing advanced on Kotelnikovo, his right wing swung northward toward Kalach where he linked up with Rokossovski on November 22. This meant that the Sixth Army, of about 200,000 combatants and 70,000 non-combatants, was surrounded; but the Russians were not sufficiently organized to prevent von Paulus from breaking out, which in all probability he could have done at any time during the following week.

When the news of the Russian offensive was received at Hitler's headquarters, General Zeitzler urged Hitler to order Paulus to cut his way out, and he nearly persuaded him to do so, but Göring—an incorrigible boaster—guaranteed that he would supply him by air with 500 tons a day of munitions, fuel, and rations. On November 24, because of this vain boast, Hitler ordered Paulus to 'hedgehog' himself in, and commanded that his army should become known as 'Fortress Stalingrad'. The next problem was how to relieve it.

For once Hitler did the right thing. He called to his aid the ablest of his subordinates, Field-Marshal von Manstein, then at Vitebsk; renamed his Eleventh Army—largely dispersed—'Army Group Don', and subordinated to it the Sixth Army, Fourth Panzer Army, and the Third and Fourth Rumanian Armies. Manstein's task was not to open a way for the Sixth Army's retreat, because Hitler had no intention to withdraw it, but instead it was to defeat the Russians who encircled it and to re-establish the Stalingrad front.

Because of his indifferent railroad communications, Paulus's supply situation had throughout been precarious; now it grew critical. His army needed 700 tons of supplies daily and, according to General Anders, O.K.W. were aware that once his reserves were exhausted he would require over double this amount. Göring had guaranteed to deliver 500 tons although there was only sufficient transport aircraft to lift 300 tons, and this amount did not allow for losses or the weather. The tonnage delivered between November 26—when the operation was initiated—and January 3 is not specified by Greiner, but he records that on January 4 250 tons were delivered, on the 5th 150 tons, on the 6th 45, and from then to January 21, when it would appear that air supply ceased, the average was well under 100 tons daily.

When, on November 27, Manstein took over command of Army Group Don the situation with which he was faced was as follows: The remnants of the Third Rumanian Army, reinforced by improvised bodies of Germans, under command of General Karl Hollidt, precariously held the northern front from Veshenskaya on the Don southward along the river Chir. On the southern front about Kotelnikovo stood Hoth's Fourth Panzer Army and remnants of the Fourth Rumanian Army, and to this group reinforcements were rushed from the north and the Caucasus. The Sixth Army was sandwiched between these two fronts in and around Stalingrad. Disturbing reports came in that the Russians north of the Don were concentrating large forces opposite the Eighth Italian and Second Hungarian Armies.

Manstein's plan, largely dictated by Hitler, was to advance Hoth's Fourth Panzer Army up the Kotelnikovo–Stalingrad railway against Yeremenko; to throw him back, and then to wheel against Rokossovski's right flank while Paulus struck at it from Stalingrad. Then he intended to launch the Hollidt group eastward over the Chir against Rokossovski's right—in brief, to defeat Yeremenko and then to encircle Rokossovski. The latter operation was an impossible task, and it would seem that Hitler had little information about the strength of Vatutin's army.

On December 12 Manstein's counter-offensive opened, and it made good progress for two days before it slowed. Nevertheless, by December 21 it was pushed forward to within 30 miles of the Stalingrad 'hedgehog'. Manstein's situation then became so critical that he decided to defy Hitler, and sent to von Paulus an order to be prepared to break out and join him within 24 hours. Paulus replied that he was unable to do so because his tanks had fuel only for 20 miles, and although he was urged by his generals to abandon his impedimenta and cut his way out with his infantry, he refused to do so. The truth would appear to be that he had no intention to withdraw from Stalingrad without a direct order from Hitler.

Why Manstein's request was so urgent was that on December 14 Hollidt had been violently attacked by Vatutin. On the

17th his front on the Chir collapsed, and on the following day Vatutin's right and centre crossed the frozen Don and struck at the Italian Eighth Army; on the 19th it was thrown back in rout toward the Donetz. Threatened as he was by encirclement, on December 24 Manstein ordered Hoth to send reinforcements to Hollidt, and then rapidly withdrew westward. On Christmas Day Hoth was in full retreat.

On December 29 von Paulus sent General Hube, commander of his XIVth Corps, by air to place the situation of the Sixth Army before Hitler. It was a futile journey, for the order Hitler sent back was to hold fast to Stalingrad until the spring. Nevertheless, on the same day, after he had repeatedly been pressed by Zeitzler to withdraw Army Group A from the Caucasus, he consented.

The next weeks were spent by Manstein in a desperate struggle to keep a corridor open for the retreat of Army Group A. He succeeded, and on January 18 Kleist reached the Don, and crossed it by the 22nd. While this retreat was in progress Gorlikov struck at the Second Hungarian Army and sent it back in rout. By the end of January, 1943, the whole of the German Don front had collapsed and a gap over 200 miles wide separated Manstein's left flank at Voroshilovgrad from Voronezh in the north.

The situation within Fortress Stalingrad rapidly deteriorated during Manstein's desperate struggle and Kleist's brilliant retreat. Soon rations had to be reduced to below subsistence level; artillery ammunition began to fail; medical stores and fuel, even for cooking, became exhausted; typhus and dysentery claimed thousands of victims, and frost as many more—the thermometer fell to 28 degrees below zero.

On January 8 Rokossovski called upon von Paulus to capitulate, and when he refused to do so, on the 10th Rokossovski ordered a general assault to be made on the doomed army. On the 14th the Pitomnik airfield, 14 miles west of the centre of the city, was captured by the Russians, and by then Paulus's situation had become so bad that he reported to Hitler that his troops could no longer bear their sufferings. The answer he received was: 'Capitulation is impossible. The Sixth Army will do its historic duty at Stalingrad until the last man, in order to make possible the reconstruction of the Eastern Front.'

On January 25 the Russians captured the last remaining German airfield, the loss of which deprived Paulus of all further physical contact with the outer world. On January 31 Hitler promoted him a field-marshal, and on the same day the radio of Sixth Army headquarters sent its final message: 'The Russians are before our bunker. We are destroying the station.' Immediately after this, except for the XIth Corps, commanded by General Strecker, the Sixth Army laid down its arms, and on February 2 the XIth Corps surrendered.

When Hitler received the news of the surrender, first he compared the Sixth Army with the Three Hundred at Thermopylae, and declared that it had shown the world 'the true spirit of National Socialist Germany and its loyalty to its Fuehrer,' then he raved against Paulus and shouted that, like Varus, he should have thrown himself upon his sword rather than accept captivity.

With Paulus, 23 generals, 2,000 field and junior officers, 90,000 other ranks, and about 40,000 non-combatant soldiers and civilians surrendered. About 34,000 wounded and sick had been evacuated by air during the siege, and over 100,000 were killed, died of sickness, hunger and frost, and left sick and wounded in Stalingrad. If Erich Kern is to be believed, these last-mentioned unfortunates were massacred by the Russians, who threw explosive charges into the hospital shelters, and on February 3 thousands were buried alive in the enormous Timoshenko bunker when its entrances were dynamited. Kern also informs us that 'of the 90,000 prisoners, between 40,000 and 50,000 died of starvation within the first six weeks [of captivity] in the prison camp Bektoffka on the Volga, some forty miles south of Stalingrad.' As regards losses of material, Chester Wilmot states that 'the records of the Army High Command show that at Stalingrad the Wehrmacht lost the equivalent of six months production of armour and vehicles, three to four months production of artillery, and two months production of small arms and mortars.' To these losses, according to General Pickert, who was in charge of the air supply of the Sixth Army, must be added over 500 transport aircraft.

Stalingrad was a second Poltava in which Hitler was as much the architect of his own ruin as was Charles XII in 1709. Into the minds of a hundred million Muscovites flashed the myth of Soviet invincibility, and it forged them into the Turks of the North. If they could overcome the legions of Hitler, what had they to fear from the nations he had trampled in the dust? The German victories had thrown Europe into chaos and so had blazed a trail for the Third Rome. This decisive victory, which came on the heels of El Alamein, and at the moment when in Tunisia the Fascist cause had reached its nadir, inspired propaganda intoxicated peoples of the west. Stalingrad exalted Stalin into the champion of all for which they so ardently yearned.

HEINZ KNOKE
A Bit of Luck

Heinz Knoke was a Luftwaffe fighter pilot during WWII. The event described here took place in April 1944.

IN WHAT I THINK COULD be a lucky break, I get a Yank in my sights. I open fire with all guns. The crate goes up in a steep climb. Then all his comrades are back again on my tail.

In spite of the freezing cold, sweat pours down my face. This kind of dog-fight is hell. One moment I am thrust down into the seat in a tight turn; the next I am upside down, hanging in the safety-harness with my head practically touching the canopy roof and the guts coming up into my mouth.

Every second seems like a lifetime.

The Focke-Wulfs have meanwhile done a good job. I have seen nearly thirty of the Fortresses go down in flames. But there are still several hundred more of the heavy bombers winging their way eastwards undaunted. Berlin is in for another hot day.

My fuel indicator needle registers zero. The red light starts to flicker its warning. Ten more minutes only, and my tank will be empty. I go down in a tight spiral dive. The Thunderbolts break away.

Just above the clouds, at an altitude of 3,000 feet, I slowly level off. I estimate that I am probably somewhere in the vicinity of Brunswick or Hildesheim.

I look at my watch. Perhaps in another forty-five minutes I shall be over the 'bomber-alley' again. Perhaps then I shall be able to get a fat bomber in front of my guns. . . .

Overhead, the sky is still streaked with vapour-trails, stamped with the imprint of that infernal dog-fight. Suddenly the wing-man beside me flicks his aircraft round and vanishes into the cloudbank.

So what the hell . . .?

In a flash I glance round, and then instinctively duck my head. There is a Thunderbolt sitting right on my tail, followed by seven more. All eight open fire. Their salvoes slam into my plane. My right wing bursts into flames.

I spiral off to the left into the clouds. A shadow looms ahead: it is a Thunderbolt. I open fire. Its tail is soon in flames.

Now I can see the ground. I jettison the canopy and am ready to bale out. There is another rat-tat-tat sound of machine-guns close to my ear and more hammer-blows hit my flaming crate. That Thunderbolt is there again, not 100 feet behind me.

Blast! I shall be chewed to mincemeat in his airscrew if I try to bale out now. I huddle down and crouch low in my seat, trying to make myself as small as possible. The armour plate at my back protects me from the otherwise fatal shots. Wings and fuselage are riddled. A large hole gapes beside my right leg. The flames are licking closer now: I can feel the heat.

Crash! The instrument panel flies into splinters in front of my eyes. Something strikes me on the head. Then my engine stops: not a drop of fuel left.

Blast! There is no chance for me now.

My forward speed, of course, rapidly decreases. This causes my opponent to overshoot and pass me. For a few seconds only he is in my sights; but it is a chance to take him with me. I press both triggers. I feel myself trembling all over from the nervous tension. If I can only take him with me!

My salvo scores a perfect bull's-eye in the centre of his fuselage. He pulls up his smoking plane in a steep climb. In a moment he is in flames. The canopy opens and the body of the pilot emerges.

The ground comes up with a rush. Too late for me to bale out now. I cross some large fields. Down goes the nose and the plane settles. The flames come up reaching for my face. Earth flies into the air. There is a dull, heavy thud. The crate skids along in a cloud of dust, then digs its own grave in the soft earth. I throw up my arms to cover my face, and brace my legs against the rudder-bar. It is all over in a split second. Something crashes with stunning force on to my head.

So this must be the end! It is my last thought before losing consciousness. . . .

I have no recollection of getting clear of that burning wreck, but

I suppose I must have done so. Coherent thought is beyond me: there is only that dreadful pain in my head. I remember bullets flying past my ears as the ammunition explodes. I stumble and fall, but somehow stagger to my feet again. My one idea is to get away before the final explosion. The bright flames consuming my aircraft contrast vividly against the dark smoke-pall rising into the sky behind it.

A second wreck is burning only a few hundred yards away. Dimly I realise that it must be my Yank. If only the pain would stop! My head! my head!—I hold it in both hands and sink to my knees. The world spins crazily in front of my eyes. I am overcome by recurrent nausea, until only the taste of green bile remains.

The other seven Thunderbolts keep diving at me. They are firing. It seems a long way to the edge of the field and comparative safety. I finally roll into the shallow ditch and pass out again. I am at the end of my tether. . . .

When next I recover consciousness, I become aware of a man standing motionless and staring down at me. He is as tall as a young tree—an American!

I try to sit up on the edge of the ditch. The big fellow sits down beside me. At first neither of us speak. It is all I can do to prop my elbows on my knees and hold my splitting head in my hands. Then the Yank offers me a cigarette. I thank him and refuse, at the same time offering him one of mine. He also refuses; so we both light up our own fags.

'Was that you flying the Messerschmitt?'

'Yes.'

'You wounded?'

'Feels like it.'

'The back of your head is bleeding.'

I can feel the blood trickling down my neck.

The Yank continues: 'Did you really shoot me down?'

'Yes.'

'But I don't see how you could! Your kite was a mass of flames.'

'Don't I know it!'

The tall American explains how he spotted me above the clouds and went down after me with his men. 'It sure seemed like a bit of luck,' he added.

I ask him in turn: 'What was your idea in getting out in front of me when my engine died?'

'Too much forward speed. Besides, it never occurred to me that you would still be firing.'

'That is where you made your mistake.'

He laughs. 'Guess I'm not the first you bagged, am I?'

'No; you are my twenty-sixth.'

The American tells me that he has shot down seventeen Germans. In a few more days he was due to go home. He notices the ring on my finger, and asks if I am married.

'Yes; and I have two little children.' I show him a picture of Lilo and Ingrid.

'Very nice,' he remarks, nodding in appreciation, 'very, very nice indeed.'

I am glad he likes them.

He also is married. His wife over there will have to wait for him in vain now. Rather anxiously, the big fellow asks what is going to happen to him.

I explain that he will be sent to a special P.O.W. camp for American airmen. 'Are you an officer?'

'Yes; a Captain.'

'In that case, you will go to a camp for officers. You will be well treated. Our prisoners are just as well treated as yours.'

We have a friendly chat for about half an hour. He seems like a decent fellow. There is no suggestion of hatred between us, nor any reason for it. We have too much in common. We are both pilots, and we have both just narrowly escaped death.

A squad of soldiers from a nearby searchlight battery arrives, and we are covered with raised rifles.

'Put away that damned artillery, you clods,' I call over to them.

On the highway there is a truck waiting for us. Six Yanks from a Fortress are huddled in the back. They look rather gloomy. My Captain and I sit beside them. Although feeling like death myself, I try to cheer up the party with a few jokes.

On the road we collect more Yanks who were shot down. One of them is badly wounded in the leg. I see that our men lift him up carefully into the truck.

We are driven to the Brunswick airfield at Broitzum. There I say farewell to my fellow-sufferers, and we all shake hands.

'Good luck!'

'All the best!'

'*Auf Wiedersehen!*'

One hour later Barran flies over and collects me in an Aroda. The Squadron all returned without further casualties. I am the only one who was caught.

HUGH TREVOR-ROPER
The Last Days of Adolf Hitler

Hugh Trevor-Roper (later Lord Dacre) was an intelligence officer during World War II. After the defeat of Germany in May 1945, he was given the task of reconstructing the last days of Adolf Hitler's life in the Berlin Bunker.

WHEN VON BULOW LEFT THE BUNKER, Hitler was already preparing for the end. During the day the last news from the outside world had been brought in. Mussolini was dead. Hitler's partner in crime, the herald of Fascism, who had first shown to Hitler the possibilities of dictatorship in modern Europe, and had preceded him in the stages of disillusion and defeat, had now illustrated in a signal manner the fate which fallen tyrants must expect. Captured by Partisans during the general uprising of northern Italy, Mussolini and his mistress Clara Petacci had been executed, and their bodies suspended by the feet in the market-place of Milan to be beaten and pelted by the vindictive crowd. If the full details were ever known to them, Hitler and Eva Braun could only have repeated the orders they had already given: their bodies were to be destroyed 'so that nothing remains'; 'I will not fall into the hands of an enemy who requires a new spectacle to divert his hysterical masses.' In fact it is improbable that these details were reported, or could have strengthened an already firm decision. The fate of defeated despots has generally been the same; and Hitler, who had himself exhibited the body of a field-marshal on a meat-hook, had no need of remote historical examples or of a new and dramatic instance, to know the probable fate of his own corpse, if it should be found.

In the afternoon, Hitler had had his favourite Alsatian dog, Blondi, destroyed. Professor Haase, his former surgeon, who was now tending the wounded in his clinic in Berlin, had come round to the Bunker and killed it with poison. The two other dogs belonging to the household had been shot by the sergeant who looked after them. After this, Hitler had given poison capsules to his two secretaries, for use in extremity. He was sorry, he said, to give them no better parting gift; and praising them for their courage, he had added, characteristically, that he wished his generals were as reliable as they.

In the evening, while the inhabitants of the two outer bunkers were dining in the general dining-passage of the Führerbunker, they were visited by one of the SS guard, who informed them that the Führer wished to say goodbye to the ladies and that no one was to go to bed till orders had been received. At about half-past two in the morning the orders came. They were summoned by telephone to the Bunker, and gathered again in the same general dining-passage, officers and women, about twenty persons in all. When they were assembled, Hitler came in from the private part of the Bunker, accompanied by Bormann. His look was abstracted, his eyes glazed over with that film of moisture which Hanna Reitsch had noticed. Some of those who saw him even suggested that he had been drugged; but no such explanation is needed of a condition upon which more familiar observers had often commented. He walked in silence down the passage and shook hands with all the women in turn. Some spoke to him, but he said nothing, or mumbled inaudibly. Ceremonies of silent handshaking had become quite customary in the course of that day.

When he had left, the participants in this strange scene remained for a while to discuss its significance. They agreed that it could have one meaning only. The suicide of the Führer was about to take place. Thereupon an unexpected thing happened. A great and heavy cloud seemed to roll away from the spirits of the Bunker-dwellers. The terrible sorcerer, the tyrant who had charged their days with intolerable melodramatic tension, would soon be gone, and for a brief twilight moment they could play. In the canteen of the Chancellery, where the soldiers and orderlies took their meals, there was a dance. The news was brought; but no one allowed that to interfere with the business of pleasure. A message from the Führerbunker told them to be quieter; but the dance went on. A tailor who had been employed in the Führer's headquarters, and who was now immured with the rest in the Chancellery, was surprised when Brigadeführer Rattenhuber, the head of the police guard and a general in the SS, slapped him cordially on the back and greeted him with democratic familiarity. In the strict hierarchy of the Bunker the tailor felt bewildered. It was as if he had been a high officer. 'It was the first time I had ever heard a high officer say "good evening",' he said; 'so I noticed that the mood had completely changed.' Then, from one of his equals, he learned the reason of this sudden and irregular affability. Hitler had said goodbye, and was going to commit suicide. There are few forces so solvent of class distinctions as common danger, and common relief.

Though Hitler might already be preparing for death, there was still one man at least in the Bunker who was thinking of life: Martin Bormann. If Bormann could not persuade the German armies to come and rescue Hitler and himself, at least he would insist on revenge. Shortly after the farewell ceremony, at a quarter-past three in the morning of 30 April, he sent another of those telegrams in which the neurosis of the Bunker is so vividly preserved. It was addressed to Dönitz at Ploen; but Bormann no longer trusted the ordinary communications, and sent it through the Gauleiter of Mecklenburg. It ran:

> DÖNITZ!—Our impression grows daily stronger that the divisions in the Berlin theatre have been standing idle for several days. All the reports we receive are controlled, suppressed, or distorted by Keitel. In general we can only communicate through Keitel. The Führer orders you to proceed at once, and mercilessly, against all traitors.—BORMANN

A postscript contained the words: 'The Führer is alive, and is conducting the defence of Berlin.' These words, containing no hint of the approaching end—indeed seeming to deny its imminence—suggest that Bormann was reluctant even now to admit that his power would soon be over, or must be renewed from another, less calculable, source.

Later in the same morning, when the new day's work had begun, the generals came as usual to the Bunker with their military reports. Brigade-führer Mohnke, the commandant of the Chancellery, announced a slight improvement: the Schlesischer railway station had been recaptured from the Russians; but in other respects the military situation was unchanged. By noon the news was worse again. The underground railway tunnel in the Friedrichstrasse was reported in Russian hands; the tunnel in the Vostrasse, close to the Chancellery, was partly occupied; the whole area of the Tiergarten had been taken; and Russian forces had reached the Potsdamer Platz and the Weidendammer Bridge over the River Spree. Hitler received these reports without emotion. At about two o'clock he took lunch. Eva Braun was not there; evidently she did not feel hungry, or ate alone in her room; and Hitler shared his meal, as usually in her absence, with his two secretaries and the cook. The conversation indicated nothing unusual. Hitler remained quiet, and did not speak of his intentions. Nevertheless, preparations were already being made for the approaching ceremony.

In the morning, the guards had been ordered to collect all their rations for the day, since they would not be allowed to pass through the corridor of the Bunker again; and about lunchtime Hitler's SS adjutant, Sturmbannführer Guensche, sent an order to the transport officer and chauffeur, Sturmbannführer Erich Kempka, to send two hundred litres of petrol to the Chancellery garden. Kempka protested that it would be difficult to find so large a quantity at once, but he was told that it must be found. Ultimately he found about 180 litres and sent it round to the garden. Four men carried it in jerricans and placed it at the emergency exit of the Bunker. There they met one of the police guards, who demanded an explanation. They told him that it was for the ventilating plant. The guard told them not to be so silly, for the plant was oil-driven. At this moment Hitler's personal servant, Heinz Linge, appeared. He reassured the guard, terminated the argument, and dismissed the men. Soon afterwards all the guards except those on duty were ordered to leave the Chancellery, and to stay away. It was not intended that any casual observer should witness the final scene.

Meanwhile Hitler had finished lunch, and his guests had been dismissed. For a time he remained behind; then he emerged from his suite, accompanied by Eva Braun, and another farewell ceremony took place. Bormann and Goebbels were there, with Burgdorf,

Krebs, Hewel, Naumann, Voss, Rattenuber, Hoegl, Guensche, Linge, and the four women, Frau Christian, Frau Junge, Fräulein Krueger, and Fräulein Manzialy. Frau Goebbels was not present; unnerved by the approaching death of her children, she remained all day in her own room. Hitler and Eva Braun shook hands with them all, and then returned to their suite. The others were dismissed, all but the high-priests and those few others whose services would be necessary. These waited in the passage. A single shot was heard. After an interval they entered the suite. Hitler was lying on the sofa, which was soaked with blood. He had shot himself through the mouth. Eva Braun was also on the sofa, also dead. A revolver was by her side, but she had not used it; she had swallowed poison. The time was half-past three.

Shortly afterwards, Artur Axmann, head of the Hitler Youth, arrived at the Bunker. He was too late for the farewell ceremony, but he was admitted to the private suite to see the dead bodies. He examined them, and stayed in the room for some minutes, talking with Goebbels. Then Goebbels left, and Axmann remained for a short while alone with the dead bodies. Outside, in the Bunker, another ceremony was being prepared: the Viking funeral.

After sending the petrol to the garden, Kempka had walked across to the Bunker by the subterranean passage which connected his office in the Hermann Goering Strasse with the Chancellery buildings. He was greeted by Guensche with the words, 'The Chief is dead'. At that moment the door of Hitler's suite was opened, and Kempka too became a participant in the funeral scene.

While Axmann was meditating among the corpses, two SS men, one of them Hitler's servant Linge, entered the room. They wrapped Hitler's body in a blanket, concealing the bloodstained and shattered head, and carried it out into the passage, where the other observers easily recognized it by the familiar black trousers. Then two other SS officers carried the body up the four flights of stairs to the emergency exit, and so out into the garden. After this, Bormann entered the room and took up the body of Eva Braun. Her death had been tidier, and no blanket was needed to conceal the evidence of it. Bormann carried the body into the passage, and then handed it to Kempka, who took it to the foot of the stairs. There it was taken from him by Guensche; and Guensche in turn gave it to the third SS officer, who carried it too upstairs to the garden. As an additional precaution, the other door of the Bunker, which led into the Chancellery, and some of the doors leading from the Chancellery to the garden, had been hastily locked against possible intruders.

Unfortunately, the most careful precautions are sometimes unavailing; and it was as a direct result of this precaution that two unauthorized persons in fact witnessed the scene from which it was intended to exclude them. One of the police guards, one Erich Mansfeld, happened to be on duty in the concrete observation tower at the corner of the Bunker, and noticing through the opaque, sulphurous air a sudden, suspicious scurrying of men and shutting of doors, he felt it his duty to investigate. He climbed down from his tower into the garden and walked round to the emergency exit to see what was afoot. In the porch he collided with the emerging funeral procession. First there were two SS officers carrying a body wrapped in a blanket, with black-trousered legs protruding from it. Then there was another SS officer carrying the unmistakable corpse of Eva Braun. Behind them were the mourners—Bormann, Burgdorf, Goebbels, Guensche, Linge, and Kempka. Guensche shouted at Mansfeld to get out of the way quickly; and Mansfeld, having seen the forbidden but interesting spectacle, returned to his tower.

After this interruption, the ritual was continued. The two corpses were placed side by side, a few feet from the porch, and petrol from the can was poured over them. A Russian bombardment added to the strangeness and danger of the ceremony, and the mourners withdrew for some protection under the shelter of the porch. There Guensche dipped a rag in petrol, set it alight, and flung it out upon the corpses. They were at once enveloped in a sheet of flame. The mourners stood to attention, gave the Hitler salute, and withdrew again into the Bunker, where they dispersed. Guensche afterwards described the spectacle to those who had missed it. The burning of Hitler's body, he said, was the most terrible experience in his life.

Meanwhile yet another witness had observed the spectacle. He was another of the police guards, and he too came accidentally upon the scene in consequence of the precautions which should have excluded him. His name was Hermann Karnau. Karnau, like others of the guard who were not on duty, had been ordered away from the Bunker by an officer of the SS Escort, and had gone to the Chancellery canteen; but after a while, in spite of his orders, he had decided to return to the Bunker. On arrival at the door of the Bunker, he had found it locked. He had therefore made his way out into the garden, in order to enter the Bunker by the emergency exit. As he turned the corner by the tower where Mansfeld was on duty, he was surprised to see two bodies lying side by side, close to the door of the Bunker. Almost at the same time they burst, spontaneously it seemed, into flame. Karnau could not explain this sudden combustion. He saw no one, and yet it could not be the result of enemy fire, for he was only three feet away. 'Possibly someone threw a match from the doorway,' he suggested; and his suggestion is essentially correct.

Karnau watched the burning corpses a moment. They were easily recognizable, though Hitler's head was smashed. The sight, he says, was 'repulsive in the extreme'. Then he went down into the Bunker by the emergency exit. In the Bunker, he met Sturmbannführer Franz Schedle, the officer commanding the SS Escort. Schedle had recently been injured in the foot by a bomb. He was distracted with grief. 'The Führer is dead,' he said; 'he is burning outside'; and Karnau helped him to limp away.

Mansfeld, on duty in the tower, also watched the burning of the bodies. As he had climbed the tower, after Guensche had ordered him away, he had seen through a loophole a great column of black smoke rising from the garden. As the smoke diminished, he saw the same two bodies which he had seen being brought up the stairs. They were burning. After the mourners had withdrawn, he continued to watch. At intervals he saw SS men come out of the Bunker and pour more petrol on the bodies to keep them alight. Some time afterwards he was relieved by Karnau, and when Karnau had helped him to climb out of the tower, the two went together to look at the bodies again. By now the lower parts of both bodies had been burned away and the shinbones of Hitler's legs were visible. An hour later, Mansfeld visited the bodies again. They were still burning, but the flame was low.

In the course of the afternoon a third member of the police guard sought to watch the spectacle of the burning bodies. His name was Hans Hofbeck. He went up the stairs from the Bunker and stood in the porch; but he did not stay there. The stench of burning flesh was intolerable and drove him away.

Late that night Brigadeführer Rattenhuber, the head of the police guard, entered the Dog-bunker where the guards were spending their leisure, and spoke to a sergeant of the SS Escort. He told him to report to his commanding officer, Schedle, and to pick three trustworthy men to bury the corpses. Soon afterwards Rattenhuber returned to the Dog-bunker and addressed the men there. He made them promise to keep the events of the day a holy secret. Anyone talking about them would be shot. Shortly before midnight Mansfeld returned to duty in the tower. Russian shells were still falling, and the sky was illuminated by flares. He noticed that a bomb crater in front of the emergency exit had been newly worked upon, and that the bodies had disappeared. He did not doubt that the crater had been converted into a grave for them; for no shell could have piled the earth around it in so neat a rectangle. About the same time, Karnau was on parade with the other guards in the Vossstrasse, and one of his comrades said to him: 'It is sad that none of the officers seems to worry about the Führer's body. I am proud that I alone know where he is.'

That is all that is known about the disposal of the remnants of Hitler's and Eva Braun's bodies. Linge afterwards told one of the secretaries that they had been burned as Hitler had ordered, 'till nothing remained'; but it is doubtful whether such total combustion could have taken place; 180 litres of petrol, burning slowly on a sandy bed, would char the flesh and dissipate the moisture of the bodies, leaving only an unrecognizable and fragile remainder; but the bones would withstand the heat. These bones have never been found. Perhaps they were broken up and mixed with the other bodies, the bodies of soldiers killed in the defence of the Chancellery, and the body of Fegelein, which were also buried in the garden. The Russians have occasionally dug in that garden, and many such bodies have been unearthed there. Perhaps, as Guensche is said to have stated, the ashes were collected in a box and conveyed out of the Chancellery. Or perhaps no elaborate explanation is necessary. Perhaps such investigations as have been made have been somewhat perfunctory. Investigators who left Hitler's engagement diary unobserved in his chair for five months may easily have overlooked other relics which were more deliberately concealed. Whatever the explanation, Hitler achieved his last ambition. Like Alaric, buried secretly under the riverbed of Busento, the modern destroyer of mankind is now immune from discovery.

While these last rites and pieties were being observed by guards and sentries, the regents of the Bunker were busy with more practical matters. Having set the bodies alight and paid their last summary respects, they had returned to safety underground, there to contemplate the future. Once again, as after Hitler's first leave-taking, a great cloud seemed to have been lifted from their spirits. The nightmare of ideological repression was over, and if the prospect before them remained dark and dubious, at least they were now free to consider it in a business-like manner. From this moment nobody seems to have bothered about the past or the two corpses still sizzling in the garden. That episode was over, and in the short space of time remaining they had their own problems to face. As the tragically-minded guard observed, it was sad to see everyone so indifferent to the Führer's body.

The first evidence of the changed atmosphere in the Bunker was noticed by the secretaries, who had been dismissed during the ceremony, but who now returned to their stations. On arrival they learned the details from Guensche and Linge; but it was not from such second-hand information only that they knew that Hitler was dead. Everyone, they observed, was smoking in the Bunker. During Hitler's lifetime that had been absolutely forbidden; but now the headmaster had gone and the boys could break the rules. Under the soothing influence of nicotine, whose absence must have increased the nervous tension of the past week, they were able to consider the administrative problems which the Führer had left them to face.

RICHARD DIMBLEBY
The Cess Pit Beneath

Six million people, mostly East European Jews, died in the SS extermination camps. Richard Dimbleby visited Belsen just after its liberation in April 1945.

19 April 1945

I PICKED MY WAY OVER corpse after corpse in the gloom, until I heard one voice raised above the gentle undulating moaning. I found a girl, she was a living skeleton, impossible to gauge her age for she had practically no hair left, and her face was only a yellow parchment sheet with two holes in it for eyes. She was stretching out her stick of an arm and gasping something, it was 'English, English, medicine, medicine', and she was trying to cry but she hadn't enough strength. And beyond her down the passage and in the hut there were the convulsive movements of dying people too weak to raise themselves from the floor.

In the shade of some trees lay a great collection of bodies. I walked about them trying to count, there were perhaps 150 of them flung down on each other, all naked, all so thin that their yellow skin glistened like stretched rubber on their bones. Some of the poor starved creatures whose bodies were there looked so utterly unreal and inhuman that I could have imagined that they had never lived at all. They were like polished skeletons, the skeletons that medical students like to play practical jokes with.

At one end of the pile a cluster of men and women were gathered round a fire; they were using rags and old shoes taken from the bodies to keep it alight, and they were heating soup over it. And close by was the enclosure where 500 children between the ages of five and twelve had been kept. They were not so hungry as the rest, for the women had sacrificed themselves to keep them alive. Babies were born at Belsen, some of them shrunken, wizened little things that could not live, because their mothers could not feed them.

One woman, distraught to the point of madness; flung herself at a British soldier who was on guard at the camp on the night that it was reached by the 11th Armoured Division; she begged him to give her some milk for the tiny baby she held in her arms. She laid the mite on the ground and threw herself at the sentry's feet and kissed his boots. And when, in his distress, he asked her to get up, she put the baby in his arms and ran off crying that she would find milk for it because there was no milk in her breast. And when the soldier opened the bundle of rags to look at the child, he found that it had been dead for days.

There was no privacy of any kind. Women stood naked at the side of the track, washing in cupfuls of water taken from British Army trucks. Others squatted while they searched themselves for lice, and examined each other's hair. Sufferers from dysentery leaned against the huts, straining helplessly, and all around and about them was this awful drifting tide of exhausted people, neither caring nor watching. Just a few held out their withered hands to us as we passed by, and blessed the doctor, whom they knew had become the camp commander in place of the brutal Kramer.

I have never seen British soldiers so moved to cold fury as the men who opened the Belsen camp this week, and those of the police and the R.A.M.C. who are now on duty there, trying to save the prisoners who are not too far gone in starvation.

M.R.D. FOOT
The Face of Courage

While most people were trying to get out of the Nazi death camps, Witold Pilecki, a Polish army officer, was determined to get into Auschwitz so that he could set up a resistance movement there.

PILECKI, THOUGH STILL ONLY a junior officer in his middle forties, was someone of enormous force of character, even in a society that teemed with people of strong character and intense individuality. He belonged to a body called the *Tajna Armia Polska*, the Secret Polish Army; a body that was merged eventually in the AK, the Home Army. It would be misleading to say he played a prominent part in the TAP, because as every Pole knew it was indispensable not to be prominent, for anyone working clandestinely against an occupier; but he was extremely active. Several much more senior people knew and trusted him, and he was aware of a great deal that was going on.

Reports of the camp under construction at Oswięcim—as the Poles called Auschwitz—reached and impressed him, and he conceived a daring plan to do something about it. The plan was so daring that for several weeks his colonel hesitated to approve. It was simply—most daring plans are simple—to let himself get arrested, and sent to Auschwitz as a prisoner. Having got there, he was to send out reports of what was really happening inside the camp, to see whether he could organize resistance, and then, if he could, to escape.

On top of the military difficulties of these tasks, the personal ones were severe. He had married a dozen years earlier, and had a daughter; but Poland's crisis was such that merely personal troubles just had to be brushed aside. Mobilization overrode the marriage tie; his heart could and did stay with his wife and child, but his body had to go elsewhere.

A little time had to be spent on arranging the essential details about communication; a very few addresses, reckoned perfectly safe, which he had to memorize, and a safe, simple password sys tem by which a messenger could establish good faith, were all that were needed. The TAP was a brisk and efficient body, though its leaders were already on the run from the Gestapo. It could clear up promptly business of this sort, over which café-conversationalist resisters in Bucarest or Paris could dally for months, even years.

And by a stroke of luck, Pilecki secured a false identity which, he reckoned, ought to earn him a sentence to Auschwitz, his first objective: the identity of Tomasz Serafiński's, a reserve officer who had gone underground instead of reporting to the Germans as ordered. Pilecki did not know—he did not need to know—where Serafiński had gone. He found out instead enough about Serafiński's past to survive cross-questioning in his new character; and he knew that the German secret police, as methodical as they were cruel, had secured a list of all the peacetime officers in the Polish army, active and reserve. To be on this list, and (like the other 19,600) not to have surrendered oneself, would—he reckoned—be crime enough to merit consignment to Auschwitz.

His reckoning proved correct.

It was not difficult to get arrested. He just failed to run away down the nearest side street, one early morning in September 1940 when the Germans made a routine rush-hour check on people walking into central Warsaw to work. He shortly found himself, with a thousand companions, lying face down on the damp sawdust floor of a nearby riding school. Their hands were stretched out flat in front of them, palms down. Machine guns covered them from the galleries. SS-men walked among them, whipping those who fidgeted. Pilecki did not fidget.

Two days later, he was received (as Serafiński) in Auschwitz, and became prisoner number 4,859. In his own words, as he and his companions were marched from the railway station into the camp:

> On the way one of us was ordered to run to a post a little off the road and immediately after him went a round from a machine-gun. He was killed. Ten of his casual comrades were pulled out of the ranks and shot on the march with pistols on the ground of 'collective responsibility' for the 'escape', arranged by the SS-men themselves. The eleven

were dragged along by straps tied to one leg. The dogs were teased with the bloody corpses and set onto them. All this to the accompaniment of laughter and jokes.

They reached the camp as glum, they thought, as could be; marched in under the slogan *Arbeit macht frei* (work sets you free); and were then made glummer still by being made to strip, and to have *all* their hair, body hair as well as head hair, shaved off, and to put on the prison uniform of striped canvas.

Pilecki was lucky enough to get an indoor job, as one of the cleaning staff for his hut; but lost it before long, as the German criminal in charge of the hut would only employ on his staff those who, like himself, habitually clubbed their fellow-prisoners before speaking to them. Not only did he lose his soft job, as well as many other illusions, promptly, he soon almost lost his health, which in such a camp was equivalent to losing one's life.

On 28 October 1940, a man ran away from an outside working-party, and was found to be missing at the noon roll-call. All the prisoners were kept standing at attention on the parade-ground from noon till nine in the evening; in an icy north-east wind that bore heavy rain and sleet, turn and turn about. Anyone who moved was liable to be shot—200 died of exposure. Pilecki was among several hundred more who collapsed, but was nursed back to a semblance of health in the camp hospital, and rapidly returned to work.

The work consisted of building more huts to hold the increased numbers of prisoners who were expected, to store the belongings they brought with them, and in the end to dispose of them and their bodies.

All nazi concentration camps were run by the SS. Most existed for two reasons: as prisons to sequester those the SS wanted out of the way, and as factories to provide the SS with profits. For this peculiar organization, originally Hitler's small personal bodyguard, grew to be a state-within-a-state of an unusually intricate kind; financing itself in part from the products of its slave labour; and with its own private army, the *Waffen-SS*. Through this army's ranks a million men passed; it provided the hard core of nazi Germany's armed forces, nearly forty divisions strong, and included many crack units. Some of its weapons and equipment were, for economy's sake, turned out by the camps that were under SS control.

At and near Auschwitz there were a few arms factories; but the Auschwitz–Birkenau group of camps existed for a third reason also, more secret and more sinister. Here among other places, here above all, the SS proposed to get on with the *Endlösung*, the final solution of the Jewish problem: the killing of all the Jews they could catch. As Himmler put it to Rudolf Hoess, the founder-commandant of Auschwitz, in the late summer of 1941, 'The Jews are the sworn enemies of the German people and must be eradicated. Every Jew that we can lay our hands on is to be destroyed now during the war, without exception.'

The method chosen was by cyanide gas poisoning. At Auschwitz and Birkenau, as at other extermination camps such as Treblinka, Maidanek, Sobibór, windowless concrete huts were built, with nozzles in their ceilings, into which Jews—or any other prisoners of whom the SS wanted to dispose—were herded, naked, in large crowds; believing they were to have a shower. They were showered with cyanide gas, their bodies were then hauled and shovelled across to the building next door, also prisoner-built, where they were cremated. On the way from gas chamber to crematorium, the bodies were checked for gold teeth or for rings, which were removed (it was simplest to remove ringed fingers with a garden chopper), to keep the SS profits up.

It took time, again, for a scheme of this size and this elaboration to get moving. Auschwitz was founded in 1940, the big killings did not start there till 1942; in January 1945 it was overrun by the Red Army. Twelve hundred prisoners were left in it at that moment, all too ill to move; in Birkenau there were about 5,800 more invalids, two-thirds of them women. Something approaching four million people had been killed in the complex meanwhile, during the 1,688 days of Auschwitz's existence.

During Pilecki's first three months in the camp, nearly 3,000 more prisoners joined it; they were only the beginners. By the summer of 1944 the Auschwitz–Birkenau group of camps had about 130,000 current inmates, sometimes 140,000; but the rate of turnover was very high. For instance, during that summer 437,000 Hungarian Jews were admitted to the camps, almost all of whom were killed when, or soon after, they arrived. In such cases people would be sent straight from the train to the gas chambers, pausing only on the way to undress—several large huts were filled, quite full, with their clothing. They were spared the body-shave Pilecki had gone through; their head hair was shorn after death, on their way to the crematoria, and made into mattresses, to keep the SS profits up.

Nearly a thousand prisoners were employed in the *Sonderkommandos*, the special squads that ran the actual process of extermination. All were Jews; they were housed, in the end, in the crematorium attics. Each squad worked a twelve-hour shift, turn and turn about with its alternate; about once a quarter, each squad was itself led into the gas chambers by its successor. 'The members of the *Sonderkommando*, speaking many languages and dialects, could quieten down those being driven to their death, and this they did in the knowledge that they would gain nothing by behaving differently and that by kindly treatment they could at least mitigate the anguish of the victims' last moments.' The death squads themselves knew only too well what awaited them.

All this apparatus of terror was under the guard of about 3,250 SS men. They never moved unarmed, seldom moved singly, and had all the usual adjuncts of a terror camp: tracker dogs, lighted electrified fences, torture chambers, above all, atmosphere. As Pilecki's example showed us, from the moment they came under SS guard, prisoners were aware that their captors were entirely ruthless. The inmates were encouraged to believe that, as the crematorium squads mostly came to do, they should accept their fate as stoically as they could. They were there to die; they might as well die in a calm and orderly way.

Yet, diabolical as their captors were, they were not diabolically efficient. And in the early months of the camp, they even now and again let people out; it was still just possible to persuade even a member of the Gestapo that he might have made a mistake.

As early as November 1940, two months after his arrest, Pilecki was able to send his first report out of Auschwitz to Warsaw. It was memorized by one of his earliest recruits, a perfectly innocent and inoffensive citizen who had friends in Warsaw powerful enough to persuade the Germans that he had in fact been arrested in error. He was made to swear the customary oaths that he would reveal nothing about what went on inside the camp, but was a good enough Pole and a good enough catholic to know that oaths sworn under duress have no value. When he made touch with Pilecki's superiors, he talked.

There was not yet much to say. At this date the gas chambers, and the whole Birkenau camp, were no more than gleams in Himmler's and Eichmann's eyes. But at least Home Army headquarters now knew that Auschwitz was a concentration camp, and a cruel one (there were no mild ones); and that Witold Pilecki was at work inside it, seeing what he could do about resistance.

What could he do? First of all, continue to report: for which he seized every opportunity, however glancing, that appeared safe. Some of the SS garrison's laundry, for example, was done for them in Auschwitz town. The SS did not want to demean themselves by carrying laundry baskets; they contented themselves with searching the baskets very thoroughly (such baskets forming a well known means of escape), and providing a vigilant armed guard for the prisoners who toted them. Over the months, their vigilance relaxed a trifle. The camp laundry squad had meanwhile had a chance to assess the characters of the few town laundry workers whom they saw, and, given luck and daring, could slip written notes to them. Any Pole could be relied on to be anti-German, so the notes got passed on to any address they bore.

Any such system bore risks of interception, at any and every stage; people who will not run risks cannot hope to win battles. In 1942–4 a considerable body of intelligence about what was going on inside the camps got passed out of Auschwitz and Birkenau, reached Warsaw safely, and was passed on thence to Stockholm, whence it reached London from March 1941. The London Poles passed the news on to MI 6, which passed it to the foreign office; thence it went to Washington, Moscow, and any service departments that needed it. Some of it the Poles used straight away in their propaganda.

The trouble was that the news was, on the whole, too bad to be credible; and most people who heard it, did not take it in as true. Moscow was disinclined to believe anything that emanated from the London Poles, on principle. In Washington and London, everyone in authority, however bellicose towards nazism, had been brought up to believe mass murder to be utterly beyond the pale of civilized behaviour, and imagined Germany still to be a civilized state. The sheer incredulity of distant senior men lay, unknown to Pilecki, as one obstacle across his path.

Much closer obstacles were only too obvious. The main starting task was to do anything he could to encourage his fellow prisoners not to kowtow, any more than they had to, to the terrorist regime under which they had to live. As most of his fellow prisoners were Poles, this task was not insuperably difficult. In carrying it through, he was able to gauge something of his companions' characters, and to estimate which could be most useful for more advanced work.

He had had to abandon most of his preconceived ideas about what he would do, as soon as he discovered how hard conditions in the camp really were: a process of adapting idea to reality, painful enough in one's teens, that can be excruciating in manhood, especially on the morrow of a great national disaster. He wanted to set up a secret grouping among the prisoners that would be ready to try to wrest power from the SS, the moment there was a nearby allied armed force to help. He did take in that there was no probability, no outside likelihood even, that the prisoners could seize power all by themselves: the SS had too many machine guns, and were too quick to use them. He hoped for a Russian or an Anglo-American parachute landing in force; or failing that, for a coup by Polish partisans.

There were in fact some Home Army partisan groups in the neighbourhood, now and again, though they were neither strong in numbers nor heavily armed. The Home Army's weakness in arms, compared to similar groups in France or Greece or Yugoslavia, arose from two causes: Poland lay at the extreme limit of air range from Anglo-American territory, and the Russians forbade aircraft on supply sorties for the Home Army to land on soviet airfields. The few aircraft that could manage the round trip—even from Brindisi, when Brindisi became available late in 1943, it was a ten-hour flight—therefore had to take up most of their load with petrol, to get them there and back. France and Yugoslavia both got about 10,000 tons of warlike stores by air, through links with SOE and its American opposite number, OSS (the Office of Strategic Services); Poland only got 600 tons.

The People's Army does not seem to have operated in the parts of Poland annexed to the Reich. The official soviet attitude to the camps was in any case, to a western eye, slightly odd. Theoretically—in Marxist-Stalinist theory, that is—no prisoners were ever taken from the Red Army; a Red Army man's duty was to fight, never to surrender. The Germans and their satellites took over six million uniformed prisoners all the same (four-fifths of whom, by the by, succumbed in German hands: another huge item for the butchers' bill). Every single survivor who was returned—usually forcibly, by the other allies—to the USSR after the war, automatically did a punishment spell in a Siberian labour camp. All camps, of whatever kind, were looked at askance by the Russians: except for their own. And the existence of their own was inadmissible.

But we must get back from these strategic and political generalities to the hard particular facts of Pilecki's Auschwitz career. By Christmas 1940 he had already chosen his first five clandestine leaders; he added two more groups of five in the following spring. An attack of pneumonia, brought on by standing naked on parade for some hours in February while his hut and clothes were disinfested of lice, put him for a month into the camp hospital, where he organized a highly efficient cell. It was (as Peulevé later found in Buchenwald) a part of the camp well adapted for resistance and deception, and the Auschwitz hospital secured, by devious means, a wireless receiver: this freed prisoners in the know from dependence on Goebbels' propaganda bulletins, which were all that the camp loudspeakers ever provided in the way of news. There were no newspapers within the camp.

All the attempts to organize resistance were not, of course, confined to Pilecki and his groups. Several senior Polish officers set about organizing intelligence networks, with varying degrees of success. Unhappily, some among them—some even of the senior officers who became involved in Pilecki's own groupings—occasionally found they had to stand on their dignity, and insisted on receiving orders only from people senior to themselves. Such petty resentments, pathetically out of place in an SS camp, were ineradicable in the old Polish officer caste.

There were differences between Polish prisoners on more important matters than rank: they did not all see eye to eye in politics. Differences in political viewpoint grew more widespread, as the racial composition of the camp's inmates changed. At first the prisoners were nearly all Poles, with a sprinkling of senior Germans, but over thirty nationalities were represented eventually; particularly Russians and Ukrainians, as well as hordes of Jews from several different states. Pilecki preferred dealing with Poles, as communication was so much more easy through a common language and common customs, but by no means imposed any sort of racial bar. In any case, while he was in the camp it remained very largely Polish in its prisoner population.

The communists among the prisoners at first lay low; after 22 June 1941 they hurled themselves into the resistance struggle, not with any outstanding effect. The German communists in Buchenwald and other camps often held dominant positions; the Polish communists, starting later in the struggle, were not as a rule as successful. One subsequently well-known politician, Jozef Cyrankiewicz, already—though ten years younger than Pilecki—an eminent socialist, took a leading part in the politico-military fusion that Pilecki's tact and ability and common sense had created by the time Cyrankiewicz reached the camp in the autumn of 1942. He later drew apart from the right-wing elements whom Pilecki had persuaded to co-operate with the socialists; threw in his own lot with the left-wingers, and became prime minister of the new communist-dominated Poland after the war.

Such actual military organization as Pilecki was able to set up was necessarily slender and tentative; and conditions, as well as people, in the camp changed so fast that he found he had to set up different groups to cope with different contingencies. By night, with the prisoners locked in their huge huts, a different set of fighting men would be needed from the grouping that would apply during the day when prisoners were scattered at work, some inside the camp and some outside it.

A good deal of intricate, deadly secret planning was done on these necessarily conjectural lines, everyone in the early stages taking the utmost care to bring nobody else into the plot who was not wholly to be trusted. The one vital necessity was armament: which was at first glance unavailable.

Reflection showed some possibilities. A daring quartet of prisoners managed to fake up a key to the SS clothing store; and on 20 June 1942 dressed as two officers and two warrant officers, used another faked-up key to visit the arms store, stole a visiting senior officer's car, and drove away in it, being smartly saluted by the sentry, who did not bother to look at their forged passes. One of them, called Jaster, bore a report of Pilecki's which he delivered in Warsaw. Rumour swelled their numbers; the incident greatly cheered the prisoners who remained behind. They had a few rough weapons ready enough to hand: pick helves, spades, hammers, mauls, hand axes, a few two-handed felling axes: no use against an alert sub-machine-gunner, but not perfectly useless in a scrimmage, or at night. One or two attempts at mass break-outs were made with these hand weapons, all with ill result; though nine men out of one party of fifty did get clean away, and over 600 prisoners escaped altogether, one way and another. Over half of these 600 were soon recaptured, humiliated and killed.

Himmler himself visited the complex on 17–18 June 1942; watched a party of Jews reach Birkenau; saw most of them gassed; inspected the artificial-rubber works run in Auschwitz town by camp labour; asked to watch a woman being flogged; promoted Hoess a rank; and went away.

Pilecki by now had four battalions of followers organized, about 500 of whom knew him by sight and name as a secret camp resistance leader: the secret was becoming much too open for comfort. He had a fairly settled job, so far as anything in Auschwitz was settled, in the tailor's shop; and all his 500 friends were vigilantly on the watch for Gestapo informers, of whom there were many. He began to feel uneasy; before he left, he had one more macabre scheme to carry through.

The SS had a weakness for black pullovers, which they had knitted for them by women prisoners. There were quite a lot of women in Auschwitz, and hundreds of thousands died in Birkenau which was primarily a women's camp: endless opportunities for intrigue, corruption and romance resulted. Hoess himself had a prisoner mistress, though he had his own wife and small children living with him just outside the main gate; his conduct was widely enough known for him to have no hold over the misdemeanours of his own men.

Pilecki's organization exploited the double SS weakness, for pretty girls, and for warm clothes, and with the help of their hospital friends, occasionally supplied the SS with pullovers or greatcoats bearing typhus-infected lice. A very few SS died as a result.

More direct action could be taken by men who were tired of life. At Sobibor camp, near Lublin, the *Sonderkommando* of about 300 in the innermost camp decided one day to break out. SS men visited the tailor's shop one by one, to collect uniforms they had left there for pressing before they went on leave. A prisoner stood behind the shop door with a spade, and hit each SS man as hard as he could on the back of the head. When the tailors had collected fifteen corpses, and a pistol from each, the whole squad rushed the gate of the inner compound; got to the main gate; rushed that too, and were out in the open. Half of them were brought back by the surrounding peasantry, because they were Jews. A few got away. Himmler was so put out that he had the whole camp closed down.

This escape was not till 14 October 1943; by which time Pilecki was well away from Auschwitz.

His escape was straightforward. He decided to leave in the spring of 1943; for another body of four escapers from Auschwitz, who had got out on the previous 29 December, included a dentist called Kuczbara who knew only too much about him, and had fallen back into Gestapo hands on 20 March. So it was dangerous for him to stay, and he was anxious also to impress in person on his superiors in Warsaw the readiness of the camp to rise, and the need for some positive partisan demonstration to give it the signal to do so.

He handed over military command to Major Bończa, and all the innumerable liaison details he carried in his head to Henryk Bartosiewicz—both were his friends—and was ready to leave. He secured—this was child's play to someone by now so experienced underground—a forged pass to join the bakery squad: the bakery was outside the wire. By now he had left the tailor's shop for the parcel office, and he faked illness on Easter Saturday, 24 April, to get out of that. Hospital friends discharged him in time to join his bakery squad on the next Monday/Tuesday night—like Peulevé, he was supposed to have typhus, but in this case he was not really ill at all. The prisoner boss of the bakery group was bribed with a piece of chicken; and a friend in the locksmith's squad produced a key to the bakery door. Two companion bakers were to leave with him; all had plain clothes beneath their camp uniforms.

After several sweltering hours—Pilecki had never been in a bakery before—one of them cut the telephone wires, another unlocked the door, and at a moment when none of the SS was in sight they all went through it: and ran.

It was a fine night for escape, dark and pouring with rain, and they got to the bank of the Vistula—several miles away—unchallenged. They had everything they needed except food. 'This had crossed their minds in the bakery, but at the last moment, in the heat of the dash for freedom, they had forgotten to grab a few loaves.' Pilecki moreover was racked by sciatica. Luck stayed with them: they found a dinghy on the river bank, padlocked, and by a miracle the bakery key opened the padlock.

They hid in a wood all day on Tuesday, and in another wood farther east all Wednesday. Next night, with a priest's help, they crossed into the General Government, kept south of Cracow, and came on 2 May to a safe address at Bochnia, a town some twenty miles east of it. There Pilecki inquired for the nearest Home Army unit, and found it, by a singular freak, to be commanded by Tomasz Serafiński whose name he had been using in captivity.

Cracow District of the Home Army could not be got to take any interest in Auschwitz. Pilecki persevered, and went to main headquarters in Warsaw. There they had 'a heap of files', with all his reports in them and others; but could not be persuaded that the risks of an action against it were worth the running. If ever there were a countrywide rising, he was assured, Auschwitz would not be forgotten; and that was all.

He turned to other duties; fought through the Warsaw rising of August–September 1944; survived even that catastrophe; and spent the rest of the war, under a different false identity, in a prisoner-of-war camp in Germany. Auschwitz had been an experience so shattering that he was looking for no more adventures; having lived through that and the Warsaw rising was, he felt, enough.

Or was it? When the Third Reich crumbled quite away, he moved southward in the crowds of what were pathetically named 'displaced persons', and reported to the Polish army in Italy. It was put to him that someone of his almost uncanny tenacity in adversity would be just the man to go back into Russian-occupied Poland on a mission for the Polish government-in-exile, in London.

He went; was arrested almost immediately he got there; and was executed in 1948—no one outside the Polish and Russian secret police forces is quite sure when, or where. His wife and daughter, who still live in Poland, do not even know where he is buried.

R.J. MINNEY
Carve Her Name With Pride

Courage is by no means the prerogative of men. Violette Szabo was a Special Operations Executive agent dropped into occupied France during WWII, where she distinguished herself by her heroism while working with the Resistance.

VIOLETTE AND HER PARTY ARRIVED AT SUSSAC in the small hours of the morning of June 7th, 1944. The Allied landings of twenty-four hours earlier had already established a foothold in Normandy and the Germans were rushing troops at reckless speed from all parts of France and Germany in order to dislodge them and drive them back into the sea. For months all the valiant endeavours of the French Section of SOE had been directed to the one end of preventing the German divisions from getting there now, or at any rate hampering and delaying their progress. Every group of Resistance workers behind the enemy lines had been allotted a specific task. Roads and bridges had to be blown up. Acts of sabotage had been arranged at factories and on the railways, at lock gates and at power stations. It was their purpose to cause the greatest possible destruction and to create a confusion that would distract and bewilder the enemy. Staunton's task in the Limoges area was to harness the Maquis most effectively to this same end.

He saw around him vast sections of Maquis, numbering 3000 men in all. They were spread out across a hundred miles of country from Sussac northwards to Châteauroux. Through this great expanse of wooded land the Maquis roved as they pleased, save for the occasional raids by detachments of heavily armed Germans. Two main roads to Normandy ran through this region—one from Toulouse, the other from Bordeaux. In its midst was the large industrial town of Limoges, which was completely under German control. The town was heavily guarded by German troops. There were road blocks at all points leading into the town and passes were required to enter and leave it. The Gestapo also had their headquarters for the area in Limoges.

Around Sussac were the Haute Vienne Maquis, numbering about 600. On learning of the Allied landings, the 200 gendarmes Pétain had in the area instantly joined forces with the Maquis. One of the chief figures in this group was a young man known by the code name of Anastasie. His real name was Jacques Dufour. He was tall, dark, heavy-browed and had sparkling eyes. He was born at Salon-la-Tour, a village not far from Sussac. For his daring exploits against them, the Germans had singled him out as 'the greatest bandit in the Limoges area'. They knew his real name and were determined to get him. A large sum of money was offered for Anastasie alive or dead and the Germans had even rounded up some Dufours who had a hotel in Salon-la-Tour, but were in no way related. To the south were the Corrèze Maquis, to the east the Creuse Maquis. Others stretched westward into the Dordogne.

For the most part these Maquis were farm hands and peasants. There was a sprinkling among them of Spaniards who had fought in the Civil War and refused to live under Franco, and just a handful of Poles. They dressed themselves in any uniform they could find or devise and looked like assorted figures out of a musical comedy. Some had bright jackets with gold epaulettes and wore feathers in their hats, others went about in khaki shorts or wore a khaki béret with their workaday corduroys.

Staunton says in his report: 'When I left London I was given to understand that I would find on arrival a very well-organized Maquis, strictly devoid of any political intrigues, which would constitute a very good basis for extending the circuit throughout the area. On arrival I did find a Maquis, which was roughly 600 strong, plus 200 French gendarmes who joined up on D-Day. But these men were strictly not trained, and were commanded by the most incapable people I have ever met, as was overwhelmingly proved by the fact that none of the D-Day targets had been attended to and that each time it took me several hours of discussions to get one small turnout, either to the railway or the telephone lines.'

The members of this force were indeed highly individualistic. When arms and explosives had been dropped to them in the past, instead of guarding them for co-ordinated and advantageous use on selected targets at the arranged signal, their one resolve had been to settle the war there and then by themselves. Buckling on their equipment and shouldering their rifles they set out in immediate quest of the enemy, provoked a battle and, having neither discipline nor a plan of campaign, suffered heavily in such engagements.

Staunton realized that his task was not going to be easy. In Rouen, starting from scratch, he had been able to recruit men and women who were willing to serve and to accept both discipline and training. Here he found disorganized bands who wanted only to go their own way. No doubt all the other groups of Maquis around here were similar in composition and attitude. At the head of them all, with the entire force of 3000 nominally under his control, was a remote figure in Châteauroux. 'The Chief of this Maquis,' states Staunton in his report, 'a man who calls himself Colonel Charles, was by trade a saxophonist in a Bal Musette; a soldier of the second class with no war experience. He had been for Hector, Samuel and Anastasie (the leaders of the separate sections) their only contact with the neighbouring Maquis, which none of these leaders had ever really visited, relying on Charles for their information.'

Staunton, who had come here with his team for the express purpose of organizing and directing them, was resolved to get the entire Maquis force into immediate action. The German divisions were already on the march, so not a moment could be lost. Had Hitler listened to what Rommel had been urging for many months, these scattered divisions would already have been in the north, for that obviously was where they would be needed. But Hitler had an eye on the possibility of a landing in the South of France (which did indeed come not long after Normandy) and he felt that, by keeping his army dispersed, he would provide them with greater mobility and striking power. The most formidable of these divisions in the south was Das Reich SS Panzer division stationed at Toulouse and already on its way to Normandy to aid the hard-pressed German forces there.

Soon it would be entering Maquis country. That was the time to strike and strike hard.

Staunton called an immediate council of action. Anastasie, as the chief of the local Maquis, listened attentively and expressed his readiness to co-operate to the full. What they needed was a plan of operation. Now that the Allies had landed and things were moving so fast, the Maquis, he said, could be relied upon absolutely to strike at the enemy whenever and wherever required. He knew the country well—they all did. He would get his men into position at points of vantage with their explosive charges, their hand grenades and Tommy guns. 'You can rely on us. Das Reich division will never get through,' he said. The words, Staunton felt, had the swagger of the Maquis, but the spirit was there, he knew.

He thanked Anastasie. 'That takes care of this territory. Now what about the others?'

'They will act too. I am sure of it,' Anastasie said. 'But we must take the plan to them—and it will have to be explained to them very carefully. We must send someone . . .' He glanced round the room.

'Violette will take it,' said Staunton.

Anastasie looked at the girl. 'Good,' he said. 'I will take her along to the Maquis nearest to us in the Corrèze.'

'We need you here,' said Staunton.

'But someone must give the girl the backing of our authority. They know me in the Corrèze. I will hand her over to Samuel, who is the leader there, and I shall be back in three—at most four hours.'

'All right.'

'She will explain the plan of operation—and Samuel will take her on personally, like me, to the next group of Maquis in the Creuse area. And so on, till in the end she gets to Colonel Charles at Châteauroux and tells him how we have decided to act.'

'That sounds fine,' said Staunton. 'But remember there's a price on your head.'

'Oh, I shall be all right. I'll be back in the afternoon,' Anastasie assured him.

Turning to Violette, Staunton added: 'Whatever happens we need Anastasie here. I want you to remember that. He is vital to our plans.'

She nodded. 'I understand.'

Anastasie got busy at once. Things had to be got going quickly. On the morning of June 10th, that is to say three days after Violette's arrival, all was ready for her to start on her mission. The Maquis had collected in the preceding months vast stores of arms and explosives which were secreted in various dumps. They also had quite a number of motor cars. Most of these were driven by wood fuel, but for this journey they brought out a large black Citroën and filled it up with petrol. The party assembled in the small square in Sussac in front of the grocer's where Violette, Staunton and the others lived. Violette was dressed in a light tailored suit, flat-heeled shoes and no stockings. She took a small suitcase with her and her Sten gun with eight magazines of ammunition. Anastasie, who had on his corduroys and a leather jacket, took his Tommy gun. It was a warm day, though the sun was obscured by clouds. Indeed the sky looked threatening, as though a storm might blow up at any minute.

The two got into the car and with a resounding cheer and a volley of good wishes set off at about half-past nine. Anastasie intended to take her to Pompadour, a charming little village about thirty miles away in the very heart of the Corrèze country. Pompadour is dominated by the fifteenth-century castle from which Antoinette Poisson, the mistress of Louis the Fifteenth, took her name.

The journey there was not expected to take much more than an hour. Almost all of it lay through narrow winding country lanes, not leafy but flanked by rocks and scrub. But they would have at some point to cross the main road from Toulouse to Normandy, and it was very possible that here they might encounter a Nazi division moving northward to Normandy with its tanks and fleet of lorries carrying supplies.

Anastasie had arranged to pick up on the way the son of a doctor who lived at La Croisille, about four miles from Sussac. The boy, who was not quite twelve years old, was going beyond Pompadour and was delighted to get a lift in the car, but brought his bicycle for the journey back. Violette and Anastasie helped him to rope it on to the side of the car. They placed it against the side Violette was sitting, so as to leave the door to the driver's seat clear. The boy got in at the back. The two in front kept their guns handy just in case there was trouble.

Anastasie decided to cross the main road at Salon-la-Tour. He felt it would be an advantage to go through a village he knew so well. The people there, with whom he had lived since his childhood, would readily inform him of any activity by the Germans along the road.

They sang, as they went, French songs that they all knew. As they passed under the railway bridge and approached the quiet sleepy little village of Salon-la-Tour, the storm clouds overhead descended in a heavy but brief downpour. Their lane swept westward and Anastasie pointed eagerly through the rain at the church, the huddle of white houses and the ivy-clad tower from which the village gets its name. 'Look,' he said, 'I climbed up to the very top of that when I was nine and took lots of photographs with my small box camera.'

They peered at the rain-slashed landscape on the right. 'That's where I used to live. I'll take you right past it. On this other side, beyond the farms, is a little stream where my sister and I used to come and fish as children. We once saw a snake swallow a frog there.'

The boy said: 'It's going to be pretty slippery cycling back.'

'Nonsense,' said Anastasie. 'Here's the sun trying to break through. This storm will be over in no time.'

They went on towards the village street, beyond which lay the main road. Suddenly Anastasie pulled up. With lowered voice he said, 'There's something behind that hedge—the further side—right in that field beyond.'

'They're Germans,' said Violette. 'You can just see their caps.'

The boy leapt out of the back of the car and ran into the nearest field. Anastasie got out too, Tommy gun in hand, and flung himself into a shallow ditch at the side of the road. Violette had to squeeze herself past the steering-wheel of the car. Seizing her Sten gun, she crossed the road to a tree. 'Run,' she called to the boy, but he was already scurrying fast across the fields.

Instantly the Germans began to shoot from the further side of the hedge. Violette turned her gun on them and blazed away too.

'Are you mad?' cried Anastasie. 'Get down here. Come on. You haven't a dog's chance out there.'

With a quick glance towards the boy, who was tearing towards home but was not yet out of sight, she sent a further burst of fire at the Germans.

'For Heaven's sake,' shouted Anastasie. 'Come down here.'

'All right. All right,' she cried. She crossed the lane, looked at the ditch. 'That's not going to do much good,' she said.

The Germans had by now emerged. There appeared to be about thirty of them. She saw that it was better to leave the lane and dash across the fields, where they might have a chance.

'This way,' she said, prodding Anastasie with her foot.

Crouching, for the Germans had begun to fire again with their very rapid Schmeissers, Violette crept along the ditch to the wooden fence of a farmhouse and leapt over it. Anastasie followed instantly and they both flung themselves down on the wet earth. A woman tending her cows turned to see the cause of all this startling activity. She was caught in the German line of fire and was killed instantly.

The storm had by now blown over and the sun was out. Anastasie motioned to Violette, both rose quickly and ran forward. The bullets flew around them. One tore through Anastasie's jacket but did not even graze his skin. Both were running hard. Violette dashed out of the small field, crossed a narrow farm track and entered the yard of the adjoining farm, with Anastasie close at her heels. The farmer, who had come in to get a jacket because of the storm, gazed with alarm through his window at the fleeing figures. He saw Anastasie stuff a piece of paper into his mouth and, running to the further hedge, leap across it to the wide sloping meadows which swept down to the stream. Violette sped after him. By the time the Germans came up the figures were out of sight. Calling angrily to the farmer, they demanded the way the fugitives had gone. He said, being indoors and they tearing by so fast, he couldn't exactly tell, but thought they had gone that way. He pointed in the wrong direction.

By now still more Germans had come up. They were in fact the advance guard of Das Reich SS Panzer division, sweeping the villages to make sure the division could proceed along the road unhindered. Four hundred strong, with armoured cars in support, they were clearing the surrounding countryside of Maquis assailants who, they felt, might be lying in wait with hand grenades and Tommy guns. Into the farmer's yard they poured in groups of twenty and fanned out, some taking the direction indicated, others tearing through the hedge to the meadows which sloped down to the stream. They were all heavily armed. Two armoured cars now appeared travelling along almost parallel farm tracks.

After some moments Violette and Anastasie, having waded through the stream, emerged, wet and out of breath, and could be seen dashing up the further slope towards a distant cornfield. Instantly the entire German advance guard dashed after them and the armoured cars turned and bounced along their tracks which, they all knew, converged at the far end.

Bullets began to fly fast now from the machine-guns of the two armoured cars and the Schmeissers of the pursuing Germans. Violette received a slight flesh wound in her left arm. In a moment the two distant figures were lost in the cornfield amid the tall golden corn. They knew, since both had been well trained, that their progress would have to be zigzag or the bending corn would leave a revealing trail for the marksmen.

The German volleys continued, tearing into the corn.

'All right?' called Anastasie, who was a few yards in front.

'Fine,' she called back.

'I've swallowed the code,' he said. 'So all's well.'

Then suddenly Violette fell. Anastasie turned back in alarm and found her lying on the earth.

'It's nothing,' she said. 'Go on. I'm doing fine.'

It was not a bullet, he found, that had brought her down, but her ankle, already damaged during her jumps at Ringway; it gave in the swift zigzagging to right and to left.

He picked her up in his arms, but she struggled hard to get free.

'Don't be a damned fool,' she said. 'We can't both be saved. You won't stand a chance if you're caught. Besides, you've work to do. Go on. Get out.'

He carried her while she struggled. She beat hard against his shoulders with her fists, kicked and wriggled. The bullets still breezed past them and the chattering guns came even nearer. With a final desperate thrust Violette succeeded in bringing them both down. As they fell amid the corn, with her Sten gun clutched in her hands, she crawled to the edge of the cornfield, clamped a new magazine in and, crouching, limped her way to an apple tree.

She was an easy mark now. The bullets pinged and spat up spurts of earth. It was a miracle that she was not killed. She stood up, cocked her gun and began firing at the oncoming Germans.

'Run!' she called. 'Run! For God's sake, make a run for it.'

Some Germans were seen to fall, whether killed or wounded none could tell.

Anastasie saw that it was utterly hopeless now to go to her aid. 'It's your last chance,' she called again. 'You can just make it.' With that she pressed a fresh magazine into the gun and resumed her firing.

Anastasie rose, glanced about him like a hunted animal, and with a last burst at the Germans from his Tommy gun, ran out of the cornfield to the road at the top. The two armoured cars were not far away now. Both were making for the same point. There was just a chance that he would get there first.

Crouching, half dropping with exhaustion, he ran on and reached at last the railway bridge at the top and the small farmhouse beside it. At the corner of the road, by the bridge, lay a pile of logs. Anastasie decided to worm his way into their midst. They should with luck provide him with enough cover. From the window of the farmhouse the farmer watched with apprehension. At other windows stood his wife and two daughters. They knew Anastasie well. Both girls had been to school with him.

Quickly the girls came out. They piled the logs upon him and had just got him covered up when the first of the two armoured cars turned towards them. With the greatest alarm suddenly one of the girls saw that Anastasie's foot was exposed, so she sat down on it.

The Germans leapt down from the car and started their questioning. The girls admitted they had seen a man run by. He had leapt, they said, down to the railway lines.

Meanwhile, swarming across the fields, shot at continuously as they came, the Germans, numbering many hundreds, firing all the time, closed in on Violette. By now all the magazines of her Sten gun had been emptied. As they came to take her she fought them with immense strength for one so small. She kicked and struggled and struck at them with her fists, and bit their hands as they seized her. But she was no match for so many. Two Nazi soldiers eventually succeeded in pinioning her by the arms and half carried, half dragged her to the top, for she was utterly exhausted and in great pain.

They brought her, hot and dishevelled, to the heap of logs under which Anastasie was hidden and stood within a pace of him. The second armoured car now came up. A young officer, eyeing Violette with admiration, said: 'I like your spirit. You put up a wonderful fight—right up to the end.' Then, motioning to his men to let go her arms, he took out his cigarette case, selected one for her and stuck it between her lips.

Some weeks before, while travelling with Germans in the train to Rouen, she had to appear to be affable in order to allay suspicion. But now the mask was off. She was no longer prepared to engage in an exchange of courtesies. She spat out the cigarette. Her eyes blazing with fury, she said: 'You dirty cowards. You filthy German swine. I don't want your cigarettes—' and with that, leaning forward, she spat full in the young officer's face.

His eyes narrowed. Drawing his handkerchief, he wiped the spittle off his eyes and cheek. Then suddenly he threw his head back and laughed.

'All right,' he said. 'Take her away.' He motioned towards the nearer armoured car. The two soldiers seized her and lifted her on to it. She refused the seat offered her.

The officer sprang on to the car himself. Hundreds of German soldiers meanwhile were swarming across the railway lines and beating the bushes in their search for Anastasie.

'We'll be back presently,' the officer told the farmer, who was now standing at his door. 'Get inside all of you. Not one of you must leave the house.'

The girl sitting on Anastasie's foot hesitated for a moment. 'Go on, get inside,' the German officer commanded.

'All right, I'm going,' she said casually.

She began to rise. With her body still covering the exposed foot, she waited until the armoured cars moved off. She heard Violette say: 'Will you tell your men to let go my arms? I'd like to have one of my own cigarettes.'

As the two armoured cars turned into the village street hundreds standing at their windows saw her go by in the leading car, with a cigarette between her lips, shouting death and damnation to the Germans. 'Your fate is sealed. The end is drawing near. It won't be long now. Then you swine will get your deserts in full.'

Many Germans were seen to fall when they closed in on her, for they presented a wide semicircle which she raked with her gun. But none can tell the exact number, as the entire village remained behind closed doors for the rest of the day. No bodies were found. The Germans were not likely to leave their dead and wounded on the fields for the villagers to dispose of.

Anastasie lay under the logs for many hours. By adjusting one of the logs after the Germans left, the girls were able to keep the foot concealed until night fell. Then they came out and took him into the house. The farmer's wife had prepared a meal for him. He ate it ravenously. 'If I live a hundred years,' he said, 'I shall never forget today.' But as things turned out he was killed the following year in Indo–China. His body was brought home and lies in the little cemetery within sight of the fields across which he and Violette were pursued for close on two miles, fighting all the way.

In Salon-la-Tour even now they talk of that heroic day when *'la petite Anglaise'* held four hundred Germans of Das Reich SS Panzer division at bay, with a complete disregard of all personal risk. It gave the boy they knew his chance to get away. Of the girl's real name they are unaware. They heard later that it was Corinne. That was the name entered in her forged papers. By it she is still known in the area.*

* *Szabo was executed by the SS just a few days before the end of the war. She was posthumously awarded the George Cross, the first woman to receive it.*

PETER FLEMING
Invasion of Spies

After the fall of France in 1940, Hitler planned to invade Britain. The prospective invasion was code-named 'Sea Lion', and was preceded by a period of German spying activity which bordered on the farcical.

AS THE PLANS FOR 'SEA LION' took shape, the extent to which they were hampered by lack of accurate intelligence came to be appreciated by the German Supreme Command, and the *Abwehr*, whose reputation at the time was high, endeavoured to remedy this state of affairs by large-scale improvisation. In September a shower of spies descended on the United Kingdom; all were taken into custody by the British authorities. They were for the most part low-grade agents who had not completed their training. The *Abwehr* seems to have realized that their chances of doing useful work or even of escaping detection were not high; but they were only expected to remain in the field for a few weeks, and it was hoped that any who got into trouble would be got out of it when the German troops arrived. At any rate a number of inferior spies were more likely to produce results than no spies at all, and early in September this clandestine traffic began in earnest. Let us follow the fortunes of two parties sent across; they give an adequate idea of the *Abwehr*'s methods at this time.

On 2 September 1940 four German agents embarked at Le Touquet in a fishing boat which was escorted across the Channel by two minesweepers. According to one of the men the fishing boat's crew consisted, improbably, of three Russians and a Latvian; another said it was manned by two Norwegians and one Russian. All had confused memories of the voyage, and it seems possible that they were drunk.

The spies were to hunt in couples. One pair, after transhipping to a dinghy, landed near Hythe in the early hours of 3 September. They had a wireless set and an elementary form of cipher, and their orders were to send back information of military importance; they had been given to understand that an invasion of the Kentish coast was imminent. By 5.30 a.m. on the same morning both men, although they separated on landing, had been challenged and made prisoner by sentries of a battalion of the Somersetshire Light Infantry.

This was hardly surprising. The two men were of Dutch nationality. They were completely untrained for their difficult task; their sole qualification for it seems to have lain in the fact that each, having committed some misdemeanour which was known to the Germans, could be blackmailed into undertaking the enterprise. Neither had more than a smattering of English; and one suffered, by virtue of having had a Japanese mother, from the additional hazard of a markedly Oriental appearance; he it was who, when first sighted by an incredulous private of the Somersets in the early dawn, had binoculars and a spare pair of shoes slung round his neck.

The other pair of spies consisted of a German, who spoke excellent French but no English at all, and a man of abstruse origins who claimed to be a Dutchman and who, alone of the four, had a fluent command of English. They landed at Dungeness under cover of darkness on 3 September, and soon after daybreak were suffering acutely from thirst, a fact which lends colour to the theory that on the previous night the whole party had relied on Dutch courage to an unwise extent. The English-speaker, pardonably ignorant of British licensing laws, tried to buy cider at breakfast-time in a public house at Lydd. The landlady pointed out that this transaction could not legally take place until ten o'clock and suggested that meanwhile he should go and look at the church. When he returned (for she was a sensible woman) he was arrested.

His companion, the only German in the party, was not caught until the following day. He had rigged up an aerial in a tree and had begun to send messages (in French) to his controllers. Copies of three of these messages survived and were used in evidence against him at his trial. They were short and from an operational point of view worthless; the news (for instance) that 'this is exact position yesterday evening six o'clock three messerschmitt fired machine guns in my direction three hundred metres south of water reservoir painted red' was in no way calculated to facilitate the establishment of a German bridgehead in Kent.

All four spies were tried, under the Treason Act, 1940, in November. One of the blackmailed Dutchmen was acquitted; the other three were hanged in Pentonville Prison in the following month. Their trials were conducted *in camera*, but short, factual obituary announcements were published after the executions.

Two men and a woman, who on the night of 30 September 1940 were landed by a rubber dinghy on the coast of Banffshire after being flown thither from Norway in a seaplane, had—and, except by virtue of their courage, deserved—no more luck than the agents deposited in Kent. They were arrested within a few hours of their arrival. During those hours their conduct had been such as to attract the maximum of suspicion. This—since both men spoke English with a strong foreign accent and the documents of all three were clumsily forged—they were in no position to dispel; and the first of them to be searched by the police was found to have in his possession, *inter alia*: a wireless set; a loaded Mauser automatic; an electric torch marked 'made in Bohemia'; a list of bomber and fighter stations in East Anglia; £327 in English notes; and a segment of German sausage. Both men—one a German, the other a Swiss—were in due course hanged.

JULIUS CAESAR
The Second Invasion of Britain

Julius Caesar was born in Rome in 102 BC. In 55 BC he made a landing in Britain but then withdrew. He invaded again the following year and proceeded to subjugate most of the country. Caesar was assassinated by a group of Roman conspirators in 44 BC.

CAESAR TOOK WITH HIM FIVE legions and the remaining two thousand cavalry, and putting out about sunset was at first carried on his way by a light southwesterly breeze. But about midnight the wind dropped, with the result that he was driven far out of his course by the tidal current and at daybreak saw Britain left behind on the port side. When the set of the current changed he went with it, and rowed hard to make the part of the island where he had found the best landing-places the year before. The soldiers worked splendidly, and by continuous rowing enabled the heavily laden transports to keep up with the warships. When the whole fleet reached Britain about midday, no enemy was to be seen. Caesar discovered afterwards from prisoners that, although large numbers had assembled at the spot, they were frightened by the sight of so many ships and had quitted the shore to conceal themselves on higher ground.

Caesar disembarked his army and chose a suitable spot for a camp. On learning from prisoners where the enemy were posted, he left ten cohorts and three hundred cavalry on the coast to guard the fleet and marched against the Britons shortly after midnight, feeling little anxiety about the ships because he was leaving them anchored on an open shore of soft sand. The fleet and its guard were put under the command of Quintus Atrius. A night march of about twelve miles brought Caesar in sight of the enemy, who advanced to a river with their cavalry and chariots, and tried to bar his way by attacking from a position on higher ground.

Repulsed by his cavalry they hid in the woods, where they occupied a well-fortified post of great natural strength, previously prepared, no doubt, for some war among themselves, since all the entrances were blocked by felled trees laid close together. Scattered parties made skirmishing attacks out of the woods, trying to prevent the Romans from penetrating their defences. But the soldiers of the 7th legion, locking their shields together over their heads and piling up earth against the fortifications, captured the place and drove them out of the woods at the cost of only a few men wounded. Caesar forbad them to pursue far, however, because he did not know the ground, and because he wanted to devote the few remaining hours of the day to the fortification of his camp.

The next morning he sent out a force of infantry and cavalry in three columns to pursue the fleeing enemy. They had advanced some way and were in sight of the nearest fugitives, when dispatch-riders brought news from Atrius of a great storm in the night, by which nearly all the ships had been damaged or cast ashore; the anchors and cables had not held, and the sailors and their captains could not cope with such a violent gale, so that many vessels were disabled by running foul of one another.

Caesar at once ordered the legions and cavalry to be halted and recalled. He himself went back to the beach, where with his own eyes he saw pretty much what the messengers and the dispatch described. About forty ships were a total loss; the rest looked as if they could be repaired at the cost of much trouble. Accordingly he called out all the skilled workmen from the legions, sent to the continent for more and wrote to tell Labienus to build as many ships as possible with the troops under his command. Further, although it was a task involving enormous labour, he decided that it would be best to have all the ships beached and enclosed together with the camp by one fortification. This work, although it was continued day and night, took some ten days to complete.

As soon as the ships were hauled up and the camp strongly fortified, Caesar left the same units as before to guard them, and returned to the place from which he had come. On arriving there he found that larger British forces had now been assembled from all sides by Cassivellaunus, to whom the chief command and direction of the campaign had been entrusted by common consent. Cassivellaunus' territory is separated from the maritime tribes by a river called the Thames, and lies about seventy-five miles from the sea. Previously he had been continually at war with the other tribes, but the arrival of our army frightened them into appointing him their supreme commander.

The British cavalry and charioteers had a fierce encounter with our cavalry on the march, but our men had the best of it everywhere and drove them into the woods and hills, killing a good many, but also incurring some casualties themselves by a too eager pursuit. The enemy waited for a time, and then, while our soldiers were off their guard and busy fortifying the camp, suddenly dashed out of the woods, swooped upon the outpost on duty in front of the camp, and started a violent battle. Caesar sent two cohorts—the first of their respective legions—to the rescue, and these took up a position close together; but the men were unnerved by the unfamiliar tactics, and the enemy very daringly broke through between them and got away unhurt. That day Quintus Laberius Durus, a military tribune, was killed. The attack was eventually repulsed by throwing in some more cohorts.

Throughout this peculiar combat, which was fought in front of the camp in full view of everyone, it was seen that our troops were too heavily weighted by their armour to deal with such an enemy: they could not pursue them when they retreated, and dared not get separated from their standards. The cavalry, too, found it very dangerous work fighting the charioteers; for the Britons would generally give ground on purpose, and after drawing them some distance from the legions would jump down from their chariots and fight on foot, with the odds in their favour. In engaging their cavalry our men were not much better off: their tactics were such that the danger was exactly the same for both pursuers and pursued. A further difficulty was that they never fought in close order, but in very open formation, and had reserves posted here and there; in this way the various groups covered one another's retreat, and fresh troops replaced those who were tired.

Next day the enemy took up a position on the hills at a distance from the camp. They showed themselves now only in small parties and harassed our cavalry with less vigour than the day before. But at midday, when Caesar had sent three legions and all the cavalry on a foraging expedition under his general Gaius Trebonius, they suddenly swooped down on them from all sides, pressing their attack right up to the standards of the legions. The legionaries drove them off by a strong counter-attack, and continued to pursue until the cavalry, emboldened by the support of the legions which they saw close behind them, made a charge that sent the natives flying headlong. A great many were killed, and the rest were given no chance of rallying or making a stand or jumping from their chariots. This rout caused the immediate dispersal of the forces that had assembled from various tribes to Cassivellaunus' aid, and the Britons never again joined battle with their whole strength.

ALEXANDER MERCER
Waterloo

On 18 June 1815, the armies of Napoleon and the Duke of Wellington met at Waterloo, a village in Belgium. Wellington's army was composed of various nationalities, including Britons, Hanoverians and Belgians, and numbered around 70,000. The French army was a similar size. Alexander Mercer was a Field Captain in the British Royal Horse Artillery.

WE WERE TALKING WHEN SUDDENLY a dark mass of cavalry appeared for an instant on the main ridge, and then came sweeping down the slope in swarms, reminding me of an enormous surf bursting over the prostrate hull of a stranded vessel, and then running, hissing and foaming, up the beach. The hollow space became in a twinkling covered with horsemen, apparently without any object. Sometimes they came pretty near us, then would retire a little. There were lancers amongst them, hussars, and dragoons—it was a complete *mêlée*. On the main ridge no squares were to be seen; the only objects were a few guns standing in a confused manner, with muzzles in the air, and not one artillery-man. After caracoling about for a few minutes, the crowd began to separate and draw together in small bodies, which continually increased; and now we really apprehended being overwhelmed, as the first line had apparently been. For a moment an awful silence pervaded that part of the position to which we anxiously turned our eyes. 'I fear all is over,' said Colonel Gould, who still remained by me. The thing seemed but too likely, and this time I could not withhold my assent to his remark, for it did indeed appear so. Meantime the 14th, springing from the earth, had formed their square, whilst we, throwing back the guns of our right and left divisions, stood waiting in momentary expectation of being enveloped and attacked. Still they lingered in the hollow, when suddenly loud and repeated shouts (not English hurrahs) drew our attention to the other side. There we saw two dense columns of infantry pushing forward at a quick pace towards us, crossing the fields, as if they had come from Merke Braine. Everyone, both of the 14th and ourselves, pronounced them French, yet still we delayed opening fire on them. Shouting, yelling, and singing, on they came, right for us; and being now not above 800 or 1,000 yards distant, it seemed folly allowing them to come nearer unmolested. The commanding officer of the 14th, to end our doubts, rode forward and endeavoured to ascertain who they were, but soon returned, assuring us they were French. The order was already given to fire, when, luckily, Colonel Gould recognized them as Belgians. Meantime, whilst my attention was occupied by these people, the cavalry had all vanished, nobody could say how or where.

We breathed again. Such was the agitated state in which we were kept in our second position. A third act was about to commence of a much more stirring and active nature.

It might have been, as nearly as I can recollect about 3 p.m., when Sir Augustus Frazer galloped up, crying out, 'Left limber up, and as fast as you can.' The words were scarcely uttered when my gallant troop stood as desired in column of subdivisions, left in front, pointing towards the main ridge. 'At a gallop, march!' and away we flew, as steadily and compactly as if at a review. I rode with Frazer, whose face was as black as a chimney-sweep's from the smoke, and the jacket-sleeve of his right arm torn open by a musket-ball or case-shot, which had merely grazed his flesh. As we went along, he told me that the enemy had assembled an enormous mass of heavy cavalry in front of the point to which he was leading us (about one-third of the distance between Hougoumont and the Charleroi road), and that in all probability we should immediately be charged on gaining our position. 'The Duke's orders, however, are positive,' he added, 'that in the event of their persevering and charging home, you do not expose your men, but retire with them into the adjacent squares of infantry.' As he spoke, we were ascending the reverse slope of the main position. We breathed a new atmosphere—the air was suffocatingly hot, resembling that issuing from an oven. We were enveloped in thick smoke, and, malgré the incessant roar of cannon and musketry, could distinctly hear around us a mysterious humming noise, like that which one hears of a summer's evening proceeding from myriads of black beetles; cannon-shot, too, ploughed the ground in all directions, and so thick was the hail of balls and bullets that it seemed dangerous to extend the arm lest it should be torn off. In spite of the serious situation in which we were, I could not help being somewhat amused at the astonishment expressed by our kind-hearted surgeon (Hitchins), who heard for the first time this sort of music. He was close to me as we ascended the slope, and, hearing this infernal *carillon* about his ears, began staring round in the wildest and most comic manner imaginable, twisting himself from side to side, exclaiming, 'My God, Mercer, what *is* that? What *is* all this noise? How curious!—how very curious!' And then when a cannon-shot rushed hissing past, '*There!—there!* What *is* it all?' It was with great difficulty that I persuaded him to retire: for a time he insisted on remaining near me, and it was only by pointing out how important it was to us, in case of being wounded, that he should keep himself safe to be able to assist us, that I prevailed on him to withdraw. Amidst this storm we gained the summit of the ridge, strange to say, without a casualty; and Sir Augustus, pointing out our position between two squares of Brunswick infantry, left us, with injunctions to remember the Duke's order, and to economize our ammunition. The Brunswickers were falling fast—the shot every moment making great gaps in their squares, which the officers and sergeants were actively employed in filling up by pushing their men together, and sometimes thumping them ere they could make them move. These were the very boys whom I had but yesterday seen throwing away their arms, and fleeing, panic-stricken, from the very sound of our horses' feet. Today they fled not bodily, to be sure, but spiritually, for their senses seemed to have left them. There they stood, with recovered arms, like so many logs, or rather like the very wooden figures which I had seen them practising at in their cantonments. Every moment I feared they would again throw down their arms and flee; but their officers and sergeants behaved nobly, not only keeping them together, but managing to keep their squares closed in spite of the carnage made amongst them. To have sought refuge amongst men in such a state were madness—the very moment our men ran from their guns I was convinced, would be the signal for their disbanding. We had better, then, fall at our posts than in such a situation. Our coming up seemed to reanimate them, and all their eyes were directed to us—indeed, it was providential, for, had we not arrived as we did, I scarcely think there is a doubt of what would have been their fate. Our first gun had scarcely gained the interval between their squares, when I saw through the smoke the leading squadrons of the advancing column coming on at a brisk trot, and already not more than one hundred yards distant, if so much, for I don't think we could have seen so far. I immediately ordered the line to be formed for action—*case-shot*! and the leading gun was unlimbered and commenced firing almost as soon as the word was given: for activity and intelligence our men were unrivalled. The very first round, I saw, brought down several men and horses. They continued, however, to advance. I glanced at the Brunswickers, and that glance told me it would not do; they had opened a fire from their front faces, but both squares appeared too unsteady, and I resolved to say nothing about the Duke's order, and take our chance—a resolve that was strengthened by the effect of the remaining guns as they rapidly succeeded in coming to action, making terrible slaughter, and in an instant covering the ground with men and horses. Still they persevered in approaching us (the first round had brought them to a walk), though slowly, and it did seem they would ride over us. We were a little below the level of the ground on which they moved—having in front of us a bank of about a foot and a half or two feet high, along the top of which ran a narrow road—and this gave more effect to our case-shot, all of which almost must have taken effect, for the carnage was frightful. I suppose this state of things occupied but a few seconds, when I observed symptoms of hesitation, and in a twinkling, at the instant I thought it was all over with us, they turned to either flank and filed away rapidly to the rear. Retreat of the mass, however, was not so easy. Many facing about and trying to force their way through the body of the column, that part next to us became a complete mob, into which we kept a steady fire of case-shot from our six pieces. The effect is hardly conceivable, and to paint this scene of slaughter and confusion impossible. Every discharge was followed by the fall of numbers, whilst the survivors struggled with each other, and I actually saw them using the pommels of their swords to fight their way out of the *mêlée*. Some, rendered desperate at finding themselves thus pent up at the muzzles of our guns, as it were, and others carried away by their horses, maddened with wounds, dashed through our intervals—few thinking of using their swords, but pushing furiously onward, intent only on saving themselves. At last the rear of the column, wheeling about, opened a passage, and the whole swept away at a much more rapid pace than they had advanced, nor stopped until the swell of the ground covered them from our fire. We then ceased firing; but as they were still not far off, for we saw the tops of their caps, having reloaded, we stood ready to receive them should they renew the attack.

One of, if not the first man who fell on our side was wounded by his own gun. Gunner Butterworth was one of the greatest pickles in the troop, but, at the same time, a most daring, active soldier; he was No 7 (the man who sponged, etc.) at his gun. He had just finished ramming down the shot, and was stepping back outside the wheel, when his foot stuck in the miry soil, pulling him forward at the moment the gun was fired. As a man naturally does when falling, he threw out both his arms before him, and they were blown off at the elbows. He raised himself a little on his two stumps, and looked up most piteously in my face. To assist him was impossible—the safety of all, everything, depended upon not slackening our fire, and I was obliged to turn from him. The state of anxious activity in which we were kept all day, and the numbers who fell almost immediately afterwards, caused me to lose sight of poor Butterworth; and I afterwards learned that he had succeeded in rising and was gone to the rear; but on inquiring for him next day, some of my people who had been sent to Waterloo told me that they saw his body lying by the roadside near the farm of Mount St Jean—bled to death! The retreat of the cavalry was succeeded by a shower of shot and shells, which must have annihilated us had not the little bank covered and threw most of them over us. Still some reached us and knocked down men and horses.

At the first charge, the French column was composed of grenadiers à cheval and cuirassiers, the former in front. I forget whether they had or had not changed this disposition, but think, from the number of cuirasses we afterwards found, that the cuirassiers led the second attack. Be this as it may, their column reassembled. They prepared for a second attempt, sending up a cloud of skirmishers, who galled us terribly by a fire of carbines and pistols at scarcely forty yards from our front. We were obliged to stand with port-fires lighted, so that it was not without a little difficulty that I succeeded in restraining the people from firing, for they grew impatient under such fatal results. Seeing some exertion beyond words necessary for this purpose, I leaped my horse up the little bank, and began a promenade (by no means agreeable) up and down our front, without even drawing my sword, though these fellows were within speaking distance of me. This quieted my men; but the tall blue gentlemen, seeing me thus dare them, immediately made a target of me, and commenced a very deliberate practice, to show us what very bad shots they were and verify the old artillery proverb, 'The nearer the target, the safer you are.' One fellow certainly made me flinch, but it was a miss; so I shook my finger at him, and called him *coquin*, etc. The rogue grinned as he reloaded, and again took aim. I certainly felt rather foolish at that moment, but was ashamed, after such bravado, to let him see it, and therefore continued my promenade. As if to prolong my torment, he was a terrible time about it. To me it seemed an age. Whenever I turned, the muzzle of his infernal carbine still followed me. At length bang it went, and whiz came the ball close to the back of my neck, and at the same instant down dropped the leading driver of one of my guns (Miller), into whose forehead the cursed missile had penetrated.

The column now once more mounted the plateau, and these popping gentry wheeled off right and left to clear the ground for their charge. The spectacle was imposing, and if ever the word sublime was appropriately applied, it might surely be to it. On they came in compact squadrons, one behind the other, so numerous that those of the rear were still below the brow when the head of the column was but at some sixty or seventy yards from our guns. Their pace was a slow but steady trot. None of your furious galloping charges was this, but a deliberate advance, at a deliberate pace, as of men resolved to carry their point. They moved in profound silence, and the only sound that could be heard from them amidst the incessant roar of battle was the low thunder-like reverberation of the ground beneath the simultaneous tread of so many horses. On our part was equal deliberation. Every man stood steadily at his post, the guns ready, loaded with a round-shot first and a case over it; the tubes were in the vents; the port-fires glared and sputtered behind the wheels; and my word alone was wanting to hurl destruction on that goodly show of gallant men and noble horses. I delayed this, for experience had given me confidence. The Brunswickers partook of this feeling, and with their squares—much reduced in point of size—well closed, stood firmly, with arms at the recover, and eyes fixed on us, ready to commence their fire with our first discharge. It was indeed a grand and imposing spectacle! The column was led on this time by an officer in a rich uniform, his breast covered with decorations, whose earnest gesticulations were strangely contrasted with the solemn demeanour of those to whom they were addressed. I thus allowed them to advance unmolested until the head of the column might have been about fifty or sixty yards from us, and then gave the word, 'Fire!' The effect was terrible. Nearly the whole leading rank fell at once; and the round-shot, penetrating the column carried confusion throughout its extent. The ground, already encumbered with victims of the first struggle, became now almost impassable. Still, however, these devoted warriors struggled on, intent only on reaching us. The thing was impossible. Our guns were served with astonishing activity, whilst the running fire of the two squares was maintained with spirit. Those who pushed forward over the heaps of carcasses of men and horses gained but a few paces in advance, there to fall in their turn and add to the difficulties of those succeeding them. The discharge of every gun was followed by a fall of men and horses like that of grass before the mower's scythe. When the horse alone was killed, we could see the cuirassiers divesting themselves of the encumbrance and making their escape on foot. Still, for a moment, the confused mass (for all order was at an end) stood before us, vainly trying to urge their horses over the obstacles presented by their fallen comrades, in obedience to the now loud and rapid vociferations of him who had led them on and remained unhurt. As before, many cleared everything and rode through us; many came plunging forward only to fall, man and horse, close to the muzzles of our guns; but the majority again turned at the very moment when, from having less ground to go over, it were safer to advance than retire, and sought a passage to the rear. Of course the same confusion, struggle amongst themselves, and slaughter prevailed as before, until gradually they disappeared over the brow of the hill. We ceased firing, glad to take breath. Their retreat exposed us, as before, to a shower of shot and shells: these last, falling amongst us with very long fuses, kept burning and hissing a long time before they burst, and were a considerable annoyance to man and horse. The bank in front, however, again stood our friend, and sent many over us innocuous.

Lieutenant Breton, who had already lost two horses and had mounted a troop-horse, was conversing with me during this our leisure moment. As his horse stood at right angles to mine, the poor jaded animal dozingly rested his muzzle on my thigh; whilst I, the better to hear amidst the infernal din, leant forward, resting my arm between his ears. In this attitude a cannon-shot smashed the horse's head to atoms. The headless trunk sank to the ground—Breton looked pale as death, expecting, as he afterwards told me, that I was cut in two. What was passing to the right and left of us I know no more about than the man in the moon—not even what corps were beyond the Brunswickers. The smoke confined our vision to a very small compass, so that my battle was restricted to the two squares and my own battery; and, as long as we maintained our ground, I thought it a matter of course that others did so too. It was just after this accident that our worthy commanding officer of artillery, Sir George Adam Wood, made his appearance through the smoke a little way from our left flank. As I said, we were doing nothing, for the cavalry were under the brow re-forming for a third attack, and we were being pelted by their artillery. 'D—n it, Mercer,' said the old man, blinking as a man does when facing a gale of wind, 'you have hot work of it here.' 'Yes, sir, pretty hot'; and I was proceeding with an account of the two charges we had already discomfited, and the prospect of a third, when, glancing that way, I perceived their leading squadron already on the plateau. 'There they are again!' I exclaimed; and, darting from Sir George *sans cérémonie*, was just in time to meet them with the same destruction as before. This time, indeed, it was child's play. They could not even approach us in any decent order, and we fired most deliberately; it was folly having attempted the thing. I was sitting on my horse near the right of my battery as they turned and began to retire once more. Intoxicated with success, I was singing out,

'Beautiful!—beautiful!' and my right arm was flourishing about, when someone from behind, seizing it, said quietly, 'Take care, or you'll strike the Duke'; and in effect our noble chief, with a serious air, and apparently much fatigued, passed close by me to the front, without seeming to take the slightest notice of the remnant of the French cavalry still lingering on the ground. This obliged us to cease firing; and at the same moment I, perceiving a line of infantry ascending from the rear, slowly, with ported arms, and uttering a sort of feeble, suppressed hurrah—ankle-deep in a thick tenacious mud, and threading their way amongst or stepping over the numerous corpses covering the ground, out of breath from their exertions, and hardly preserving a line, broken everywhere into large gaps the breadth of several files—could not but meditate on the probable results of the last charge had I, in obedience to the Duke's order, retired my men into the squares and allowed the daring and formidable squadrons a passage to our rear, where they must have gone thundering down on this disjointed line. The summit gained, the line was amended, files closed in, and the whole, including our Brunswickers, advanced down the slope towards the plain.

Although the infantry lost several men as they passed us, yet on the whole the cannonade began to slacken on both sides (why, I know not), and, the smoke clearing away a little, I had now, for the first time, a good view of the field. On the ridge opposite to us dark masses of troops were stationary, or moving down into the intervening plain. Our own advancing infantry were hid from view by the ground. We therefore recommenced firing at the enemies' masses, and the cannonade, spreading, soon became general again along the line. Whilst thus occupied with our front, we suddenly became sensible of a most destructive flanking fire from a battery which had come, the Lord knows how, and established itself on a knoll somewhat higher than the ground we stood on, and only about 400 or 500 yards a little in advance of our left flank. The rapidity and precision of this fire were quite appalling. Every shot almost took effect, and I certainly expected we should all be annihilated. Our horses and limbers, being a little retired down the slope, had hitherto been somewhat under cover from the direct fire in front; but this plunged right amongst them, knocking them down by pairs, and creating horrible confusion. The drivers could hardly extricate themselves from one dead horse ere another fell, or perhaps themselves. The saddle-bags, in many instances, were torn from the horses' backs, and their contents scattered over the field. One shell I saw explode under the two finest wheel-horses in the troop—down they dropped. In some instances the horses of a gun or ammunition waggon remained, and all their drivers were killed. The whole livelong day had cost us nothing like this. Our gunners too—the few left fit for duty of them—were so exhausted that they were unable to run the guns up after firing, consequently at every round they retreated nearer to the limbers; and as we had pointed our two left guns towards the people who were annoying us so terribly, they soon came altogether in a confused heap, the trails crossing each other, and the whole dangerously near the limbers and ammunition waggons, some of which were totally unhorsed, and others in sad confusion from the loss of their drivers and horses, many of them lying dead in their harness attached to their carriages. I sighed for my poor troop—it was already but a wreck.

I had dismounted, and was assisting at one of the guns to encourage my poor exhausted men, when through the smoke a black speck caught my eye, and I instantly knew what it was. The conviction that one never sees a shot coming towards you unless directly in its line flashed across my mind, together with the certainty that my doom was sealed. I had barely time to exclaim 'Here it is then!'—much in that gasping sort of way one does when going into very cold water takes away the breath—'whush' it went past my face, striking the point of my pellisse collar, which was lying open, and smash into a horse close behind me. I breathed freely again.

Under such a fire, one may be said to have had a thousand narrow escapes; and, in good truth, I frequently experienced that displacement of air against my face caused by the passing of shot close to me; but the two above recorded, and a third which I shall mention, were remarkable ones, and made me feel in full force the goodness of Him who protected me among so many dangers. Whilst in position on the right of the second line, I had reproved some of my men for lying down when shells fell near them until they burst. Now my turn came. A shell, with a long fuse, came slop into the mud at my feet, and there lay fizzing and flaring, to my infinite discomfiture. After what I had said on the subject, I felt that I must act up to my own words, and, accordingly, there I stood, endeavouring to look quite composed until the cursed thing burst—and, strange to say, without injuring me, though so near. The effect on my men was good. We had scarcely fired many rounds at the enfilading battery when a tall man in the black Brunswick uniform came galloping up to me from the rear, exclaiming, 'Ah! mine Gott!—mine Gott! vat is it you doos, sare? Dat is your friends de Proosiens; an you kills dem! Ah, mine Gott!—mine Gott! vill you no stop, sare?—vill you no stop? Ah! mine Gott!—mine Gott! vat for is dis? De Inglish kills dere friends de Proosiens! Vere is de Dook von Vellington?—vere is de Dook von Vellington? Oh, mine Gott!—mine Gott!' etc. etc., and so he went on raving like one demented. I observed that if these were our friends the Prussians they were treating us very uncivilly; and that it was not without sufficient provocation we had turned our guns on them, pointing out to him at the same time the bloody proofs of my assertion. Apparently not noticing what I said, he continued his lamentations, and, 'Vill you no stop, sare, I say?' Wherefore, thinking he might be right, to pacify him I ordered the whole to cease firing, desiring him to remark the consequences. *Psieu, psieu, psieu*, came our *friends'* shot, one after another; and our friend himself had a narrow escape from one of them. 'Now, sir,' I said, 'you will be convinced; and we will continue our firing, whilst you can ride round the way you came, and tell them they kill their friends the English; the moment their fire ceases, so shall mine.' Still he lingered, exclaiming, 'Oh, dis is terreebly to see de Proosien and de Inglish kill vonanoder!' At last darting off I saw no more of him. The fire continued on both sides, mine becoming slacker and slacker, for we were reduced to the last extremity, and must have been annihilated but for the opportune arrival of a battery of Belgic artillery a little on our left, which, taking the others in flank nearly at point blank, soon silenced and drove them off. Our strength was barely sufficient to fire three guns out of our six.

These Belgians were all beastly drunk, and, when they first came up, not at all particular as to which way they fired; and it was only by keeping an eye on them that they were prevented treating us, and even one another. The wretches had probably already done mischief elsewhere—who knows? My recollections of the latter part of this day are rather confused; I was fatigued, and almost deaf. I recollect clearly, however, that we had ceased firing—the plain below being covered with masses of troops, which we could not distinguish from each other. Captain Walcot of the horse-artillery had come to us, and we were all looking out anxiously at the movements below and on the opposite ridge, when he suddenly shouted out, 'Victory!—victory! they fly!—they fly!' and sure enough we saw some of the masses dissolving, as it were, and those composing them streaming away in confused crowds over the field, whilst the already desultory fire of their artillery ceased altogether. I shall never forget this joyful moment!—this moment of exultation! On looking round I found we were left almost alone. Cavalry and infantry had all moved forward, and only a few guns here and there were to be seen on the position. A little to our right were the remains of Major M'Donald's troop under Lieutenant Sandilands, which had suffered much, but nothing like us. We were congratulating ourselves on the happy results of the day, when an aide-de-camp rode up, crying 'Forward, sir!—forward! It is of the utmost importance that this movement should be supported by artillery!' at the same time waving his hat much in the manner of a huntsman laying on his dogs. I smiled at his energy, and, pointing to the remains of my poor troop, quietly asked, 'How, sir?' A glance was sufficient to show him the impossibility, and away he went.

Our situation was indeed terrible: of 200 fine horses with which we had entered the battle, upwards of 140 lay dead, dying, or severely wounded. Of the men, scarcely two-thirds of those necessary for four guns remained, and these so completely exhausted as to be totally incapable of further exertion. Lieutenant Breton had three horses killed under him; Lieutenant Hincks was wounded in the breast by a spent ball; Lieutenant Leathes on the hip by a splinter; and although untouched myself, my horse had no less than eight wounds, one of which—a graze on the fetlock joint—lamed him for ever. Our guns and carriages were, as before mentioned, altogether in a confused heap, intermingled with dead and wounded horses, which it had not been possible to disengage from them. My poor men, such at least as were untouched, fairly worn out, their clothes, faces, etc., blackened by the smoke and spattered over with mud and blood, had seated themselves on the trails of the carriages, or had thrown themselves on the wet and polluted soil, too fatigued to think of anything but gaining a little rest. Such was our situation when called upon to advance! It was impossible, and we remained where we were.

ROBERT SOUTHEY
Nelson at Trafalgar

The battle of Trafalgar, 1805, was the decisive naval engagement of the Napoleonic Wars, and resulted in a victory for the British over the French and Spanish fleets led by Villeneuve. However, the action—which was fought to the west of the Spanish port of Cadiz—also saw the death of Admiral the Lord Nelson.

ABOUT HALF-PAST NINE IN THE morning of the 19th, the *Mars*, being the nearest to the fleet of the ships which formed the line of communication with the frigates inshore, repeated the signal that the enemy were coming out of port. The wind was at this time very light, with partial breezes, mostly from the S.S.W. Nelson ordered the signal to be made for a chase in the south-east quarter. About two, the repeating-ships announced that the enemy were at sea. All night the British fleet continued under all sail, steering to the south-east. At daybreak they were in the entrance of the Straits, but the enemy were not in sight. About seven, one of the frigates made signal that the enemy were bearing north. Upon this the *Victory* hove to; and shortly afterwards Nelson made sail again to the northward. In the afternoon the wind blew fresh from the south-west, and the English began to fear that the foe might be forced to return to port. A little before sunset, however, Blackwood, in the *Euryalus*, telegraphed that they appeared determined to go to the westward. 'And that,' said the admiral in his diary, 'they shall not do, if it is in the power of Nelson and Bronte to prevent them.' Nelson had signified to Blackwood that he depended upon him to keep sight of the enemy. They were observed so well, that all their motions were made known to him; and, as they wore twice, he inferred that they were aiming to keep the port of Cadiz open, and would retreat there as soon as they saw the British fleet; for this reason he was very careful not to approach near enough to be seen by them during the night. At daybreak the combined fleets were distinctly seen from the *Victory's* deck, formed in a close line of battle ahead, on the starboard tack, about twelve miles to leeward, and standing to the south. Our fleet consisted of twenty-seven sail of the line and four frigates; theirs of thirty-three and seven large frigates. Their superiority was greater in size and weight of metal than in numbers. They had four thousand troops on board; and the best riflemen who could be procured, many of them Tyrolese, were dispersed through the ships. Little did the Tyrolese, and little did the Spaniards, at that day, imagine what horrors the wicked tyrant whom they served was preparing for their country.

Soon after daylight Nelson came upon deck. The 21st of October was a festival in his family, because on that day his uncle, Captain Suckling, in the *Dreadnought*, with two other line-of-battle ships, had beaten off a French squadron of four sail of the line and three frigates. Nelson, with that sort of superstition from which few persons are entirely exempt, had more than once expressed his persuasion that this was to be the day of his battle also; and he was well pleased at seeing his prediction about to be verified. The wind was now from the west, light breezes, with a long heavy swell. Signal was made to bear down upon the enemy in two lines; and the fleet set all sail. Collingwood, in the *Royal Sovereign*, led the lee line of thirteen ships; the *Victory* led the weather line of fourteen. Having seen that all was as it should be, Nelson retired to his cabin, and wrote the following prayer:-

'May the great God, whom I worship, grant to my country, and for the benefit of Europe in general, a great and glorious victory; and may no misconduct in any one tarnish it; and may humanity after victory be the predominant feature in the British fleet! For myself individually, I commit my life to Him that made me; and may His blessing alight on my endeavours for serving my country faithfully! To Him I resign myself, and the just cause which is entrusted to me to defend. Amen, Amen, Amen.'

Having thus discharged his devotional duties, he annexed, in the same diary, the following remarkable writing:-

October 21st, 1805.—Then in sight of the combined fleets of France and Spain, distant about ten miles.

'Whereas the eminent services of Emma Hamilton, widow of the Right Honourable Sir William Hamilton, have been of the very greatest service to my king and country, to my knowledge, without ever receiving any reward from either our king or country;

'First: That she obtained the King of Spain's letter, in 1796, to his brother, the King of Naples, acquainting him of his intention to declare war against England; from which letter the ministry sent out orders to the then Sir John Jervis, to strike a stroke, if opportunity offered, against either the arsenals of Spain or her fleets. That neither of these was done is not the fault of Lady Hamilton; the opportunity might have been offered.

'Secondly: The British fleet under my command could never have returned the second time to Egypt, had not Lady Hamilton's influence with the Queen of Naples caused letters to be written to the governor of Syracuse, that he was to encourage the fleet's being supplied with everything, should they put into any port in Sicily. We put into Syracuse, and received every supply; went to Egypt, and destroyed the French fleet.

'Could I have rewarded these services, I would not now call upon my country; but as that has not been in my power, I leave Emma Lady Hamilton therefore a legacy to my king and country, that they will give her an ample provision to maintain her rank in life.

'I also leave to the beneficence of my country my adopted daughter, Horatia Nelson Thompson; and I desire she will use in future the name of Nelson only.

'These are the only favours I ask of my king and country, at this moment when I am going to fight their battle. May God bless my king and country, and all those I hold dear! My relations it is needless to mention: they will, of course, be amply provided for.

'NELSON AND BRONTE.

'Witness HENRY BLACKWOOD.
T. M. HARDY.'

The child of whom this writing speaks was believed to be his daughter, and so, indeed, he called her the last time that he pronounced her name. She was then about five years old, living at Merton, under Lady Hamilton's care. The last minutes which Nelson passed at Merton were employed in praying over this child, as she lay sleeping. A portrait of Lady Hamilton hung in his cabin; and no Catholic ever beheld the picture of his patron saint with devouter reverence. The undisguised and romantic passion with which he regarded it amounted almost to superstition; and when the portrait was now taken down, in clearing for action, he desired the men who removed it to 'take care of his guardian angel.' In this manner he frequently spoke of it, as if he believed there were a virtue in the image. He wore a miniature of her, also, next his heart.

Blackwood went on board the *Victory* about six. He found him in good spirits, but very calm; not in that exhilaration which he had felt upon entering into battle at Aboukir and Copenhagen: he knew that his own life would be particularly aimed at, and seems to have looked for death with almost as sure an expectation as for victory. His whole attention was fixed upon the enemy. They tacked to the northward, and formed their line on the larboard tack; thus bringing the shoals of Trafalgar and St Pedro under the lee of the British, and keeping the port of Cadiz open for themselves. This was judiciously done; and Nelson, aware of all the advantages which it gave them, made signal to prepare to anchor.

Villeneuve was a skilful seaman; worthy of serving a better master, and a better cause. His plan of defence was as well conceived, and as original, as the plan of attack. He formed the fleet in a double line; every alternate ship being about a cable's length to windward of her second ahead and astern. Nelson, certain of a triumphant issue to the day, asked Blackwood what he should consider as a victory. That officer answered, that, considering the handsome way in which battle was offered by the enemy, their apparent determination for a fair trial of strength, and the situation of the land, he thought it would be a glorious result if fourteen were captured. He replied, 'I shall not be satisfied with less than twenty.' Soon afterwards he asked him, if he did not think there was a signal wanting. Captain Blackwood made answer, that he thought the whole fleet seemed very clearly to understand what they were about. These words were scarcely spoken before that signal was made, which will be remembered as long as the language, or even the memory, of England shall endure—Nelson's last signal: 'ENGLAND EXPECTS EVERY MAN TO DO HIS DUTY!' It was received throughout the fleet with a shout of answering acclamation, made sublime by the spirit which it breathed, and the feeling which it expressed. 'Now,' said Lord Nelson, 'I can do no more. We must trust to the great Disposer of all events, and the justice of our cause. I thank God for this great opportunity of doing my duty.'

He wore that day, as usual, his admiral's frockcoat, bearing on the left breast four stars, of the different orders with which he was invested. Ornaments which rendered him so conspicuous a mark for the enemy were beheld with ominous apprehensions by his officers. It was known that were there riflemen on board the French ships; and it could not be doubted but that his life would be particularly aimed at. They communicated their fears to each other; and the surgeon, Mr Beatty, spoke to the chaplain, Dr Scott, and to Mr Scott, the public secretary, desiring that some person would entreat him to change his dress, or cover the stars; but they knew that such a request would highly displease him. 'In honour I gained them,' he had said, when such a thing had been hinted to him formerly, 'and in honour I will die with them.' Mr Beatty, however, would not have been deterred by any fear of exciting his displeasure, from speaking to him himself upon a subject in which the weal of England, as well as the life of Nelson, was concerned—but he was ordered from the deck before he could find an opportunity. This was a point upon which Nelson's officers knew that it was hopeless to remonstrate or reason with him; but both Blackwood and his own captain, Hardy, represented to him how advantageous to the fleet it would be for him to keep out of action as long as possible; and he consented at last to let the *Leviathan* and the *Téméraire*, which were sailing abreast of the *Victory*, be ordered to pass ahead. Yet even here the last infirmity of this noble mind was indulged; for these ships could not pass ahead if the *Victory* continued to carry all her sail; and so far was Nelson from shortening sail, that it was evident he took pleasure in pressing on, and rendering it impossible for them to obey his own orders. A long swell was setting into the Bay of Cadiz: our ships, crowding all sail, moved majestically before it, with light winds from the south-west. The sun shone on the sails of the enemy; and their well-formed line, with their numerous three-deckers, made an appearance which any other assailants would have thought formidable; but the British sailors only admired the beauty and the splendour of the spectacle; and, in full confidence of winning what they saw, remarked to each other, what a fine sight yonder ships would make at Spithead!

The French admiral, from the *Bucentaure*, beheld the new manner in which his enemy was advancing—Nelson and Collingwood each leading his line; and, pointing them out to his officers, he is said to have exclaimed that such conduct could not fail to be successful. Yet Villeneuve had made his own dispositions with the utmost skill, and the fleets under his command waited for the attack with perfect coolness. Ten minutes before twelve they opened their fire. Eight or nine of the ships immediately ahead of the *Victory*, and across her bows, fired single guns at her, to ascertain whether she was yet within their range. As soon as Nelson perceived that their shot passed over him, he desired Blackwood, and Captain Prowse, of the *Sirius*, to repair to their respective frigates; and, on their way, to tell all the captains of the line-of-battle ships that he depended on their exertions; and that, if by the prescribed mode of attack they found it impracticable to get into action immediately, they might adopt whatever they thought best, provided it led them quickly and closely alongside an enemy. As they were standing on the front of the poop, Blackwood took him by the hand, saying, he hoped soon to return and find him in possession of twenty prizes. He replied, 'God bless you, Blackwood; I shall never see you again!'

Nelson's column was steered about two points more to the north than Collingwood's, in order to cut off the enemy's escape into Cadiz: the lee line, therefore, was first engaged. 'See,' cried Nelson, pointing to the *Royal Sovereign*, as she steered right for the centre of the enemy's line, cut through it astern of the *Santa Anna*, three-decker, and engaged her at the muzzle of her guns on the starboard side—'see how that noble fellow, Collingwood, carries his ship into action!' Collingwood, delighted at being first in the heat of the fire, and knowing the feelings of his commander and old friend, turned to his captain, and exclaimed, 'Rotherham, what would Nelson give to be here!' Both these brave officers, perhaps, at this moment, thought of Nelson with gratitude, for a circumstance which had occurred on the preceding day. Admiral Collingwood, with some of the captains, having gone on board the *Victory* to receive instructions, Nelson inquired of him where his captain was; and was told, in reply, that they were not upon good terms with each other. 'Terms!' said Nelson—'good terms with each other!' Immediately he sent a boat for Captain Rotherham; led him, as soon as he arrived, to Collingwood, and saying, 'Look; yonder are the enemy!' bade them shake hands like Englishmen.

The enemy continued to fire a gun at a time at the *Victory*, till they saw that a shot had passed through her main-top-gallant sail; then they opened their broadsides, aiming chiefly at her rigging, in the hope of disabling her before she could close with them. Nelson, as usual, had hoisted several flags, lest one should be shot away. The enemy showed no colours till late in the action, when they began to feel the necessity of having them to strike. For this reason, the *Santissima Trinidad*, Nelson's old acquaintance, as he used to call her, was distinguishable only by her four decks: and to the bow of this opponent he ordered the *Victory* to be steered. Meantime, an incessant raking fire was kept up upon the *Victory*. The admiral's secretary was one of the first who fell; he was killed by a cannon-shot while conversing with Hardy. Captain Adair of the marines, with the help of a sailor, endeavoured to remove the body from Nelson's sight, who had a great regard for Mr Scott; but he anxiously asked, 'Is that poor Scott that's gone?' and being informed that it was indeed so, exclaimed, 'Poor fellow!' Presently a double-headed shot struck a party of marines, who were drawn up on the poop, and killed eight of them: upon which Nelson immediately desired Captain Adair to disperse his men round the ship, that they might not suffer so much from being together. A few minutes afterwards a shot struck the fore-brace bits on the quarter-deck, and passed between Nelson and Hardy, a splinter from the bit tearing off Hardy's buckle, and bruising his foot. Both stopped, and looked anxiously at each other: each supposed the other to be wounded. Nelson then smiled, and said, 'This is too warm work, Hardy, to last long.'

The *Victory* had not yet returned a single gun; fifty of her men had been by this time killed or wounded, and her main-topmast, with all her studding-sails and their booms, shot away. Nelson declared, that, in all his battles, he had seen nothing which surpassed the cool courage of his crew on this occasion. At four minutes after twelve, she opened her fire from both sides of her deck. It was not possible to break the enemy's line without running on board one of their ships; Hardy informed him of this, and asked him which he would prefer. Nelson replied, 'Take your choice, Hardy; it does not signify much.' The master was ordered to put the helm to port, and the *Victory* ran on board the *Redoubtable*, just as her tiller-ropes were shot away. The French ship received her with a broadside; then instantly let down her lower-deck ports, for fear of being boarded through them, and never afterwards fired a great gun during the action. Her tops, like those of all the enemy's ships, were filled with riflemen. Nelson never placed musketry in his tops; he had a strong dislike to the practice: not merely because it endangers setting fire to the sails, but also because it is a murderous sort of warfare, by which individuals may suffer, and a commander now and then be picked off, but which never can decide the fate of a general engagement.

Captain Harvey, in the *Téméraire*, fell on board the *Redoubtable* on the other side. Another enemy was in like manner on board the *Téméraire*, so that these four ships formed as compact a tier as if they had been moored together, their heads lying all the same way. The lieutenants of the *Victory*, seeing this, depressed their guns of the middle and lower decks, and fired with a diminished charge, lest the shot should pass through and injure the *Téméraire*. And because there was danger that the *Redoubtable* might take fire from the lower-deck guns, the muzzles of which touched her side when they were run out, the fireman of each gun stood ready with a bucket of water; which, as soon as the gun was discharged, he dashed into the hole made by the shot. An incessant fire was kept up from the *Victory* from both sides; her larboard guns playing upon the *Bucentaure* and the huge *Santissima Trinidad*.

It had been part of Nelson's prayer, that the British fleet might be distinguished by humanity in the victory which he expected. Setting an example himself, he twice gave orders to cease firing upon the *Redoubtable*, supposing that she had struck, because her great guns were silent; for, as she carried no flag, there was no means of instantly ascertaining the fact. From this ship, which he had thus twice spared, he received his death. A ball fired from her mizen-top, which, in the then situation of the two vessels, was not more than fifteen yards from that part of the deck where he was standing, struck the epaulette on his left shoulder, about a quarter after one, just in the heat of action. He fell upon his face, on the spot which was covered with his poor secretary's blood. Hardy, who was a few steps from him, turning round, saw three men raising him up. 'They have done for me at last, Hardy!' said he. 'I hope not!' cried Hardy. 'Yes,' he replied; 'my back-bone is shot through!' Yet even now, not for a moment losing his presence of mind, he observed, as they were carrying him down the ladder, that the tiller-ropes, which had been shot away, were not yet replaced, and ordered that new ones should be rove immediately. Then, that he might not be seen by the crew, he took out his handkerchief, and covered his face and his stars. Had he but concealed these badges of honour from the enemy, England, perhaps, would not have had cause to receive with sorrow the news of the battle of Trafalgar. The cockpit was crowded with wounded and dying men; over whose bodies he was with some difficulty conveyed, and laid upon a pallet in the midshipmen's berth. It was soon perceived, upon examination, that the wound was mortal. This, however, was concealed from all, except Captain Hardy, the chaplain, and the medical attendants. He himself being certain, from the sensation in his back, and the gush of blood he felt momently within his breast, that no human care could avail him, insisted that the surgeon should leave him, and attend to those to whom he might be useful. 'For,' said he, 'you can do nothing for me.' All that could be done was to fan him with a paper, and frequently to give him lemonade to alleviate his intense thirst. He was in great pain, and expressed much anxiety for the event of the action, which now began to declare itself. As often as a ship struck, the crew of the *Victory* huzzaed; and at every huzza, a visible expression of joy gleamed in the eyes, and marked the countenance, of the dying hero. But he became impatient to see Captain Hardy; and as that officer, though often sent for, could not leave the deck, Nelson feared that some fatal cause prevented him, and repeatedly cried, 'Will no one bring Hardy to me? He must be killed! He is surely dead!'

An hour and ten minutes elapsed from the time when Nelson received his wound, before Hardy could come to him. They shook hands in silence; Hardy in vain struggling to suppress the feelings of that most painful and yet sublimest moment. 'Well, Hardy,' said Nelson, 'how goes the day with us?' 'Very well,' replied Hardy; 'ten ships have struck, but five of the van have tacked, and show an intention to bear down upon the *Victory*. I have called two or three of our fresh ships round, and have no doubt of giving them a drubbing.' 'I hope,' said Nelson, 'none of our ships have struck?' Hardy answered, 'There was no fear of that.' Then, and not till then, Nelson spoke of himself. 'I am a dead man, Hardy,' said he: 'I am going fast; it will be all over with me soon. Come nearer to me. Let my dear Lady Hamilton have my hair, and all other things belonging to me.' Hardy observed, that he hoped Mr Beatty could yet hold out some prospect of life. 'Oh no!' he replied; 'it is impossible; my back is shot through. Beatty will tell you so.' Captain Hardy then, once more, shook hands with him; and with a heart almost bursting, hastened upon deck.

By this time all feeling below the breast was gone; and Nelson, having made the surgeon ascertain this, said to him, 'You know I am gone. I know it. I feel something rising in my breast' (putting his hand on his left side) 'which tells me so.' And upon Beatty's inquiring whether his pain was very great, he replied, 'So great, that he wished he was dead. Yet,' said he, in a lower voice, 'one would like to live a little longer too!' And after a few minutes, in the same under-tone, he added, 'What would become of poor Lady Hamilton if she knew my situation!' Next to his country, she occupied his thoughts. Captain Hardy, some fifty minutes after he had left the cockpit, returned, and again taking the hand of his dying friend and commander, congratulated him on having gained a complete victory. How many of the enemy were taken he did not know, as it was impossible to perceive them distinctly; but fourteen or fifteen at least. 'That's well!' cried Nelson; 'but I bargained for twenty.' And then, in a stronger voice, he said, 'Anchor, Hardy; anchor.' Hardy, upon this, hinted that Admiral Collingwood would take upon himself the direction of affairs. 'Not while I live, Hardy,' said the dying Nelson, ineffectually endeavouring to raise himself from the bed; 'do you anchor.' His previous order for preparing to anchor had shown how clearly he foresaw the necessity of this. Presently, calling Hardy back, he said to him, in a low voice, 'Don't throw me overboard;' and he desired that he might be buried by his parents, unless it should please the king to order otherwise. Then reverting to private feelings,—'Take care of my dear Lady Hamilton, Hardy; take care of poor Lady Hamilton. Kiss me, Hardy,' said he. Hardy knelt down and kissed his cheek; and Nelson said, 'Now I am satisfied. Thank God, I have done my duty!' Hardy stood over him in silence for a moment or two, then knelt again, and kissed his forehead. 'Who is that?' said Nelson; and being informed, he replied, 'God bless you, Hardy!' And Hardy then left him—for ever.

Nelson now desired to be turned upon his right side, and said, 'I wish I had not left the deck; for I shall soon be gone.' Death was, indeed, rapidly approaching. He said to the chaplain, 'Doctor, I have *not* been a *great* sinner;' and after a short pause, 'Remember that I leave Lady Hamilton and my daughter Horatia as a legacy to my country.' His articulation now became difficult; but he was distinctly heard to say, 'Thank God, I have done my duty!' These words he repeatedly pronounced; and they were the last words which he uttered. He expired at thirty minutes after four,—three hours and a quarter after he had received his wound.

JEAN DE JOINVILLE
Knight of the Crusades

Joinville was a French knight on the Christian Crusades to the Holy Land in the 13th Century. Here he describes the battle against the Muslim Turks and Saracens at Mansourah in February 1250 AD.

IN THE MEANTIME, I AND MY KNIGHTS had decided to go and attack some Turks who were loading their baggage in their camp on our left; so we fell on them. As we were pursuing them through the camp I caught sight of a Saracen on the point of mounting his horse; one of his knights was holding the bridle. At the moment he had both his hands on the saddle to pull himself up, I gave him a thrust with my lance just under the arm-pits and struck him dead. On seeing this, his knight left his lord and the horse, and thrusting his lance at me as I passed, caught me between the shoulders, pinning me down to the neck of my horse in such a way that I could not draw the sword at my belt. I therefore had to draw the sword attached to my horse. When he saw me with my sword drawn he withdrew his lance and left me.

When I and my knights came out of the Saracens' camp we found what we reckoned to be about six thousand Turks, who had left their tents and retreated into the fields. As soon as they saw us they came charging towards us, and killed Hugues de Trichâtel, Lord of Conflans, who was with me bearing a banner. I and my knights spurred on our horses and went to the rescue of Raoul de Wanou, another of my company, whom they had struck to the ground.

As I was coming back, the Turks thrust at me with their lances. Under the weight of their attack my horse was brought to its knees, and I went flying forward over its ears. I got up as soon as ever I could, with my shield at my neck and sword in hand. One of my knights, named Érard de Siverey—may God grant him grace!—came to me and advised our drawing back towards a ruined house where we could wait for the king, who was on his way. As we were going there, some on foot and some on horseback, a great body of Turks came rushing at us, bearing me to the ground and riding over my body, so that my shield went flying from my neck.

As soon as they had passed, Érard de Siverey came back to me and took me with him to the walls of the tumble-down house. Here we were joined by Hugues d'Écot, Frédéric de Loupey, and Renaud de Menoncourt. While we were there the Turks attacked us from all sides. Some of them got into the house and pricked us with their lances from above. My knights asked me to hold on to their horses' bridles, which I did, for fear the beasts should run away. Then they put up a vigorous defence against the Turks, for which, I may say, they were afterwards highly praised by all men of good standing in the army, both those who witnessed their bravery and those who heard of it later.

During this incident, Hugues d'Écot received three wounds in the face from a lance, and so did Raoul de Wanou, while Frédéric de Loupey had a lance-thrust between his shoulders, which made so large a wound that the blood poured from his body as if from the bung-hole of a barrel. A blow from one of the enemy's swords landed in the middle of Érard de Siverey's face, cutting through his nose so that it was left dangling over his lips. At that moment the thought of Saint James came into my mind, and I prayed to him: 'Good Saint James, come to my help, and save us in our great need.'

Just as I had uttered this prayer Érard de Siverey said to me: 'My lord, if you think that neither I nor my heirs will incur reproach for it, I will go and fetch you help from the Comte d'Anjou, whom I see in the fields over there.' I said to him: 'My dear man, it seems to me you would win great honour for yourself if you went for help to save our lives; your own, by the way, is also in great danger.' (I spoke truly, for he died of his wound.) He consulted the other knights who were there, and they all gave him the same advice as I had given him. After hearing what they said, he asked me to let go his horse, which I was holding by the bridle; so I let him take it.

He went over to the Comte d'Anjou and begged him to come to the rescue of me and my people. A person of some importance who was with the count tried to dissuade him, but he said he would do as my knight had asked. So he turned his horse's head to come to our help, and a number of his sergeants set spurs to their horses as well. As soon as the Saracens saw them coming, they turned to leave us. Pierre d'Auberive, who was riding in front of the sergeants with his sword clenched in his fist, saw them leaving and charged right into the midst of the Saracens who were holding Raoul de Wanou, and rescued him, sorely wounded.

As I stood there on foot with my knights, wounded as I have told you, King Louis came up at the head of his battalions, with a great sound of shouting, trumpets, and kettledrums. He halted with his troops on a raised causeway. Never have I seen a finer or more handsome knight! He seemed to tower head and shoulders above all his people; on his head was a gilded helmet, and a sword of German steel was in his hand.

The moment he stopped, those good knights in his division whom I have already named to you, together with other valiant knights of his, flung themselves right at the Turks. It was, I can assure you, a truly noble passage of arms, for no one there drew either bow or crossbow; it was a battle of maces against swords between the Turks and our people, with both sides inextricably entangled.

One of my squires, who had fled away with my banner, but had rejoined me, brought up one of my Flemish horses, on which I mounted and rode to take up my place beside the king. While we were there together, the worthy knight Jean de Valery came up to the king and said he advised him to bear to the right towards the river, so as to have the support of the Duc de Bourgogne, and also to give his Majesty's sergeants a chance of something to drink, for by now the day had grown very hot.

The king ordered his sergeants to go and fetch the good knights of his council who were round about, indicating each of them by name. The sergeants went and summoned them from the thick of the fight, where the struggle between the Turks and our people was most intense. They came to the king, who asked them what they advised. They replied that they considered Jean de Valery's advice very sound. So the king ordered his standard-bearers to move with the great flag of Saint Denis to the right towards the river. As the royal army began to move there was once again a great sound of trumpets, kettledrums, and Saracen horns.

The king had scarcely advanced more than a few paces when he received several messages from the Comte de Poitiers, the Comte de Flandre, and other men in high command who were there with their troops, all begging him not to move, because they were so hard pressed by the Turks that they could not possibly follow him. The king summoned the worthy knights of his council once more, and they all advised him to wait. Shortly after, Jean de Valery came back, and reproached the king and his council for remaining stationary. On this all the members of his council recommended the king to move towards the river as Jean de Valery advised.

At this moment the Constable Imbert de Beaujeu came to tell the king that his brother the Comte d'Artois was defending himself in a house in Mansourah, and begged his Majesty to go to his relief. 'You go on ahead of me, Constable,' said the king, 'and I will follow.' I told the constable I would accompany him as his knight, for which he thanked me heartily. So we both began to make our way towards Mansourah.

As we were going there, a sergeant armed with a mace came after the constable in a terrible state of fright, and told him that the king's advance was halted, and that the Turks had placed themselves between his Majesty and us. We turned round, and saw that there were more than a thousand of them between us and the king's army; and we were no more than six. So I said to the constable: 'My lord, we can't get back to the king through this mass of men, so let's go upstream, and place this gully you can see in front of you between the enemy and ourselves. In this way we may manage to get back to the king.' The constable took my advice; but I can assure you that if the Turks had paid any attention to us they would certainly have killed us all. However at the time they were giving no thought to anything except the king and the big battalions of men, and so assumed we were some of their own people.

While we were coming back down the bank of the river, between a brooklet and the main stream, we saw that the king had come up close to the river. The Turks were driving back his other battalions, slashing and striking at them with swords and maces, and gradually forcing them, together with the king's own battalion, back upon the river. The rout there was so complete that many of our people attempted to swim across to join the Duc de Bourgogne; but they were unable to do so, for their horses were weary, and the day had become very hot. So, as we were coming downstream towards them, we saw the river strewn with lances and shields, and full of men and horses drowning in the water.

As we came to a little bridge that spanned the brook I said to the constable: 'Let's stay here and defend this bridge, for if we abandon it the Turks will hurl themselves against the king from this side too, and if our people are attacked from two sides they may well be overpowered.' So we did as I advised. Later on we learnt that we should have all been lost that day if it had not been for the king. For, as Pierre de Courtenay and Jean de Saillenay told me, six Turks had seized the king's horse by the bridle and were leading him away captive, when he delivered himself without anyone's help by slashing at them with great strokes of his sword. When his men saw how the king was defending himself their courage revived, and many of them, giving up all thought of escaping across the river, rallied round to help him.

Riding straight towards us, as we were holding the little bridge, came the Comte Pierre de Bretagne, with a sword-cut across his face from which blood ran down into his mouth. He was mounted on a very handsome pony. He had thrown its reins over the pummel of his saddle, which he was gripping with both his hands, for fear his men, who were following him too close for comfort, might jostle him out of position as they crossed the narrow bridge. It would seem he had a very poor opinion of them; for as he spat the blood out of his mouth he kept ejaculating: 'Good Lord, did you ever see such scum!' Behind his men came the Comte de Soissons and Pierre de Neuville who was nicknamed 'Caier'; they had both received blows enough that day.

After these men had crossed the bridge, the Turks, seeing that we were guarding it with our faces turned towards them, stopped following the Comte Pierre and his party. I went up to the Comte de Soissons, who happened to be my wife's cousin, and said to him: 'I think it would be a good thing, sir, if you stayed to hold this bridge, for if we leave it unguarded the Turks over there will rush across it, and the king will be attacked both from the front and rear.' He asked me whether, if he stayed, I would remain there with him. 'I most certainly will,' I replied. On hearing this the constable told me not to move from the place till he returned, and said he would go in search of help for us.

I remained there, mounted on my sturdy cob, with the Comte de Soissons on my right hand, and Pierre de Neuville on my left. Suddenly a Turk came riding towards us from the direction of the king's troops, which were to our rear, and struck Pierre such a fierce blow from behind with his mace that he forced him down on to the neck of his horse; then, darting across the bridge, he rushed in amongst his own people.

When the Turks saw that we were not going to abandon the little bridge, they crossed the brook and placed themselves between it and the river, as we had done when we were going downstream. Thereupon we moved towards them so as to be ready to charge them if they attempted either to go in the direction of the king's troops or to cross our little bridge.

Just ahead of us were two of the king's sergeants—one called Guillaume of Boon and the other Jean of Gamaches. The Turks who had come between the brook and the river had brought along a large number of peasants on foot, who kept on pelting these two men with clods of earth, but were never able to force them back to where we stood. Finally the Turks brought up a low fellow who threw Greek fire at them three times in succession. Once Guillaume of Boon warded off a bucket-load of the stuff by catching it on his shield, for if the flames had caught any of his clothing he would certainly have been burnt alive.

We were all covered with the darts that failed to hit the sergeants. By some lucky chance I happened to find a Saracen's tunic, padded with tow. I turned the open side towards me and used the garment as a shield. It did me good service, for I was only wounded by the enemy's darts in five places, though my horse was wounded in fifteen. It also happened that a certain worthy fellow from Joinville brought me a pennon with my arms affixed to a lance head, and every time we saw the Turks pressing too hardly on the sergeants we charged them and sent them flying.

The good Comte de Soissons, hard put to it as we were at that moment, still made a joke of it and said to me gaily: 'Seneschal, let these dogs howl as they will. By God's bonnet'—that was his favourite oath—'we shall talk of this day yet, you and I, sitting at home with our ladies!'

That evening, as the sun was setting, the constable came up with a company of the king's unmounted crossbowmen, who drew up in rank in front of us. As soon as the Saracens saw them setting foot to the stirrup of their crossbows, they left us and fled. Then the constable said to me: 'Seneschal, that's a good thing done. Now go to the king and don't leave his side till he's back again in his pavilion.' Just as I reached the king, Jean de Valery came up to him and said: 'Your Majesty, the Lord of Châtillon asks you to give him command of the rear-guard.' The king consented very willingly, and then rode on. As we were going, I made him take off his helmet, and lent him my steel cap so that he might have some air.

After the king had crossed the river, Brother Henri de Ronnay, Provost of the Hospitallers, came up to him and kissed his mailed hand. The king asked him if he had any news of the Comte d'Artois, to which the provost replied that indeed he had news of him, for he was certain that his Majesty's brother was now in paradise. 'Ah, your Majesty,' added the provost, 'take comfort in the thought that no King of France has gained such honour as you have gained today. For, in order to fight your enemies, you swam across a river, to rout them utterly and drive them from the field. Besides this, you have captured their machines, and also their tents, in which you will be sleeping tonight.' 'May God be worshipped for all He has given me,' replied the king; and then big tears began to fall from his eyes.

When we reached the camp we found some of the unmounted Saracen troops pulling at the ropes of a tent they had just taken down, while some of our own troops were tugging away on the other side. The Master of the Temple and I charged in among them, so that the enemy fled and the tent remained in our hands.

In the course of that day's battle there had been many people, and of fine appearance too, who had come very shamefully flying over the little bridge you know of and had fled away so panic-stricken that all our attempts to make them stay with us had been in vain. I could tell you some of their names, but shall refrain from doing so, because they are now dead.

I shall not however fail to mention the name of Guy Mauvoisin, for he returned with honour from Mansourah. All the way the constable and I had followed up the river, he followed down. And just as the Turks had pressed hard on the Comte de Bretagne and his men, so they harassed Guy Mauvoisin and his; but Mauvoisin's men, as well as he, won great honour for their part in that day's fighting. Nor is it to be wondered at that they acquitted themselves so well, since—as I learnt from those who knew of the arrangement of his troops—his whole company, with very few exceptions, was composed of knights who were either members of his family or his own vassals.

After we had routed the Turks and driven them from their tents, and while our people had left their camp empty, the Bedouins rushed in to plunder it, for the Turks who had been quartered there were men of high rank and great possessions. The marauders left nothing at all behind them, but carried away everything the Turks had left. I did not, however, hear that the Bedouins, though they were subject to the Saracens, were any less well thought of for stealing and carrying off this booty—it being well known that the habit of these people is to regard the weaker side as their lawful prey.

As it is connected with my subject, I will now tell you what kind of people the Bedouins are. They do not follow Mahomet, but accept the teaching of Ali, who was Mahomet's uncle. (The Old Man of the Mountain, who maintains the Assassins, is of this persuasion too.) These people believe that when a man dies for his lord, or in any other good cause, his soul goes into another body, a better and a happier one than before. That is why the Assassins care little whether they are killed when carrying out their master's commands. However, I will say no more about the Old Man of the Mountain for the present, but speak only of the Bedouins.

These people do not live in villages, or cities, or castles, but sleep always out in the open fields. At night, or by day when the weather is bad, they house their servants, their wives, and their children in a sort of shelter they make with the hoops of barrels tied to poles, somewhat like ladies' litters. Over these hoops they throw sheepskins, cured with alum, which are known as Damascus hides.

The Bedouins themselves wear great hairy mantles that cover the whole of the body, including the legs and feet. When it rains in the evening, or the weather is bad by night, they wrap themselves up in these mantles, and taking the bits from their horses' mouths, leave them to browse on the grass near by. In the morning they spread out their mantles in the sun, then rub them and give them a new dressing of alum, after which there remains no trace of their ever having been wetted.

They believe that no one can die before the appointed day, and for this reason refuse to wear any sort of armour. Whenever they wish to curse their children they say to them: 'Be accursed like a Frank, who puts on armour for fear of death!' In battle they carry nothing but swords or spears.

Nearly all of them wear a long tunic like the surplice worn by priests. Their heads are all bound round with cloths that go underneath the chin, so that, what with these and the jet-black colour of their hair and their beards, they are an ugly people, and frightful to look at.

They live on the milk from their beasts, paying rent to the wealthy men who own the plains for the pasturage on which these animals subsist. No man can tell the number of these people; for they are to be found in the kingdom of Egypt, the kingdom of Jerusalem, and in all the other lands belonging to the Saracens and other heathen peoples, to whom they pay a large sum of money in tribute every year.

In our own country, since I returned from the land oversea, I have come across certain disloyal Christians who follow the Bedouin faith in holding that no man can die except on the appointed day. This belief is in effect a denial of our religion, since it amounts to saying that God has no power to help us. For those of us who serve God would indeed be fools if we did not think He has power to prolong our lives, and to preserve us from evil and misfortune. Most certainly we ought to put our faith in Him, seeing that He has power to do all things.

JOHN SHIPP
A Soldier's Life

John Shipp was born in 1782 in England. Below he describes how he was dressed for parade on joining the 22nd Regiment of Foot in 1797.

I WENT INTO TOWN TO PURCHASE a few requisites, such as a powder-bag, puff, soap, candles, grease, & c.; and, having procured what I stood in need of, I returned to my barrack, where I underwent the operation of having my hair tied for the first time, to the no small amusement of all the boys assembled. A large piece of candle-grease was applied, first, to the sides of my head, then to the hind long hair; after this, the same kind of operation was performed with nasty stinking soap—sometimes the man who was dressing me applied his knuckles, instead of the soap, to the delight of the surrounding boys, who were bursting their sides with laughter, to see the tears roll down my cheeks. When this operation was over, I had to go through one of a more serious nature. A large pad, a bag filled with sand, was poked into the back of my head, round which the hair was gathered tight, and the whole tied round with a leather thong. When I was dressed for parade, I could scarcely get my eyelids to perform their office, the skin of my eyes and face was drawn so tight by the plug that was stuck in the back of my head, that I could not possibly shut my eyes; add to this, an enormous high stock was poked under my chin; so that, altogether, I felt as stiff as if I had swallowed a ramrod, or a sergeant's halberd. Shortly after I was thus equipped, dinner was served; but my poor jaws refused to act on the offensive, and when I made an attempt to eat, my pad behind went up and down like a sledgehammer.

GEORGE SMALLEY
Antietam

The battle at Antietam, 17 September 1862, was the bloodiest single-day engagement of the American Civil War, costing 12,500 Union killed and wounded and 13,000 Confederate. George Smalley wrote this historic dispatch from the battlefield for the New York Daily Tribune.

FIERCE AND DESPERATE BATTLE BETWEEN 200,000 men has raged since daylight, yet night closes on an uncertain field. It is the greatest battle since Waterloo—all over the field contested with an obstinacy equal even to Waterloo. If not wholly a victory to-night, I believe it is the prelude to victory tomorrow. But what can be foretold of the future of a fight in which from 5 in the morning till 7 at night the best troops of the continent have fought without decisive result?

I have no time for speculation—no time even to gather detail of the battle—only time to state its broadest features—then mount and spur for New York.

After the brilliant victory near Middletown, Gen. McClellan pushed forward his army rapidly, and reached Keedysville with three corps on Monday night. That march has already been described. On the day following the two armies faced each other idly, until night. Artillery was busy at intervals; once in the morning with spirit, and continuing for half an hour, with vigor, till the Rebel battery, as usual, was silenced.

McClellan was on the hill where Benjamin's battery was stationed and found himself suddenly under rather heavy fire. It was still uncertain whether the Rebels were retreating or re-enforcing—their batteries would remain in position in either case, and as they had withdrawn nearly all their troops from view, there was only the doubtful indications of columns of dust to the rear.

On the evening of Tuesday, Hooker was ordered to cross Antietam Creek with his corps, and feeling the left of the enemy, to be ready to attack next morning. During the day of apparent inactivity, McClellan had been maturing his plan of battle, of which Hooker's movement was one development.

The position on either side was peculiar. When Richardson advanced on Monday he found the enemy deployed and displayed in force on a crescent-shaped ridge, the outline of which followed more or less exactly the course of Antietam Creek. Their lines were then forming, and the revelation of force in front of the ground which they really intended to hold, was probably meant to delay our attack until their arrangements to receive it were complete.

During that day they kept their troops exposed and did not move them even to avoid the artillery fire, which must have been occasionally annoying. Next morning the lines and columns which had darkened cornfields and hill crests, had been withdrawn. Broken and wooded ground behind the sheltering hills concealed the Rebel masses. What from our front looked like only a narrow summit fringed with woods was a broad table-land of forest and ravine cover for troops everywhere, nowhere easy access for an enemy. The smoothly sloping surface in front and the sweeping crescent of slowly mingling lines was only a delusion. It was all a Rebel stronghold beyond.

Under the base of those hills runs the deep stream called Antietam Creek, fordable only at distant points. Three bridges cross it, one on the Hagerstown road, one on the Sharpsburg pike, one to the left in a deep recess of steeply falling hills. Hooker passed the first to reach the ford by which he crossed, and it was held by Pleasanton with a reserve of cavalry during the battle. The second was close under the Rebel center, and no way important to yesterday's fight. At the third, Burnside attacked and finally crossed. Between the first and third lay most of the battle lines. They stretched four miles from right to left.

Unaided attack in front was impossible. McClellan's forces lay behind low, disconnected ridges, in front of the Rebel summits, all or nearly all unwooded. They gave some cover for artillery, and guns were therefore massed on the center. The enemy had the Shepherdstown road and the Hagerstown and Williamsport road open to him in the rear for retreat. Along one or the other, if beaten, he must fly. This, among other reasons, determined, perhaps, the plan of battle which McClellan finally resolved on.

The plan was generally as follows: Hooker was to cross on the right, establish himself on the enemy's left if possible, flanking his position, and to open the fight. Sumner, Franklin and Mansfield were to send their forces also to the right, co-operating with and sustaining Hooker's attack while advancing also nearer the center. The heavy work in the center was left mostly to the batteries, Porter massing his infantry supports in the hollows. On the left Burnside was to carry the bridge already referred, advancing then by a road which enters the pike at Sharpsburg, turning at once the Rebel left flank and destroying his line of retreat. Porter and Sykes were held in reserve. It is obvious that the complete success of a plan contemplating widely divergent movements of separate corps, must largely depend on accurate timing, that the attacks should be simultaneous and not successive.

Hooker moved on Tuesday afternoon at four, crossing the creek at a ford above the bridge and well to the right, without opposition. Fronting south-west his line advanced not quite on the Rebel flank but over-lapping and threatening it. Turning off from the road after passing the stream, he sent forward cavalry skirmishers straight into the woods and over the fields beyond. Rebel pickets withdrew slowly before them, firing scattering and harmless shots. Turning again to the left, the cavalry went down on the Rebel flank, coming suddenly close to a battery which met them with unexpected grape shot. It being the nature of cavalry to retire before batteries, this company loyally followed the law of its being, and came swiftly back without pursuit.

Artillery was sent to the front, infantry was rapidly deployed, and skirmishers went out in front and on either flank. The corps moved forward compactly, Hooker as usual reconnoitering in person. They came at last to an open grass-sown field inclosed on two sides with woods, protected on the right by a hill, and entered through a corn field in the rear. Skirmishers entering these woods were instantly met by Rebel shots, but held their ground, and as soon as supported advanced and cleared the timber. Beyond, on the left and in front, volleys of musketry opened heavily, and a battle seemed to have begun a little sooner than it was expected.

General Hooker formed his lines with precision and without hesitation. Rickett's Division went into the woods on the left in force. Meade, with the Pennsylvania Reserves, formed in the center. Doubleday was sent out on the right, planting his batteries on the hill, and opening at once on a Rebel battery that began to enfilade the central line. It was already dark, and the Rebel position could only be discovered by the flashes of their guns. They pushed forward boldly on the right, after losing ground on the other flank, but made no attempt to regain their first hold on the woods. The fight flashed; and glimmered, and faded, and finally went out in the dark.

Hooker had found out what he wanted to know. When the firing ceased the hostile lines lay close to each other—their pickets so near that six Rebels were captured during the night. It was inevitable that the fight should commence at daylight. Neither side had suffered considerable loss; it was a skirmish, not a battle. 'We are through for to-night, gentlemen,' remarked the General, 'but to-morrow we fight the battle that will decide the fate of the Republic.'

Not long after the firing ceased, it sprang up again on the left. General Hooker, who had taken up his headquarters in a barn, which had been nearly the focus of the Rebel artillery, was out at once. First came rapid and unusually frequent picket shots, then several heavy volleys. The General listened a moment and smiled grimly. 'We have no troops there. The Rebels are shooting each other. It is Fair Oaks over again.' So everybody lay down again, but all the night through there were frequent alarms.

McClellan had been informed of the night's work, and of the certainties awaiting the dawn. Sumner was ordered to move his corps at once, and was expected to be on the ground at daylight. From the extent of the Rebel lines developed in the evening, it was plain that they had gathered their whole army behind the heights and were waiting for the shock.

The battle began with the dawn. Morning found both armies just as they had slept, almost close enough to look into each others eyes. The left of Meade's reserves and the right of Rickett's line became engaged at nearly the same moment, one with artillery, the other with infantry. A battery was almost immediately pushed forward beyond the central woods, over a plowed field, near the top of the slope where the corn-field began. On this open field, in the corn beyond, and in the woods which stretched forward into the broad-fields, like a promontory into the ocean, were the hardest and deadliest struggles of the day.

For half an hour after the battle had grown to its full strength, the line of fire swayed neither way. Hooker's men were fully upto their work. They saw their General everywhere in front, never away from the fire, and all the troops believed in their commander, and fought with a will. Two-thirds of them were the same men who under McDowall had broken at Manassas.

The half hour passed, the Rebels began to give way a little, only a little, but at the first indication of a receding fire, Forward, was the word, and on went the line with a cheer and a rush. Back across the corn-field, leaving dead and wounded behind them, over the fence, and across the road, and then back again into the dark woods which closed around them, went the retreating Rebels.

Meade and his Pennsylvanians followed hard and fast—followed till they came within easy range of the woods, among which they saw their beaten enemy disappearing—followed still, with another cheer, and flung themselves against the cover.

But out of those gloomy woods came suddenly and heavily terrible volleys – volleys which smote, and bent, and broke in a moment that eager front, and hurled them swiftly back for half the distance they had won. Not swiftly, nor in panic, any further. Closing up their shattered lines, they came slowly away – a regiment where a brigade had been, hardly a brigade where a whole division had been victorious. They had met from the woods the first volleys of musketry from fresh troops—had met them and returned them till their line had yielded and gone down before the might of fire, and till their ammunition was exhausted.

In ten minutes the fortune of the day seemed to have changed—it was the Rebels now who were advancing, pouring out of the woods in endless lines, sweeping through the corn-field from which their comrades had just fled. Hooker sent in his nearest brigade to meet them, but it could not do the work. He called for another. There was nothing close enough unless he took it from his right. His right might be in danger if it was weakened, but his center was already threatened with annihilation. Not hesitating one moment, he sent to Doubleday: 'Give me your best brigade instantly.'

The best brigade came down the hill on the run, went through the timber in front through a storm of shot and bursting shell and crashing limbs, over the open field beyond, and straight into the corn-field, passing as they went the fragments of three brigades shattered by the Rebel fire, and streaming to the rear. They passed by Hooker, whose eyes lighted as he saw these veteran troops led by a soldier whom he knew he could trust. 'I think they will hold it,' he said.

General Hartstuff took his troops very steadily, but now they they were under fire, not hurriedly, up the hill from which the corn-field begins to descend, and formed them on the crest. Not a man who was not in full view—not one who bent before the storm. Firing at first in volleys, they fired them at will with wonderful rapidity and effect. The whole line crowned the hill and stood out darkly against the sky, but lighted and shrouded ever in flame and smoke. There were the 12th and 18th Massachusetts and another regiment which I cannot remember—old troops all of them.

There for half an hour they held the ridge unyielding in purpose, exhaustless in courage. There were gaps in the line, but it nowhere quailed. Their General was wounded badly early in the fight, but they fought on. Their supports did not come—they were determined to win without them. They began to go down the hill and into the corn, they did not stop to think their ammunition was nearly gone; they were there to win the field and they won it. The Rebel line for the second time fled though the corn into the woods. I cannot tell how few of Hartsuff's brigade were left when the work was done, but it was done. There was no more gallant, determined heroic fighting in all this desperate day. General Hartsuff is very severely wounded, but I do not believe he counts his success too dearly purchased.

The crisis of the fight at this point had arrived: Rickett's division, vainly endeavoring to advance and exhausted by the effort had fallen back. Part of Mansfield's corps was ordered in to their relief but Mansfield's troops came back again, and their General was mortally wounded. The left nevertheless was too extended to be turned, and too strong to be broken. Rickett sent word he could not advance, but could hold his ground. Doubleday had kept his guns at work on the right, and had finally silenced a Rebel battery that for half an hour had poured in a galling enfilading fire along Hooker's central line.

There were woods in front of Doubleday's hill which the Rebels held, but so long as those guns pointed that way they did not care to attack. With his left then able to take care of itself, with his right impregnable with two brigades of Mansfield still fresh and coming rapidly up, and with his center a second time victorious, Gen. Hooker determined to advance. Orders were given to Crawford and Gordon—the two Mansfield brigades—to move directly forward at once, the batteries in the center were ordered on, the whole line was called on, and the General himself went forward.

To the right of the corn-field and beyond it was a point of woods. Once carried and firmly held, it was the key of the position. Hooker determined to take it. He rode out in front of his furthest troops on a hill to examine the ground for a battery. At the top he dismounted and went forward on foot, completed his reconnaissance, returned and remounted. The musketry fire from the point of woods was all the while extremely hot. As he put his foot in the stirrup a fresh volley of rifle bullets came whizzing by. The tall soldierly figure of the General, the white horse which he rode, the elevated place where he was—all made him a most dangerously conspicuous mark. So he had been all day, riding often without a staff officer or an orderly near him—all sent off on urgent duty—visible everywhere on the field. The Rebel bullets had followed him all day, but they had not hit him, and he would not regard them. Remounting on this hill he had not ridden five steps when he was struck in the foot by a ball.

Three men were shot down at the same moment by his side. The air was alive with bullets. He kept on his horse for a few moments, though the wound was severe and excessively painful, and he would not dismount till he had given his last order to advance. He was himself in the very front. Swaying unsteadily on his horse, he turned in his seat to look about him. 'There is a regiment to the right. Order it forward! Crawford and Gordon are coming up. Tell them to carry these woods and hold them—and it is our fight!'

It was found that the bullet had passed completely through his foot. The surgeon who examined it on the spot could give no opinion whether bones were broken, but it was afterward ascertained that though grazed they were not fractured. Of course the severity of the wound made it impossible for him to keep the field which he believed already won, so far as it belonged to him to win it. It was nine o'clock. The fight had been furious since five. A large part of his command was broken, but with his right still untouched and with Crawford's and Gordon's brigades just up, above all, with the advance of the whole central line which the men had heard ordered, with a regiment already on the edge of the woods he wanted, he might well leave the field, thinking the battle won—that *his* battle was won, for I am writing, of course, only about the attack on the Rebel left.

I see no reason why I should disguise my admiration of Gen. Hooker's bravery and soldierly ability. Remaining nearly all the morning on the right, I could not help seeing the sagacity and promptness of his maneuvers, how completely his troops were kept in hand, how devotedly they trusted to him, how keen was his insight into the battle; how every opportunity was seized and every reverse was checked and turned into another success. I say this the more unreservedly, because I have no personal relation whatever with him, never saw him till the day before the fight, and don't like his politics or opinions in general. But what are politics in such a battle?

Sumner arrived just as Hooker was leaving, and assumed command. Crawford and Gordon had gone into the woods, and were holding them stoutly against heavy odds. As I rode over toward the left I met Sumner at the head of his column advancing rapidly through the timber, opposite the point where Crawford was fighting. The veteran General was riding alone in the forest far ahead of his leading brigade, his hat off, his gray hair and beard contrasting strangely with the fire in his eyes and his martial air, as he hurried on to where the bullets were thickest.

Sedgwick's division was in advance, moving forward to support Crawford and Gordon. Rebel re-enforcements were approaching also, and the struggle for the roads was again to be renewed. Sumner sent forward two divisions, Richardson and French, on the left. Sedgwick moving in column of divisions through the woods in the rear, deployed and advanced in line over the corn-field. There was a broad interval between him and the nearest division, and he saw that if the Rebel line was complete his own division was in immediate danger of being flanked. But his orders were to advance, and those are the orders which a soldier—and Sedgwick is every inch a soldier—loves best to hear. To extend his own front as far as possible, he ordered the 34th New York to move by the left flank. The maneuver was attempted under a fire of the greatest intensity, and the regiment broke. At the same moment the enemy, perceiving their advantage, came round on that flank. Crawford was obliged to give on the right, and his troops pouring in confusion through the ranks of Sedgwick's advance brigade, threw it into disorder and back on the second and third lines. The enemy advanced, their fire increasing.

General Sedgwick was three times wounded, in the shoulder, leg and wrist, but he persisted in remaining on the field so long as there was a chance of saving it. His Adjutant-General, Major Sedgwick, bravely rallying and trying to reform the troops, was shot through the body, the bullet lodging in the spine, and fell from his horse. Severe as the wound is it is probably not mortal. Lieutenant Howe of Gen. Sedgwick's staff endeavoured vainly to rally the 34th New York. They were badly cut up and would not stand. Half their officers were killed or wounded, their colours shot to pieces, the Colour-Sergeant killed, everyone of the colour-guard wounded. Only thirty-two were afterward got together.

The 15th Massachusetts went into action with 17 officers and nearly 600 men. Nine officers were killed or wounded, and some of the latter are prisoners. Captain Simons, Capt. Saunders of the Sharpshooters, Lieut. Derby and Lieut. Berry are killed. Captain Bartlett and Capt. Jocelyn, Lieut. Sourr, Lieut. Gale and Lieut. Bradley are wounded. One hundred and thirty four men were the only remnant that could be collected of this splendid regiment.

General Dans was wounded. General Howard, who took command of the division after Gen. Sedgwick was disabled, exerted himself to restore order, but it could not be done there. General Sumner ordered the line to be reformed under fire. The test was too severe for volunteer troops under such fire. Sumner himself attempted to arrest the disorder, but to little purpose. Lieutenant-Colonel Revere and Capt. Andenried of his staff were wounded severely, but not dangerously. It was impossible to hold the position. General Sumner withdrew the division to the rear, and once more the corn-field was abandoned to the enemy.

French sent word he would hold his ground. Richardson, while gallantly leading a regiment under heavy fire, was severely wounded in the shoulder. General Meagher was wounded at the head of his brigade. The loss in general officers was becoming frightful.

At 1 o'clock affairs on the right had a gloomy look. Hooker's troop were greatly exhausted, and their General away from the field. Mansfield's were no better. Sumner's command had lost heavily, but two of his divisions were still comparatively fresh. Artillery was yet playing vigorously in front, though the ammunition of many of the batteries was entirely exhausted, and they had been compelled to retire.

Doubleday held the right inflexibly. Sumner's headquarters were now in the narrow field where the night before, Hooker had begun the fight. All that had been gained in front had been lost! The enemy's batteries, which if advanced and served vigorously might have made sad work with the closely massed troops were fortunately either partially disabled or short of ammunition. Sumner was confident that he could hold his own; but another advance was out of the question. The enemy on the other hand, seemed to be too much exhausted to attack.

At this crisis Franklin came up with fresh troops and formed on the left. Slocum, commanding one division of the corps, was sent forward along the slopes lying under the first range of rebel hills, while Smith, commanding the other division, was ordered to retake the corn-fields and woods which all day had been so hotly contested. It was done in the handsomest style. His Maine and Vermont regiments and the rest went forward on the run, and cheering as they went, swept like an avalanche through the corn-fields, fell upon the woods, cleared them in ten minutes, and held them. They were not again retaken.

The field and its ghastly harvest which the reaper had gathered in those fatal hours remained finally with us. Four times it had been lost and won. The dead are strewn so thickly that as you ride over it you cannot guide your horse's steps too carefully. Pale and bloody faces are everywhere upturned. They are sad and terrible, but there is nothing which makes one's heart beat so quickly as the imploring look of sorely wounded men who beckon wearily for help which you cannot stay to give.

General Smith's attack was so sudden that his success was accomplished with no great loss. He had gained a point, however, which compelled him to expect every moment an attack, and to hold which, if the enemy again brought up reserves, would take his best energies and best troops. But the long strife, the heavy losses, incessant fighting over the same ground repeatedly lost and won inch by inch, and more than all, perhaps, the fear of Burnside on the left and Porter in front, held the enemy in check. For two or three hours there was a lull even in the cannonade on the right which hitherto had been incessant. McClellan had been over on the field after Sumner's repulse, but had speedily returned to his headquarters. Sumner again sent word that he was able to hold his position, but could not advance with his own corps.

Meanwhile where was Burnside, and what was he doing? On the right where I had spent the day until two o'clock, little was known of the general fortunes of the field. We had heard Porter's guns in the center, but nothing from Burnside on the left. The distance was too great to distinguish the sound of his artillery from Porter's left. There was no immediate prospect of more fighting on the right, and I left the field which all day long had seen the most obstinate contest of the war, and rode over to McClellan's headquarters. The different battle-fields were shut out from each other's view, but all partially visible from the central hill which General McClellan had occupied during the day. But I was more than ever impressed on returning with the completely deceitful appearance of the ground the Rebels had chosen when viewed from the front.

Hooker's and Sumner's struggle had been carried on over an uneven and wooded surface, their own line of battle extending in a semi-circle not less than a mile and a half. Perhaps a better notion of their position can be got by considering their right, center and left as forming three sides of a square. So long therefore as either wing was driven back, the center became exposed to a dangerous enfilading fire, and the further the center was advanced the worse off it was, unless the lines on its side and rear were firmly held. This formation resulted originally from the efforts of the enemy to turn both flanks. Hooker at the very outset, threw his column so far into the center of the Rebel lines that they were compelled to threaten him on the flank to secure their own center.

Nothing of all this was perceptible from the hills in front. Some directions of the Rebel lines had been disclosed by the smoke of their guns, but the whole interior formation of the country beyond the hills was completely concealed. When McClellan arranged his order of battle, it must have been upon information, or have been left to his corps and division commander to discover for themselves.

Up to 3 o'clock Burnside had made little progress. His attack on the bridge had been successful, but the delay had been so great that to the observer it appeared as if McClellan's plans must have been seriously disarranged. It is impossible not to suppose that the attacks on the right and left were meant in a measure to correspond, for otherwise the enemy had only to repel Hooker on the one hand, then transfer his troops, and hurl them against Burnside.

Finally, at 4 o'clock, McClellan sent simultaneous orders to Burnside and Franklin; to the former to carry the batteries in his front at all hazards and at any cost; to the latter to carry the woods next in front of him to the right, which the rebels still held. The order to Franklin, however, was practically countermanded in consequence of a message from Gen. Sumner that if Franklin went on and was repulsed, his own corps was not yet sufficiently reorganised to be depended on as a reserve.

Franklin, thereon, was directed to run no risk of losing his present position, and, instead of sending his infantry into the woods, contented himself with advancing his batteries over the breadth of the fields in front, supporting them with heavy columns of infantry, and attacking with energy the Rebel batteries immediately opposed to him. His movement was a success so far as it went, the batteries maintaining their new ground and sensibly affecting the steadiness of the Rebel fire. That being accomplished, and all hazard of the right being again forced back having been dispelled, the movement of Burnside became at once the turning point of success and the fate of the day depended on him.

How extraordinary the situation was may be judged from a moment's consideration of the facts. It is understood that from the outset Burnside's attack was expected to be decisive; it certainly must have been if things went well elsewhere, and if he succeeded in establishing himself on the Sharpsburg road in the Rebel rear.

Yet Hooker, and Sumner, and Franklin, and Mansfield were all sent to the right three miles away while Porter seems to have done double duty with his single corps in front, both supporting the batteries and holding himself in reserve. With all this immense force on the right, but 16,000 then were given to Burnside for the decisive movement of the day.

Still more unfortunate in its results was the total failure of these separate attacks on the right and left to sustain, or in any manner co-operate with each other. Burnside hesitated for hours in front of the bridge which should have been carried at once by a *coup de main.* Meantime, Hooker had been fighting for four hours with various fortune, but final success. Sumner had come up too late to join in the decisive attack which his earlier arrival would probably have converted into a complete success; and Franklin reached the scene only when Sumner had been repulsed. Probably before his arrival the Rebels had transferred a considerable number of troops to their right to meet the attack of Burnside, the direction of which was then suspected or developed.

Attacking first with one regiment, then with two, and delaying both for artillery, Burnside was not over the bridge before 2 o'clock—perhaps not till 3. He advanced slowly up the slope in his front, his batteries in rear covering, to some extent, the movements of the infantry. A desperate fight was going on in a deep ravine on his right, the Rebel batteries were in full play and, apparently, very annoying and destructive, while heavy columns of Rebel troops were plainly visible, advancing as if careless of concealment, along the road and over the hills in the direction of Burnside's forces. It was at this point of time that McClellan sent him the order above given.

Burnside obeyed it most gallantly. Getting his troops well in hand, and sending a portion of his artillery to the front, he advanced them with rapidity and the most determined vigor, straight up the hill in front, on top of which the Rebels had maintained their most dangerous battery. The movement was in plain view of McClellan's position, and as Franklin, on the other side sent his batteries into the field about the same time, the battle seemed to open in all directions with greater severity than ever.

The fight in the ravine was in full progress, the batteries which Porter supported were firing with new vigor. Franklin was blaring away on the right, and every hill-top ridge and woods along the whole line was crested and vailed with clouds of smoke. All day had been clear and bright since the early cloudy morning, and now this whole magnificent, unequalled scene shone with the splendor of an afternoon September sun. Four miles of battle, its glory all visible, its horrors all vailed, the fate of the Republic hanging on the hour – could anyone be insensible of its grandeur.

There are two hills on the left of the road, the furthest the lowest. The Rebels have batteries on both. Burnside is ordered to carry the nearest to him, which is the furthest from the road. His guns opening first from this new position in front, soon entirely controlled and silenced the enemy's artillery. The infantry came on at once, moving rapidly and steadily up long dark lines, and broad, dark masses, being plainly visible without a glass as they moved over the green hill-side.

The next moment the road in which the Rebel battery was planted was canopied with clouds of dust swiftly descending into the valley. Underneath was a tumult of wagons, guns, horses, and men flying at speed down the road. Blue flashes of smoke burst now and then among them, a horse or a man or half a dozen went down, and then the whirlwind swept on.

The hill was carried, but could it be held? The Rebel columns, before seen moving to the left, increased their pace. The guns, on the hill above, sent an angry tempest of shell down among Burnside's guns and men. He had formed his columns apparently in the near angles of two fields bordering the road—high ground about them everywhere except in the rear.

In another moment a Rebel battle-line appears on the brow of the ridge above them, moves swiftly down in the most perfect order, and though met by incessant discharge of musketry, of which we plainly see the flashes, does not fire a gun. White spaces show where men are falling, but they close up instantly, and still the line advances. The brigades of Burnside are in heavy column; they will not give way before a bayonet charge in line. The rebels think twice before they dash into those hostile masses.

There is a halt, the Rebel left gives way and scatters over the field, the rest stand fast and fire. More infantry comes up, Burnside is outnumbered; flanked, compelled to yield the hill he took so bravely. His position is no longer one of attack; he defends himself with unfaltering firmness, but he sends to McClellan for help. McClellan's glass for the last hour has seldom been turned away from the left.

He sees clearly enough that Burnside is pressed—he needs no messengers to tell him that. His face grows darker with anxious thought. Looking down into the valley where 15,000 troops are lying, he turns a half-questioning eye on Fitz John Porter, who stands by his side, gravely scanning the field. They are Porter's troops below, are fresh and only impatient to share in this fight. But Porter slowly shakes his head, and one may believe that the same thought is passing through the minds of both generals: 'They are the only reserves of the army; they cannot be spared.'

McClellan remounts his horse, and with Porter and a dozen officers of his staff rides away to the left in Burnside's direction. Sykes meets them on the road—a good soldier, whose opinion is worth taking. The three Generals talk briefly together. It is easy to see that the moment has come when everything may turn on one order given or withheld, when the history of the battle is only to be written in thoughts and purposes and words of the General.

Burnside's messenger rides up. His message is 'I want troops and guns. If you do not send them I cannot hold my position for half an hour.' McClellan's only answer for the moment is a glance at the western sky. Then he turns and speaks very slowly, 'Tell Gen. Burnside that this is the battle of the war. He must hold his ground till dark at any cost. I will send him Miller's battery. I can do nothing more. I have no infantry.' Then as the messenger was riding away he called him back. 'Tell him if he *cannot* hold his ground, then the bridge, to the last man!—always the bridge! If the bridge is lost, all is lost.'

The sun is already down; not half an hour of daylight is left. Till Burnside's message came, it had seemed plain to everyone that the battle could not be finished today. None suspected how near was the peril of defeat; of sudden attack on exhausted forces—how vital to the safety of the army and the nation were those fifteen thousand waiting troops of Fitz John Porter in the hollow. But the Rebels halted instead of pushing on, their vindictive cannonade died away as the light faded. Before it was quite dark, the battle was over. Only a solitary gun of Burnside's thundered against the enemy, and presently this also ceased, and the field was still.

The peril came very near, but it has passed, and in spite of the peril, at the close the day was partly a success—not a victory, but an advantage had been gained. Hooker, Sumner, and Franklin held all the ground they had gained, and Burnside still held the bridge and his position beyond. Everything was favourable for a renewal of the fight in the morning. If the plan of the battle is sound, there is every reason why McClellan should win it. He may choose to postpone the battle to await his reinforcements.

The Rebels may choose to retire while it is still possible. Fatigue on both sides might delay the deciding battle, yet, if the enemy means to fight at all, he cannot afford to delay. His re-enforcements may be coming, his losses are enormous. His troops have been massed in woods and hollows, where artillery has its most terrific effect. Ours have been deployed and scattered. From infantry fire there is less difference.

It is hard to estimate losses on a field of such extent, but I think ours cannot be less than six thousand killed and wounded—it may be much greater. Prisoners have been taken from the enemy—I hear of a regiment captured entire, but I doubt it. All the prisoners whom I saw agree in saying that their whole army is there.

DEE BROWN
Little Bighorn

An account of Custer's defeat at the battle of Little Bighorn in 1876 from the American Indian perspective.

AFTER THE FIGHT ON THE Rosebud, the chiefs decided to move west to the valley of the Greasy Grass (Little Bighorn). Scouts had come in with reports of great herds of antelope west of there, and they said grass for the horses was plentiful on the nearby benchlands. Soon the camp circles were spread along the west bank of the twisting Greasy Grass for almost three miles. No one knew for certain how many Indians were there, but the number could not have been smaller than ten thousand people, including three or four thousand warriors. 'It was a very big village and you could hardly count the tepees,' Black Elk said.

Farthest upstream toward the south was the Hunkpapa camp, with the Blackfoot Sioux nearby. The Hunkpapas always camped at the entrance, or at the head end of the circle, which was the meaning of their name. Below them were the Sans Arcs, Minneconjous, Oglalas, and Brulés. At the north end were the Cheyennes.

The time was early in the Moon When the Chokecherries Are Ripe, with days hot enough for boys to swim in the melted snow water of the Greasy Grass. Hunting parties were coming and going in the direction of the Bighorns, where they had found a few buffalo as well as antelope. The women were digging wild turnips out on the prairies. Every night one or more of the tribal circles held dances, and some nights the chiefs met in councils. 'The chiefs of the different tribes met together as equals,' Wooden Leg said. 'There was only one who was considered as being above all the others. This was Sitting Bull. He was recognized as the one old man chief of all the camps combined.'

Sitting Bull did not believe the victory on the Rosebud had fulfilled his prophecy of soldiers falling into the Indian camp. Since the retreat of Three Stars, however, no hunting parties had sighted any Bluecoats between the Powder and the Bighorn.

They did not know until the morning of June 24 that Long Hair Custer was prowling along the Rosebud. Next morning scouts reported that the soldiers had crossed the last high ridge between the Rosebud and the Indian camp and were marching toward the Little Bighorn.

The news of Custer's approach came to the Indians in various ways:

'I and four women were a short distance from the camp digging wild turnips,' said Red Horse, one of the Sioux council chiefs. 'Suddenly one of the women attracted my attention to a cloud of dust rising a short distance from camp. I soon saw that the soldiers were charging the camp. To the camp I and the women ran. When I arrived a person told me to hurry to the council lodge. The soldiers charged so quickly that we could not talk. We came out of the council lodge and talked in all directions. The Sioux mount horses, take guns, and go fight the soldiers. Women and children mount horses and go, meaning to get out of the way.'

Pte-San-Waste-Win, a cousin of Sitting Bull, was one of the young women digging turnips that morning. She said the soldiers were six to eight miles distant when first sighted. 'We could see the flashing of their sabers and saw that there were very many soldiers in the party.' The soldiers first seen by Pte-San-Waste-Win and other Indians in the middle of the camp were those in Custer's battalion. These Indians were not aware of Major Marcus Reno's surprise attack against the south end of camp until they heard rifle fire from the direction of the Blackfoot Sioux lodges. 'Like that the soldiers were upon us. Through the tepee poles their bullets rattled. . . . The women and children cried, fearing they would be killed, but the men, the Hunkpapa and Blackfeet, the Oglala and Minneconjou, mounted their horses and raced to the Blackfoot tepees. We could still see the soldiers of Long Hair marching along in the distance, and our men, taken by surprise, and from a point whence they had not expected to be attacked, went singing the song of battle into the fight behind the Blackfoot village.'

Black Elk, a thirteen-year-old Oglala boy, was swimming with his companions in the Little Bighorn. The sun was straight above and was getting very hot when he heard a crier shouting in the Hunkpapa camp: 'The chargers are coming! They are charging! The chargers are coming!' The warning was repeated by an Oglala crier, and Black Elk could hear the cry going from camp to camp northward to the Cheyennes.

Low Dog, an Oglala chief, heard this same warning cry. 'I did not believe it. I thought it was a false alarm. I did not think it possible that any white man would attack us, so strong as we were. . . . Although I did not believe it was a true alarm, I lost no time getting ready. When I got my gun and came out of my lodge the attack had begun at the end of the camp where Sitting Bull and the Hunkpapas were.'

Iron Thunder was in the Minneconjou camp. 'I did not know anything about Reno's attack until his men were so close that the bullets went through the camp, and everything was in confusion. The horses were so frightened we could not catch them.'

Crow King, who was in the Hunkpapa camp, said that Reno's pony soldiers commenced firing at about four hundred yards' distance. The Hunkpapas and Blackfoot Sioux retreated slowly on foot to give the women and children time to go to a place of safety. 'Other Indians got our horses. By that time we had warriors enough to turn upon the whites.'

Near the Cheyenne camp, three miles to the north, Two Moon was watering his horses. 'I washed them off with cool water, then took a swim myself. I came back to the camp afoot. When I got near my lodge, I looked up the Little Bighorn toward Sitting Bull's camp. I saw a great dust rising. It looked like a whirlwind. Soon a Sioux horseman came rushing into camp shouting: "Soldiers come! Plenty white soldiers!"'

Two Moon ordered the Cheyenne warriors to get their horses, and then told the women to take cover away from the tepee village. 'I rode swiftly toward Sitting Bull's camp. Then I saw the white soldiers fighting in a line [Reno's men]. Indians covered the flat. They began to drive the soldiers all mixed up—Sioux, then soldiers, then more Sioux, and all shooting. The air was full of smoke and dust. I saw the soldiers fall back and drop into the riverbed like buffalo fleeing.'

The war chief who rallied the Indians and turned back

Reno's attack was a muscular, full-chested, thirty-six-year-old Hunkpapa named Pizi, or Gall. Gall had grown up in the tribe as an orphan. While still a young man he distinguished himself as a hunter and warrior, and Sitting Bull adopted him as a younger brother. Some years before, while the commissioners were attempting to persuade the Sioux to take up farming as a part of the treaty of 1868, Gall went to Fort Rice to speak for the Hunkpapas. 'We were born naked,' he said, 'and have been taught to hunt and live on the game. You tell us that we must learn to farm, live in one house, and take on your ways. Suppose the people living beyond the great sea should come and tell you that you must stop farming and kill your cattle, and take your houses and lands, what would you do? Would you not fight them?' In the decade following that speech, nothing changed Gall's opinion of the white man's self-righteous arrogance, and by the summer of 1876 he was generally accepted by the Hunkpapas as Sitting Bull's lieutenant, the war chief of the tribe.

Reno's first onrush caught several women and children in the open, and the cavalry's flying bullets virtually wiped out Gall's family. 'It made my heart bad,' he told a newspaperman some years later. 'After that I killed all my enemies with the hatchet.' His description of the tactics used to block Reno was equally terse: 'Sitting Bull and I were at the point where Reno attacked. Sitting Bull was big medicine. The women and children were hastily moved downstream. . . . The women and children caught the horses for the bucks to mount them; the bucks mounted and charged back Reno and checked him, and drove him into the timber.'

In military terms, Gall turned Reno's flank and forced him into the woods. He then frightened Reno into making a hasty retreat which the Indians quickly turned into a rout. The result made it possible for Gall to divert hundreds of warriors for a frontal attack against Custer's column, while Crazy Horse and Two Moon struck the flank and rear.

Meanwhile Pte-San-Waste-Win and the other women had been anxiously watching the Long Hair's soldiers across the river. 'I could hear the music of the bugle and could see the column of soldiers turn to the left to march down to the river where the attack was to be made. . . . Soon I saw a number of Cheyennes ride into the river, then some young men of my band, then others, until there were hundreds of warriors in the river and running up into the ravine. When some hundreds had passed the river and gone into the ravine, the others who were left, still a very great number, moved back from the river and waited for the attack. And I knew that the fighting men of the Sioux, many hundreds in number, were hidden in the ravine behind the hill upon which Long Hair was marching, and he would be attacked from both sides.'

Kill Eagle, a Blackfoot Sioux chief, later said that the movement of Indians toward Custer's column was 'like a hurricane . . . like bees swarming out of a hive.' Hump, the Minneconjou comrade of Gall and Crazy Horse during the old Powder River days, said the first massive charge by the Indians caused the long-haired chief and his men to become confused. 'The first dash the Indians made my horse was shot from under me and I was wounded—shot above the knee, and the ball came out at the hip, and I fell and lay right there.' Crow King, who was with the Hunkpapas, said: 'The greater portion of our warriors came together in their front and we rushed our horses on them. At the same time warriors rode out on each side of them and circled around them until they were surrounded.' Thirteen-year-old Black Elk, watching from across the river, could see a big dust whirling on the hill, and then horses began coming out of it with empty saddles.

'The smoke of the shooting and the dust of the horses shut out the hill,' Pte-San-Waste-Win said, 'and the soldiers fired many shots, but the Sioux shot straight and the soldiers fell dead. The women crossed the river after the men of our village, and when we came to the hill there were no soldiers living and Long Hair lay dead among the rest. . . . The blood of the people was hot and their hearts bad, and they took no prisoners that day.'

Crow King said that all the soldiers dismounted when the Indians surrounded them. 'They tried to hold on to their horses, but as we pressed closer they let go their horses. We crowded them toward our main camp and killed them all. They kept in order and fought like brave warriors as long as they had a man left.'

According to Red Horse, toward the end of the fighting with Custer, 'these soldiers became foolish, many throwing away their guns and raising their hands, saying, "Sioux, pity us;

take us prisoners." The Sioux did not take a single soldier prisoner, but killed all of them; none were alive for even a few minutes.'

Long after the battle, White Bull of the Minneconjous drew four pictographs showing himself grappling with and killing a soldier identified as Custer. Among others who claimed to have killed Custer were Rain-in-the-Face, Flat Hip, and Brave Bear. Red Horse said that an unidentified Santee warrior killed Custer. Most Indians who told of the battle said they never saw Custer and did not know who killed him. 'We did not know till the fight was over that he was the white chief,' Low Dog said.

In an interview given in Canada a year after the battle, Sitting Bull said that he never saw Custer, but that other Indians had seen and recognized him just before he was killed. 'He did not wear his long hair as he used to wear it,' Sitting Bull said. 'It was short, but it was the color of the grass when the frost comes. . . . Where the last stand was made, the Long Hair stood like a sheaf of corn with all the ears fallen around him.' But Sitting Bull did not say who killed Custer.

An Arapaho warrior who was riding with the Cheyennes said that Custer was killed by several Indians. 'He was dressed in buckskin, coat and pants, and was on his hands and knees. He had been shot through the side, and there was blood coming from his mouth. He seemed to be watching the Indians moving around him. Four soldiers were sitting up around him, but they were all badly wounded. All the other soldiers were down. Then the Indians closed in around him, and I did not see any more.'

Regardless of who had killed him, the Long Hair who made the Thieves' Road into the Black Hills was dead with all his men. Reno's soldiers, however, reinforced by those of Major Frederick Benteen, were dug in on a hill farther down the river. The Indians surrounded the hill completely and watched the soldiers through the night, and next morning started fighting them again. During the day, scouts sent out by the chiefs came back with warnings of many more soldiers marching in the direction of the Little Bighorn.

After a council it was decided to break camp. The warriors had expended most of their ammunition, and they knew it would be foolish to try to fight so many soldiers with bows and arrows. The women were told to begin packing, and before sunset they started up the valley toward the Bighorn Mountains, the tribes separating along the way and taking different directions.

RUDYARD KIPLING
Skirmish at Kari Siding

The skirmish at Kari Siding took place during the Boer War, and was part of Lord Roberts' mopping-up operation before advancing on Kruger's base in the Transvaal. At the time of the incident Kipling was working on the Friend, *a newspaper for British soldiers.*

SO THERE HAD TO BE a battle, which was called the Battle of Kari Siding. All the staff of the Bloemfontein *Friend* attended. I was put in a Cape cart, with native driver, containing most of the drinks, and with me was a well-known war-correspondent. The enormous pale landscape swallowed up seven thousand troops without a sign, along a front of seven miles. On our way we passed a collection of neat, deep and empty trenches well undercut for shelter on the shrapnel side. A young Guards officer, recently promoted to *Brevet-Major*—and rather sore with the paper that we had printed it *Branch*—studied them interestedly. They were the first dim lines of the dug-out, but his and our eyes were held. The Hun had designed them *secundum artem*, but the Boer had preferred the open within reach of his pony. At last we came to a lone farmhouse in a vale adorned with no less that five white flags. Beyond the ridge was a sputter of musketry and now and then the whoop of a field-piece. 'Here,' said my guide and guardian, 'we get out and walk. Our driver will wait for us at the farmhouse.' But the driver loudly objected. 'No, sar. They shoot. They shoot me.' 'But they are white flagged all over,' we said. 'Yess, sar. That *why*,' was his answer, and he preferred to take his mules down into a decently remote donga and wait our return.

The farm-house (you will see in a little why I am so detailed) held two men and, I think, two women, who received us disinterestedly. We went on into a vacant world full of sunshine and distances, where now and again a single bullet sang to himself. What I most objected to was the sensation to being under aimed fire—being, as it were, required as a head. 'What are they doing this for?' I asked my friend. 'Because they think we are the Something Light Horse. They ought to be just under this slope.' I prayed that the particularly Something Light Horse would go elsewhere, which they presently did, for the aimed fire slackened and a wandering Colonial, bored to extinction, turned up with news from a far flank. 'No; nothing doing and no one to see.' Then more cracklings and a most cautious move forward to the lip of a large hollow where sheep were grazing. Some of them began to drop and kick. 'That's both sides trying sighting-shots,' said my companion. 'What range do you make it?' I asked. 'Eight hundred, at the nearest. That's close quarters nowadays. You'll never see anything closer than this. Modern rifles make it impossible. We're hung up till something cracks somewhere.' There was a decent lull for meals on both sides, interrupted now and again by sputters. Then one indubitable shell—ridiculously like a pipsqueak in that vastness but throwing up much dirt. 'Krupp!' Four or six pounder at extreme range,' said the expert. 'They still think we're the—Light Horse. They'll come to be fairly regular from now on.' Sure enough, every twenty minutes or so, one judgmatic shell pitched on our slope. We waited, seeing nothing in the emptiness, and hearing only a faint murmur as of wind along gas-jets, running in and out of the unconcerned hills.

Then pom-poms opened. These were nasty little one-pounders, ten in a belt (which usually jammed about the sixth round). On soft ground they merely thudded. On rock-face the shell breaks up and yowls like a cat. My friend for the first time seemed interested. 'If these are *their* pom-poms, it's Pretoria for us,' was his diagnosis. I looked behind me—the whole length of South Africa down to Cape Town—and it seemed very far. I felt that I could have covered it in five minutes under fair conditions, but—*not* with those aimed shots up my back. The pom-poms opened again at a bare rock-reef that gave the shells full value. For about two minutes a file of racing ponies, their tails and their riders' heads well down, showed and vanished northward. 'Our pom-poms,' said the correspondent. 'Le Gallais, I expect. *Now* we shan't be long.' All this time the absurd Krupp was faithfully feeling for us, *vice*—Light Horse, and, given a few more hours, might perhaps hit one of us. Then to the left, almost under us, a small piece of hanging woodland filled and fumed with our shrapnel much as a man's moustache fills with cigarette-smoke. It was most impressive and lasted for quite twenty minutes. Then silence; then a movement of men and horses from our side up the slope, and the hangar our guns had been hammering spat steady fire at them. More Boer ponies on more skylines; a flurry of pom-poms on the right and a little frieze of far-off meek-tailed ponies, already out of rifle range.

'*Maffeesh*,' said the correspondent, and fell to writing on his knee. 'We've shifted 'em.'

Leaving our infantry to follow men on ponyback towards the Equator, we returned to the farm-house. In the donga where he was waiting someone squibbed off a rifle just after we took our seats, and our driver flogged out over the rocks to the danger of our sacred bottles.

Then Bloemfontein, and Gwynne storming in late with his accounts complete—one hundred and twenty-five casualties, and the general opinion that 'French was a bit of a butcher' and a tale of the General commanding the cavalry who absolutely refused to break up his horses by galloping them across raw rock—'not for any dam' Boer'.

Months later, I got a cutting from an American paper, on information from Geneva—then a pest-house of propaganda—describing how I and some officers—names, date, and place correct—had entered a farm-house where we found two men and three women. We had dragged the women from under the bed where they had taken refuge (I assure you that no Tantie Sannie of that day could bestow herself beneath any known bed) and, giving them a hundred yards' start, had shot them down as they ran.

Even then, the beastliness struck me as more comic than significant. But by that time I ought to have known that it was the Hun's reflection of his own face as he spied at our back-windows. He had thrown in the 'hundred yards' start' touch as a tribute to our national sense of fair play.

From the business point of view the war was ridiculous. We charged ourselves step by step with the care and maintenance of all Boerdom—women and children included. Whence horrible tales of our atrocities in the concentration-camps.

One of the most widely exploited charges was our deliberate cruelty in making prisoners' tents and quarters open to the north. A Miss Hobhouse among others was loud in this matter, but she was to be excused.

We were showing off our newly-built little 'Woolsack' to a great lady on her way up-country, where a residence was being built for her. At the larder the wife pointed out that it faced south—that quarter being the coldest when one is south of the Equator. The great lady considered the heresy for a moment. Then, with the British sniff which abolishes the absurd, 'Humm! I shan't allow *that* to make any difference to *me*.'

Some Army and Navy Stores Lists were introduced into the prisoners' camps, and the women returned to civil life with a knowledge of corsets, stockings, toilet-cases, and other accessories frowned upon by their clergymen and their husbands. *Qua* women they were not very lovely, but they made their men fight, and they knew well how to fight on their own lines.

In the give-and-take of our work our troops got to gauge the merits of the commando-leaders they were facing. As I remember the scale, De Wet, with two hundred and fifty men, was to be taken seriously. With twice that number he was likely to fall over his own feet. Smuts (of Cambridge), warring, men assured me, in a black suit, trousers rucked to the knees, and a top-hat, could handle five hundred but, beyond that, got muddled. And so with the others. I had the felicity of meeting Smuts as a British General, at the Ritz during the Great War. Meditating on things seen and suffered, he said that being hunted about the veldt on a pony made a man think quickly, and that perhaps Mr Balfour (as he was then) would have been better for the same experience.

Each commando had its own reputation in the field, and the grizzlier their beards the greater our respect. There was an elderly contingent from Wakkerstroom which demanded most cautious handling. They shot, as you might say, for the pot. The young men were not so good. And there were foreign contingents who insisted on fighting after the manner of Europe. These the Boers wisely put in the forefront of the battle and kept away from. In one affair the Zarps—the Transvaal Police—fought brilliantly and were nearly all killed. But they were Swedes for the most part, and we were sorry.

Occasionally foreign prisoners were gathered in. Among them I remember a Frenchman who had joined for pure logical hatred of England, but, being a professional, could not resist telling us how we ought to wage the war. He was quite sound but rather cantankerous.

The 'war' became an unpleasing compost of 'political considerations', social reform, and housing; maternity-work and variegated absurdities. It is possible, though I doubt it, that first and last we may have killed four thousand Boers. Our own casualties, mainly from preventible disease, must have been six times as many.

The junior officers agreed that the experience ought to be a 'first-class dress-parade for Armageddon', but their practical conclusions were misleading. Long-range, aimed rifle-fire would do the work of the future: troops would never get near each other than half a mile, and Mounted Infantry would be vital. This was because, having found men on foot cannot overtake men on ponies, we created eighty thousand of as good Mounted Infantry as the world had seen. For these Western Europe had no use. Artillery preparation of wire-works, such as were not at Magersfontein, was rather overlooked in the reformers' schemes, on account of the difficulty of bringing up ammunition by horse-power. The pom-poms, and Lord Dundonald's galloping light gun-carriages, ate up their own weight in shell in three or four minutes.

In the ramshackle hotel at Bloemfontein, where the correspondents lived and the officers dropped in, one heard free and fierce debate as points came up, but—since no one dreamt of the internal-combustion engine that was to stand the world on its thick head, and since our wireless apparatus did not work in those landscapes—we were all beating the air.

Eventually the 'war' petered out on political lines. Brother Boer—and all ranks called him that—would do everything except die. Our men did not see why they should perish chasing stray commandos, or festering in block-houses, and there followed a sort of demoralizing 'handy-pandy' of alternate surrenders complicated by exchange of Army tobacco for Boer brandy which was bad for both sides.

At long last, we were left apologizing to a deeply-indignant people, whom we had been nursing and doctoring for a year or two; and who now expected, and received, all manner of free gifts and appliances for the farming they had never practised. We put them in a position to uphold and expand their primitive lust for racial domination, and thanked God we were 'rid of a knave'.

JOHN REED
Ten Days That Shook the World

The Bolshevik Revolution began on 6 November 1917 in Petrograd, and was the first act in a civil war which lasted until 1922. John Reed, later to be immortalised in the film Reds, *was in Petrograd at the time.*

SATURDAY, NOVEMBER 10 . . .

Quiet lay the city. By night armed patrols went through the silent streets, and on the corners soldiers and Red Guards stood around little fires, laughing and singing.

In the day-time great crowds walked in the streets, listening to hot debates between students and soldiers, businessmen and workmen. The citizens stopped each other and said,

'Are the Cossacks coming?'

'No . . .'

'What is the latest?'

'I don't know anything. Where's Kerensky?'

'They say only eight versts from Petrograd . . .'

'It is true that the Bolsheviki have fled to the cruiser *Aurora*?'

'They say so . . .'

All the walls of the houses were covered with proclamations, decrees, posters, appeals . . . But the bourgeois press had disappeared for a time . . .

Pravda had an account of the first meeting of the new *Tsay-ee-kah*, now the parliament of the Russian Soviet Republic. It was announced that an All-Russian Peasant Congress would be called on December 13. Three decrees were read and approved, first, Lenin's 'General Rules for the Press', ordering the suppression of all newspapers opposing the new Government; the Decree of Moratorium for House-rents; and the Decree Establishing a Workers' Militia.

As we came up to Smolny,—busier than ever, we saw workers and soldiers running in and out, and doubled guards everywhere. We met the reporters for the bourgeois and 'moderate' Socialist papers.

'Threw us out!' cried one of them, from *Volya Naroda*. 'Bonch-Bruevich came down to the Press Bureau and told us to leave. He said we were spies!' They all began to talk at once, 'Insult! Insult!'

In the lobby we saw great tables with bundles of appeals, proclamations and orders of the Military Revolutionary Committee. Workmen and soldiers were carrying them to waiting automobiles.

As we came out into the dark cold day, all around the city factory whistles were blowing, a nervous sound.

Tens of thousands of working-people poured out of the factories, men and women. Red Petrograd was in danger! Cossacks!

South and south-west the people poured through the streets toward the Moskovsky Gate, men, women and children, with rifles, spades, rolls of wire, cartridge-belts over their working clothes . . .

They walked along, companies of soldiers were with them, guns, motor-trucks, wagons—the revolutionary proletariat, defending with its breast the capital of the Workers' and Peasants' Republic!

Before the door of Smolny was an automobile. A thin man with thick glasses stood with his hands in the pockets of his old coat. A great bearded soldier with clear eyes of a youth was playing with a big blue-steel revolver, which never left his hand. These were Antonov and Dybenko.

Some soldiers were trying to fasten two military bicycles on the running-board of the automobile. The driver protested,—the paint would get scratched, he said. True, he was a Bolshevik, and the automobile was confiscated from a bourgeois; true, the bicycles were for the use of orderlies. But the driver's professional pride protested . . . So the bicycles were left behind.

The People's Commissars for War and Marine were going to inspect the revolutionary front. Could we go with them? Certainly not. The automobile only held five—the two Commissars, two orderlies and the driver.

We were left behind and went to the Tsarskoye Selo railway station. Up the Nevsky, as we passed, Red Guards were marching, all armed, some with bayonets and some without. The early winter darkness was falling. Heads up they marched, irregular lines of four, without music, without drums. A red flag with letters in gold, 'Peace! Land!' was flying over them.

At the railway station nobody knew just where Kerensky was, or where the front lay. Trains went no further, however, than Tsarskoye Selo . . .

Our car was full of country people going home with bundles and evening papers. The talk was all of the Bolshevik uprising.

Through the window we could see, in growing darkness, masses of soldiers going along the road toward the city. Back along the horizon, the lights of the city were seen.

Tsarskoye Selo station was quiet, but groups of soldiers stood here and there, talking in low voices and looking uneasily down the empty road in the direction of Gatchina.

I asked some of them which side they were on.

'Well,' said one, 'we don't know the rights of the matter. There is no doubt that Kerensky is a provocator, but we don't think it is right for Russian men to kill Russian men . . .'

In the station commandant's office was a big bearded soldier with the red arm-band of a regimental committee. Our papers from Smolny made a good impression on the man. He was plainly for the Soviets, but felt somehow lost.

'The Red Guards were here two hours ago, but they went away again,' he said. 'A Commissar came this morning, but he returned to Petrograd when the Cossacks arrived.'

'Are the Cossacks here then?'

'Yes. There has been a battle. The Cossacks came early in the morning. They captured two or three hundred of our men, and killed about twenty-five.'

'Where are the Cossacks?'

'Well, they didn't get this far. I don't know just where they are. Off that way . . .' He waved his arm westward.

We had dinner in the station restaurant—a very good dinner, better and cheaper than we could get in Petrograd. Then we went out into the town.

Just at the door of the station stood two soldiers with rifles, bayonets fixed. They were surrounded by about a hundred businessmen, government officials and students, who attacked them with argument.

The soldiers were uncomfortable. A tall young man, dressed in the uniform of a student was leading the attack.

'You understand,' he said to the soldiers, 'that by taking up arms against your brothers you are making yourselves the tools of murderers and traitors?'

'Now, brother,' answered one of the soldiers, 'you don't understand. There are two classes, don't you see, the proletariat and the bourgeoisie . . .'

We walked up the street, where the lights were few and far apart and where very few people passed. A silence hung over the place, a political No Man's Land. Only the barber-shops were all lighted and crowded and a line of people formed at the doors of the public baths.

The nearer we came to the Imperial Park, the more deserted were the streets. A frightened priest pointed out the headquarters of the Soviets, and hurried on. It was in the wing of one of the palaces.

The windows were dark, the door locked. A soldier standing at the door looked us up and down with suspicion.

'The Soviet went away two days ago,' he said.

'Where?'

'I don't know.'

We went toward the Palaces, along the dark gardens, fantastic pavilions, bridges and fountains.

At one place we saw a dozen big armed soldiers. They were looking at us from a terrace. I climbed up to them.

'Who are you?' I asked.

'We are the guard,' answered one.

'Are you Kerensky's troops, or the Soviets'?'

There was silence for a moment, then one of them said,

'We are neutral.'

We went on through the arch of the Ekaterina Palace, into the Palace itself, asking for the headquarters. A sentry outside the door said that the commandant was inside.

In a white great room with a fire-place, a group of officers stood, talking anxiously. They were pale and seemed tired, and evidently had not slept. There was an older man with a white beard, a colonel. We showed him our Bolshevik papers. He seemed surprised.

'How did you get here without being killed?' he asked politely. 'It is very dangerous in the streets just now. There was a battle this morning, and there will be another tomorrow morning. Kerensky is to enter the town at eight o'clock.'

'Where are the Cossacks?' we asked.

'About a mile over that way.' He waved his arm.

'And will you defend the town against them?'

'Oh, dear, no.' He smiled. 'We are holding the town for Kerensky.'

Our hearts sank, for our passes showed that we were revolutionary.

The colonel said,

'About those passes of yours. Your lives will be in danger if you are arrested. Therefore, if you want to see the battle I will give you an order for rooms in the officers' hotel. And if you come here at seven o'clock in the morning, I will give you new passes.'

'So you are for Kerensky?' we asked.

'Well, not exactly for Kerensky. You see, most of the soldiers in the garrison are Bolsheviki, and today, after the battle, they all went away in the direction of Petrograd, taking the artillery with them. You might say that none of the soldiers are for Kerensky; but some of them just don't want to fight at all. The officers have almost all gone over to Kerensky's forces, or simply gone away. We are—in a most difficult situation as you see . . .'

We did not believe that there would be any battle next morning, so the colonel politely sent his orderly to take us to the railway station.

'Ah,' the orderly kept saying, 'it is not danger I mind, but being so long, three years, away from my mother . . .'

Looking out of the window of the train, as we went through the dark night toward Petrograd, I saw groups of soldiers talking and gesticulating in the light of fires. And there were many armoured cars at cross-roads . . .

All the troubled night groups of soldiers and Red Guards wandered and the Commissars of the Military Revolutionary

Committee hurried from one group to another, trying to organise a defence . . .

Back in Petrograd, excited crowds of citizens were moving up and down the Nevsky. Something was in the air. From the Warsaw Railway station far-off cannonade could be heard.

Next morning, Sunday the 11th, the Cossacks entered Tsarskoye Selo; Kerensky himself rode a white horse. There was no battle. But Kerensky made a fatal mistake.

At seven in the morning he sent word to the soldiers of the Second Tsarskoye Selo Rifles to lay down their arms. The soldiers answered that they would remain neutral but would not disarm. Kerensky gave them ten minutes in which to obey. This angered the soldiers . . . A few minutes later Cossack artillery opened fire on the barracks, killing eight men. From that moment there were no more 'neutral' soldiers in Tsarskoye . . .

Petrograd woke to the sound of rifle-fire and marching men. Under the high dark sky a cold wind smelt of snow.

All day long in every district of the city there was fighting between *Yunkers* and Red Guards, battles between armoured cars . . .

The sound of machine-guns and shots could be heard far and near. The shutters of the shops were drawn, but business still went on. Even the moving-picture shows played to crowded houses. The trams were running. The telephones were all working; when you called Central, shooting could be heard over the wire . . .

Smolny was cut off, but the Duma and the Committee for Salvation were in communication with all the *yunker* schools and with Kerensky at Tsarskoye Selo.

At seven in the morning the Vladimir *yunker* school was visited by a patrol of soldiers, sailors and Red Guards who gave the *yunkers* twenty minutes to lay down their arms.

The ultimatum was rejected. Soviet troops surrounded the building and opened fire. The *yunkers* telephoned for help. The Cossacks answered that they dare not come, because a large body of sailors with two cannons stood at the barracks.

The Pavlovsk school was surrounded too. Most of the Mikhailov school *yunkers* were fighting in the streets . . .

At half past eleven three field-guns arrived. Another demand to surrender was met by the *yunkers* by shooting down two of the Soviet delegates under the white flag.

Now began a real bombardment. Great holes were torn in the walls of the school. The *yunkers* defended themselves desperately. At half past two *yunkers* threw out a white flag.

With a rush and a shout thousands of soldiers and Red Guards poured through windows, doors and holes in the walls. About two hundred *yunkers* were captured and taken to the Peter-Paul Fortress.

All the other *yunker* schools surrended without fighting, and the *yunkers* were sent to the Peter-Paul Fortress and Kronstadt.

The telephone exchange held out until afternoon, when a Bolshevik armoured car appeared, and the sailors stormed the place.

The frightened telephone girls ran to and fro. The terrified *yunkers* tore from their uniforms all the marks; one *yunker* offered my friend Williams anything for his overcoat, as a disguise . . .

'They will kill us! They will kill us!' the *yunkers* cried, for many of them had given their word at the Winter Palace not to take up arms against the people.

Williams agreed to help them, if they set Antonov free. This was immediately done; Antonov and Williams made speeches to the victorious sailors, asking them to set the *yunkers* free.

All the *yunkers* went free, except a few of them, who in their panic tried to flee over the roofs, or to hide in the attic. When they were found the sailors threw them out of the building into the street.

Tired, bloody, triumphant, the sailors and workers went into the switchboard room, and finding so many pretty telephone girls, stopped at the door awkwardly. Not a girl was injured, not onc insulted.

Frightened girls stood in the corners of the room, and then, finding themselves safe, began screaming,

'Ugh! The dirty ignorant people! The fools!'

The sailors and Red Guards did not know what to do.

'Fools! Pigs!' screamed the girls angrily, putting on their coats and hats. Their experience had been dramatic that day. During the fighting they were passing up cartridges and helping wounded *yunkers*, their young and noble defenders. And these were just common workmen, peasants, 'dark people'.

The Commissar of the Military Revolutionary Committee tried to make the girls remain. He was very polite.

'You have been badly treated. The telephone system is controlled by the Municipal Duma. You are paid sixty roubles a month, and have to work ten hours and more . . . From now on all that will be changed. The Government will put the telephones under control of the Ministry of Posts and Telegraphs. Your pay will be immediately raised to one hundred and fifty roubles, and you will work less. As members of the working class you should be happy . . .'

Members of the working class indeed! Did he mean to say that there was anything in common between these—these animals—and us? Remain? Not if they offered a thousand roubles! . . . The angry girls left the place . . .

The employees of the building and workers—they remained. But the switch-boards must be operated—the telephone was quite necessary.

Only half a dozen trained operators were available. Volunteers were called for; a hundred sailors, soldiers and workers were willing to help. Six operators rushed backward and forward, instructing, helping . . .

So slowly the wires began to hum. The first thing was to connect Smolny with the barracks and the factories; the second, to cut off the Duma and the *yunker* schools . . .

It was getting dark and a cold wind was blowing when we walked down the Nevsky and saw a crowd of people before the Kazan Cathedral, continuing the endless debate; a few workmen, some soldiers, and the rest shop-keepers, clerks and the like.

'But Lenin won't get Germany to make peace!' cried one.

'And whose fault is it?' a young soldier said. 'Your damn Kerensky, dirty bourgeois! To hell with Kerensky! We don't want him. We want Lenin . . .'

Outside the Duma an officer with a white arm-band was tearing down Bolshevik posters and proclamations from the wall of the house . . .

Far away separate shots still sounded, but the city lay quiet.

In the Nikolai Hall of the Duma, the session was coming to an end. One after another the Commissars reported—capture of the telephone exchange by sailors and Red Guards, street-fighting, the taking of the Vladimir *yunker* school . . . The members of the Duma were startled.

Only three newspapers were out—*Pravda, Dyelo Naroda* and *Novaya Zhizn*. All of them wrote about new 'coalition' government.

The Socialist Revolutionary paper demanded a cabinet without either Cadets or Bolsheviki.

As for *Pravda*, it wrote:

'We laugh at these coalitions with political parties whose most important members are petty journalists of doubtful reputation; our 'coalition' is that of the proletariat and the revolutionary army with the poor peasants . . .'

In Smolny there were thousands of people in action.

In the Trade Union headquarters I met a delegate of the railway workers of the Nikolai railway line, who said that there were mass-meetings everywhere . . .

'All power to the Soviets!' he cried.

On the top floor, the Military Revolutionary Committee was working continuously. Men went in, fresh and energetic; night and day and night and day they threw themselves into the terrible machine; and came out dead tired to fall on the floor and sleep . . .

The Committee for Salvation had been outlawed.

From Moscow word came that the *yunkers* and Cossacks had surrounded the Kremlin . . . Small forces of Bolsheviki had been driven from the telephone and telegraph offices; the *yunkers* now held the centre of Moscow . . .

But all around them the Soviets troops were concentrating. Street fighting was slowly gathering way, all attempts at compromise had failed . . . On the side of the Soviets ten thousand garrison soldiers and a few Red Guards; on the side of the Provisional Government six thousand *yunkers*, twenty-five hundred Cossacks, and two thousand white guards.

The Petrograd Soviet was meeting, and next door the new *Tsay-ee-kah* acting on the decrees and orders. They came down in a stream from the Council of People's Commissars in session upstairs . . ., establishing an eight hour day for workers, and Lunacharsky's 'Basis for a System of Popular Education'.

Only a few hundred people were present at the two meetings, most of them armed. Smolny was almost deserted, except for the guards, who were busy at the hall windows, setting up machine-guns . . .

Meanwhile all was not well on the revolutionary front. The enemy had brought up armoured trains with cannon. The Soviet forces, mostly untrained Red Guards, were without officers and without a definite plan. Only five thousand regular soldiers had joined them; the rest of the garrison was either fighting against the *yunkers* revolt, guarding the city, or undecided what to do.

At ten in the evening Lenin addressed a meeting of delegates from the city regiments who voted to fight. A committee of five soldiers was elected to serve as General Staff, and in the small hours of the morning the regiments left their barracks in full battle array . . . Going home I saw them pass, bayonets fixed, in regular formations, through the deserted streets of the city . . .

GEORGE ORWELL
The Spanish Front

The Spanish Civil War of 1936–1939, between General Franco's Nationalists and Spain's elected leftist Republican Government, fired political passions around the world. Although the Republic's army was poorly trained and equipped, its ranks were swelled by a number of anti-fascist volunteers from outside Iberia. Among these was the English writer George Orwell, who fought with the Republican militia on the Ebro front, in north-western Spain.

BARBASTRO, THOUGH A LONG WAY from the front line, looked bleak and chipped. Swarms of militiamen in shabby uniforms wandered up and down the streets, trying to keep warm. On a ruinous wall I came upon a poster dating from the previous year and announcing that 'six handsome bulls' would be killed in the arena on such and such a date. How forlorn its faded colours looked! Where were the handsome bulls and the handsome bull-fighters now? It appeared that even in Barcelona there were hardly any bullfights nowadays; for some reason all the best matadors were Fascists.

They sent my company by lorry to Sietamo, then westward to Alcubierre, which was just behind the line fronting Zaragoza. Sietamo had been fought over three times before the Anarchists finally took it in October, and parts of it were smashed to pieces by shell-fire and most of the houses pockmarked by rifle-bullets. We were 1500 feet above sea level now. It was beastly cold, with dense mists that came swirling up from nowhere. Between Sietamo and Alcubierre the lorry-driver lost his way (this was one of the regular features of the war) and we were wandering for hours in the mist. It was late at night when we reached

Alcubierre. Somebody shepherded us through morasses of mud into a mule-stable where we dug ourselves down into the chaff and promptly fell asleep. Chaff is not bad to sleep in when it is clean, not so good as hay but better than straw. It was only in the morning light that I discovered that the chaff was full of breadcrusts, torn newspapers, bones, dead rats, and jagged milk tins.

We were near the front line now, near enough to smell the characteristic smell of war—in my experience a smell of excrement and decaying food. Alcubierre had never been shelled and was in a better state than most of the villages immediately behind the line. Yet I believe that even in peacetime you could not travel in that part of Spain without being struck by the peculiar squalid misery of the Aragonese villages. They are built like fortresses, a mass of mean little houses of mud and stone huddling round the church, and even in spring you see hardly a flower anywhere; the houses have no gardens, only back-yards where ragged fowls skate over the beds of mule-dung. It was vile weather, with alternate mist and rain. The narrow earth roads had been churned into a sea of mud, in places two feet deep, through which the lorries struggled with racing wheels and the peasants led their clumsy carts which were pulled by strings of mules, sometimes as many as six in a string, always pulling tandem. The constant come-and-go of troops had reduced the village to a state of unspeakable filth. It did not possess and never had possessed such a thing as a lavatory or a drain of any kind, and there was not a square yard anywhere where you could tread without watching your step. The church had long been used as a latrine; so had all the fields for a quarter of a mile round. I never think of my first two months at war without thinking of wintry stubble fields whose edges are crusted with dung.

Two days passed and no rifles were issued to us. When you had been to the Comité de Guerra and inspected the row of holes in the wall—holes made by rifle-volleys, various Fascists having been executed there—you had seen all the sights that Alcubierre contained. Up in the front line things were obviously quiet; very few wounded were coming in. The chief excitement was the arrival of Fascist deserters, who were brought under guard from the front line. Many of the troops opposite us on this part of the line were not Fascists at all, merely wretched conscripts who had been doing their military service at the time when war broke out and were only too anxious to escape. Occasionally small batches of them took the risk of slipping across to our lines. No doubt more would have done so if their relatives had not been in Fascist territory. These deserters were the first 'real' Fascists I had ever seen. It struck me that they were indistinguishable from ourselves, except that they wore khaki overalls. They were always ravenously hungry when they arrived—natural enough after a day or two of dodging about in no man's land, but it was always triumphantly pointed to as a proof that the Fascist troops were starving. I watched one of them being fed in a peasant's house. It was somehow rather a pitiful sight. A tall boy of twenty, deeply windburnt, with his clothes in rags, crouched over the fire shovelling a pannikinful of stew into himself at desperate speed; and all the while his eyes flitted nervously round the ring of militiamen who stood watching him. I think he still half-believed that we were bloodthirsty 'Reds' and were going to shoot him as soon as he had finished his meal; the armed man who guarded him kept stroking his shoulder and making reassuring noises. On one memorable day fifteen deserters arrived in a single batch. They were led through the village in triumph with a man riding in front of them on a white horse. I managed to take a rather blurry photograph which was stolen from me later.

On our third morning in Alcubierre the rifles arrived. A sergeant with a coarse dark-yellow face was handing them out in the mule-stable.I got a shock of dismay when I saw the thing they gave me. It was a German Mauser dated 1896—more than forty years old! It was rusty, the bolt was stiff, the wooden barrel-guard was split; one glance down the muzzle showed that it was corroded and past praying for. Most of the rifles were equally bad, some of them even worse, and no attempt was made to give the best weapons to the men who knew how to use them. The best rifle of the lot, only ten years old, was given to a half-witted little beast of fifteen, known to everyone as the *maricón* (Nancy-boy). The sergeant gave us five minutes' 'instruction', which consisted in explaining how you loaded a rifle and how you took the bolt to pieces. Many of the militiamen had never had a gun in their hands before, and very few, I imagine, knew what the sights were for. Cartridges were handed out, fifty to a man, and then the ranks were formed and we strapped our kits on our backs and set out for the front line, about three miles away.

The *centuria*, eighty men and several dogs, wound raggedly up the road. Every militia column had at least one dog attached to it as a mascot. One wretched brute that marched with us had had P.O.U.M. branded on it in huge letters and slunk along as though conscious that there was something wrong with its appearance. At the head of the column, beside the red flag, Georges Kopp, the stout Belgian commandante, was riding a black horse; a little way ahead a youth from the brigand-like militia cavalry pranced to and fro, galloping up every piece of rising ground and posing himself in picturesque attitudes at the summit. The splendid horses of the Spanish cavalry had been captured in large numbers during the revolution and handed over to the militia, who, of course, were busy riding them to death.

The road wound between yellow infertile fields, untouched since last year's harvest. Ahead of us was the low sierra that lies between Alcubierre and Zaragoza. We were getting near the front line now, near the bombs, the machine-guns, and the mud. In secret I was frightened. I knew the line was quiet at present, but unlike most of the men about me I was old enough to remember the Great War, though not old enough to have fought in it. War, to me, meant roaring projectiles and skipping shards of steel; above all it meant mud, lice, hunger, and cold. It is curious, but I dreaded the cold much more than I dreaded the enemy. The thought of it had been haunting me all the time I was in Barcelona; I had even lain awake at nights thinking of the cold in the trenches, the stand-to's in the grisly dawns, the long hours on sentry-go with a frosted rifle, the icy mud that would slop over my boot-tops. I admit, too, that I felt a kind of horror as I looked at the people I was marching among. You cannot possibly conceive what a rabble we looked. We straggled along with far less cohesion than a flock of sheep; before we had gone two miles the rear of the column was out of sight. And quite half of the so-called men were children—but I mean literally children, of sixteen years old at the very most. Yet they were all happy and excited at the prospect of getting to the front at last. As we neared the line the boys round the red flag in front began to utter shouts of 'Visca P.O.U.M.!' 'Fascistas-maricones!' and so forth—shouts which were meant to be war-like and menacing, but which, from those childish throats, sounded as pathetic as the cries of kittens. It seemed dreadful that the defenders of the Republic should be this mob of ragged children carrying worn-out rifles which they did not know how to use. I remember wondering what would happen if a Fascist aeroplane passed our way—whether the airman would even bother to dive down and give us a burst from his machine-gun. Surely even from the air he could see that we were not real soldiers?

As the road struck into the sierra we branched off to the right and climbed a narrow mule-track that wound round the mountain-side. The hills in that part of Spain are of a queer formation, horseshoe-shaped with flattish tops and very steep sides running down into immense ravines. On the higher slopes nothing grows except stunted shrubs and heath, with the white bones of the limestone sticking out everywhere. The front line here was not a continuous line of trenches, which would have been impossible in such mountainous country; it was simply a chain of fortified posts, always known as 'positions', perched on each hill-top. In the distance you could see our 'position' at the crown of the horseshoe; a ragged barricade of sand-bags, a red flag fluttering, the smoke of dug-out fires. A little nearer, and you could smell a sickening sweetish stink that lived in my nostrils for weeks afterwards. Into the cleft immediately behind the position all the refuse of months had been tipped—a deep festering bed of breadcrusts, excrement, and rusty tins.

The company we were relieving were getting their kits together. They had been three months in the line; their uniforms were caked with mud, their boots falling to pieces, their faces mostly bearded. The captain commanding the position, Levinski by name, but known to everyone as Benjamin, and by birth a Polish Jew, but speaking French as his native language, crawled out of his dug-out and greeted us. He was a short youth of about twenty-five, with stiff black hair and a pale eager face which at this period of the war was always very dirty. A few stray bullets were cracking high overhead. The position was a semi-circular enclosure about fifty yards across, with a parapet that was partly sand-bags and partly lumps of limestone. There were thirty or forty dug-outs running into the ground like rat-holes. Williams, myself, and Williams's Spanish brother-in-law made a swift dive for the nearest unoccupied dug-out that looked habitable. Somewhere in front an occasional rifle banged, making queer rolling echoes among the stony hills. We had just dumped our kits and were crawling out of the dug-out when there was another bang and one of the children of our company rushed back from the parapet with his face pouring blood. He had fired his rifle and had somehow managed to blow out the bolt; his scalp was torn to ribbons by the splinters of the burst cartridge-case. It was our first casualty, and, characteristically, self-inflicted.

In the afternoon we did our first guard and Benjamin showed us round the position. In front of the parapet there ran a system of narrow trenches hewn out of the rock, with extremely primitive loopholes made of piles of limestone. There were twelve sentries, placed at various points in the trench and behind the inner parapet. In front of the trench was the barbed wire, and then the hillside slid down into a seemingly bottomless ravine; opposite were naked hills, in places mere cliffs of rock, all grey and wintry, with no life anywhere, not even a bird. I peered cautiously through a loophole, trying to find the Fascist trench.

'Where are the enemy?'

Benjamin waved his hand expansively. 'Over zere.' (Benjamin spoke English—terrible English.)

'But *where*?'

According to my ideas of trench warfare the Fascists would be fifty or a hundred yards away. I could see nothing—seemingly their trenches were very well concealed. Then with a shock of dismay I saw where Benjamin was pointing; on the opposite hill-top, beyond the ravine, seven hundred metres away at the very least, the tiny outline of a parapet and a red-and-yellow flag—the Fascist position. I was indescribably disappointed. We were nowhere near them! At that range our rifles were completely useless. But at this moment there was a shout of excitement. Two Fascists, greyish figurines in the distance, were scrambling up the naked hill-side opposite. Benjamin grabbed the nearest man's rifle, took aim, and pulled the trigger. Click! A dud cartridge; I thought it a bad omen.

The new sentries were no sooner in the trench than they began firing a terrific fusillade at nothing in particular. I could see the Fascists, tiny as ants, dodging to and fro behind their parapet, and sometimes a black dot which was a head would pause for a moment, impudently exposed. It was obviously no use firing. But presently the sentry on my left, leaving his post in the typical Spanish fashion, sidled up to me and began urging me to fire. I tried to explain that at that range and with these rifles you could not hit a man except by accident. But he was only a child, and he kept motioning with his rifle towards one of the dots, grinning as eagerly as a dog that expects a pebble to be thrown. Finally I put my sights up to seven hundred and let fly. The dot disappeared. I hope it went near enough to make him jump. It was the first time in my life that I had fired a gun at a human being.

Now that I had seen the front I was profoundly disgusted. They called this war! And we were hardly even in touch with the enemy! I made no attempt to keep my head below the level of the trench. A little while later, however, a bullet shot past my ear with a vicious crack and banged into the parados behind. Alas! I ducked. All my life I had sworn that I would not duck the first time a bullet passed over me; but the movement appears to be instinctive, and almost everybody does it at least once.

ERNESTO 'CHE' GUEVARA
Guerilla Attack on the Barracks at La Plata

The Marxist guerilla fighter describes a classic operation from the first year of the Cuban Revolutionary War.

THE ATTACK ON THE SMALL BARRACKS at the mouth of the La Plata river in the Sierra Maestra brought us our first victory, and had repercussions which reached far beyond the craggy region where it took place. It came to everyone's attention, proving that the Rebel Army existed and was ready to fight. For us, it was the reaffirmation of the possibility of our final triumph.

On 14 January 1957, a little over a month after the surprise attack at Alegría de Pío, we stopped at the Magdalena river which is separated from the La Plata by a range of the Sierra which ends in the ocean, separating the two small river valleys. Here, on Fidel's order, we trained the men in the elements of marksmanship; some of them held guns for the first time in their lives. Here we also washed, after many days of ignoring hygiene, and those who could changed their clothes. At that time we had twenty-three usable weapons: nine rifles with telescopic sights, five semi-automatics, four bolt-action rifles, two Thompson submachine-guns, two machine pistols, and a 16-gauge shotgun. That afternoon we climbed the last hillock to reach the environs of the La Plata. We walked along a narrow, deserted footpath in the woods, following machete slashes left especially for us by a local peasant named Melquiades Elias. His name had been given to us by our guide, Eutimio, who at that time was indispensable to us and was a model peasant rebel. Some time later Eutimio was captured by Casillas who, instead of killing him, bribed him with the offer of 10,000 pesos and a rank in the Army if he would murder Fidel. He came very close to carrying out this plan, but he lacked the courage to do it. Nevertheless, by revealing our camp-sites, he proved important to the enemy.

At that period, Eutimio served us loyally; he was one of the many peasants who had fought for his land against the landlords, and who, in so doing, fought also against the Guardia Rural.

During that day's march we captured two *guajiros* (peasants). They turned out to be relatives of our guide; we released one of them, but kept the other as a precautionary measure. The following day, 15 January, we sighted the half-constructed zinc-roofed barracks of La Plata. We saw a group of men who, although half-clothed, sported the enemy uniform. We saw that at six in the evening, just before sunset, a launch loaded with guards arrived. Some disembarked, others got on. Since we did not clearly understand these manoeuvres, we decided to postpone the attack until the following day.

From dawn on the 16th the barracks was under constant surveillance. The coast guards had retired for the night; we sent out a few scouts who saw no soldiers anywhere. At three in the afternoon, in order to see more, we decided to move up the path leading to the barracks and bordering the river. At nightfall we crossed the shallow La Plata river and posted ourselves on the path. After five minutes two *guajiros* passed and we took them prisoner. One of them was a known informer. Once they knew who we were and believed our threats, they gave us vital information. We found out that there were about fifteen soldiers in the barracks; furthermore, we were told that in a while one of the three most infamous foremen in the region, Chicho Osorio, would pass along the road. These foremen worked on the Laviti plantation, an enormous fief run by means of terror with the help of individuals like Chicho Osorio. After a while Chicho appeared, drunk and mounted on a mule, which he was sharing with a little Negro boy. Universo Sánchez called to him to halt in the name of the Guardia Rural, and he immediately answered 'mosquito', the password.

Despite our ragged appearance, we were able to trick Chicho Osorio, maybe because he was so drunk. Fidel, in an indignant manner, told him he was an Army colonel, that he had come to find out why the rebels had not yet been destroyed, that *he* was going into the mountains to find them (that was why he had a beard), and that what the Army was doing was 'garbage'. All in all he spoke quite contemptuously of the enemy's efficiency. With great submissiveness, Chicho Osorio said that it was true, the guards spent their time inside the barracks, eating and doing nothing but carry out unimportant manoeuvres; all the rebels, he said strongly, should be destroyed. We began to ask Chicho discreetly about friendly and unfriendly people in the region, naturally reversing the roles: when Chicho said someone was bad, we then had reason to believe he was good. In this way we collected about twenty names, and the scoundrel continued jabbering. He told us that he had killed two men, 'but *mi general Batista* let me go free immediately'; he told us how he had just beaten some peasants who had 'gotten a bit uppity' and that, in fact, the Guardia Rural were incapable of doing anything like that; they allowed the peasants to talk back with impunity. Fidel asked him what he would do with Fidel Castro if he captured him, and Chicho answered with an unmistakable gesture that he would cut off his——, as he would also do with Crescencio. Look, he said, pointing to the Mexican-made boots he wore (and which we wore also), 'I got them off one of those sons of——we killed.' There, without knowing it, Chicho Osorio had signed his own death sentence. In the end, on Fidel's suggestion, he agreed to lead us to the barracks in order to surprise the soldiers and show them that they were poorly prepared and were neglecting their duty.

We approached the barracks, with Chicho Osorio leading us; personally, I was not too sure that the man had not already caught on to our game. However, he continued in all innocence: he was so drunk his judgement was impaired. As we crossed the river once again in order to come closer to the barracks, Fidel told him that according to military regulations prisoners had to be bound; Chicho did not resist and he unknowingly continued as a real prisoner. He explained that the only guard post was between the partly constructed barracks and the house of one of the other overseers, Honorio, and he led us to a place near the barracks where the road to El Macío passed. Comrade Luis Crespo, today a major, was sent to reconnoitre and returned with the news that Chicho's information was correct, for Luis had seen the two buildings and the red point of the guard's cigarette between them.

We were about to move in when three guards passed by on horses, and we had to hide. Before them walked a prisoner whom they were driving like a mule. The prisoner passed near me and I remember the words of that poor peasant: 'I am a man just like you,' and the answer that one of the guards gave (we later identified him as Corporal Basól): 'Shut up and move, or we'll whip you on.' At the time we thought the peasant would be out of danger by not being in the barracks, and would escape the bullets at the moment of the attack; however, the following day, when they found out about the battle and its outcome, he was brutally murdered in El Macío.

We prepared to attack with the twenty-two available weapons. It was an important moment, for we had few bullets; we had to take the barracks no matter what, for otherwise we would spend all our ammunition and remain practically defenceless. Comrade Lieutenant Julito Díaz (who died heroically at El Uvero), with Camilo Cienfuegos, Benítez, and Calixto Morales, all with semiautomatic rifles, were to surround the overseer's palm-thatched house from the extreme right. Fidel, Universo Sánchez, Luis Crespo, Calixto García, Fajardo (now a Major), and I would attack from the centre. Raúl with his squad and Almeida with his would attack the barracks from the left.

Thus, we slowly approached the enemy positions until we got within forty metres. There was a full moon. Fidel started the shooting with two bursts of machine-gun fire and was followed by all the available guns. Immediately, we called on the soldiers to surrender, but with no result. The moment the shooting began, Chicho Osorio, the murdering informer, was executed.

The attack began at 2.40 in the morning and the guards resisted more than we had expected. In the barracks there was a sergeant with an M-1, and each time we suggested surrender, he answered with a volley of shots. We were ordered to throw our old Brazilian-type grenades; Luis Crespo threw his, and I threw mine; neither one exploded. Raúl Castro threw dynamite and this also had no effect. So we then had to move in closer and set fire to the houses, although it was at the risk of our lives. First Universo Sánchez tried but failed, then Camilo Cienfuegos tried and also failed. Finally Luis Crespo and I approached the building and set fire to it. In the light of the fire we were able to see that it was simply a coconut warehouse attached to a nearby coconut palm plantation; but we had already intimidated the soldiers into abandoning the fight. One of them, fleeing, almost collided with Luis Crespo's rifle and was wounded in the chest; Luis took the soldier's weapon and we continued firing at the house. Camilo Cienfuegos, sheltered behind a tree, fired on the fleeing sergeant and used up his few cartridges.

The soldiers, almost defenceless, were cut to pieces by our merciless fire. Camilo Cienfuegos was the first to enter the house and we heard cries of surrender. We quickly counted the weapons, with which the battle had left us: eight Springfields, a Thompson submachine-gun, and some thousand rounds; we had used about five hundred rounds. In addition, we had cartridge belts, fuel, knives, clothing, and some food. The casualty list was as follows: they had two dead and five wounded, and three of them were our prisoners. Some, along with the wretched Honorio, had escaped. On our side, not even a scratch. We set the soldiers' houses on fire and withdrew, after attending to the wounded as best we could. There were three seriously wounded who subsequently died, as we found out after the final victory. We left them in the care of the captured soldiers. One of the soldiers later joined the troops of Major Raúl Castro and reached the rank of lieutenant, dying in an airplane crash after the end of the war.

Our attitude towards the wounded contrasted sharply with that of the Army. The Army not only murdered our wounded, but also abandoned their own. In time, this difference began having its effect, and constituted one of the factors in our victory. To my despair, Fidel ordered us to leave all our medicines with the prisoners who were to treat the wounded; I wanted to conserve our reserves for our fighting troops. We also freed the civilians and, at 4.30 on the morning of the 17th, we left for Palma Mocha, where we arrived at dawn, immediately seeking the most rugged and inaccessible regions of the Sierra Maestra.

We were met with a pitiful sight: the day before, a corporal and a foreman had informed all the local peasant families that the Air Force was going to bomb the whole region and this sparked an exodus to the coast. Since no one knew of our presence, this was clearly a manoeuvre among the overseers and the rural guards to rob the *guajiros* of their land and belongings. But their lie had coincided with our attack and now became a reality, so that real terror spread and it was impossible to stop the peasant exodus.

This was the Rebel Army's first victorious battle. This and the following battle were the only occasions in the life of our troop when we had more weapons than men. The peasants were not yet prepared to join the struggle and communication with urban bases was practically non-existent.

MAX HASTINGS
The First Man into Port Stanley

The war between Britain and Argentina for the Falkland Islands (Malvinas) in the South Atlantic, came to an end on 14 June 1982, with the surrender of the Argentinian forces under their commander, General Menendez. The first Briton into Port Stanley, the Falkland's capital, was not a soldier, but the war correspondent, Max Hastings.

BRITISH FORCES ARE IN PORT STANLEY. At 2.45 p.m. British time today, men of the 2nd Parachute Regiment halted on the outskirts at the end of their magnificent drive on the capital pending negotiations.

There, we sat on the racecourse until, after about 20 minutes I was looking at the road ahead and there seemed to be no movement. I thought, well I'm a civilian so why shouldn't I go and see what's going on because there didn't seem to be much resistance.

So I stripped off all my combat clothes and walked into Stanley in a blue civilian anorak with my hands in the air and my handkerchief in my hand.

The Argentinians made no hostile movement as I went by the apparently undamaged but heavily bunkered Government House.

I sort of grinned at them in the hope that if there were any Argentinian soldiers manning the position they wouldn't shoot at me.

Nobody took any notice so I walked on and after a few minutes I saw a group of people all looking like civilians a hundred yards ahead and I shouted at them.

I shouted: 'Are you British?' and they shouted back: 'Yes, are you?' I said 'Yes.'

They were a group of civilians who had just come out of the civil administration building where they had been told that it looked as if there was going to be a ceasefire.

We chatted for a few moments and then I walked up to the building and I talked to the senior Argentinian colonel who was standing on the steps. He didn't show any evident hostility.

They were obviously pretty depressed. They looked like men who had just lost a war but I talked to them for a few moments and I said: 'Are you prepared to surrender West Falkland as well as East?'

The colonel said: 'Well, maybe, but you must wait until four o'clock when General Menendez meets your general.'

I said: 'May I go into the town and talk to civilians?' He said: 'Yes,' so I started to walk down the main street past Falklanders who were all standing outside their houses.

They all shouted and cheered and the first person I ran into was the Catholic priest, Monsignor Daniel Spraggon, who said: 'My God, it's marvellous to see you.'

That wasn't directed at me personally but it was the first communication he had had with the British forces.

I walked on and there were hundreds, maybe thousands, of Argentinian troops milling around, marching in columns through the streets, some of them clutching very badly wounded men and looking completely like an army in defeat with blankets wrapped around themselves.

There were bits of weapons and equipment all over the place and they were all moving to central collection points before the surrender or ceasefire.

Eventually I reached the famous Falklands hotel, the Upland Goose. We had been dreaming for about three months about walking into the Upland Goose and having a drink, and I walked in and again it was marvellous that they all clapped and cheered.

They offered me gin on the assumption that this is the traditional drink of British journalists, but I asked if they could make it whisky instead and I gratefully raised my glass to them all.

Owner of the Upland Goose, Desmond King said: 'We never

doubted for a moment that the British would turn up. We have just been waiting for the moment for everybody to come.'

The last few days had been the worst, he said, because Argentinian guns had been operating from among the houses of Stanley and they had heard this terrific, continuous battle going on in the hills.

They were afraid that it was going to end up with a house-to-house fight in Stanley itself. The previous night when I had been with the Paras we were getting a lot of shell fire coming in on us and eventually we sorted out the co-ordinates from which it was firing. Our observation officer tried to call down to fire on the enemy batteries and the word came back that you could not fire on them because they are in the middle of Stanley.

So the battalion simply had to take it and suffer some casualties.

Anyway, there we were in the middle of the Upland Goose with about 20 or 30 delighted civilians who said that the Argentinians hadn't done anything appalling. It depends what one means by appalling, but they hadn't shot anybody or hung anybody up by their thumbs or whatever.

They had looted a lot of houses that they had taken over. At times they got very nervous and started pushing people around with submachine guns in their backs and the atmosphere had been pretty unpleasant.

Robin Pitaleyn described how he had been under house arrest in the hotel for six weeks, since he made contact by radio with the Hermes. He dismissed criticism of the Falkland Island Company representatives who had sold goods to the occupiers.

'We were all selling stuff,' he said. 'You had a simple choice—either you sold it or they took it. I rented my house to their air force people. They said—either you take rent or we take the house. What would you have done?'

Adrian Monk described how he had been compulsorily evicted from his own house to make way for Argentinian soldiers who had then totally looted it. There appears to have been widespread looting in all the houses of Stanley to which the Argentinians had access.

The houses on the outskirts of the town in which the Argentinians had been living were an appalling mess full of everything from human excrement all over the place to just property lying all over the place where soldiers had ransacked through it. But they were all alive and they all had plenty of food and plenty to drink and they were all in tremendous spirits.

It wasn't in the least like being abroad. One talks about the Falklanders and yet it was as if one had liberated a hotel in the middle of Surrey or Kent or somewhere.

It was an extraordinary feeling just sitting there with all these girls and cheerful middle-age men and everybody chatting in the way they might chat at a suburban golf club after something like this had happened.

I think everybody did feel a tremendous sense of exhilaration and achievement. I think the Paras through all their tiredness knew they had won a tremendous battle.

It was the Paras' hour and, after their heavy losses and Goose Green and some of the fierce battles they had fought, they had made it all the way to Stanley and they were enjoying every moment of their triumph.

A question that has to be answered is how the Argentinian troops managed to maintain their supplies of food and ammunition.

I think it's one of the most remarkable things. I think intelligence hasn't been one of our strong points throughout the campaign.

Even our commanders and people in London agree that we have misjudged the Argentinians at several critical points in the campaign.

Our soldiers have been saying in the last couple of days how astonished they were when they overran enemy positions. We have been hearing a great deal about how short of food and ammunition they were supposed to be but whatever else they lacked it certainly was not either of those.

They had hundreds of rounds of ammunition, masses of weapons and plenty of food.

The civilians told me they had been running Hercules on to the runway at Port Stanley despite all our efforts with Naval gunnery, with Vulcans, with Harriers up to and including last night and, above all, at the beginning of May they ran a very big container ship called the Formosa through the blockade and got her back to Buenos Aires again afterwards. She delivered an enormous consignment of ammunition which really relieved the Argentinians' serious problems on that front for the rest of the campaign.

I think in that sense we have been incredibly lucky. The British forces have been incredibly lucky.

Considering the amount of stuff the Argentinians got in, we have done incredibly well in being able to smash them when they certainly had the ammunition and equipment left to keep fighting for a long time.

So why did they surrender? I think their soldiers had simply decided that they had had enough. Nobody likes being shelled and even well-trained troops find it an ordeal.

Even the Paras freely admit that it's very, very unpleasant being heavily shelled.

The last two nights, the Argentinian positions had been enormously heavily shelled by our guns. They gave them a tremendous pounding and when an Army starts to crumble and collapse it's very, very difficult to stop it.

I think that the Argentinian generals simply had to recognise that their men no longer had the will to carry on the fight.

This story of the fall of Port Stanley begins last night, when men of the Guards and the Gurkhas and the Parachute Regiment launched a major attack supported by an overwhelming British bombardment on the last line of enemy positions on the high ground above the capital.

Three civilians died in British counter-battery fire the night before last, as far as we know the only civilian casualties of the war. Mrs Doreen Burns, Mrs Sue Whitney and 82-year-old Mrs Mary Godwin were all sheltering together in a house hit by a single shell. Altogether only four or five houses in Stanley have been seriously damaged in the battle.

At first light the Paras were preparing to renew their attack in a few hours after seizing all their objectives on Wireless Ridge under fierce shell and mortar fire. Suddenly, word came that enemy troops could be seen fleeing for their lives in all directions around Port Stanley. They had evidently had enough. The decision was taken to press on immediately to complete their collapse.

Spearheaded by a company of the Parachute Regiment commanded by Major Dare Farrar-Hockley, son of the regiment's colonel, British forces began a headlong dash down the rocky hills for the honour of being first into Stanley.

I marched at breakneck speed with Major Farrar-Hockley through the ruins of the former Royal Marine base at Moody Brook, then past the smoking remains of buildings and strong-points destroyed by our shelling and bombing.

Our route was littered with the debris of the enemy's utter defeat.

We were already past the first houses of the town, indeed up to the War Memorial beside the sea, when the order came through to halt pending negotiations and to fire only in self-defence.

The men, desperately tired after three night without sleep, exulted like schoolboys in this great moment of victory.

The Parachute Regiment officer with whom I was walking had been delighted with the prospect that his men who had fought so hard all through this campaign were going to be the first British troops into Stanley. But they were heartbroken when, just as we reached the racecourse the order came to halt.

Major Farrar-Hockley ordered off helmets, on red berets. Some men showed their sadness for those who hadn't made it all the way, who had died even during the last night of bitter fighting.

The Regiment moved on to the racecourse and they tore down the Argentinian flag flying from the flagpole. Afterwards they posed for a group photograph . . . exhausted, unshaven but exhilarated at being alive and having survived a very, very bitter struggle.

After half an hour with the civilians I began to walk back to the British lines. Scores of enemy were still moving through the town, many assisting badly wounded comrades, all looking at the end of their tether.

Damaged enemy helicopters were parked everywhere among the houses and on the racecourse. Argentine officers still looked clean and soldierly, but they made no pretence of having any interest in continuing the struggle.

Each one spoke only of 'four o'clock', the magic moment at which General Moore was scheduled to meet General Menendez and the war presumably come to a halt.

Back in the British lines. Union Jacks had been hoisted and Brigadier Julian Thompson and many of his senior officers had hastened to the scene to be on hand for the entry into the capital.

Men asked eagerly about the centre of Stanley as if it was on the other side of the moon.

By tomorrow, I imagine, when everyone has seen what little there is of this little provinicial town to be seen, we shall all be asking ourselves why so many brave men had to die because a whimsical dictator, in a land of which we knew so little, determined that his nation had at all costs to possess it.

CHAIM HERZOG
Tank Battle on the Golan Heights

The Syrian and Egyptian armies launched a surprise attack on Israel on 6 October 1973, and almost succeeded in achieving a decisive breakthrough. The Israelis, however, rallied under the leadership of Lt.-Col. Yossi and managed to block the assault.

THEY HAD BEEN FIGHTING FOR four days and three nights, without a moment's rest or respite, under constant fire. On average each tank was left with three or four shells. At the height of battle Avigdor turned and spoke to his operations officer. The officer began to reply but suddenly in the middle of his sentence slid to the floor of the armoured carrier, fast asleep. Avigdor spoke to Raful and told him that he did not know if he could hold on. Already in a daze, he described the condition of his brigade. Raful, as ever quiet, calm and encouraging, pleaded with him, 'For God's sake, Avigdor, hold on! Give me another half an hour. You will soon be receiving reinforcements. Try, please, hold on!'

At this critical moment, Lieut.-Col. Yossi, leading remnants of the Barak Brigade with a force of eleven tanks, entered the divisional area and was directed by Raful to Avigdor. Yossi had handed over command of his battalion in the Barak Brigade on 4 September and decided that his honeymoon would be a non-conventional one. So with his newly wed wife, Naty, he flew to the Himalayas. On Yom Kippur eve they rode by motorbike to the Chinese frontier. Back in Katmandu for Yom Kippur, the receptionist in the hotel said to him, 'You're from Israel, aren't you? Something is happening in your area. You ought to listen to the news.' Racing against time Yossi and Naty, using every form of subterfuge, managed to fly back to

Israel via Teheran and Athens. From Athens Yossi phoned his family to bring his uniform and equipment to the airport. As he rushed northwards, little did he realize that he would receive command of the remnants of his former brigade. He hurried to Hofi's advanced headquarters and heard what had happened to the Barak Brigade. It was Tuesday morning.

When Dov had reached the Barak Brigade centre, remnants of the brigade began to arrive in dribs and drabs. Oded had in the meantime evacuated from the area of Tel Faris, taking with him some 140 infantry men who arrived on foot down the Gamla Rise. Dov and the other officers organized technical teams and began to recover abandoned tanks in the field, while ordnance units began to repair them. At noon on Tuesday a psychiatrist arrived from the medical centre of Tel Hashomer to take care of the soldiers of the Barak Brigade. He stood and looked at the dishevelled, unshaven, gaunt-eyed soldiers, some of them burnt and most of them blackened by the smoke and flames, working silently on the damaged tanks and putting them in shape. It was a moving and sobering sight. He asked them what they were doing and they explained that they were preparing the tanks to take them back into battle again. 'If they are going into battle again, I had better forget everything I ever learnt,' he remarked.

Dov notified command headquarters that he already had thirteen tanks ready for battle. He organized crews, brought in ammunition, begged some mortars and then he heard from command headquarters that Yossi was arriving to take command. The news of Yossi's arrival spread and Shmulick, who had been Yossi's second-in-command and who had been wounded in the first day of battle, escaped from the hospital in Safed and came to rejoin him and go back into battle. Conscious of the fact that they were to avenge the comrades of their brigade, Dov led Yossi's force to the front in a jeep. As they approached and received orders to join the 7th Brigade, Yossi heard on the radio that Tiger on the southern sector of the brigade front was out of ammunition and unable to hold out on the slopes of the 'Booster' against the Syrian advance.

Tiger's force was by now left with two shells per tank. 'Sir,' he radioed in a tone of desperation to the brigade commander, 'I can't hold on.' 'For heaven's sake hold on for only ten minutes,' implored Avigdor. 'Help is on the way.' When Tiger ran out of shells completely, he began to fill his pockets with hand grenades and withdraw. At this moment Yossi moved up to the 'Booster', opened fire and in the initial clash destroyed some thirty Syrian tanks. He had arrived just as the 7th Brigade, left with 7 running tanks out of an original total of approximately 100, was on the verge of collapse. Both sides had fought to a standstill. Avigdor had told Raful that he could not hold the Syrian attack, but suddenly a report came in from the A3 fortification (surrounded by Syrians and well behind the Syrian advance forces), that the Syrian supply trains were turning round and withdrawing. The Syrian attack had been broken; their forces broke and began to withdraw in panic.

The remnants of the 7th Brigade, including Yossi's reinforcements, totalled some twenty tanks. Exhausted, depleted to a minimum, many wounded, with their tanks bearing the scars of war, they now began to pursue the Syrians, knocking out tanks and armoured personnel carriers as they fled. On the edge of the anti-tank ditch, they stopped: the brigade had reached the limits of human exhaustion.

Avigdor stood in a daze looking down on the Valley of the Tears. Some 260 Syrian tanks and hundreds of armoured personnel carriers and vehicles lay scattered and abandoned across this narrow battlefield between the Hermonit and the 'Booster'. In the distance he could see the Syrians withdrawing in a haze of smoke and dust, the Israeli artillery following them. Raful's quiet voice came through on the earphones as he addressed them on the network of the 7th Brigade. 'You have saved the people of Israel.'

ANON
Brutal Cannon

A reminiscence of Nam from an anonymous helicopter pilot.

SOMEWHERE ALONG THE LINE IN the early stages of the war, some observation chopper pilot got tired of being shot at all the time. The guy rigged up three rocket tubes to the side of his helicopter, tied them into his electrical system and it worked. So they started arming helicopters very heavily. Basic American ingenuity.

Our gunship was a UH-1C Bell helicopter. On a really good day it was capable of flying 100 knots per hour. The later models, the Delta and the Hotel models, were faster and stronger but they weren't as manoeuvrable. There were two rocket pods on each side, seven 2.5-inch rockets. They were fired electrically by the pilot. Inside it also had two XM-21 systems—the Miniguns. Each gun was capable of firing 6,000 rounds a minute. But, on our helicopters they had inhibitor cards in the electronics so they only fired 2,000 rounds per minute. The guns were equipped with what was called a ten-degree pivot. The Miniguns would automatically track from side to side five degrees off centre.

In training films, a helicopter with one Minigun mounted in the nose would make a pass over a football field—fifty yards wide and a hundred yards long. They'd turn a rabbit loose on the field and let him run around. Consistently, the ship would make one pass and kill the rabbit. Every time. The noise that they made was not like a gun. It was a long, deep, very loud belch. *BRAAAAAAAAAAAAAH.*

In a light fire team, two helicopters, you dive into a position from maybe 1,500 feet up, firing the rockets and maybe the Miniguns. As you come up out of the dive, you make a very sharp turn. That's the break. Depending on who the pilot is, you could make the break as low as 100 feet above where you're shooting at. During that critical turn, the Miniguns weren't much help and the helicopter was extremely vulnerable. That's when the door gunner became important. I had an M-60 machine gun in the door. I'd do a whole acrobatic trip of shooting behind and underneath the helicopter to spray the area. By the time we were coming out of the break and I was out of range, the other helicopter would be coming in behind us and shooting their Miniguns or their 40mm cannon or whatever.

These helicopters were never intended to carry troops or supplies or letters. They were just these big pieces of death machine that flew around and that's all they did. Some of the more inventive crew chiefs would crawl under the helicopter and paint things on them like, 'Be nice or I'll kill you.' We had some colourful names: The Bounty Hunters, The Sting Ray Light Fire Team, Magic Turban. We were Brutal Cannon.

Most of the time, we would just hang out in the stand-by shack close to the airfield and wait to get a call. There was a lot of bullshitting, but it was fairly good bullshit. I remember talking about philosophy, the universe as a single-entity with One Pilot. There was this one guy who was a real fan of Isaac Asimov, always talking about Einstein's theory of relativity.

Then the telephone in the shack would ring: 'It's a scramble.' It was right out of the movies. We'd go racing like hell across the airfield, dive into our helicopter, take off and go blow the hell out of whatever section of earth they had pointed us at.

Sometimes, if troops were being dropped into what was suspected to be a hot area, we'd fly in before they landed and blow the shit out of it. A lot of times, we'd fly counter-mortar. The fastest way to stop somebody from mortaring the base was not to hit them with artillery or to send out reconnaissance patrols, but to have a helicopter team standing by. When the base got mortared, we race out to the field, take off like mad and then fly up and look for the next mortar flash. When we've spotted it, we dive in on that position and blow the shit out of it.

The Viet Cong, being no dummies, discovered what we were doing. They'd start to mortar the generators and they'd allow a minute and a half to go by, figuring that would be the reaction time for us to get out to the helicopters. Three or four times, we'd be racing across the airfield and they would begin to mortar us.

Twice all of us were recommended for the Distiguished Flying Cross for running through the barrage to our helicopters.

One night we were flying pretty far south and got a call in flight. A whole area was involved in a fire fight, on the ground, in the air. It was really something. We landed to pick up fuel. We're sitting there on the flight deck and we look over to where the battle was. Usually, it would be the gunships working out, shooting down with the Miniguns, sporadic fire coming back up. This night you could see the gunships firing, but even more fire was coming back up, .50 calibres.

'Whoa, let's think this one over, man. I am serious. This doesn't look good. Not good at all.' A .50 calibre machine gun is nothing to be fucked with. Movies have done a disservice to that weapon. What they fail to convey is that a .50 calibre machine gun is big and bad enough that if you look around a city block, you will see almost no structure standing that you can hide behind safely if somebody is firing one of those things at you. It just goes through everything.

'Hey, we're going to go over there and really kick ass. Those sons of bitches can't get away with that.' We got into a pitched battle, the worst I'd ever been in. When they would fire from the ground the bullets looked like baseballs or beer cans coming up at you. They'd kind of float up in your direction slowly. When they'd get closer, they'd suddenly seem to speed up and whiz by. Have you ever been drunk and stood on a dark street corner where there's a lot of traffic? Your vision is a little blurry and you see all the taillights flashing by you. This was like being in the middle of the intersection with the lights flashing *at* you. They had green tracers and white tracers and red tracers.

I guess we flew six sorties. Go out, expend all of our ammunition, fly back and load up. Go out again. Finally, dawn came. The battle broke off.

There were literally hundreds and hundreds of Vietnamese fleeing the area, any way they could. Panic. The sun was up and that was it. Time to get the hell out of Dodge. This wasn't a village. It was a big swampy area. They were leaving in boats, slogging on foot, anything. I don't know if they ran out of ammunition or what, but we were taking very little fire at that point and we were just killing everybody.

It turned into a turkey shoot. They were defenceless. There

were three or four light fire teams working the area. Hundreds of people were being mowed down. Bodies were floating in the water. Insane.

I was in there with the best of them. Blowing people off the boats, out of the paddies, down from the trees for Chrissake. Blood lust. I can't think of a better way to describe it. Caught up in the moment. I remember thinking this insane thought, that I'm God and retribution is here, now, in the form of my machine gun and the Miniguns that I take care of and the rockets that we are firing. It was a slaughter. No better than lining people up on the edge of a ditch and shooting them in the back of the head. I was doing it enthusiastically.

You begin at that point to understand how genocide takes place. I consider myself a decent man, but I did mow those people down from my helicopter. A lot of people we were killing in the morning were the same people who were trying to kill us that night. I tried to compensate in my head that most of the people we were wasting were the enemy. But I could appreciate in a black way that you can take anybody given the right circumstances and turn him into a wholesale killer. That's what I was. I did it. Bizarre. That's what it was. It was very bizarre.

MICHAEL HERR
The Nights at Khe Sahn

On 21 January 1968, the US Marine Corps firebase at Khe Sahn, just to the south of the Demilitarized Zone in central Vietnam, was invested by substantial forces of the North Vietnamese Army and Viet Cong. The subsequent fighting at Khe Sahn was the most intense of the Vietnam War. Michael Herr, author of the Vietnam classic, Dispatches, *remembers the nights at Khe Sahn during the battle.*

SOMETIMES YOU'D STEP FROM THE bunker, all sense of time passing having left you, and find it dark out. The far side of the hills around the bowl of the base was glimmering, but you could never see the source of the light, and it had the look of a city at night approached from a great distance. Flares were dropping everywhere around the fringes of the perimeter, laying a dead white light on the high ground rising from the piedmont. There would be dozens of them at once sometimes, trailing an intense smoke, dropping white-hot sparks, and it seemed as though anything caught in their range would be made still, like figures in a game of living statues. There would be the muted rush of illumination rounds, fired from 60-mm mortars inside the wire, dropping magnesium-brilliant above the NVA trenches for a few seconds, outlining the gaunt, flat spread of the mahogany trees, giving the landscape a ghastly clarity and dying out. You could watch mortar bursts, orange and grey-smoking, over the tops of trees three and four kilometres away, and the heavier shelling from support bases farther east along the DMZ, from Camp Carrol and the Rockpile, directed against suspected troop movements or NVA rocket and mortar positions. Once in a while—I guess I saw it happen three or four times in all—there would be a secondary explosion, a direct hit on a supply of NVA ammunition. And at night it was beautiful. Even the incoming was beautiful at night, beautiful and deeply dreadful.

I remembered the way a Phantom pilot had talked about how beautiful the surface-to-air missiles looked as they drifted up towards his plane to kill him, and remembered myself how lovely .50-calibre tracers could be, coming at you as you flew at night in a helicopter, how slow and graceful, arching up easily, a dream, so remote from anything that could harm you. It could make you feel a total serenity, an elevation that put you above death, but that never lasted very long. One hit anywhere in the chopper would bring you back, bitten lips, white knuckles and all, and then you knew where you were. It was different with the incoming at Khe Sanh. You didn't get to watch the shells very often. You knew if you heard one, the first one, that you were safe, or at least saved. If you were still standing up and looking after that, you deserved anything that happened to you.

Nights were when the air and artillery strikes were heaviest, because that was when we knew that the NVA was above ground and moving. At night you could lie out on some sandbags and watch the C-47s mounted with Vulcans doing their work. The C-47 was a standard prop flareship, but many of them carried .20- and .762-mm guns on their doors, Mike-Mikes that could fire out 300 rounds per second, Gatling style, 'a round in every square inch of a football field in less than a minute,' as the handouts said. They used to call it Puff the Magic Dragon, but the Marines knew better: they named it Spooky. Every fifth round fired was a tracer, and when Spooky was working, everything stopped while that solid stream of violent red poured down out of the black sky. If you watched from a great distance, the stream would seem to dry up between bursts, vanishing slowly from air to ground like a comet tail, the sound of the guns disappearing too, a few seconds later. If you watched at a close range, you couldn't believe that anyone would have the courage to deal with that night after night, week after week, and you cultivated a respect for the Viet Cong and NVA who had crouched under it every night now for months. It was awesome, worse than anything the Lord had ever put down on Egypt, and at night, you'd hear the Marines talking, watching it, yelling, 'Get some!' until they grew quiet and someone would say, 'Spooky understands.' The nights were very beautiful. Night was when you really had the least to fear and feared the most. You could go through some very bad numbers at night.

Because, really, what a choice there was; what a prodigy of things to be afraid of! The moment that you understood this, really understood it, you lost your anxiety instantly. Anxiety was a luxury, a joke you had no room for once you knew the variety of deaths and mutilations the war offered. Some feared head wounds, some dreaded chest wounds or stomach wounds, everyone feared the wound of wounds, the Wound. Guys would pray and pray—Just you and me, God. Right?—offer anything, if only they could be spared that: Take my legs, take my hands, take my eyes, take my fucking *life*, You Bastard, but please, please, please, don't take *those*. Whenever a shell landed in a group, everyone forgot about the next rounds and skipped back to rip their pants away, to check, laughing hysterically with relief even though their legs might be shattered, their kneecaps torn away, kept upright by their relief and shock, gratitude and adrenalin.

There were choices everywhere, but they were never choices that you could hope to make. There was even some small chance for personal style in your recognition of the one thing you feared more than any other. You could die in a sudden bloodburning crunch as your chopper hit the ground like dead weight, you could fly apart so that your pieces would never be gathered, you could take one neat round in the lung and go out hearing only the bubble of the last few breaths, you could die in the last stage of malaria with that faint tapping in your ears, and that could happen to you after months of firefights and rockets and machine guns. Enough, too many, were saved for that, and you always hoped that no irony would attend your passing. You could end in a pit somewhere with a spike through you, everything stopped forever except for the one or two motions, purely involuntary, as though you could kick it all away and come back. You could fall down dead so that the medics would have to spend half an hour looking for the hole that killed you, getting more and more spooked as the search went on. You could be shot, mined, grenaded, rocketed, mortared, sniped at, blown up and away so that your leavings had to be dropped into a sagging poncho and carried to Graves Registration, that's all she wrote. It was almost marvellous.

And at night, all of it seemed more possible. At night in Khe Sanh, waiting there, thinking about all of them (40,000, some said), thinking that they might really try it, could keep you up. If they did, when they did, it might not matter that you were in the best bunker in the DMZ, wouldn't matter that you were young and had plans, that you were loved, that you were a non-combatant, an observer. Because if it came, it would be in a bloodswarm of killing, and credentials would not be examined. (The only Vietnamese many of us knew was the words 'Bao Chi! Bao Chi!'—Journalist! Journalist! or even 'Bao Chi Fap!'—French journalist!, which was the same as crying, Don't shoot! Don't shoot!) You came to love your life, to love and respect the mere fact of it, but often you became heedless of it in the way that somnambulists are heedless. Being 'good' meant staying alive, and sometimes that was only a matter of caring enough at any given moment. No wonder everyone became a luck freak, no wonder you could wake at four in the morning some mornings and *know* that tomorrow it would finally happen, you could stop worrying about it now and just lie there, sweating in the dampest chill you ever felt.

But once it was actually going on, things were different. You were just like everyone else, you could no more blink than spit. It came back the same way every time, dreaded and welcome, balls and bowels turning over together, your senses working like strobes, free-falling all the way down to the essences and then flying out again in a rush to focus, like the first strong twinge of tripping after an infusion of psilocybin, reaching in at the point of calm and springing all the joy and all the dread ever known, *ever* known by *everyone* who *ever* lived, unutterable in its speeding brilliance, touching all the edges and then passing, as though it had all been controlled from outside, by a god or by the moon. And every time, you were so weary afterwards, so empty of everything but being alive that you couldn't recall any of it, except to know that it was like something else you had felt once before. It remained obscure for a long time, but after enough times the memory took shape and substance and finally revealed itself one afternoon during the breaking off of a firefight. It was the feeling you'd had when you were much, much younger and undressing a girl for the first time.

TATSUICHIRO AKIZUKI
Nagasaki 1945

Tatsuichiro Akizuki was working as a doctor in Nagasaki when the atomic bomb dropped on the city at 11.02 a.m. on 9 August 1945. (The world's first atomic bomb had been dropped on Hiroshima two days earlier). Around 30,000 people were instantly killed in the bombing, and another 70,000 have died since from injuries, burns and radiation poisoning.

On Thursday, 9 August, the boundless blue sky, the loud shrilling of cicadas, promised another day as hot and as sultry as the day before.

At 8.30 I began the medical examination and treatment of out-patients. Nearly thirty had turned up by ten o'clock. Some were patients requiring artificial pneumo-thorax (the temporary collapsing of a lung); they had been entrusted to us by Takahara Hospital, 5,000 metres away. Miss Yoshioka, a woman doctor in her mid-thirties who came from there, arrived to assist me with the operations, as well as two nurses also belonging to Takahara Hospital. Our hospital was in something of a turmoil.

During the morning Mr Yokota turned up to see his daughter, who was one of our in-patients. He lived at the foot of Motohara Hill, and was an engineer in the research department of the Mitsubishi Ordnance Factory, then one of the centres of armament manufacture in Japan. The torpedoes used in the attack on Pearl Harbor had been made there. Mr Yokota always had something interesting to say. He used to visit me now and again, often passing on some new piece of scientific information.

He said: 'I hear Hiroshima was very badly damaged on the sixth.'

Together we despaired over the destiny of Japan, he as an engineer, I as a doctor.

Then he said gloomily: 'I don't think the explosion was caused by any form of chemical energy.'

'What then?' I inquired, eager to know about the cause of the explosion, even though my patients were waiting for me.

He said: 'The power of the bomb dropped on Hiroshima is far stronger than any accumulation of chemical energy produced by the dissolution of a nitrogen compound, such as nitro-glycerine. It was an *atomic* bomb, produced by atomic fission.'

'Good heavens! At last we have atomic fission!' I said, though somewhat doubtfully.

Just then the long continuous wail of a siren arose.

'Listen . . . Here comes the regular air-raid.'

'The first warning . . . The enemy are on their way.'

Mr Yokota hurried back down the hill to his factory and all at once I began to feel nervous. It was now about 10.30. When such a warning sounded we were supposed to make sure our patients took refuge in our basement air-raid shelter. We were meant to do likewise. But recently I had become so accustomed to air-raids that, even though it was somewhat foolhardy, I no longer bothered with every precaution. In any case, breakfast was about to begin. At the time our diet at the hospital consisted of two meals a day of unpolished rice. The patients were waiting for their breakfast to be served, and so remained on the second and third floors.

I went out of the building. It was very hot. The sky had clouded over a little but the familiar formation of B29 bombers was neither to be seen nor heard. I asked myself: 'What route will our dear enemies choose to take today?'

I went in again to warn my patients to stay away from the windows—they could be swept by machine-gun fire. Recently we had been shot up once or twice by fighter-planes from American aircraft carriers in neighbouring waters.

About thirty minutes later the all-clear sounded. I said to myself: In Nagasaki everything is still all right. *Im Westen Nichts Neues*—All quiet on the Western Front.

I went down to the consulting room, humming cheerfully. Now that the all-clear had been given I felt free from danger. I entered the room and found Dr Yoshioka about to carry out an artificial pneumo-thorax operation on one of the male out-patients. 'You ought to stop working when the air-raid warning goes, at least for a little while,' I told her.

'Thank you,' she replied. 'But there were so many patients waiting.'

She looked tired. She had come to the hospital that morning on foot, walking 5,000 metres across Nagasaki, and since then she had been very busy treating the patients who needed attention.

'Please have a rest,' I said. 'I'll carry on in your place.'

'Well . . . Thank you for your kindness,' she said, and went upstairs to her room to rest. I began the pneumo-thorax. Miss Sugako Murai, one of our few trained nurses, was there by my side to help me. She was two years younger than me and came from Koshima in Nagasaki; she had been at Urakami Hospital for about four months, since April.

It was eleven o'clock. Father Ishikawa, who was Korean, aged about thirty-six and the hospital chaplain, was listening in the hospital chapel to the confessions of those Catholics who had gone to him to confess, one after the other, before the great festival, on 15 August, of the Ascension of the Virgin Mary, which was only a week away. Brother Joseph Iwanaga was toiling outside the hospital with some farm workers, digging another air-raid shelter in the shrubbery in the centre of the hospital yard. Mr Noguchi had just begun to repair the apparatus used to lift water from the well. Other members of staff were busy providing a late breakfast. Some were filling big bowls with miso soup; others were carrying them through the corridors or up the stairs. The hospital was a hive of activity after the all-clear.

'Well, we'll soon be getting our breakfast,' I said to Miss Murai. 'The patients must be hungry.'

So was I, but before we had our breakfast we would have to finish treating all the out-patients.

I stuck the pneumo-thorax needle into the side of the chest of the patient lying on the bed. It was just after 11 a.m.

I heard a low droning sound, like that of distant aeroplane engines.

'What's that?' I said. 'The all-clear has gone, hasn't it?'

At the same time the sound of the plane's engines, growing louder and louder, seemed to swoop down over the hospital.

I shouted: 'It's an enemy plane! Look out—take cover!'

As I said so, I pulled the needle out of the patient and threw myself beside the bed.

There was a blinding white flash of light, and the next moment—*Bang! Crack!* A huge impact like a gigantic blow smote down upon our bodies, our heads and our hospital. I lay flat—I didn't know whether or not of my own volition. Then down came piles of debris, slamming into my back.

The hospital has been hit, I thought. I grew dizzy, and my ears sang.

Some minutes or so must have passed before I staggered to my feet and looked around. The air was heavy with yellow smoke; white flakes of powder drifted about; it was strangely dark.

Thank God, I thought—I'm not hurt! But what about the patients?

As it became brighter, little by little our situation grew clearer. Miss Murai, who had been assisting me with the pneumo-thorax, struggled to her feet beside me. She didn't seem to have been seriously injured, though she was completely covered with white dust. 'Hey, cheer up!' I said. 'We're not hurt, thank God!'

I helped her to her feet. Another nurse, who was also in the consulting room, and the patient, managed to stand up. The man, his face smeared white like a clown and streaked with blood, lurched towards the door, holding his bloody head with his hands and moaning.

I said to myself over and over again: Our hospital has suffered a direct hit—We've been bombed! Because the hospital stood on a hill and had walls of red brick, it must, I thought, have attracted the attention of enemy planes. I felt deeply and personally responsible for what had happened.

The pervading dingy yellow silence of the room now resounded with faint cries—'Help!' The surface of the walls and ceiling had peeled away. What I had thought to be clouds of dust or smoke was whirling brick-dust and plaster. Neither the pneumo-thorax apparatus nor the microscope on my desk were anywhere to be seen. I felt as if I were dreaming.

I encouraged Miss Murai, saying: 'Come on, we haven't been hurt at all, by the grace of God. We must rescue the in-patients.' But privately I thought it must be all over with them—the second and third floors must have disintegrated, I thought.

We went to the door of the consulting room which faced the main stairway, and there were the in-patients coming down the steps, crying: 'Help me, doctor! Oh, help me, sir.' The stairs and the corridor were heaped with timbers, plaster, debris from the ceiling. It made walking difficult. The patients staggered down towards us, crying: 'I'm hurt! Help me!' Strangely, none seemed to have been seriously injured, only slightly wounded, with fresh blood dripping from their faces and hands.

If the bomb had actually hit the hospital, I thought, they would have been far more badly injured.

'What's happened to the second and third floors?' I cried. But all they answered was—'Help me! Help!'

One of them said: 'Mr Yamaguchi has been buried under the debris. Help him.'

No one knew what had happened. A huge force had been released above our heads. What it was, nobody knew. Had it been several tons of bombs, or the suicidal destruction of a plane carrying a heavy bomb-load?

Dazed, I retreated into the consulting room, in which the only upright object on the rubbish-strewn floor was my desk. I went and sat on it and looked out of the window at the yard and the outside world. There was not a single pane of glass in the window, not even a frame—all had been completely blown away. Out in the yard dun-coloured smoke or dust cleared little by little. I saw figures running. Then, looking to the south-west, I was stunned. The sky was as dark as pitch, covered with dense clouds of smoke; under that blackness, over the earth, hung a yellow-brown fog. Gradually the veiled ground became visible, and the view beyond rooted me to the spot with horror.

All the buildings I could see were on fire: large ones and small ones and those with straw-thatched roofs. Further off along the valley, Urakami Church, the largest Catholic church in the east, was ablaze. The technical school, a large two-storeyed wooden building, was on fire, as were many houses and the distant ordnance factory. Electricity poles were wrapped in flame like so many pieces of kindling. Trees on the near-by hills were smoking, as were the leaves of sweet potatoes in the fields. To say that everything burned is not enough. It seemed as if the earth itself emitted fire and smoke, flames that writhed up and erupted from underground. The sky was dark, the ground was scarlet, and in between hung clouds of yellowish smoke. Three kinds of colour—black, yellow and scarlet—loomed ominously over the people, who ran about like so many ants seeking to escape. What had happened? Urakami Hospital had not been bombed—I understood that much. But that ocean of fire, that sky of smoke! It seemed like the end of the world.

I ran out into the garden. Patients who were only slightly hurt came up to me, pleading for aid.

I shouted at them: 'For heaven's sake! You're not seriously wounded!'

One patient said: 'Kawaguchi and Matsuo are trapped in their rooms! They can't move. You must help them!'

I said to myself: Yes, we must first of all rescue those seriously ill tubercular patients who've been buried under the ruins.

I looked southwards again, and the sight of Nagasaki city in a sea of flames as far as the eye could reach made me think that such destruction could only have been caused by thousands of bombers, carpet-bombing. But not a plane was to be seen or heard, although even the leaves of potatoes and carrots at my feet were scorched and smouldering. The electricity cables must have exploded underground, I thought.

And then at last I identified the destroyer—'That's it!' I cried. 'It was the new bomb—the one used on Hiroshima!'

'Look—there's smoke coming from the third floor!' exclaimed one of the patients, who had fled for safety into the hospital yard.

I turned about and looked up at the roof.

The hospital was built of brick and reinforced concrete, but the main roof was tiled, sloping in the Japanese style, and in the middle of the roof was another small, ridged roof, from whose end a little smoke was issuing, as if something was cooking there. Almost all the tiles had fallen off, leaving the roof timbers exposed.

That's odd, I said to myself, not heeding what I saw.

The smoke from the hospital looked just like that of a cigarette in comparison with the masses billowing above the technical school, Urakami Church, near-by houses, and the Convent of the Holy Cross, which were now blazing with great ferocity. The sky was dark, as if it were threatening to rain.

'As soon as we have some rain,' I said, 'these fires will quickly be extinguished.' So saying, I began to dash about in the confusion.

The fire in the hospital roof spread little by little. It was rather strange how the roof was the first thing in the hospital to catch fire. But the temperature at the instant the bomb exploded would have been thousands of degrees Centigrade at the epicentre and hundreds of degrees Centigrade near the hospital. Wooden buildings within 1,500 metres of the epicentre instantly caught fire. Within 1,000 metres, iron itself melted. The hospital stood 1,800 metres away from the epicentre. Probably, coming on top of the scorching heat of the sun, which had shone for more than ten days running, the blasting breath of hundreds of degrees Centigrade had dried out the hospital timbers and ignited them. The attics under the roof were wooden and used as a store-house; the fire now spread through them. Upset as I was, at first I wasn't too concerned, thinking it was only a small fire. But before long the main roof of the building was enveloped in flames.

'Doctor! Doctor!' people shouted. 'There are still many patients on the third floor!'

I went up to the third floor many times, and ran down just as often. As I rushed about like a madman, the damage sustained by the hospital became much clearer. Brother Iwanaga and Mr Noguchi, who were both fit and well, also raced up and down in the work of rescue.

'Dr Yoshioka has been badly hurt. I'm afraid she's going to die.'

That cry was heard several times, and it so discouraged me that, for a while, my feet would hardly move.

I also heard someone say: 'Brother Iwanaga is taking Dr Yoshioka to the hill opposite the hospital, carrying her on his back. Please come quickly, sir!'

Another voice cried from somewhere a bit later: 'The chief nurse has been injured, and is being taken to the hill where Dr Yoshioka is.'

Meanwhile we were carrying those patients who were seriously ill down from the third floor, even as the fire was spreading along the hospital roof. But thanks to the unselfish devotion of the nurses and the co-operation of the in-patients, we were able to bring out all the serious tubercular cases, until only two remained. Pinned under fallen beams, they could not be pulled away, despite all our efforts. At that point I came close to running away myself, to giving them up in despair. But something had to be tried to rescue them. Brother Iwanaga and Mr Noguchi brought a saw with which we cut through the beams until at last the two could be freed.

Miss Murai wept with happiness, overjoyed that no patients would now be burnt to death in the hospital.

'We have rescued every one of them!' she cried.

Ten or twenty minutes after the smoke had cleared outside, people began coming up the hill from the town below, crying out and groaning: 'Help me, help!' Those cries and groans seemed not to be made by human voices; they sounded unearthly, weird.

About ten minutes after the explosion, a big man, half-naked, holding his head between his hands, came into the yard towards me, making sounds that seemed to be dragged from the pit of his stomach.

'Got hurt, sir,' he groaned; he shivered as if he were cold. 'I'm hurt.'

I stared at him, at the strange-looking man. Then I saw it was Mr Zenjiro Tsujimoto, a market-gardener and a friendly neighbour to me and the hospital. I wondered what had happened to the robust Zenjiro.

'What's the matter with you, Tsujimoto?' I asked him, holding him in my arms.

'In the pumpkin field over there—getting pumpkins for the patients—got hurt . . .' he said, speaking brokenly and breathing feebly.

It was all he could do to keep standing. Yet it didn't occur to me that he had been seriously injured.

'Come along now,' I said. 'You are perfectly all right, I assure you. Where's your shirt? Lie down and rest somewhere where it's cool. I'll be with you in a moment.'

His head and his face were whitish; his hair was singed. It was because his eyelashes had been scorched away that he seemed so bleary-eyed. He was half-naked because his shirt had been burned from his back in a single flash. But I wasn't aware of such facts. I gazed at him as he reeled about with his head between his hands. What a change had come over this man who was stronger than a horse, whom I had last seen earlier that morning. It's as if he's been struck by lightning, I thought.

After Mr Tsujimoto came staggering up to me, another person who looked just like him wandered into the yard. Who he was and where he had come from I had no idea. 'Help me,' he said, groaning, half-naked, holding his head between his hands. He sat down, exhausted. 'Water . . . Water . . .' he whispered.

'What's the trouble? What's wrong with you? What's become of your shirt?' I demanded.

'Hot—*hot* . . . Water . . . I'm burning.' They were the only words that were articulate.

As time passed, more and more people in a similar plight came up to the hospital—ten minutes, twenty minutes, an hour after the explosion. All were of the same appearance, sounded the same. 'I'm hurt, *hurt*! I'm burning! Water!' They all moaned the same lament. I shuddered. Half-naked or stark naked, they walked with strange, slow steps, groaning from deep inside themselves as if they had travelled from the depths of hell. They looked whitish; their faces were like masks. I felt as if I were dreaming, watching pallid ghosts processing slowly in one direction—as in a dream I had once dreamt in my childhood.

These ghosts came on foot uphill towards the hospital, from the direction of the burning city and from the more easterly ordnance factory. Worker or student, girl or man, they all walked slowly and had the same mask-like face. Each one groaned and cried for help. Their cries grew in strength as the people increased in number, sounding like something from the Buddhist scriptures, re-echoing everywhere, as if the earth itself were in pain.

One victim who managed to reach the hospital yard asked me, 'Is this a hospital?' before suddenly collapsing on the ground. There were those who lay stiffly where they fell by the roadside in front of the hospital; others lay in the sweet-potato fields. Many went down to the steep valley below the hospital where a stream ran down between the hill of Motohara and the next hill. 'Water, water,' they cried. They went instinctively down to the banks of the stream, because their bodies had been scorched and their throats were parched and inflamed; they were thirsty. I didn't realize then that these were the symptoms of 'flash-burn'.

Many times I met with and separated from Brother Iwanaga as each of us toiled wherever we happened to be. Earlier, Brother

Iwanaga had rescued a farmer, Mr Yamano, by sawing through the boughs of a tree that had fallen upon him in the yard. Now Brother Iwanaga said to me: 'Father Ishikawa has been hurt, some part of his head.'

After mass that morning Father Ishikawa had listened to the confessions of the Catholics, who had grown in number as the festival of the Ascension of the Virgin Mary approached. Towards eleven o'clock, he had returned to his room on the third floor to fetch a book he needed, and then hurried back to the chapel. He was passing along the corridor in the middle of the first floor when a sudden white flash filled the corridor with light; there was a great roar and he was hurled head over heels through the air, striking his head against a concrete post. But although he was in some pain, he returned to the chapel, where such thick yellowish smoke and white dust hung over the broken furnishings he could hardly tell where he was. Not a person was in sight. It was there that Brother Iwanaga found him. When I saw Father Ishikawa, lying down in a shaded part of the yard, one of his eyes had swollen purple. Fortunately, the bleeding from his injured head had stopped.

Black smoke was now billowing up from the hospital roof. By the time the rescue of all the patients had been achieved, the top floor was enveloped in smoke and the fire in the roof burned furiously.

'Ah, the X-ray machines will be burnt!' I exclaimed, in spite of myself.

Miss Murai and some of the patients took up my cry. We had thought the fire would be held back by the ceiling of the third floor, which was made of thick concrete. But when a lift was installed in the hospital, a shaft three metres square had been built in the middle of the building, from the basement to the third floor. Into that shaft burning timbers now fell, crashing down into the basement, where three of the most up-to-date X-ray machines were stored, Half of the best X-ray machines in Nagasaki city were, in fact, in the care of our hospital, thought to be the safest place for them. In the transformer of every X-ray machine there was a quantity of insulation oil. The transformers blew up in the intense heat and the machines caught fire.

'There they go,' I murmured sadly.

The sun shone dim and reddish through the south-westerly veil of black smoke over the city. It seemed a long time since the explosion. I thought it must now be evening, but only three hours had passed. It was just two o'clock and still broad daylight. I had completely lost any sense of time. And I was not alone—it was a timeless day for everyone. It seemed as if years had passed, maybe because so many houses continued to burn and because so many badly injured people appeared one after another before my eyes. On the other hand, it felt as if only a moment had passed, because all around us people and houses and fields seemed unbelievably changed.

Not every part of the hospital was beset with fire. Brother Iwanaga and I went in and out of the building many times, for I still had to make sure that all the patients and staff were safe and to check for any dead or wounded. We couldn't imagine how everything had looked before the explosion—rooms, corridors, furniture and the rest. The ceilings had all been stripped of their planks and plaster, the walls of their panelling. Desks, cupboards, bookcases, instrument boxes, medicine chests had all been overturned. Whatever had escaped the onslaught had been emptied—drawers were open and their contents lost. I never found out what happened to the contents of my desk. A gigantic wind had struck the hospital, shattered the windows, torn through every room, swept along the corridors and ravaged everything inside the hospital with a force beyond human comprehension.

It is the mark of the devil, I thought—of the devil's claw.

Clothes which the chief nurse and the nurses once wore were lying about as if torn off their bodies. The mere sight of them made me afraid that they had been killed. But in fact it was only that the door of the wardrobe in the room had been torn off and the clothing inside blown out.

I noticed other unusual facts. The ceremonial robes usually kept by the altar in the chapel were discovered far away, torn to shreds. The books from the library were scattered in unimaginable places. As for my own office, where many important records and instruments were kept—the whole room had been wrecked. I couldn't find a thing. The clothes I had put on that morning were all that remained of my possessions. My shoes were straw sandals. I felt uneasy about them. There had been three pairs of fine leather shoes in my room, but I couldn't find any of them, hard as I tried. In the end I ran about for several days with only straw sandals on my feet. My soles must have been infected by radioactivity but I was unaware of the danger.

In the afternoon a change was noticeable in the appearance of the injured people who came up to the hospital. The crowd of ghosts which had looked whitish in the morning were now burned black. Their hair was burnt; their skin, which was charred and blackened, blistered and peeled. Such were those who now came toiling up to the hospital yard and fell there weakly.

'Are you a doctor? Please, if you wouldn't mind, could you examine me?' So said a young man.

'Cheer up!' I said. It was all I could say.

He died in the night. He must have been one of the many medical students who were injured down at the medical college. His politeness and then his poor blackened body lying dead on the concrete are things I shall never forget.

Neither shall I ever forget the countenance of a father who came stumbling up to me, carrying his baby in his arms. The father begged me to try to do something for his baby. I examined the child. The wall of its stomach had been sliced open and part of its intestines protruded. The baby's face was purple. No pulse could be felt.

I said, 'It's hopeless.'

The father, laying his baby on the grass in the yard, sat down exhausted and said: 'Would you do what you can?'

I shook my head. There was nothing that I could do. I had neither medical instruments nor medicine. He wouldn't leave the child.

The brick wall around the hospital was in ruins, blown down by the blast. The wall, hundreds of metres long, had like everything else been crushed by a devilish force. A child who had been playing near the wall lay beneath it on the road, his skull broken like a pomegranate.

Gradually the severity of cases increased: a person whose body had been riven by pieces of glass or splinters blown by the colossal force of the blast; a person who had been battered by heavy objects falling upon him; a person who had been blown off his feet and thrown against something hard—people with such serious injuries appeared one after the other. None of them, however, knew how they had come to be so badly injured. They all trembled with fear and pain, each thinking that the bomb had fallen only on them.

The southern sky was still dark. After the strange clouds caused by the explosion had thinned, smoke from the burning city obscured the sky. Through it the sun shone redly now and again. Sometimes the sound of aeroplane engines could be heard overhead—not Japanese planes, but those of the enemy. Because of the smoke, we couldn't see them. The droning sound of the enemy's low-altitude flights was repeated several times, and every time the sound was heard the injured trembled, fled and hid, fearing that another bomb would be dropped or that machine-gun fire would sweep through them. Whenever the sound of the engines was heard we stopped whatever we were doing and hid, thinking the enemy were about to attack again with even greater ferocity.

I thought it unlikely, however, that they would drop any more bombs on us after the new bomb. Possibly the planes were flying over on reconnaissance, checking on the damage the bomb had done. But the injured who ran about below, seeking to survive any further attack, and the people caring for the injured could not reason as objectively as I. The throb of engines made all of us tremble and cower, and the hateful sound continued off and on, endlessly, as it would do even through the night, droning above the city where the black smoke hung in heavy clouds.

'Isn't all this destruction enough?' I cried, and bit my lip in mortification.

The Book Lady

May 29, 2013

Dolly Parton

sharing books

founder -

Imagination Library
(Severe Tennessee) Giving

books begins at birth

started 17 yrs ago

120 million budget

distributes 700,000

books a month

~~Has~~ given children
(about 50 million
new books)